Joanna Southcott

The Woman Clothed with the Sun

'And there appeared a great wonder in heaven;
a woman clothed with the sun, and the moon under her feet,
and upon her head a crown of twelve stars:
And she being with child cried, travailing in birth,
and pained to be delivered. . . . and she brought forth a man child,
who was to rule all nations with a rod of iron.'

Revelation 12:1, 5

Joanna Southcott

The Woman Clothed with the Sun

Frances Brown

The Lutterworth Press

For
Peter and Sheila Goldsmith

The Lutterworth Press
P.O. Box 60
Cambridge
CB1 2NT

www.lutterworth.com
publishing@lutterworth.com

ISBN 0 7188 3018 0

British Library Cataloguing in Publication Data
A catalogue record is available from the British Library

First Published in 2002

Printed in the United Kingdom by
MFP Print, Manchester

Contents

List of Illustrations

Colour Illustrations

Acknowledgements

This book owes an immeasurable debt to libraries, museums and record offices throughout the country, but I am particularly grateful to the staffs of the British Library; the Devon and Exeter Institution; the Guildhall Library; the London Metropolitan Archive; the Harry Price Library, University of London; John Rylands Library, Manchester; Dr Williams's Library, London; Rochdale Library; Salford Museum; Local Studies Libraries at Bristol, Plymouth, Stourbridge and Taunton; and both the West Country Studies Library and the Royal Albert Memorial Museum at Exeter. I am also indebted to members of Devon Family History Society and to the staff of the Public Record Office and the Record Offices of Devon, Gloucestershire, Somerset, Wiltshire and Worcestershire.

I should especially like to thank David Bromige of Taunton Local Studies Library who was so helpful at the start of my project, Marilyn Ferris, Major Martin Keer, Gillian Lindsay and Dorothy Weyers who sent me valuable information, and Helga Harman whose hospitality made my research trips to London such a pleasure. In Exeter Ian Maxted painstakingly guided me through the Joanna Southcott material in the West Country Studies Library, John Draisey located relevant documents, and Shelley Tobin shared her expertise on the Southcott relics at Rougemont House. The Reverend Canon Richard Saunders provided valuable information about Gittisham and Roy Langworthy entertained me with memories of his boyhood home, the cottage where Joanna Southcott's family lived. At Blockley Professor J.D.M.Derrett kindly enabled me to examine the Southcottian manuscripts in his care and gave me useful advice. In Bedford David McLynn was very helpful and I spent unforgettable days with Ruth Klein and John Coghill whose quiet passion for the Panacea Society will always remain with me.

Finally I wish to record my gratitude to my husband, Henry Brown, for his unfailing support and encouragement.

Illustrations

The illustrations used in this book are courtesy of the following sources: Royal Albert Memorial Museum, Exeter, 16; C1; C3; C6; C7; C8; C9; Devon Library and Information Services, 4; 5; 7; 18; 20; 22; C4; Panacea Society, Bedford, 11; 14; 15; C5; C7 (ladle); London Metropolitan Archive, 13; Harry Price Library, Senate House, London, C2; Roy Langworthy, 2; Joan Roebuck, 3; Author, 1; 6; 8; 9; 10; 12; 17; 19; 21; 23; 24.

Introduction

Joanna Southcott – the name may be vaguely familiar to most people, if only in connection with an advertisement placed regularly in the national press urging the bishops to open her Box of Sealed Prophecies. But few know anything about the woman herself – who she was, what she did, why nearly two hundred years after her death her life still excites controversy. In Britain, the USA, Australia and New Zealand, groups of her followers continue to wait expectantly for the return of Shiloh, the divine child to whom they claim Joanna Southcott gave birth in 1814. Scholars still study her contribution to millenarian thought. Believers pore over her prophecies.

Joanna Southcott was forty-two years old and earning her living as a domestic servant in Exeter when she claimed that God had chosen her to announce the Second Coming. In normal times perhaps few would have taken her seriously. But this was 1792 and times were far from normal. The American War and the Revolution in France had shattered everyday certainties for many who, turning to their Bible for consolation and guidance, read in the prophetic book of Revelation that they must expect just such upheavals in the Last Days. That they were living through a time that would encompass the final overthrow of Satan and usher in the Second Coming was a possibility being explored even by advanced thinkers such as Joseph Priestley, Presbyterian minister and chemist.

In his sermon published in 1794, *The Present State of Europe Compared with Ancient Prophecies,* Priestley warned that if anything could be learned from the language of prophecy it was that greater calamities than the world had yet known would precede that happy state of affairs in which 'the kingdoms of this world will become the kingdom of our Lord Jesus Christ.' Priestley not only saw the disturbances in Europe as the beginning of these calamitous times but believed that the French Revolution was the fulfilment of Revelation 11:13: 'And the same hour was there a great earthquake, and the tenth part of the city fell, and in the earthquake were slain of men seven thousand: and the remnant were affrighted, and gave glory to the God of heaven'.

Against this background of war on the Continent, the fall of the French monarchy, bad harvests, food shortages and freakish weather people's thoughts turned easily to apocalypse and predisposed them to listen to Joanna. Socially and geographically her appeal was broad-based.

Numbered among her followers were scores of country folk like herself, reared on a diet of traditional piety spiced with superstition, people who looked naturally to their Bible for an explanation of whatever troubled them. She also attracted support from Anglican clergymen such as Thomas Foley, Thomas Webster, Stanhope Bruce, Samuel Eyre and Hoadley Ashe. Other adherents included William Sharp, famous engraver; Owen Pughe, lexicographer and close friend of Blake; Elias Carpenter, wealthy paper manufacturer; George Turner, a Leeds merchant; and Colonel William Tooke Harwood. At the peak of her career, her following numbered many thousands and her influence stretched from the West Country to the Midlands, the industrial cities of the North, and was particularly strong in London.

Nevertheless, Joanna's early hope of securing support from the Methodists in Exeter was disappointed. She had assumed that Dissenters would be her natural allies because they shared some of her millennial beliefs and, like her, regarded the Bible as the record of a golden age when perfect communion had existed between God and His people. If this golden age was ever to return, it seemed to her, then it must be through the restoration of both the form and substance of apostolic Christianity – which was exactly what she thought Methodists were trying to achieve. Their eventual rejection of her message was all the more bitter for the hopes they had aroused. 'I was deeply wounded with the conduct of the Methodists, who said that my writings were not from the Lord,' she wrote, castigating both kinds of Methodism found in Exeter at that time, Wesley's Arminianism and Whitefield's Calvinism.

Despite this experimentation Joanna always regarded herself as a devout daughter of the Church of England and even while going to Methodist meetings never neglected her regular attendance at Anglican services. Frequently she declared, 'Back to the Church all must come,' meaning that all sects were to seek in her their way back to the Anglican fold. That the clergy of the Established Church failed to appreciate this was a source of great disappointment to Joanna, for she believed that they had a crucial role to play in the accomplishment of her mission. Without their endorsement she feared that she might not be taken seriously. For this reason she made innumerable overtures to the Church hierarchy expecting them to examine her writings and arrange a formal hearing of her claims. Their disdainful reaction alienated Joanna from the clergy, if not from the Church. In one of her early pamphlets, *The Answer of the Lord to the Powers of Darkness,* Joanna's Spirit said, 'It is no Love to Me that man aspireth to be a bishop, a chancellor, an archdeacon, or a shepherd of the flock, it is their love to themselves, for they all preach for hire.'

The Anglican establishment's hostility towards Joanna had important consequences. It meant that the Southcottians inevitably turned to other forms of worship and, like the Methodists, founded their own chapels. Yet Joanna never gave up her attempts to find accommodation within the Church. To do this she had to establish her credibility beyond doubt. Knowing that if she were ever caught out in a deception all her claims would be open to question, she staged three formal 'trials' at which her writings and character were examined. Personal invitations were sent to the bishops and prominent clergy, but since none of these would attend, Joanna was each time denied the possibility of official sanction – or reproof.

There is no shortage of material when it comes to studying the life of Joanna Southcott, for she herself published sixty-five books detailing her exploits, visions and prophecies. Most of these books follow a basic pattern. First there is a description of some incident, dream, or prophecy. Then the 'Voice' of her Spirit takes over and in both prose and verse interprets the initial passage, seeing every event as a biblical 'type' that symbolises the present or predicts the future. For the biographer Joanna Southcott's books are a mixed blessing. They are not journals, but simply reflect whatever was in her head at the time, and her ideas tumble out in such confusion that they have to be pieced together, fragment by fragment, to form a shape. On the other hand, whilst they are not great literature, her jumbled reflections contain a wealth of intimate, and at times exuberant, detail that makes the woman, her family and her circle of friends come alive.

Contemporary observers dismissed Joanna as a fanatic, or worse, a cunning manipulator who exploited her followers for pecuniary gain. In 1812 Hewson Clarke, editor of *The Scourge,* admitted that he had no foundation for the scurrilous articles he had published about Joanna, but that 'being a prophetess, she was fair game for anyone to shoot at.' Caricaturists clearly thought so too and she became the butt of artists like Rowlandson and Cruikshank. In 1820 a defamatory account of her appeared in R.S.Kirby's *Wonderful and Eccentric Museum; Or Magazine of Remarkable Characters.* Fifty years later she received similar treatment in *The Book of Wonderful Characters: Memoirs and Anecdotes of Remarkable and Eccentric Persons in All Ages and Countries.* More recent studies have sought to place Joanna Southcott in a more meaningful context and give credit to the thousands of followers who gave her career its significance. In 1956 G. R. Balleine provided an accessible account of her life in *Past Finding Out: The Tragic Story of Joanna Southcott and Her Successors,* but his book suffers from an uncritical reliance on Joanna's own writings and a failure to quote sources. Since then J. F. C. Harrison's *The Second Coming* has included a judicious treatment of Joanna Southcott in his wide-ranging study of millenarianism, whilst at the same time stressing that she 'still awaits a modern published biography'. Similarly, J. K. Hopkins, in *A Woman to Deliver Her People,* has provided a stimulating study of Joanna Southcott and her followers by placing them in the social, intellectual and political setting of their time.

Earlier in the twentieth century Alice Seymour had revived public interest in Joanna by founding the Southcottian Society and publishing *The Express*, a two-volume biography drawn almost entirely from Joanna Southcott's own writings. Seymour confessed that many had been baffled in trying to write a satisfactory account of Joanna:

> [T]he incidents of her life are so scattered throughout so many books, and the trifling events that are mentioned, are nearly all set as types and prophetic to the nation at large, that one cannot but acknowledge that her life was indeed 'hid in God'. She could not understand why she was ordered to chronicle such ordinary everyday occurrences. . . .

For the present writer the challenge has been to extricate these 'ordinary everyday occurrences' and test them against other sources without becoming embroiled in the need to prove or deny Joanna's own 'spin' on events. To this end, Joanna's own propaganda has been checked against the evidence – contemporary letters, diaries, parish records and newspapers – with the result that many new and revealing facts have emerged about her family, early relationships and the events which led to her remarkable career as a visionary prophetess.

By any reckoning Joanna was a fascinating woman who exerted a powerful influence over her contemporaries. In her lifetime she had tens of thousands of followers and even today passions run high on the vexed question of her character. She was certainly charismatic, but was she a genuine spiritual leader? Was she naïve, or manipulative? Prophet, or impostor? Cunning cheat, or long-suffering saint? Because the jury is still out on these questions, this book aims to convey Joanna Southcott's story – without fear or favour – just as it happened, leaving readers to form their own judgement on the controversial character who dared to identify herself as the *Woman Clothed with the Sun*.

GROWING UP IN GITTISHAM, 1750-1765

Children, why do you blame your father? If he is passionate, he
is compassionate, and he doth not do like many men, spend his
time and his money in public houses, to bring you children to
the parish.

Copies & Parts of Copies, 1804

A stolid little girl with curly brown hair surveyed a flower bed, carefully
checking the carnations she had sown.[1] Examining each plant, she
excitedly pictured the wonderful blossoms that would be coming out
soon. What colour would they be? Red, perhaps. Or white. Time would
show, if she were patient, but patience was not one of her virtues. She
was not prepared to wait. Slowly and methodically she passed down the
row, pinching out the tip of every top bud. Curiosity satisfied, she wandered
away. Picture her chagrin, then, when in the course of time her flowers
blossomed and she found that every stem was topped by a withered bud.

What lesson should she draw from this? To take more notice of her
elders and betters? Develop more humility in the face of Creation? Of
course not. She was just a little girl growing flowers in her garden, but
she never forgot her mistake and brought it out years later to illustrate
the Lord's working – for nothing in Joanna Southcott's life was ever
wasted.[2] How could it be, when right from the day of her birth everything
was a sign and a wonder?

Old Moore's Almanac for 1750 showed angels trumpeting great joy
from heaven whilst a woman sat astride a dragon, piercing its head with
her spear.[3] It was the kind of glorious vision which later Southcottians
saw as heralding the birth of their Spiritual Mother, the Woman clothed
with the Sun, the Woman of Revelation. According to them this was the
exalted being born in Devon that year. No one at the time would have
recognised such a personage in the six-week old infant taken to the
church of Ottery St Mary on 6 June to be christened Joanna.

Joanna was the fourth surviving child of William and Hannah
Southcott, a hard-working, God-fearing couple who, after marrying in
Ottery, had spent the next seven years in Exmouth where their three
older children – William, Hannah and Lucy – were born. When Hannah's
father, John Godfrey, died in 1747, she and William had returned to take

Taleford Farm, near Ottery St Mary, Devon, where Joanna Southcott was born in April, 1750. Formerly the home of her maternal grandparents, John and Hannah Godfrey, the farm was very run down when the Southcotts took possession in 1747, and they tried to improve it.

over his farm in what should have been a beneficial move for the young family. Agricultural reform was in the air and Taleford Farm ripe for all the improvements which William set about introducing. His wife must have rejoiced at renewing acquaintance with old friends such as the Channons, who lived nearby at Fairmile. But her homecoming was marred by the fact that they had hardly settled in when baby Lucy sickened and died; although Hannah, already pregnant again, probably had her hands too full to grieve long. A third daughter, Susanna, was born in 1748 and Joanna less than two years later. After similar intervals of time, she gave birth to two more sons: John in 1752, and Joseph in 1755.[4] By that date, however, the family had moved to Gittisham, their fortunes having tumbled as a result of William Southcott's hasty temper.

Trouble arose from the fact that agricultural improvements cost money and although William and Hannah worked hard and long (it was said that a more industrious couple never came together) there were hurdles to jump before they could see profits.

Nevertheless, William set to work with a will, ploughing up the furze, thickets and barren ground, bringing it all into good heart. He even began excitedly to calculate what he would get from it – £50 a year, if he was lucky – a prize that attracted the covetous eyes of his neighbour, Mr Anley. Anley went to Mr Brooke, William's landlord, and slyly asked if he did not sometimes need more money? When Mr Brooke gave the predictable response, Anley asked whether William Southcott always paid his rent? He did, his landlord replied, but not always on time. In that case, suggested Anley, he had a proposition to make.

Brooke should let Southcott fall behind with his rent and then turn him out so that he, Anley, could take on the farm, paying twelve months' rent in advance.

This was an offer Mr Brooke could not refuse; the next time he met Southcott driving his sheep to Exeter market, he asked why he was selling at such a bad time.

'I must sell them, sir, to get your honour the rent,' William explained.
'Never mind that, I will wait. If it be a bad market,' Brooke advised,
'don't sell them.'

William thanked him and, finding prices low, drove the flock home
again and so did not have his rent ready in August. Come harvest time,
in the midst of reaping, he was shocked to hear that Mr Brooke had sent
two bailiffs to his house to seize for the half-year's rent. In this crisis,
Hannah rushed to Fairmile to borrow money from their friend, Edward
Channon, the blacksmith, who returned with her to tell Mr Brooke what
an ungrateful, wicked thing he had done after all the improvements
Southcott had made on his farm.

'If you are afraid to trust the farmer, I am not,' he declared, slapping
down the money.

There the matter might have rested had it not been for William's
temper. As it was, words rose high and when Mr Brooke suggested a
change in their agreement, William refused in no uncertain manner and
in a fit of pique gave notice to quit on Lady-day. Having previously
received many offers of farms, he thought it would be easy to find
another as good, but he proved wrong. Now, when he applied for these
farms, their owners asked Mr Brooke for his character and were told
that he was honest but poor. Concluding that he had too little money to
make improvements, they withdrew their offers.

Lady-day found William Southcott obliged to sell off part of his stock
and take a small farm three miles away at Gittisham.[5] It was a move
which proved heart-breaking, for the new land was so impoverished
that it took a year for him to make enough money even to pay the rent.[6]

Lying in the Otter valley about sixteen miles from Exeter, Gittisham is
a pretty cob-and-thatch village remarkably little changed in appearance
since the eighteenth century. Riding through East Devon in the summer
of 1794 the Reverend John Swete followed 'the windings of the Otter
which as a silver serpent rolled itself through a most enchanting expanse
of greenest pastures' before arriving in Gittisham

> which had a neat trim appearance and was most charmingly
> situated in a rich, well-wooded valley. [H]aving forded a little
> river which descended from the neighbouring hills, I passed
> through a grove of venerable elms casting a solemn shade,
> impervious to the sun, and alighted at the gate of the school
> house.[7]

No doubt the 'neat trim appearance' of the village owed much to the
influence of its lords of the manor, the Putt family, whose ancient
mansion, Combe, was situated in a woody vale beyond the church and
whose domain included most of the parish. Certain it was that Squire

Putt dominated the intimate world of Gittisham which the Southcotts entered in the 1750s.

Joanna, under five years old when her family moved, was too young to be aware of all the hardship involved. They took possession of a farm which, surrounded by its own fields and cider orchards, had the usual range of outbuildings as well as a dilapidated lower house which had stood empty since its last occupant drowned himself in the nearby well. William Southcott agreed to let one of his sons use this building for breeding rabbits. The enterprise, however, brought friction with the village when the rabbits jumped around so noisily at night that rumours spread of sinister goings-on at the lonely site. No one thought of rabbits as the culprits. The place was being used by smugglers, it was whispered.

Squire Putt summoned William Southcott into the schoolhouse one Sunday to answer the charge. Naturally William denied any connection with smugglers and luckily Squire Putt believed him, even going on to persuade him to serve a second term as poor warden after examining his 'peevishly honest' accounts.[8]

Nevertheless, William must have found it galling to tug his forelock to the squire, for he was wont to dream of his own lost inheritance. Insisting that he was the first in his family who knew what it was to work, he often fell to telling his children the saga of how he might have been a rich landowner in Hertfordshire had it not been for a series of dire misadventures.

William's grandfather – so the story went – had taken a second wife who made life so wretched for his eldest son, John, that he ran away to sea in an attempt to reach an uncle who had settled in Pennsylvania. Working his passage in a ship bound for Topsham in Devon, John confided in the captain who promptly wrote on his behalf to his father. He received back a money-draft for £200 and the news that his father, though still angry, would never disinherit him or cut off the entail of the land, which had been in succession for seven generations. The captain declared:

> Mr Southcott, why had not you made yourself known to me sooner? I used to call you John, but I should never have treated you in the manner I have, if I had known you were that gentleman's son.

After leaving the ship, John married Miss Mauditt, a local girl with a moderate fortune, and they lived at Topsham till William was born. Then John visited the uncle in Pennsylvania who, turning out to be the richest man in the place and childless to boot, promptly promised to leave everything to his nephew.

John returned to Topsham to fetch his wife and son only to find his wife reluctant to go to Pennsylvania. He begged her. She refused. He

Hayne Cottage, Gittisham, was Joanna's childhood home. The photograph, taken in 1927, shows its owner, Olive May Langworthy, standing outside her home in Hayne's Lane. A place of pilgrimage for many Southcottians in the 1920s, 'Joanna's Cottage' was destroyed by fire in 1971; no trace now remains.

stayed long enough for a second son to be born, then took sail for America again. The ship foundered and he was drowned.

William's mother, left destitute, farmed him out to her uncle, Mr Mills, who had an estate of £50 a year which he promised to leave him. Another relation took in the younger boy, John. The widow soon remarried.

Then old William Southcott in Hertfordshire died and his youngest son wrote that, since he was not married, nor ever likely to be, his sister-in-law should send him her two sons so that the elder could inherit the Southcott estate and the younger all the remaining fortune. At last the sun seemed about to shine, but no! William's mother, ashamed of her feckless new husband, failed to reply to her brother-in-law's letter. Offended, he wrote no more.

Young William's hopes were further blasted when his guardian, Mr Mills, got drunk and signed away his whole estate for £50.

'My dear boy, my dear child, I have ruined thee for ever!' he sobbed, as depression and drink dragged him into a pauper's grave. Left to make shift as best he could, William took a humble post as farm servant near Ottery St Mary.

By his own account William Southcott succeeded in breaking many hearts in the neighbourhood before 1737 when, at the age of twenty-one, he married Elizabeth Sayer – marrying her out of pity, he said, after being told that she was ill and could not live without him.

Two years later Elizabeth, frail and expecting a child, asked one of her closest friends, Hannah Godfrey, to keep her company. Seeing this young woman in his wife's sickroom, William allowed himself to entertain the idea that, should his Elizabeth die, he would – as soon as decency allowed – address his attentions to her attractive friend.

Hannah, a devout chapel-goer, would have been horrified by such thoughts. William Southcott? He was the last man she would marry, she had protested after hearing her father's servant repeat a conversation he had had with other young men about the relative virtues of local girls. One had declared his fancy for Hannah Godfrey as a wife only to hear another object: 'I would never go a-courting there; for men enough have tried, and she hath refused them all. She looks with scorn on every man.'

But William Southcott had spoken up: 'You know not how to go a-courting to a religious woman: I'll be bound for it, if I was a widower I would gain her.'

His words left Hannah indignant and promising herself that William Southcott would never find her such easy game. Nursing her sick friend in child-bed, however, gave Hannah the chance to see William in a different light – as a man made distraught by his wife's sufferings, a man full of tender feelings who was, when Elizabeth died, torn with self-reproach. In these circumstances her heart was touched to the extent that, in February 1740, less than three months after her friend's death, Hannah agreed to become the widower's wife.

At Exmouth, where the Southcotts spent the first seven years of marriage, William caught another tantalising glimpse of his lost inheritance. A local solicitor, also called Southcott, after seeing William snubbed, sprang to his defence by explaining how he was legal heir to estates which had been in his family for seven generations. Furthermore, he promised to get those estates for £5 if William went to London and proved his grandfather's will. So there it was again – his birthright beckoning. This time there should have been nothing to stand in William's way, except . . . there was a war being waged and William was afraid of being pressganged, so he put off going until peace returned – by which time Hannah's father had died and, taking over Taleford Farm, William declared that now he would live by his own hands.[9]

Such was the oft-told tale of the Southcotts' lost inheritance. Regardless of how much was true, this long saga left an indelible impression not only on William himself who, as he grew older, fell to brooding over his misfortunes, but also on his children. They all, especially Joanna, grew up with a sense of being born for higher things.

Nevertheless, while they were young, it was not their family's past

Gittisham church and the school that Joanna may have attended – a pen and ink sketch made in 1975 by Julian Roebuck, A.R.C.A. Gittisham school house was founded in the early eighteenth century by Sir Thomas Putt, lord of the manor and head of the family that dominated village affairs for more than two hundred years. The church retains its eighteenth century box-pews, decorated ceiling in the chancel and several impressive monuments to the Putt family. With its pale stone houses and charming cob-and-thatch cottages Gittisham has remained in many ways little changed since Joanna Southcott lived here.

but their father's ever-present moods that filled them with awe, for William Southcott had a temper which he was prone to take out on his children. Brooking no interference with his authority, when his eldest son upset one of the maids, William banned him from the supper table, declaring that

> it was as good to be a toad under a pair of harrows as to be an apprentice under so many masters and mistresses. One master and mistress were enough for any one, and no apprentice in his house should have more.

Since after each explosion of rage he left his wife to act as peace-maker, there must have been times when poor Hannah ran out of excuses for him. She would chide on these occasions:

> Children, why do you blame your father? If he is passionate, he is compassionate, and he doth not do like many men, spend his time and his money in public-houses, to bring you children to the parish; but he has been a hard-working, careful, industrious man, to keep you from the parish, that you might not suffer, as other poor apprentices do.[10]

At which they were supposed to feel grateful, if no less terrified by the prospect of William's next display of wrath.

Yet by his own lights he was a good father, providing for his children's material needs and looking after their spiritual welfare. He taught them to study the Scriptures daily, regularly testing them to make sure they understood what they had read. Joanna found these sessions a dreadful ordeal for, although she knew that she could read and comprehend every bit as well as her brothers and sisters, for some reason she found herself tongue-tied when she was questioned. 'She felt but could not describe,'[11] she recalled later, remembering how often she had run off into the fields to weep and pray that she could learn better.[12]

She also remembered the time when, after reading about the disciples in the Bible, she had taken herself off to a shady grove some distance from the house and there solemnly prayed to God not to let her ever be like Peter to deny Christ.[13]

So what was she like, this impressionable little girl growing up in Gittisham? An imaginative child, fond of her own company, often hiding herself away to think and dream – she liked nothing better than to walk in the fields singing her favourite hymns to the wind.[14] She found little enough time to read, even though both parents encouraged her to study the Bible. Like most farmers' daughters she was from an early age expected to work hard[15] so, always anxious to please,[16] she joined her sisters in cooking, washing and sewing clothes, milking cows, feeding hens, and any other jobs she could manage.

But lest all work make Joanna sound a dull child, there were also times for play. One winter, for example, when their pond froze over, she was soon out on the shiny ice, sliding up and down, oblivious to danger and had reached the far end when the ice cracked. She went under and would have drowned had not her father, threshing in his barn, seen what was happening and rushed to her rescue, breaking the ice to get her out.[17]

As for her character, her younger brother Joseph remembered Joanna as a mild, placid, well-behaved and truthful child. And to her own mind Joanna appeared unselfish to a fault, always studying the happiness of her brothers and sisters and doing what she could for them. Imbibing religion with her mother's milk, she sat by a hearth where worldly and otherworldly never drew far apart. On long winter nights before the fire in the kitchen, she took her place amid the womenfolk as they cooked, sewed, cleaned and whiled away their time, as country people always have, by spinning tales of local wonders.

There was the strange story of Joanna's Uncle John, her father's younger brother who went to sea. A religious young man, the last time he left he said to William: 'My dear brother, I hope we shall meet in a better world! I don't believe I shall ever see you more in this.'

Rather than return immediately after the voyage he wrote his mother that he was taking ship for London so that he could visit Hertford to make enquiries about the family's property. She immediately asked him to come straight home, as she had had dreadful dreams about his being drowned. He complied and took passage in a ship which, racing another into Topsham, ran on to rocks and was dashed to pieces.

Then there was Granny Godfrey who lived at Cadhay and was blessed with second sight. When her son, another religious youth, heard that his close friend, Mr Dagworthy, was sick, he called round only to meet his coffin at the door. The shock sent him into such despair that, when he suddenly disappeared, his family suspected suicide. Not Granny Godfrey, though. She dreamt that he had gone to sea and, though nothing more was heard for over a year, she kept reassuring the family that he would come home safely – which, two years later, he did.

For Joanna this kind of instance was 'a sure sign that the Lord is with us as in ages past, to warn us by dreams and visions of the night.'

It was hard to be philosophical about what happened to her grandmother's maids, though. One described a dream in which she was walking in Cadhay fields between Ottery and Fairmile when a cat scratched her breast till she bled to death.[18] A few days later the poor girl was found in the same field, raped and murdered. Another maid dreamt she was walking over Sidbury Hill when she was stung to death by a serpent. She too was later found murdered on that very spot.

Such were the dark stories told at twilight, but by day Gittisham was a different place, full of sunlit scenes as in the Garden of Eden – except that, as recalled by Joanna, there was usually a snake hidden in the grass. Throughout her life her dreams and writings were full of farming images – weeds lying at the butt-end of the sheaf so that when the labourer comes to thresh, he has to spread them with a steel comb and later burn them for stroil (raked weeds) to stop their seeds returning to the soil.[19] And there were so many times she dreamt of her father with his shirt-collar unbuttoned on a hot summer's day, or bare-chested and reaping so fast that he was covered in sweat.[20] These earthy, fertile images filled Joanna's dreams as she emerged from the stolid child into a passionate young woman, who was painfully aware of the change and castigated herself for falling short of that ideal woman always before her eyes in the person of her beloved mother.

Among her neighbours Hannah Southcott was a byword for Christian charity, so it was not unusual when a local woman turned to her when her husband lay dying and asked if she could spare one of her daughters to sit by him during the night.[21] Hannah, eager to help, sent fourteen-year old Joanna. Sitting by his bed hour after hour, Joanna was deeply troubled, not by the man's imminent demise, but by the fact that he was an atheist. By midnight she was petrified and began to feel the room quake as the Devil came for his own. Nor was she alone in her fears, for the dying man reared up in his bed wailing, 'There's a great black dog down in the window.'

When Joanna tried to reassure him, he howled:

'You think I am light, but I'm not. I tell you the Devil is there.'

For the next hour he trembled so much that the bed shook under him.

'I do not remember, in all this time, that he once called on the Lord to have mercy on him,' she later recalled. 'This made a deep impression on my mind and heart, and made me fear sin more than death.'[21]

The experience reinforced her obsession with death. From childhood, she said, death was always before her. Any young person's death prompted fears for her own sudden demise,[22] setting her at war with herself – half of her striving for sainthood, the other half drawn towards something very different. She hated the idea of growing up like her sisters, both of whom were consumed by thoughts of courtship and marriage, yet the sensual part of her nature inevitably dragged her that way.

'When I came to the age of fifteen or sixteen and began to be flattered by the world, I found vanity arise,' she confessed, 'and I became vain.'[23]

Moreover, being Joanna, there was no such thing as moderation. She gave way to a passion for clothes, striving to outshine her sisters and friends, determined to be nothing less than the best dressed young woman in the neighbourhood:

> So deeply was my heart fixed on the vanity of dress that I did
> not care how hard I worked, early and late, so long as I could
> earn money to get clothes to appear smart in.

Her unworldly mother, shocked at this change in her youngest daughter, took her sternly to task.

'Joanna, my dear child,' Hannah said, relying on edifying verse to make her point,

> Wilt thou then thy bright morning waste,
> To trim and make thee fine?
> 'Twill be but bitterness at last,
> If Christ be none of thine.
> How frail is beauty, in how short a time
> 'Twill fade like roses which are past their prime.[24]

Joanna listened, but being young and in the spring of life, the wintry words had but a momentary effect. More significant was her failure to heed her father when he rounded on her, telling her that he was ashamed to see her, a farmer's daughter, dressing the way she did. In fact, his words seemed to give her satisfaction. After all, it was not her fault that he had lost his birthright and, no matter how he might disapprove, there was a big world beyond Gittisham where both she and her new finery might be better appreciated.

VANITY OF YOUTH, 1765-1770

As Noah was the only man that I said was a just and perfect man that walked before God and found favour in My sight – perfect so was the name with thee.

Answer of the Revd T.P. Foley to the World, 1805

Joanna left home in her teens to join her eldest brother William on his farm on the slopes of Bulverton Hill within view of the sea at Sidmouth.[1] If she had been hoping for an easier life here, she did not find it, for her days were still filled with the hundred and one tasks that had occupied her since childhood – picking fruit, milking cows, making butter and cheese and working in the fields. Common country chores – nothing to write home about – but scenes which formed her inner landscape and wove in and out of her dreams for the rest of her life.

William's land included five fields known as High Street – three adjoining Bulverton Hill and two called New Park and Warp on the other side of the roadway.[2] They included pasture and some rather poor arable land on which he tried to grow corn. In summer one of Joanna's tasks was to weed between the wheatstalks before the ears had grown, back-breaking work at the best of times and heart-breaking too when she knew that the crop might be ruined by rust disease and canker and have to be kept back as 'tail corn' for the chickens.[3]

But if the work was hard and at times dispiriting, there were compensations. For at Sidmouth, away from her pious mother and irascible father, Joanna was at least free to enjoy the company of her brother's friends: the Bishops and the Wests, whose families farmed nearby, Fanny Wickers, Nicholas Paige, William Carter, and Richard Isaac – all these young people engaged in similar pursuits to herself and regularly met up at local fairs and harvest-home.[4]

However, not all William's neighbours met with Joanna's approval and her sharp eyes soon noticed Mr Follard's shepherd skiving. She complained that she had been in her brother's ground weeding, and seen him ride into the fields with his dogs to inspect the flock, whilst at the same time she knew many sheep were in the ditch groaning and eaten by maggots. He then rode out of the field, taking no notice of missing sheep. Enraged, she reported this neglect to others who confirmed that they had seen the man's sheep lying dead under the bushes while he idled away his time in the pub.[5]

Such fellows got short shrift from Joanna who, though attracting attention from many young hopefuls in the area, from the start only had eyes for one. 'When I was young in years I had many lovers; but the first I indulged the company of was Noah Bishop, a farmer's son in Sidmouth,' she wrote later.[6]

Noah, a year younger than Joanna, was completely different in temperament, less complicated, more extrovert. Whereas Joanna in her late teens was riddled by self-doubt, and in matters of the heart pathetically dependent on her friends' opinions, Noah was hot-headed, impatient and known to have a temper. What made him even less suitable as a match was his lack of money and poor prospects. As a younger son there was little chance of his inheriting much – a fact her friends were keen to point out when Joanna started walking out with him. At first she tried to ignore their words, but as they kept on insisting that Noah had a terrible temper and would break her heart if she married him, she eventually decided to put him to the test. Just to see how he would react she accused him of being unfaithful.

Noah's response was predictable. Working himself into a lather, he hoped her friends' tongues would burn in hell. Ah, she replied tartly, then if she were to marry him, he might wish hers there too. No, he replied, it was his fervent love for her that provoked such fury against his detractors. Joanna was not convinced. She knew that she loved him, but was appalled by his violence. Telling herself that it was better to 'once smart than always ache', she broke off the courtship.

Here it might have stood had not the busy tongues of her friends kept wagging. Noah was so miserable, they told her. He had said he would as soon be dead as alive and made himself ill on her account. Then, finding himself unable to die of love, he had gone to sea rather than wait to see her wed another.

Their remarks rekindled Joanna's love.

'I would rather break my heart by his passions, than break my heart by my own cruelty and wound us both,' she thought, making up her mind to accept if he proposed again.

Noah returned from his sea voyage, and when they met on the morning of Sidmouth fair he asked if she was going that afternoon.

'Yes,' she replied, deciding there and then.

At the fair she tried to avoid her neighbours in favour of the one person she wanted to meet – Noah. When her friends kept pressing her to join them, she excused herself by saying that she was looking for her brother to take her home. Suddenly, going up through the fair, she caught

sight of William standing with a younger man who, glory be! turned out
to be Noah. Noah pressed her to join him, and . . . for some inexplicable
reason she couldn't. Not for the first, nor the last, time everything in
her froze as she heard herself asking her brother to take her home.

While William went obligingly into the yard for the horse, Noah begged
her to join him for a drink – in the name of old friendship, if not new.
She declined in no uncertain terms. Not for old or new, nor even if he
used as many words as there were stars in the sky or stones in the
street, would she go with him.

So that was that. Except . . . poor Noah's misery had touched her
heart and, no sooner had she mounted the horse, than she had second
thoughts and wanted to be back at the fair with him. In silence she rode
home with her brother until, noticing how depressed she was, William
pointed out, 'This is the way of women. You refused to go with him
when he entreated you, and now you are as melancholy as he.'

All that night she tossed and turned. Next day she felt worse when
one of her friends told her how a sudden downpour had driven the
young people into a public-house the night before and they had all had
their sweethearts there except Noah who, although there was a young
woman just crazy about him, took no notice of her but sat and looked
glum all evening.

Hearing this, Joanna's heart melted. Never would she spurn him again,
she resolved. So when, on the following Sunday, she was going off to
milk her brother's cows and who should appear but Noah, offering to
help – what was her response? Her limbs quaked. Her lips trembled.
And she refused. Naturally. Moreover, she had not gone twenty yards
before regretting it!

Another week passed. Sunday came round again. Noah and his friend
Richard appeared. Richard asked Joanna if he could help himself to
some pears from her brother's tree. She readily agreed. Noah asked if
he could go into the orchard to pick some too. Joanna refused him,
saying that Richard would bring him some.

And so it went on. When Noah was with her, she did not want to
know. When he was gone her heart ached for him.

At length Noah admitted defeat:

I have tried often enough and it is always the same, and all her
friends are against me; and now if I die for her sake, I'll never
try more.

Hearing this, Joanna was convinced that his passion was love –
especially when he refused to let her go before she told him who had
put her against him, gripping her hands so hard that they hurt for days
afterwards.

Now she loved him to such distraction that her sisters, alarmed by her state of mind, persuaded her to leave Sidmouth and go back to Gittisham.

'No! You may kill me or you may drown me, but I will not leave the place where he is,' she wailed. 'I must see him, if I cannot have him.'

So she stayed on, hoping to meet Noah at Newton Fair some weeks later. It was unfortunate that fair day found her not looking her best. Head in the clouds and distracted by love, she had run through the orchard and almost blinded herself by getting a 'cuckol-button' (burdock seed) in her eye. Seeing her face so swollen, her family tried to dissuade her from going, but Joanna was determined.

'There he is, there he is!' she exclaimed excitedly as she clapped eyes on Noah.

He passed her by without acknowledgement. So was the biter bit.

As her two sisters fell about with laughter, Joanna wept.

Later, on their way home, they met Noah's older brother, Nathaniel, who asked what was wrong with Joanna's eye. She explained.

'Can't Noah cure it?' he teased.

'If he can, he won't!' Joanna shrieked.

Such indiscretion shocked her sisters, who tut-tutted at her for giving herself away. But Joanna was past caring. All she wanted was to rekindle Noah's love. Indeed, she knew now that she could not live without him.

All of which her sisters repeated to their parents when they went home the following day, with no idea what dramatic affect their words would have on their father. William Southcott groaned, pacing up and down and starting to list all the women he had himself courted and not married:

> My former sins are brought to my remembrance. How many women's hearts have I broken by love! Now it is come home upon me: for that maid, who is the delight of my soul, is now wounded the same.

But for Joanna, the game was not yet over. It came to her ears that Noah was being pursued by Fanny Wickers so she taxed him with this when they met on Sidmouth beach one Sunday. Citing Fanny's loose reputation, Noah insisted that he had no more than passed the time of day with her.[7] Joanna refused to listen. Neither would she see him when he came to William's house the following Sunday until, going out to milk the cows that evening, she found him waiting at the orchard gate. With a halter in his hand, he said he had just brought up the colt and would not let her pass until he had convinced her that not only did he not like Fanny Wickers but that she, Joanna, was the only woman in the world he loved.

If that were the case, Joanna sniffed, he should have come the previous Monday night and not kept away all week, leaving her to assume he was with Fanny.

But he *had* tried to see Joanna that Monday, Noah protested. His father had sent him up Bulverton Hill to find his colts and he had come round to William's land two or three times that morning in the hope of catching her when she watered the bullocks at noon. In fact, his visits had made him so late that he failed to reach home before nightfall – a fact she could verify by asking Nathaniel and his friends.[8] Even though Joanna accepted his explanation, it made no difference to their relationship.

She loved Noah, but only at a distance. When he was with her, she found herself snubbing the fellow and sending him packing. So it should have come as no surprise when he gave up the chase, and yet regret at losing him was no less bitter for knowing that she had no one to blame but herself. Years later she was still reproaching herself:

> The fault was thine, now I'll resign,
> Thy anger rose too soon;
> Thou didst resent and then relent
> And cloud thy sun ere noon.[9]

And although her sister Susanna kept assuring her that there were plenty more fish in the sea, Joanna insisted that she would rather die than marry another. She was even prepared to listen to her mother, who urged her to follow the example of Great-aunt Sarah and seek comfort in religion.

The story of Sarah Southcott formed another romantic strand in Joanna's family saga. Sarah, sister to Joanna's grandfather, had been a great beauty who had attracted many admirers in her youth but fallen in love with a gentleman whose modest means did not meet with her father's approval. Forced to reject her lover, Sarah had found compensation in religion and spent the rest of her short life composing hymns and meditations. Some of these, printed in a book which Hannah possessed, made a profound impression on Joanna who, after breaking with Noah, fell to wandering the fields reciting Great-aunt Sarah's poems in an effort to quell her own rebellious passions.

> I love thee more than life or interest;
> Nor hast thou any rival in my breast;
> I love thee so, that for one smile of thine,
> Was all the world – the brightest gems were mine,
> Then I to fools these trifles would resign,
> And envy none the world, if Christ be mine.[10]

Verses such as this, Joanna wrote, 'have been a comfort and

consolation to me, amidst the various troubles I have passed through, to bring my heart above this world.'

It was as well for Joanna to adopt a more philosophical attitude with the world changing so rapidly about her ears. According to the records, William Southcott, husbandman, married Susannah Major, spinster, on 20 September 1768 at Gittisham church in a ceremony conducted by the Reverend William Putt in the presence of Lydia Major and William Keene. With the advent of this new Mrs Southcott, Joanna's presence was no longer so welcome in her brother's home in Sidmouth, but rather than return to her parents, she decided to take service in Honiton, a busy little market-town lying on the main London-Exeter road about three miles from Gittisham.

In Honiton she found a job with Mr and Mrs Arthur Brown, owners of a bookshop which had fortunately survived the devastating fire that had ravaged the town in 1765, destroying over a hundred houses. Joanna quickly settled in with her new employers, identifying so closely with their interests that they came to look on her more as a daughter than a servant.[11]

Arthur Brown was a member of Honiton's Independent Chapel. Besides selling books, he took in advertisements for *Trewman's Flying Post,* which in turn publicised his new stock. In 1768 this included the latest volumes of Clarendon's *History of England* – which Joanna could dip into in free moments. Arthur Brown also acted as an agent for drugs such as Dr Flugger's 'Lignorum Antiscorbutic Drops' which could 'perfectly cure the most inveterate scurvy, leprosy, pimpled face of ever so long standing. Likewise the Evil, Fistula, Piles, old obstinate sores or ulcers and is a Sovereign Remedy in all disorders arising from the Foulness of blood incident to the Fair Sex' – a concoction which sold in his shop at 5 shillings (25p) the bottle 'with directions'.[12]

However, it was her own healing salve that Mrs Brown applied to the nasty boil which came up on Joanna's shoulder where her stays rubbed. This brought temporary relief, but because the boil had already turned septic it was soon causing agony and eventually the only way to save Joanna's arm was to reopen the wound and use another ointment to draw out the poison.[13]

Although the sons of the house were too young to be tempted by Joanna's charms, it was not long before she caught the eye of an apprentice serge-maker who attended the Independent Chapel. John Thomas was considered to be 'a man of fortune' but, still heart-broken over Noah, Joanna decided to discourage his advances by making it clear that her father as a poor farmer could give her no dowry. Far from being put off, John Thomas promptly asked her to marry him. He declared,

> Money, my dear, I do not want. I have money enough for you and myself too: I have fifty pounds a year, which my uncle left me; I have money out at use, which my father gave me, which I will call in, if you will be married, and place you in a shop before my time is out; for I had rather have you without a farthing, than any other woman with five hundred pounds.[14]

A tempting offer! Joanna, though not in love, began to walk out with him. Then, just as their relationship was starting to develop, she heard her mother was sick. There was no apparent cause for alarm, but Joanna hurried home to help nurse her. She arrived to find her mother far worse than expected and for the next few days hardly ever left her side, while around them the life of the farm continued – cows being milked, butter churned and cheese made – with Susanna, playing Martha to Joanna's Mary, on hand to take charge.

Then came the night when Joanna, sitting at the bedside, heard a strange sound from her mother's throat and asked what was wrong.

'My dear child, don't you hear the rattle is upon me?' Hannah whispered.

Deeply shocked, Joanna asked if she was in pain.

'No, my dear child,' she sighed, before softly reciting:

> Jesus can make a dying bed
> As sweet as downy pillows are,
> While on his breast I lay my head
> And breathe my life out sweetly there.

Joanna shouted for Susanna and together the sisters sat at their mother's side till morning when, thinking that she seemed stronger, they went down to their dairy work while a neighbour, Mrs Venn, took their place. An hour later, at about eight o'clock, Hannah intimated that her time was short.

'As to my children,' she murmured, 'I must leave them to the Lord; but tell Joanna to come to me.'

Leaving Susanna to finish the butter, Joanna went up alone and approached the bed. Taking her hand, her mother sighed:

> My dear child, stand there and learn how to die. Live in Christ, for to die in Him is great gain. What profit would all the world be to me now, if I had it to leave to you, and I myself was lost? You are a maid of lively spirits and great courage, be strong in the Lord; cast all thy care on Him, for He careth for thee. Commit all thy ways unto the Lord, and He will direct thy goings; and the blessing of God be with thee, my dear child![15]

After which she said little beyond: 'What is not already done, must now be left undone.'[16]

Just before the end, her husband and Susanna entered the room and, although she tried to say more, her Voice failed her. She died with her hand in Joanna's and was buried near her parents in the graveyard of the Independent Chapel in Ottery St Mary.[17]

Her death left the family devastated. It was such a shock. Because she had not been ill long, nobody guessed her end was so near. On Joanna in particular her mother's death and dying words made a tremendous impact. Inevitably she compared the scene with the dreadful deathbed of their ungodly neighbour and, after a fit of soul-searching, returned to Honiton a changed person. It was as if her mother's death had left Joanna dead to the world and, in her own words, 'thoughts of the other drew my thoughts from love.' She no longer had any interest in poor John Thomas.

When, at Mr Brown's request, she went the following Sunday to hear Mr Stevens of Axminster preach on the text: 'Blessed are they that weep, for they shall be comforted', it seemed to Joanna that the minister was speaking specifically to her. Afterwards, John Thomas walked her part of the way home, the last time he was to spend in her company. Joanna was no longer susceptible to his charms. For the moment she had turned away from men to follow in the footsteps of Great-aunt Sarah and give herself up to God.[18]

STORMY COURTSHIPS, 1770-1776

All thy lovers were broken off by ME.
An Explanation of the Parables, 1804

In May 1771 Joanna's eldest sister, Hannah, had married Nicholas Paige and gone to live in Black Torrington, the village in West Devon where his family had farmed for centuries.[1] After her mother's death, Joanna travelled down to see them and their new baby daughter, but had scarcely arrived in the place before attracting the attentions of another eligible bachelor. In fact, John Rigsby declared himself smitten by love when he first laid eyes on Joanna in the local church and was soon offering her both his hand and his fortune of £60 per annum.

Financially she had received better offers, but sister Hannah favoured the match and there must have been something about the young man – his looks, perhaps, or his manner; or was it the tempting smell of forbidden fruit? Certainly Joanna was attracted despite persistent rumours about Rigsby's dark past.

He had, it was whispered, fathered a child on some poor, unfortunate girl who had died in giving birth. Or worse! After living with a woman and getting her with child, he urged her to take savine (oil extracted from juniper) to get rid of it. She did and in the process killed herself, confessing on her deathbed without blaming him so that he might avoid prosecution. Naturally his reputation had suffered as a result, but being young and possessed of a decent fortune Rigsby had soon managed to regain his neighbours' respect.

Joanna heard the stories with a sense of mounting horror. It seemed impossible that she should be attracted to such a man, but since when she was with him she could hardly trust herself there was only one thing to do. By the time Rigsby arrived at Hannah's house to press his suit, Joanna had fled back to Gittisham.

Back home, she said nothing to her father, so it was only when he went to Black Torrington himself that William heard about Rigsby's attachment to his daughter. Without waiting to hear her side of the affair, he returned home furious at Joanna for refusing such a handsome, well-heeled gentleman. Rather than stoop to give her reasons, Joanna simply said that she did not like the man, whereupon her father stormed:

I don't know what the Devil thou dost like! Thou shouldst have
a man chalked out for thee; and if thou dost not like him, he
shall be blotted out again.[2]

To which Joanna declared that all she wanted was a husband who
was noble-minded.

Her father retorted that he had seen no such men around: there were
plenty good enough for her sisters but the man was not yet born who
was good enough for Joanna.

With this Joanna might well have agreed, had she not still some
lingering hope of Noah Bishop. However, when she returned to her
brother's home in Sidmouth she found herself becoming involved, not
with Noah, but with one of his friends – Peter West, whose sister had
recently married Noah's brother, Nathaniel.[3]

'Here my heart began to be entangled again in love which I dreaded,'
she later confessed, describing how Peter was not only young and
handsome but of unexceptionable character.

Soon they were walking out together and everything seemed set for
wedding bells except . . . Joanna began to have her doubts. One Sunday
evening found her pacing up and down her room asking, in a fit of
anguish, 'Where is my foolish heart wandering?' Struggling with what
she regarded as her own weakness, she begged God not to let her 'keep
company' with any man not destined to be her husband.

She received an answer: if Peter stayed away for a month then he
was not for her.

Stay away for a month? That seemed out of the question for one so
ardent in his courtship that, as her brother joked next day, it was probably
too hot to last. When Joanna replied that if it lasted a month it would last
forever, William laughed. But the day passed and Peter made no
appearance. Nor did he come on the next, or any following day. In fact,
it was two months before Joanna set eyes on him again. Then, meeting
her by chance, Peter wanted to resume where they had left off. Joanna
declined. He promised never to deceive her again. She replied stiffly
that no man would ever deceive her twice.

Echoing her father, he snapped, 'These upright men get if you can;
but I don't know where you will find them.'

On reflection, Joanna agreed with him: 'True I found his words; as
true as he did mine; for upright men are very scarce.'[4]

Retreating from Peter West, Joanna took refuge again in Gittisham where
Susanna had been keeping house for their father since their mother's
death. A nubile, if rather solemn, young woman in her early twenties,
Susanna too had been plagued by unwanted male attention, especially

after a local farmer's son who had been courting her for years refused to take no for an answer. Having used every art to seduce her, all to no avail, he eventually resorted to such violence that William Southcott had to call on the law to restrain him. To escape this unhappy situation, Susanna paid a prolonged visit to Hannah in Black Torrington while Joanna took her turn as house-keeper.[5] However, no sooner had Joanna taken her sister's place but she became embroiled in a feud with the disappointed suitor who had now turned his malice against their father.

Everything began to go wrong for William Southcott. His stock died, his crops failed. And although his enemy's servants more or less confessed that they had caused the deaths of William's cattle, saying that their master had brought more guilt on their heads over farmer Southcott than all other sins in their lives, there was no way of proving the charge. As a result of the harassment William found himself eventually facing not only ruin but mental collapse.

Joanna was left to contemplate the spectacle of her father's mind giving way under the strain. Night after night, after listing his grievances, he went to bed in such agitation that Joanna would have to sit by his side for hours trying to reason with him.

> I have seen the sweat running down his face, in a cold winter's night, like a man in the harvest day, that I have stood hours wiping his face. He said all the sorrows and disappointments in life that he had gone through now crowded upon his mind; and the loss of his property that he was heir to, now came upon him with a double weight.[6]

Chief among William's sorrows were his children – and it can have come as no pleasure for Joanna to find that his chief concern was Susanna. Day after day she listened as he constantly lamented how his poor Susanna had been forced to flee from her home; occasionally varying the tune by complaining about his second son, John, who had brought shame on the family by getting a local girl called Jemima into trouble.[7]

For three months, while her father's mind tottered on the brink of insanity, Joanna cosseted and cajoled him, urging him to forget his losses and imagine he had never had any prospects. Refusing to listen, he sank into such a depression that he despaired of seeing another harvest. Meanwhile, it fell to Joanna to run the farm and keep it going until her father's tenure was up so that he could walk away from the business with some profit, for the fields were in good condition after all his improvements and the cider apples due to crop well that year. Throwing herself into the work, she slaved away with the zeal of a martyr, working every hour God sent in order to avoid hiring extra hands.[8]

It was a formative time in her development, for to the strong religious faith she had imbibed from her mother she now added a growing belief in her own special abilities. She became convinced, for instance, that she could foretell the future. This talent probably originated in her success at forecasting the weather – a talent especially valued by a rural community concerned for their crops, and one for which Joanna acquired such a reputation that farmers from miles around began to base their operations on her forecasts and at local markets greet each other with, 'Well, what has Joanna for us this time?'[9]

But if forecasting the weather was acceptable, extending her range of powers to include people's personal affairs was more problematic. After making some prediction concerning her father, he told her in no uncertain terms that she was crazy to believe in such things. After all, she surely didn't think the Lord would work the same kind of miracles today as He did for the children of Israel. Did she? Joanna primly replied that what the Lord did then, He could surely do now. Her words shook William. Although he had always encouraged his children to be religious, for the first time he saw danger in his youngest daughter's zeal.[10]

From Joanna's point of view, however, she needed to cultivate holiness at a time when her father's behaviour would have tried the patience of a saint. James Speerway, boarding in the house while employed to work their flax, witnessed some anguished scenes between them.

After falling out with her on one occasion, William woke in the night, raving like a madman:

Oh, my dear child, have I grieved her heart that makes herself such a slave to keep me from a prison! . . . What Devil is in me? Oh, that dear creature, how does she strive to please me! How does she strive to keep me from ruin! I must see her!

'How can you wish to disturb her? She has stayed up to work till twelve o'clock, and is but just gone to bed,' Speerway protested.

'I cannot live unless I see her,' insisted her father.

So Speerway was forced to knock at Joanna's bedroom door and wake her up. Then, when she went to her father, he seized her hand, moaning,

My dear child, dost thou forgive me? Why did I fall out with thee that is the comfort of my life, and venturest thy life to save me from ruin? Oh, my dear child! Oh, my dear child! My heart is wounded to see thy love for me!

Recalling the incident later, Joanna described how his face had been 'like a pot when you take off a cover, covered with drops', and how she had sat by his bed for hours, wiping away his sweat and comforting him, trying to soothe him into sleep. Next day he still rattled on about how dreadful he felt for having upset her.

Another time, after making cider all day, William woke at midnight and, finding Joanna still up, asked her to go and check that the cider was not running over the tub – regardless of the fact that she would have to cross two fields and an orchard to reach the poundhouse, the outbuilding where apples are crushed for cider. Grabbing a lantern because it was a dark, cloudy night, Joanna set out for the ghostly house that her brother had used for his rabbits and whose last human occupant had drowned himself in the well; and once there, pushed open the door to see, just inside, the dark shape of a man. At the same instant startled by some sort of noise, she dropped the lantern, turned and fled, taking the longer way home along a lane, wading twenty yards through a stream in her panic, sure there was a spirit chasing her.

Once home she was greeted by her father's voice wanting to know if the cider had run over. She was trembling so much she could hardly reply.

'My dear love, what is the matter?' he called.

Well might he say 'my dear love', after sending me out at this time of night, Joanna thought to herself before telling him what had happened. She confessed how she had dropped the lantern, left the poundhouse door wide open, and not even glanced at the cider. For once her father was sympathetic and helped her work out what had startled her – she must have opened the door just as the moon emerged from behind clouds to shine against the jamb and form the silhouette of a man. And as for the noise, that must have been owls dropping apples from their beaks as they flew out over her head. Joanna went to bed reassured, but angry at herself for being frightened by shadows.[11]

The fact was, William did not always show such understanding. He was truculent, demanding, and – not yet sixty – used to having a woman at his beck and call. It was probably pain at seeing another woman move into the house to take her mother's place that drove Joanna to leave home once more,[12] although another goad had been applied when she visited Sidmouth for the reaping-harvest and, meeting Noah again, caught him making eyes at Peter West's sister and sighing, 'Oh, Ann! I love the name of Ann'.[13]

It was cold comfort for Joanna to recall that years ago she had told Noah that he would one day marry Ann West only for him then to say that he did not even like the girl. Well, time had now caught up with her prophecy – yet again proving (at least to her own satisfaction) that she had special powers, even if they were not properly appreciated by those around her.

Stifling her jealousy, Joanna decided to set off for pastures new. So, in her late twenties, she took service in the home of a gentleman called Mr Smith where she found the work congenial, got on well with all the womenfolk, but – as so often before – fell foul of a man.[14]

It turned out to be the old problem. Mr Smith's footman, having taken a fancy to the new servant, was furious when she rejected his advances and went all out for revenge. The result was that poor Joanna, finding that she could do nothing right in the house, resorted to the fields and Great-aunt Sarah – wandering about reciting such edifying verses as:

> Why should my passions mix with earth,
> And thus debase my heavenly birth?
> Why should I cleave to things below,
> And let my God and Saviour go?[15]

The effect of this, together with Joanna's frequent fits of weeping and prayer, on the other servants may be imagined. Nevertheless, Great-aunt Sarah's poems helped to strengthen her religious resolve until one Sunday, after roaming the fields and praying for deliverance, she was answered by an inner Voice: 'Thou shalt not spend another sabbath in this house.'[16]

Trusting the words, she went indoors feeling much more cheerful until accosted by the footman, who had taken to shadowing her about the house. When he complained about her absence, she merely smiled and, before sailing upstairs, loftily remarked that she hoped the next servant would please him better.

This was on the Sunday evening. The following Tuesday, while she was working in the dairy, the housekeeper came, with tears flowing down her cheeks, to announce that a new maid had just come to replace Joanna who was to leave the very next day, it being Mr Smith's custom never to allow servants any warning.

The reason for her dismissal? The footman, perhaps whispering the words 'religious mania', had persuaded his master that Joanna was mentally unbalanced, an allegation against which she was given no chance to defend herself. Instead, she was told to pack up and leave, her only consolation being the muttered words of the housekeeper, 'My God! what is my master about? He has this day discharged the best servant in the house.'[17]

ON A SHELF IN EXETER, 1777-1784

No tongue can paint the horror I felt, to hear of love from a
married man. . . .   *Copies & Parts of Copies*, 1804

On the principle that any port is welcome in a storm, Joanna decided on
another visit to Hannah, intending to stay at Black Torrington while
casting around for something permanent. After spending a couple of
days with her old friends, the Channon family at Fairmile, she set out on
her journey, and was approaching Exeter when she had second thoughts.[1]

She knew that Hannah had just given birth to her fourth child and
might welcome extra help, but providing just another pair of hands had
little appeal for Joanna.[2] Besides which, there were painful memories
associated with Black Torrington and although John Rigsby was now
married and thus no threat to her virtue, she could hardly have relished
the thought of seeing him with a wife on his arm.[3]

So, where else could she go? Certainly not Gittisham. For, as if
seeing her father with another woman was not bad enough, there was
now the prospect of sister Susanna being married to William Carter, one
of the young men at Sidmouth who had previously flirted with Joanna.[4]
It must have been galling to realise that Susanna's marriage would leave
only two members of their family unattached – the youngest, Joseph,
and herself. It was an inescapable fact that no matter how much Joanna
rejoiced in being fancy-free, others no doubt considered her on the shelf.

Thinking along these lines perhaps drove her towards comfort-eating
– or, as she put it, stopping on the road to pray for guidance, she was
suddenly inspired to go and buy cakes. She went into Exeter where, as
luck would have it, she entered a shop kept by a woman from Gittisham
who, recognising her, invited her to sit down and take a rest. In the
course of their conversation Joanna asked whether there were many
domestic jobs to be had in the city. The shopkeeper shook her head, but
asked her next customer if she knew of any. 'Because if you do,' she
added, 'here is a woman of a creditable family, whose parents I well
know to be worthy good people, in want of a situation.'[5]

The woman replied that on Tuesday she had been at a house where the
master and mistress had both asked her if she knew of a servant. Tuesday,
Joanna thought; that was the day she had left Squire Smith's house.

She quizzed the woman, happy to hear her give the master a good character and say there was no man but him in the house. The situation sounded perfect – clearly the place the Lord had prepared for her. She went and offered, was accepted and started there the following week.

Her new employer, an upholsterer called William Wills, occupied a cabinet, chair, carpet and bedding warehouse at the corner of St George's Lane and Bell Hill in Southgate Street, Exeter.[6] He had a wife named Sarah and was the father of two young daughters, Ann and Mary, as well as a teenage son, William. On the surface they seemed a happy, respectable, religious family, but underneath flowed dangerous currents of a kind that would inevitably tug Joanna into difficulties.[7]

Mr Wills was a passionate man, whose loyalty had been much tried when his wife made a fool of him with a clothworker in their home town of Moretonhampstead.[8] After being driven to drink and thoughts of suicide by his wife's antics, Wills accepted money from his father-in-law to pay off his debts and start up elsewhere. He came to Exeter, established a successful upholstery business and became a pillar of the Methodist Church, all the time suspecting Sarah of still chasing other men behind his back. Small wonder then, that when it was his turn to be attracted to someone else, he failed to resist temptation.

This, however, lay in the future when Joanna joined his household, settling in happily with his family, accompanying them to their local Methodist chapel as well as attending services in St Peter's Cathedral nearby. She worked hard, picking up those upholstery skills which later enabled her to earn her own living, and after years spent in quiet backwaters seemed to enjoy life at the heart of a busy city, even if it had its dangers.

Exeter, like many other towns, suffered much from fire during the latter half of the eighteenth century – and the Wills's warehouse with its stocks of wood, textiles and mattresses was particularly vulnerable. On 29 September 1780 it was reported in the *Exeter Flying Post*:

> This afternoon fire broke out in the house of Mr Wills cabinet-maker and broker in Southgate Street but by timely assistance and a plentiful supply of water was got under [control] without any considerable damage.

By that time Joanna had been living harmoniously with the Wills' family for about three years, so it came as a great shock when Mr Wills suddenly declared himself in love with her.

> No tongue can paint the horror I felt, to hear of love from a married man. I asked him how he could make a profession of religion, and talk of love to another whilst he had a wife of his own. He said his love was not sinful; it was only religious love,

which no man that had such a wife as he had, that was roving after other men, could help. . . .[9]

Joanna, indifferent to his blandishments, even when he praised her mind 'so mild and heavenly, endowed with every virtue', chastised him for bringing shame on his religion. To which he replied that he knew his own heart and would never disgrace religion even were he offered £500.[10]

'He that trusteth his own heart is a fool,' Joanna retorted, adding that *he* might trust his heart, but *she* would never trust hers, so if his heart was inclined to love her, she would leave his home at once.

Although she received no further advances, the incident left Joanna so depressed that, coming upon her working alongside his children one day, Mr Wills asked them what was wrong with her. They told him she was very unhappy. He then became infuriated to discover that, as earnest of intent, she had already been to Mr Anthony Tremlett, a prosperous merchant, and offered her services there.

Meanwhile, a horse that Wills had bought from Joanna's brother broke out of its stable and could not be found. As she cogitated its loss, Joanna came to believe that if it was found within seven days it would be a sign that she should leave. Nevertheless, to give life a chance to decide otherwise, she rose each morning at four o'clock to walk the fields around Exeter in an effort to find it. During this time Wills approached her once more and she repeated that she would go away if he ever mentioned love again. Mindful of his children and the fact that Joanna was so well suited to his shop, he promised to desist. Furthermore, he added by way of a bribe, only if she stayed would he welcome in his house the Methodist preachers whom she respected so highly. This left Joanna in a quandary. Mr Wills was a generous patron. The last thing she wanted was to alienate him from these religious men. After praying for guidance she was told that she should not leave Mr Wills's house because the Lord had a secret purpose in keeping her there. Reluctantly she obeyed.

Eight days after the horse disappeared, Mrs Tremlett sent for Joanna's character-reference and Sarah Wills refused to give it. That very afternoon the horse was cried in the market place after it had been found and impounded one mile from Exeter. In obedience to such clear spiritual signs, Joanna stayed on and was perfectly happy in the house until joined there by Mrs Garrick, a mischief-making woman who daily regaled her with stories about Sarah Wills's lewd conduct with Mr Sanderson.

Hugh Sanderson was, ironically enough, one of the preachers whom Mr Wills took into his home as a result of Joanna's influence. Five feet two inches tall, thin and with a swaggering walk, he was a charismatic preacher who had quickly established his ascendancy over the Methodist

Society in Exeter – one moment enthralling them with accounts of his miracles, at another making them lie stiff on the floor while he drove out their evil spirits.[11] Joanna was suspicious of him from the first and used to think the room filled with spirits when he was praying. She grew even more suspicious after hearing him confess that his late wife's ghost troubled him so much that he had to have someone to sleep in his room every night, and her worst fears were confirmed when, after praying to know by what spirit he was led, she opened her Bible at random and found herself reading Revelation19: 20: 'The beast was taken, and with him the false prophet that worked miracles before him, with which he deceived them that had received the mark of the beast. . . .'

This could mean only one thing. Sanderson was the false prophet who worked his miracles through devils. Sanderson was the agent of the Devil. Joanna taxed the preacher with this damning indictment only to hear him insist that his miracles came from the Lord, who gave him power to destroy all his enemies! In fact, there was never a man so highly favoured as he was, Sanderson declared, and he would not thank God to make him anything less than the greatest man on earth with power above all men.

Choosing her words with care, Joanna observed that it was happy for him if the Lord had given him that power, but if not, he would end up in hell. At which Sanderson scoffed, 'Yes, I will take care to get a good warm corner there.'[12]

Joanna was shocked.

She had to do something in the face of such evil, but felt quite helpless for, even if Mrs Garrick and the other servants shared her misgivings they kept them to themselves after hearing that a Plymouth man had fallen down dead after reproving Sanderson.[13] So things were allowed to go from bad to worse and, while William Wills maintained Sanderson in luxury, people laughed behind his back at what was going on in his house. Eventually, convinced that the preacher was having affairs with not only Sarah Wills but her daughters too, Joanna found the situation intolerable.

But what could she do? Afraid to tell Mr Wills lest he be driven to thoughts of suicide again, Joanna at first tried to deal with the matter quietly by asking other Methodist preachers to put pressure on their colleague. They, however, were powerless, having already turned Sanderson out of their meetings for his outrageous behaviour. Indeed, when John Wesley arrived in Exeter in 1782 in the course of one of his tours, he had remarked: 'Here poor Hugh Sanderson has pitched his standard and declared open war. Part of the society have joined him; the rest go on their way quietly.'[14]

Having exhausted other avenues, there was nothing left but for Joanna to write to William Wills warning him that he was nurturing a serpent in his bosom. The result was predictable. Mr Wills exploded in fury. But it came as a surprise when the object of his rage turned out to be not his errant wife but virtuous Joanna. He saw Sarah as a paragon and Joanna as wickedly trying to cause trouble between them. As if to prove his case, Wills recalled how Joanna had previously misunderstood his own innocent feelings towards her and falsely accused him.

Joanna was dumbfounded. Retreating before such treachery, she went on a visit to her brother Joseph, who lived about twenty-five miles away in Musbury.[15] Perhaps this was the dramatic journey when she rode in the first of two coaches driven by men competing over speed and quantities of ale consumed on the way. Afraid that her coach would overturn before Honiton, Joanna asked Mr Cawley, a friend and fellow-passenger, to speak to the driver but his words had no effect and they continued to hurtle along. As they came within sight of Honiton the rear coach drew alongside, its horses running up against the hedge, knocking its drunken driver off his perch and causing their coach to overturn. Although one passenger broke his arm, Mr Cawley and Joanna got out unscathed and were even able to laugh over their adventure.[16]

Whilst staying at Joseph's home in Musbury, Joanna had time to reflect. Return to the wicked Wills she could not. But nor could she allow such infamy to flourish, so she decided to send private letters to Sarah Wills, her daughters, and Hugh Sanderson, threatening to reveal all she knew to Mr Wills if the preacher failed to leave his house.

When they took no notice, she was left with no choice. For virtue to triumph she must confront the sinners, so she charged back to Exeter, arriving at the Wills's house so early that Sarah was still in bed.

'You impudent wretch! What do you here before I am up?' Sarah screeched, coming downstairs. 'What hast thou told thy master? Thou hast told him all thou knowest and thou wantest to cut my throat.'[17]

Joanna declared that she had told Mr Wills nothing. This Sarah refused to believe even when her husband and children assured her of it. In the midst of the kerfuffle, William Wills woke up to the fact that something was being kept from him and asked what it was he was supposed not to know. Since no one knew what to say, they sent for Sanderson.

The preacher entered the house with a face like fury, swearing to God he would punish Joanna. He had forgiven many, he said, but her he would punish, calling on the Three-One-God to witness that he had never touched or kissed her in his life.

Touched or kissed Joanna?

It was a clever ruse to make Wills think all this fuss was over some

Exeter Guildhall – drawn by Baynes, engraved by W. Deeble and published by Robert Jennings in 1829. This was the scene of Joanna's courtroom triumph over Mr Wills. The stone-pillared entrance was added to its medieval structure in 1593 and remains virtually unaltered today.

dalliance between Sanderson and Joanna, and he fell into the trap, despite Joanna's insistence that she had nothing personal to lay against Sanderson, indeed had never been alone in his company. Beyond this, Joanna would say nothing until her employer left the room. After he had gone, she told Sanderson all she had seen and heard when he was with Mrs Wills and her daughters, especially how he had set them against Mr Wills. Then she repeated all that the womenfolk themselves had told

The Guildhall, 1839, showing 17th-century jury-boxes and fittings. The hall remained the city's Law Court until recently.

her, only to find them now denying everything and accusing her of wanting to cut their throats. Even though Polly Wills wanted to tell her father what Joanna had said about Sanderson and her mother, the others persuaded her to keep quiet.

At the end of this stormy session, Joanna returned to Musbury where she had already taken service with the family of a clergyman named Marshall. Only later did she hear the version of events given to Mr Wills – that all she, Joanna, had against Sanderson was that he had lied when he denied ever embracing her, for he had done so once after returning from a journey and was in the habit of embracing all the women before he went to bed.

Satisfied by this story, William Wills was now persuaded to help his wife take revenge on Joanna by going to Marshall and warning him against his new servant. Marshall summoned Joanna and told her what Wills had said. Although she denied the allegations and begged him to bring her face to face with Wills to clear up the truth, Marshall was reluctant to do this in case he upset the Wills family, who were influential in his parish. After visiting their home and hearing more of their lies, he dismissed Joanna.

For Joanna it was a turning-point. She was thirty-three years old and tired of being treated with such contempt. But who was there to stand up for her? Not her father. He had just insulted her mother's memory by leading a third woman to the altar, so she would certainly not go crawling to him.[18] Her brothers showed no interest and Mr Marshall had scorned her efforts to clear up the truth. Yet she was determined not to let a man like William Wills get the better of her. She could stand up for herself. After all, there were means at hand to seek redress. She was a citizen as good as the next and, if necessary, would go to law and sue him for defamation.

So it was that Joanna passed beneath the granite portico of Exeter's ancient Guildhall early in 1784 and entered her charge. The records show:

19 January 1784 William Wills indicted at this sessions for an

assault on Joanna Southcott entered his traverse to try the same
at the next sessions as under sd.: William Wills in £20

George Powell of the City of Exeter Joiner in £20.[19]

Once embarked on her suit, Joanna had to wait three months for a
hearing – time to contemplate the dire consequences of losing her action.
When the day came she stood in the Guildhall trembling for fear that
Wills would swear away her life, for he had hired two women to give
evidence against her and, although their testimony was false, Joanna's
counsellor, Mr Roberts, had no way of breaking their story. In fact, it
looked certain that Joanna would lose her case until, on sudden
inspiration, she asked Roberts why Wills had not produced his son to
give evidence, intimating that, unlike the others, the young man would
not perjure himself.

Roberts put this question to Charles Fanshaw, acting for Wills, who
answered that his client had brought as many witnesses as he thought
proper. 'You brought as many as did not care what they swore,' Roberts
retorted.

> Mr Wills would not perjure those in his own house, but he cared
> not how many he perjured out of the house. Let him bring the
> son; and if he swear as false as these have, I will give up my
> cause.

Since the younger Wills refused to appear, Joanna won the day.[20]

Easter Sessions 19 April 1784

> William Wills indicted last sessions for an assault on Joanna
> Southcott, singlewoman, upon trial of his Traverse was found
> guilty and fined 20s. which he paid in court.[21]

The case proved to be a milestone in Joanna's life. Her victory gave
her confidence – not in herself, but in her special relationship with the
Lord. For, on reflection, it appeared obvious that, humble as she was,
she could never have prevailed over men like Sanderson and Wills had
the Lord not been on her side. It had been the Lord Himself who inspired
her to mention the son whose refusal to testify won her the case. And it
was the Lord who, on the following day, ordered her to write down her
life history and have it printed so that thousands could learn the valuable
lesson – all they had to do was obey the Lord, then no one could stand
against them.

She embarked on the task with enthusiasm, scribbling down the story
of her life, surprised when her friends were not keen for her to publish.
Perhaps they were afraid she would waste her money, or distrusted her
version of events – whatever the reason, they did their best to discourage
her. And since the Voice of the Lord no longer pressed her either, she
put away her manuscript till a later date.[22]

STARTING TO PROPHESY, 1784-1792

Quench not the Spirit; despise not prophecy; for the time is
come, that your women shall prophesy.

Strange Effects of Faith, 1801

Joseph, who had given Joanna temporary refuge when she fled from
the Wills's household, was at that time seriously alarmed by her religious
mania. 'I . . . thought my sister so far possessed of Methodism, from
her very strong propensities for reading and perusing the Bible, that I
was afraid her intellect might be hurt,' he later wrote.[1] His fears were in
line with those of Mr Wills's attorney, who during her trial at the Guildhall,
had referred disparagingly to Joanna as an 'enthusiast'.[2]

Surprisingly enough, this 'enthusiasm' was not at all dimmed by her
sad experience with Hugh Sanderson. On the contrary, according to her
own testimony she kept up her attendance at both Anglican services and
Methodist meetings:

> I attended constantly my church, forenoons and afternoons, and
> received the Sacrament. At the same time I also attended Mr
> Wesley's preachers at eight o'clock in the mornings and at six
> in the evenings; these hours not interfering with the service of
> the established Church; but did not join their society, though I
> was much invited to do so.[3]

With such piety as recommendation, Joanna had no trouble finding
other posts. Her first was with Mrs B. Graves of Exeter who, on leaving
to go to France, gave her a glowing testimonial:

> Joanna Southcott behaved so well in my service that I am sure I
> may safely pronounce her deserving of the very good character
> which everybody who knew her will give her, and I think it my
> duty to respect and serve her, on account of the experience
> which I have had of her integrity, honesty and sobriety.[4]

After a brief period with elderly Mrs White, staying with her until she
died, Joanna took service with her late employer's daughter who had
married Anthony Tremlett, a trader in Spanish oil and iron. The Tremletts
lived in a fine house to the north-west of the city at Davids Hill and
were sufficiently wealthy for their daughter to be described as 'a very
agreeable young lady, with a genteel fortune' when she married in 1777.[5]

Joanna stayed with them for nearly two and a half years, leaving only when she was called away by a tragedy in her brother William's family.

William Southcott had by this time moved from Sidmouth to Aylesbeare where, in December 1784, his infant son Richard died. His wife, Susannah, already pregnant again, died in childbirth the following July, leaving William to cope with their newborn daughter, Hannah.[6] When Joanna left Davids Hill to go and help, it was with a tacit promise that her post would be kept open – a promise which perished when Mary Tremlett herself died in early 1787.[7]

Fortunately another opportunity opened up when Joanna renewed her connection with her old friends, the Channon sisters of Fairmile. Sarah, ten years Joanna's senior, had married Charles Minifie, a London businessman with a shop near West Gate, Exeter, selling cotton-dipped and mould candles and the best white and yellow soap.[8] In 1783 the Minifies moved into the city centre where they built a new house and soap workshops in Fore Street.[9] When, two years later, Sarah's younger sister, Mary Channon, married John Wolland, a maltster,[10] she offered Joanna employment in her new home at Heavitree on the outskirts of Exeter. Apart from possible pangs at seeing another of her contemporaries safely wed, Joanna settled in well with the Wollands, fitting in as one of the family, doing all the domestic chores she had been doing since childhood. Part of her, however, yearned to be back in the city pursuing the trade for which she had been trained by Mr Wills.

With this in mind, she popped into Mr Taylor's upholstery shop in Fore Street one day – ostensibly to buy something, but perhaps having noticed his advertisement in the *Exeter Flying Post*:

> Robert Taylor, at his Cabinet & Upholstery Warehouse, in Fore Street, acquaints that he keeps ready-made four-post and other bedsteads with Dimity, Cotton, Manchester, Check, Morine, Cheney and other furniture; Goose and other feather beds, mattresses, blankets, quilts, carpets . . . now selling at the very lowest prices.
>
> Wanted immediately 3 or 4 good Hands in the Cabinet Branch.[11]

In the course of conversation Joanna let drop that she was looking for a suitable job in her old trade. Mrs Lucy Taylor, a religious woman who had been shocked by the goings-on in Mrs Wills's household, did not respond favourably. In fact, when her husband insisted on giving Joanna a chance, she protested: 'You have hired a person I shall never like.'[12]

Joanna joined the Taylors, but finding herself still employed on domestic chores, moved on after one year to become an upper servant in the home of Mr Burrows, a druggist in Fore Street. However, Mr Burrows's large family kept her so busy that, in order to have more time to herself on Sundays, she left them after two years and moved back to the Taylors.[13] This time the situation worked better, as Lucy Taylor came to appreciate Joanna's religious values and found her marvellous with her five children who all became devoted to her. The youngest, Charles, born in 1783, listened to her for hours as she spoke of the wonderful times coming soon when Christ's Kingdom was established on earth. Hanging on her every word, the little boy became her admirer for life.[14]

Living at the hub of the city meant that Joanna was well-placed to indulge her 'enthusiasm' even if she remained chary of the Methodists whose ranks, after the Sanderson debacle, were still in disarray – a fact lamented by John Wesley on his last visit at the end of August 1789.

We set out at three in a lovely morning, and reached Exeter between twelve and one. Here the scene was much changed: many of the people were scattered, and the rest faint and dead enough. The preaching house was swiftly running to ruin, the rain running through the room into it amain, and five or six tenants living in the house were noisy enough, having none to control them. We called earnestly upon God to arise and maintain his own cause. He did so in the evening congregation (which was much larger than usual), while I strongly enforced the parable of the sower; and the dread of God seemed to rest on the whole congregation.[15]

If Joanna came to hear the eighty-six year old preacher that day, she would have appreciated his message (and the farming metaphor), but it was not until after Wesley's death in 1791 that, in the course of her 'First or Strange Visitation', she received a divine command to join the Methodists. Could she have imagined that, with the head of their Society gone, his followers might be looking for another? Whatever her motive, Joanna was warned that something would happen in the class meeting to convince people that she had a special mission.[16]

She joined a class meeting under the tutelage of a local tailor, John Eastlake, who was regarded locally as 'a man of saintly character and manners and a pattern of meek and simple goodness.'[17] It was at his home in Musgrave's Alley that John Wesley used to stay whenever he visited Exeter, being entertained by the tailor and his resourceful wife who, finding on one occasion that she had no curtains for the great man's bed, used one of her nether garments instead![18] The class was a weekly gathering of about a dozen men and women whose meetings followed a regular pattern. Starting with a hymn, they knelt while John Eastlake offered an impromptu prayer. He then launched into a critical review of his personal behaviour during the previous week before inviting the rest to bare their souls in similar fashion – the cue for members to elaborate at lugubrious length on their own shortcomings. After this, Eastlake would give each a few words of encouragement or criticism before closing the meeting with another prayer and the final hymn.

In the weeks leading up to Easter Joanna sat and listened to her fellow class-members, hearing them applauded for their candour and supported in their moral infirmities by the sympathetic group and its saintly leader. And all this time she said practically nothing.

Then, on Easter Sunday, sitting in church listening to the preacher read from Luke 24, she had a revelation. 'O fools, and slow of heart to believe all that the prophets have spoken!' – his words made her think how strange it was that she had been sent to Exeter; how nothing seemed to happen in her life by accident; how everything had been pre-ordained. And the more she thought, the more she became certain that she was the subject of a special providence. She felt sure that she had a personal guide who spoke as an inner Voice and, since its wisdom was far greater than hers, all she had to do was obey its instructions.

Nevertheless, when this inner Voice told her to go to the Methodist meeting and speak of her experiences, she felt petrified.

'No one spoke of past experience in a class meeting; how should I go to act different from others?' she queried.

Her Spirit replied with a challenge: 'If thou art afraid to speak of the goodness of God, I will take it from thee. For now thou art comforted, strengthen thy brethren.'

So, at the next meeting she tried to do just this, standing up and awkwardly making her revelations. 'I thought they might judge me simple, and I was much confused whilst I was speaking,' she later admitted.

They, it seemed, were equally confused and responded with little sympathy. Next day, feeling very depressed, Joanna prayed for an explanation and was told that the people at the meeting had acted out of jealousy because she had spoken about her personal experience of God's goodness. Loath to believe this, she said to herself, 'It cannot be; they are too religious men, and Mr Eastlake, I know to be too good a man.'

Eastlake, however, was not the cause of the trouble. It was her fellow class members who refused to hear her revelations and made such a fuss that Eastlake suggested she leave the society in order to restore peace. Hearing this, Joanna broke down and sobbed, the meeting's rejection bringing back memories of so many former 'put-downs' – especially by her father who, seeing her so affected by reading the Bible, used to say: 'Joanna, my dear child, why dost thou exercise thyself in things too high for thee? It must be milk for babes, but wine for men of stronger years.' And she, the dutiful daughter, would turn her back on the Scriptures, only to find that the more she tried to give them up, the more they came to obsess her until it seemed as if she had ministers preaching in her ears all the time.[19]

Joanna felt let down by Eastlake, whom she considered far too sure of himself. In fact, he reminded her of one of her aunts who, having decided to test her position as teacher's pet by soiling her lace with soot, found herself being beaten like any other child who had done something wrong. Well, thought Joanna, Mr Eastlake might be religious but that did not make him infallible. God could still punish him.[20]

Such angry thoughts plunged her into an emotional turmoil, which lasted the best part of a week. Peace returned only when her inner Voice ordered her back to the class meeting to tell everyone what had happened and let them know exactly what *they* were thinking and feeling about *her*. No matter how terrifying she found the idea, she knew she had to obey lest God withdraw his Spirit from her. With trembling steps she made her way to Musgrave's Alley and sat down, feeling even worse when John Eastlake began the meeting by saying: 'Let us come to the purpose of things that are present, and say no more of the things which are past.'

At one point she felt faint and thought of leaving but was told by her Spirit to stay. This divine command restored her courage so that, standing up, she told the members that she thought it must be Satan who had put her against them by revealing all that was in their minds concerning her. When she finished speaking, she waited to be contradicted. But no one spoke. They just exchanged baffled glances.

To Joanna the situation was suddenly clear. If no one had understood, then she was casting her pearls before swine and it was obvious that this class meeting was no place for her. She would therefore resign from the Society.

But when Eastlake went through the formalities of trying to persuade her to reconsider, her Spirit surprisingly took his side and told her 'to go and reprove them.' Suspecting what kind of reception she might receive, she asked whether she should consult the class leader first and was told: 'Go to Eastlake, and do as he directs thee, and thou wilt see what man *is*!'

That Saturday night Joanna dreamed she was in the Cathedral, trying to seat herself on a chair which gave way and she was close to falling when she awoke. 'So will Eastlake deceive you,' the Spirit warned.

Sure enough, next day when she came out of the Cathedral and approached John Eastlake for a word – he turned his back on her and spoke to someone else. Refusing to accept this rebuff, Joanna followed him back to his house and waited for the other man to leave him, whereupon Eastlake looked up and coolly announced that he would speak to her another time. His words cut so deep that she ran off into the fields where she could be on her own to think and weep. In the depths of despair, she felt deserted and utterly alone.

'Thy friends are like Job's friends,' her Spirit explained, 'because they cannot account for the manner of God's strange dealing with thee: they are sometimes silent, and when they speak they speak wrong.' Drawing comfort from her unseen companion, she went into a cattle-byre and pulled out her Book of Common Prayer, which fell open at Psalm 110. She was immediately struck by the words: 'Thy people shall be willing in the day of thy power.'

Again she opened the book again at random, this time at Psalm 72:

Blessed be the God, the God of Israel, who only doeth wondrous things: and blessed be his glorious name for ever and let the whole earth be filled with his glory.

Somewhat soothed, she spent the rest of the day wandering around alone, thinking about her situation. She realised that she was treading dangerous ground, for in the evening her inner Voice told her plainly that if she wanted to stay sane she should stop troubling herself so much over religion. Such a notion brought her up with a start and she replied to herself sternly: 'What then will become of me if I give up religion? I am lost for ever; and I had rather lose my senses than my soul.'

'Why canst thou not do as others, who mind the world, and all is well?' her inner Voice persisted.

Recognising these as the words of the Devil, Joanna fell into a dark mood which still hung about her the following morning when, after sitting for hours at her work pondering over the past, she found herself questioning why she had been ordered to obey Mr Eastlake only to find he had kept procrastinating and not told her to do anything. She was answered by her Spirit:

I no more intended thou shouldst go to the class-meeting to reprove them than I intended Abraham should offer up his son Isaac. I only did it to try thy obedience; and as far as thou hadst it in thy heart to obey, so far will I reward thee. For now will I swear unto thee as I did unto Abraham, that I will make with thee an everlasting covenant, and I will save thee with an everlasting salvation. Thou shalt prophesy in my name, and I will bear thee witness.[21]

Suddenly she saw the light! It did not matter that she had failed to impress Eastlake. He and the Methodists were simply the occasion of her trial. It did not matter that they had not acknowledged her mission. It was her obedience to the Voice of the Spirit that mattered and the fact that she had proved herself committed to its service – even as Abraham had shown himself committed to the Lord.

Now Joanna had cause to rejoice, for she had made contact with the inner Voice which she called the Spirit of Truth. She knew that as long as she was prepared to obey without question, the Spirit would reward her with singular strength and direction. From this moment on, wherever she went, whatever she did, there would be – could be – no self-doubt.

POMEROY AND THE PROMISE, 1792-1797

> In 1792 I was strangely visited by day and night concerning what was coming upon the whole earth. I was then ordered to set it down in writing. I obeyed, though not without strong external opposition. *Strange Effects of Faith*, 1801

Each painful confrontation with her class meeting had left Joanna in a state of stress and confusion. In the days that followed she began to hear voices and dream dreams, meeting with little sympathy from the Taylors, neither of whom took her prophecies seriously.[1] So she was still feeling very isolated when she experienced the dream that haunted her for years.

She dreamt of a woman in white walking in a garden who, as the wind blew away her clothes, was revealed as a skeleton with a full round face. As she looked at Joanna, she smiled and winked.[2]

Joanna had no doubt about the meaning. Recognising her dream as a 'type' of the famine that would occur in the last days, she immediately urged Mr Taylor to lay in stores. When he refused to listen, insisting that there were no signs of a poor harvest or dislocation of trade, Joanna grew increasingly agitated. As far as she was concerned, she could see what was coming, but no one would listen, no one understood, nobody would take her seriously.

Close to despair, she was suddenly offered a way out. Her Voice commanded,

> Leave thy work and go to thy sister's and write what I have revealed to thee, for what I have put in thy mouth I will do upon the earth. I have begun, and I will make an end.

Of course. She must go to Susanna at Plymtree. That was the obvious thing to do. Susanna was religious and she would understand, especially when she saw Joanna's miraculous prophecies put down in writing.

Next day Joanna went out and bought pens, ink and paper and made a start. Writing had never come easily to her. There had always been complaints about its illegibility, but she would not let that put her off. Painfully beginning to write what she heard her inner Voice say, her effort brought its own reward and the Spirit world drew even closer. As she was going to bed, she felt her heart glow with such warmth she found herself whispering, 'What Spirit is near me?'

A low Voice answered, 'It is thy mother and if thou hast courage to see me, I will appear to thee.' Joanna said she had that courage.

The Voice continued, 'This is a sign to thee.' There came three hard knocks on her headboard. Joanna sat up, but hearing something rustle near the bed, quickly sank back and buried her head under the blankets.

'My dear child, thou art afraid, and I cannot appear to thee,' came a soft whisper.

'My dear mother, I am not afraid,' Joanna said, sitting up again.

Then she felt the bed-clothes move and was petrified.

'Thou art afraid, and I cannot appear. But I can converse with thee invisibly, as well as visibly,' the Voice said.

Settling for this, Joanna asked her mother if she was happy.

'Yes. Mrs Channon and me are happy together in glory; and rejoice to see Mrs Minifie, Mrs Wolland and you so united together,' Hannah Southcott replied.[3]

Joanna was surprised to think that her mother knew of things that had happened after her death. Mary Channon, for instance, had married John Wolland as recently as 1785, years after Mr and Mrs Channon and Joanna's mother had died.[4] Reflecting on these deaths prompted her to wonder whether her dear brother John, who had recently died, was saved?

Her mother reassured her, 'Yes, but thou wilt be much happier in glory than he.'

So did parents know after death how their children lived in the body?

'Yes, they do,' Hannah declared before going into detail about the predicament of Mrs Channon's elder daughter, Sarah, and her errant husband, Mr Minifie. 'But the Lord will break the yoke from off her neck; and a final separation will take place between them,' she foretold, adding that Charles Minifie would die, leaving his widow to enjoy happier days.

Old Edward Channon had never trusted Charles Minifie. Suspecting that his new son-in-law might turn out to be a treasure-hunter or unstable, his will had specified that Sarah's inheritance would be for her sole and separate use and revert to the Channon family after her death.[5] Events were to prove this a very sensible precaution.

The day after her 'visitation' Joanna hurried round to Mary Wolland to tell her what her mother had said. Mary, most impressed, agreed that something tremendous must be about to happen. Joanna then left for Plymtree where, to her dismay, she found sister Susanna far more sceptical. Why should she believe what Joanna said about Sarah Minifie, she demanded, when everyone knew that spirits could not see into the mind of God? Joanna had an answer. If God had sent her mother to strengthen her faith, then naturally He would know what questions Joanna would ask and provide Hannah with the right answers. To add substance to her argument Joanna repeated their mother's advice that Susanna should sack one of her servants – something she was eventually obliged to do a few months later.[6]

After this, Joanna settled down to the serious business of penning her prophecies. And what did Susanna make of these profound revelations? Apparently not much, for she had a husband to humour and a farm to run and could probably have done without this emotional sister under her feet for the rest of that year. Joanna's mood may be gauged from the fact that, come harvest time, her thoughts were still so doom-laden that she could hardly bear to listen to jovial reapers' songs. To cheer her up, her Spirit foretold that the next refrain would be spiritual and, sure enough, she was heartened to hear everyone sing:

> Britons, to arm yourselves prepare,
> Prepare yourselves with force and might,
> And show how Christians now can fight
> For to maintain their Gospel's right –
> Then, brave England!

Soon, however, another problem emerged. Harvest-home being a Saturday, as it drew towards midnight Susanna grew upset at the prospect of hearing bawdy songs on a Sunday and had to ask the reapers to sing psalms instead. They happily obliged with Psalm 95:

> O come, loud anthems let us sing,
> Loud thanks to our almighty king:
> For we our voices high should raise,
> When our salvation's rock we praise. . . .[7]

Although Joanna was ecstatic with the words, her joy was short-lived. Such a good harvest might be cause for celebration but did nothing for her reputation as a prophet. Mentioning her fears to Susanna, her sister told her quite bluntly that she was going off her head. She scoffed,

> You say there will be a war. Who shall we go to war with? The
> French are destroying themselves. As to the dearth of provision
> you speak of, you are wrong; for corn will come down very
> low. I could not make 4s. 6d. a bushel of the very best wheat
> this year. As to the distresses of the nation, you are wrong there,
> for England was never in a more flourishing state than it is at present.

Joanna replied,

> Well, if it be of God, it will come to pass, however likely or
> unlikely it may appear at present. If not, I shall hurt no one but
> myself in writing it. I am the fool, and must be the sufferer, if it
> be not of God. If it be of God, I would not refuse for the world,
> and am determined to err on the safest side.

She would be erring on the safest side if she stopped writing down her prophecies altogether, Susanna snorted, promptly forbidding all such activity in her house. Henceforth, to avoid friction, Joanna had to wait for her sister to go out before she could take up her pen. Such constraint inevitably caused further tension, as a result of which, in February 1793, leaving her precious writings at Plymtree, Joanna returned to work for the Taylors in Exeter.[8]

Her timing was good. Robert Taylor had recently moved into new premises – a large dwelling-house, warehouses and stables, with a twenty-six foot frontage on to Fore Street and useful side entrances in Friernhay Lane.[9] Here, back at the hub of city life, Joanna was in a good position to seek out some churchman to examine her prophecies. This time she was directed towards Henry Tanner, an elderly Calvinistic lay preacher whose meetings at the Tabernacle she had attended before leaving for Plymtree. An orator so powerful that on one occasion the congregation was 'struck with awesome trembling' at his sermon, Tanner was a pious but narrow-minded man who had endured great suffering in his own life.[10] Perhaps for this reason he listened sympathetically to Joanna's complaints about the way the Wesleyans had dismissed her prophecies as coming from the Devil.

'Then they were all unconverted people,' Mr Tanner replied.

Sufficiently encouraged to reveal some of her prophecies, she was gratified when Tanner agreed with her, saying that he too had received warnings about the awful things that were hastening on, even if his were not so clear as hers. He asked to see her writings and she explained that they were at Plymtree, sealed up and not yet to be opened. They continued to chat – she telling him how, at the end of the American War, every time she opened her Bible she had alighted on significant passages in Isaiah and Jeremiah; he nodding sagely and agreeing that it must all have been alluding to the present time.

Joanna, clearly enjoying herself, must have found it wonderful to be taken seriously, especially by someone the same age as her father. Later she declared that she had been as much at her ease with Mr Tanner as with anyone and even the presence of his wife in the room had proved no bar to communication, as Mrs Tanner agreed with everything her husband said. The interview ended on a friendly note with Mr Tanner asking her to call on him again, politely adding that he would be glad to see her at any time.[11] Their relationship, however, did not flourish – perhaps because Joanna remained a member of the Established Church and could therefore not be considered one of the elect. Or perhaps he too thought she was mad but was too polite to say so.

Meanwhile events were moving on apace. In spring 1793, in

Side entrance to Robert Taylor's home and upholstery business in Friernhay Lane, Exeter. The Taylor family lived here from 1792 to 1799, when their premises comprised a large dwelling-house, warehouses, and stables, with a shop entrance in Fore Street. Today the frontage is occupied by a hairdresser's salon.

confirmation of Joanna's prophecies, war broke out between England and France and it became a matter of urgency for her to find someone in authority who would take her warnings seriously. The Spirit instructed her to approach John Leach, another Methodist preacher.[12] This seemed to be a mistake when, after listening to her in silence, Leach thundered:

> It comes from the Devil; for not one thing you have mentioned will come to pass. You have the war in your favour, which is all that will come true of your prophecies; and the war will be over in a quarter of a year. It is from the Devil to disturb your peace: Satan hath a design to sift you as wheat.

Before he finished, however, he modified his tone:

> Yet I believe you to be a good woman; your friends speak of you in the highest terms; but what you have said will never come true. Besides, if it were [to come true], the Lord would never have revealed it to you. There are a thousand in Exeter whom I could point out, to whom the Lord would have revealed it before he would to you.[13]

This unkind cut reduced Joanna to tears, but not despair. Her equanimity was restored the next day when her Spirit, reflecting her own angry thoughts, demanded, 'Who made him a judge? He neither knows thee nor thy forefathers who walked before me with a perfect and upright heart.' Though this made her feel better, she still needed somebody to take her writings seriously and in the absence of any one else, Mr Leach was her best hope, so she continued to cultivate him.

Meanwhile the signs of cosmic disaster were visible not just in Europe but in the microcosm of Joanna's circle of friends in Exeter, where Sarah Minifie was going through the marital crisis she had predicted. It seems the late Mrs Channon's warnings had fallen on deaf ears, for one year later her daughter was shocked to discover that her husband's affairs had gone disastrously wrong. Charles Minifie's business had been faltering since a new tax on candles had been imposed in 1784[14] and, although elected a Commissioner of the Poor in the following year,[15] he had remained a controversial figure in Exeter where many felt that he was unsuitable for such an office.[16]

One Sunday in October 1793 Joanna woke from a troubled dream about Sarah Minifie. After church, she called on her friend and found her very depressed but refusing to say why. Still bothered, Joanna went on to see Sarah's sister, Mary Wolland, and in the course of their conversation reminded her of Mrs Channon's warning. A few days later Charles Minifie took Joanna into his confidence. He was going to London on business, he said, and would like her to stay with Sarah during his absence. Joanna, happy to oblige, moved in the evening before he left and so was there to comfort Sarah when a letter arrived, not from her husband but his brother, explaining that the pair were off to America.

The house plunged into confusion – with poor Sarah taking to her bed, creditors on the doorstep and the bailiffs about to descend on the following Monday. Intending to spend the night in prayer, Joanna collapsed into exhausted sleep and dreamt she heard a Voice saying, 'Hurt not the man; he hath done nothing to cheat his creditors; wait but a little and the mystery will be discovered; there are writings coming from him.'[17]

When Sarah heard this next morning she said the message rang true, as she had always found her husband honest despite his unkindness. Sure enough, after breakfast letters arrived from Charles Minifie empowering his friends Mr Rowe and Mr Harris to settle his affairs and promising that, if there was insufficient money to pay his creditors, he would send more from America.

Sudden joy at this news made Sarah ill again. Joanna, having been told that Mr Minifie would not reach America with his present attitude, was less optimistic and confided her fears to Lucy Taylor. A few days later news reached Exeter that Charles Minifie had been arrested at sea and would languish in prison until his debts were paid.[18] A notice apeared in the *Flying Post* declaring him a bankrupt and his house and chandler's shop for sale.[19]

Nor was this the extent of Mrs Minifie's troubles. One night Joanna awoke in the early hours from a dreadful dream that the shop was on fire. She went down to see if the maids had left their candle burning too near the bedcurtains and opened a door to find herself almost engulfed in smoke. The shop was indeed on fire! Wick yarns had caught fire,spreading flames to masses of candles and wood near the staircase. Yelling up to Mr Pike and the maidservants, Joanna ran out into the street and as far as the Guildhall, screaming 'Fire! Fire!' at the top of her voice.[20] Had she not woken when she did, the house would almost certainly have burnt and nobody could have escaped down the stairs.

Amidst all this turmoil Joanna went to the Cathedral at Advent 1793 and found herself listening to a sermon based on the text: 'Walk ye in the light, while ye have light, lest darkness come upon you.' She was entranced. The preacher was handsome[21] and spoke with great eloquence as he ranged over the affairs of nations, the seven churches of Asia and the current situation in England before concluding, 'Yet for all this God will save you, because ye are his people if ye obey him.' She knew beyond any possibility of doubt that his words were meant for her. Moreover, his rich voice had hardly stopped echoing before her Spirit told Joanna that what she had just heard was the will of God and she could rest assured that if Leach let her down then this man, the Reverend Joseph Pomeroy, would take up her cause. She left the Cathedral with a light step, certain that her writings would soon be verified.

But having been told not to contact Pomeroy until Leach had reached his decision, she went away to practise patience. Containing her excitement as well as she could, she whispered the good news to her friends, swearing them to secrecy so that no one could be influenced before the truth of her prophecies was proved.[22]

Meanwhile Mrs Minifie's situation continued to distract her. In June 1794 the Receivers placed a notice in the Exeter newspapers ordering all Mr Minifie's debtors to pay up so that they could settle his affairs. After that Charles Minifie went to America, leaving his wife to manage on her father's legacy and, though he promised to write, week after week passed without news.[23] So, the yoke had fallen from Sarah's neck, even if not in the way Joanna had anticipated.

When corn grew dear that summer, Joanna saw this as a further sign that her warnings were coming true and sent another letter to Mr Leach. His reply was disappointing: 'The Lord may have revealed to you what he has not to me, but I am of opinion with many, we are going to see good days.' Taking his letter she sealed it together with hers, confident that time would show who was right.[24]

After her husband's desertion, Sarah Minifie moved in with her sister at Heavitree and Joanna returned to work for the Taylors in Fore Street. Here she found that the outbreak of war with France had improved her stock with Mrs Taylor, who was now convinced of her prophetic powers even if her husband remained sceptical. Moreover, the younger children still adored Joanna, hanging on her every word when she told them stories. Charles, now eleven years old and completely under her spell, was heard to ask whether, if he were good, he could hope to be a trumpeter in Heaven[25] Mr Taylor, uneasy about her influence on his children or fearing that her fervour was interfering with her work, issued an ultimatum: Joanna must either give up her prophecies or her job. She gave up her job.[26]

Joanna found the next months miserable. Lodging for a while with Miss Bird, a mantua-maker who lived on Stripcoat Hill, she felt desperately lonely. Shunned by her brothers and sisters who had made it clear that they disapproved of her spiritual antics, the only friends she had left were Sarah Minifie and Mary Wolland.[27]

Then came distressing family news. Her nephew John, William's son, had been struck down by fever, and the apothecary, whose services were all his family could afford, had declared his case hopeless. Joanna was asked if she could get a doctor for a second opinion. She rushed round to see her nephew and, judging him to be dying, decided it was useless to seek further help. But as her Spirit disagreed, she sent for a doctor, who confirmed that John was dying. Her Spirit was unimpressed, decreeing that John's fever would turn within three days, he would go into the country for a change of air and return strong enough to resume work – even if his recovery was short-lived. All this Joanna repeated to Mrs Taylor, among others who later remembered her words.[28]

Next day John took a turn for the worse and it seemed he could not live till morning, but two days later his fever broke and he was able to eat and sit on a chair while his bed was made up. A week later he was well enough to ride five miles into the country to convalesce with his Aunt Susanna before returning to work.

A miracle had happened, yet no one acknowledged it. Her family still refused to take Joanna's powers seriously and – what was worse – her claims seemed to be causing strife wherever she went. Even affable Mr Wolland fell out with his wife after calling Joanna an impostor and, hating to see her friends at odds, Joanna had to console them with the notion that on Judgment Day the husband would owe his redemption to his wife's faith.[29] To Joanna people's attitude must have seemed most unfair, especially as in obedience to the Spirit she was now living the life of a saint. Ordered to fast between Michaelmas and Christmas, she subjected herself to a strict regime, returning to her room straight from the sacrament each Sunday to see visions and have mysteries revealed. And, in view of her privations, it could have come as no surprise when she experienced another vivid series of dreams.[30]

In November she dreamt that she stood at a door and saw in the bright moonlight a troupe of men in long cloaks riding softly through the air. As she watched, one man came through their ranks directly towards her.

Another night, no sooner was her head on the pillow than she became aware of a strange light, not from the window or door but from myriads of candles hanging on lines across the room. Frightened, she hid under the bedclothes only to see a vast chamber lit by a chandelier with sparkling lustres and, on a table, so many candles that their light was like the noonday sun.

'What can this mean?' she cried.

'Arise and shine, for the light is come and the glory of the Lord is risen,' came the response.

Next day she was given the explanation: her writings must be proved by twelve men who, when they met for that purpose, would see the candle of the Lord burn brightly among them. And who would these twelve men be? Joanna sealed up their names and gave them to Mr Leach with strict instructions not to break the seals until the twelve were assembled.[31]

That year she spent Christmas as usual with the Wollands at Heavitree where she had the sad experience of seeing Mary's brother, John Channon, exhibiting signs of mental disorder. After he came into a room cursing and muttering, pursuing his interminable argument with some demon, Joanna received a long verse containing words of warning to the Devil:

I say like lightning thou shalt sure fall down
If to this house thou ever more dost come
Or trouble those on whom I put my seal
And now of Channon I shall seal him up
Thou knowest thy doom, and hast no room to hope.

After writing down this ominous message, she sealed it up and wrote on the outer paper:

For Mr Channon and the time draws near
The whether it plainly will appear.
Joanna Southcott.[32]

By now any doubts she might have entertained about her actions had been dispelled by the countless 'signs and wonders' that were appearing. At the end of 1794 newspapers reported that two large balls of fire had fallen on the ship Britannia. Riding towards Cullompton on New Year's Day, Mr May and his daughter saw three balls of fire plummeting to earth. At eight o'clock that same evening Susanna Carter at Plymtree feared the end of the world was nigh when she saw a bright flash of light and her courtyard apparently ablaze.[33]

Times were clearly dangerous and, with Christmas over and Leach still making no move to call together the twelve men who were to judge her prophecies, Joanna waited for a sign that Pomeroy, not Leach, was the ordained minister who would take over this task. The sign came on Sunday, 8 February when she went again to hear him preach.

'A new Commandment I give unto you, that ye love one another, as I have loved you,' he exhorted his congregation, quoting from St John.[34] Again it must have seemed that he was speaking specifically to Joanna. St John – the very name was significant – 'John' being the male counterpart to 'Joanna.' And 'a new Commandment' – surely referring to Joanna's own mission?

She renewed her spiritual rigours to a point where, after long hours of prayer on the morning of the Fast Day, 25 February,[35] she entered the Cathedral almost collapsing with hunger. The sight of the sanctuary crowded with soldiers and volunteers sent her into a fit of weeping. Afterwards she crossed to the little church of St Martin's, crammed into a corner of the Close next to Mol's Coffee House, and sat in its porch to hear Mr Pomeroy preach, his rich voice harking on spiritual dangers and urging people to repent.

This time, the more she listened the more she grew frustrated. The message was exactly what was needed, but oh dear! how feebly it was put across. She knew she could do better than either of the preachers she had heard that morning – if only she were given the chance. But she would not be given a chance, because as a woman she could not be ordained. No matter that she knew herself to be the inspired instrument of the Lord, the Woman sent to redress the sin of Eve, there was still no place for her in the Established Church.

Depressed, she made her way to the Wollands at Heavitree where her spirits only recovered after, in obedience to new orders, she allowed herself to eat meat. That evening Mr Wolland called all the womenfolk out to see a great circle around the moon enclosing three stars on one side and one on the other. He observed,

> The moon is circled like the globe of the world. The four stars
> are the four quarters and three of the four like a compass to
> compass in the world.[36]

The weather in the summer of 1795 was dreadful – for a month from the middle of June it was so cold that ice formed on ponds and there were severe storms. On 19 June most of the country was covered in snow which still lay thick on the ground in northern England in July.[37]

One night Joanna was at the Taylors' house, cooking for a family lodging there, when she heard a loud banging at the door. Since it was

The Cathedral Close, Exeter, 1830 – engraved by W. Deeble after A. Glennie, and published by Jennings & Chaplin. The view shows the ancient church of St Martin, Exeter, where the Revd Joseph Pomeroy occasionally preached. In the foreground is Mol's Coffee House. The building was partly occupied by Fisher's Carving, Guilding [sic] and Looking Glass Manufactory. Built in the 16th century, the Coffee House became a favourite haunt of Sir Francis Drake and Sir Walter Raleigh and was much frequented by the Cathedral clergy. In 1792 Mol's was acquired by Miss Sarah Heard who, according to her obituary, conducted the business for over twenty-five years 'with great credit to herself and satisfaction to the numerous and respectable subscribers'.

nearly midnight and the Taylors all in bed, she asked nervously who was there. When there was no answer, she asked again. Again there was no response. Hearing voices, she opened the door and called asking who was there. There was still no reply and when the wind blew out her candle and she heard what sounded like a band of robbers rushing up the steps, she slammed the door and ran upstairs to rouse the family. The Taylors, greatly alarmed, came down almost naked to look for weapons. Mr Taylor went to the door and demanded to know who was there. 'Councillor Holland,' said a voice they recognised.

Reassured, the family trooped back to bed, leaving Joanna still faint with shock.[38]

Her nerves were in shreds. She felt that she could not go on like this; it was not her work that was causing trouble, but her failure to gain recognition as a prophet. So she sent Leach another letter, reiterating that the country was in danger and would continue so until the truth of what she had written in 1792 was proved by twelve men. Leach replied that he would bring the twelve together the following Monday.

Far from being reassured, Joanna was told that Leach and others had proposed this merely to convince her of her folly, and the sign of their duplicity would be that Eastlake would come and invite her to his house, where she would meet Mr Leach.

This is exactly what happened.

On the following Monday, Eastlake came. Joanna went to his house, met Mr Leach and four other dissenters to whom she gave her reasons for believing that her writings came from God. When she finished, Joanna left the room while they consulted. Eventually they came to some agreement and asked to see the prophecies. She consented on condition that they judged them to be of God. Again they consulted before coming back to say they must know the names of the twelve judges. Joanna explained that they would only know these once the seals were broken and the seals would be broken only in the presence of the twelve themselves. These remarks stirred their curiosity to a pitch they found irresistible. They broke the seals and then sought to cover up their betrayal by declaring that her writings came either from the Devil or herself but not from God.

A week later Joanna asked Mr and Mrs Leach to breakfast at her house, but they did not come. Instead she received a message from Leach that he had given up her cause and resigned it to the other minister she had mentioned.

So now she knew. Leach's betrayal marked the end of the dissenting line for Joanna and made it clear that Pomeroy was her man. Henceforth she would turn her attention to the Established Church as embodied in him. She wrote this to him in a letter which Pomeroy acknowledged through his servant and promised to answer. She waited nearly a week before finding herself sitting upstairs at the Taylors' writing the words: 'Go down and see him.' As she descended the stairs she heard a gentleman enquiring for her at the door.

'I suppose, Sir, my letter hath surprised you,' she said, as she asked the Revd Mr Pomeroy to step in.[39]

They fell into a discussion during which she outlined her reasons for contacting him and admitted that Mr Leach had already judged that her visitation had come from the Devil. Listening politely, Pomeroy assured her that as far as he could tell nothing she said seemed to come from that source. In fact, he shared her concern about the spiritual perils facing the nation and welcomed her attempt to warn people.

His words fell like manna, confirming what she had been told years before. They proved that Pomeroy was definitely the man she had been seeking. It could not have been more encouraging.

Joanna spent Old Christmas Day (January 6) 1796 with the Wollands at Heavitree where she was ordered by her Spirit to seal up the names of the King with the loyal half of his nation and then go out and look at the sky. Seeing a great mist over the earth and a halo round the moon, she excitedly summoned Mary Wolland and Sarah Minifie to share her wonder. The two sisters came out grumbling that it was too cold to stay outdoors, and in any case what was so unusual about seeing mist?

That night, perhaps reminded of the Channons' old smithy at Fairmile, Joanna dreamt of men drying clothes in a furnace that filled the room with steam. Suddenly they took out a bundle, tied it to a pole and carried it over their shoulders into another room where they untied it to reveal a pig, which ran towards her with steam pouring from its mouth. Asked why they put it in the furnace alive, the men said they had to, but that the pig would not die nor would it do her any harm.[40]

While Joanna was staying at Heavitree her father arrived from Gittisham, about fourteen miles away, and amused everyone by announcing that he had travelled part of the way in the Bishop's carriage. Realising that no one was taking him seriously, William Southcott explained that, if he had not travelled *in* the Bishop's coach, he had ridden *behind* it.

What had happened was that Bishop Buller, travelling in his coach, saw the octogenarian walking towards Exeter and stopped to ask how far he was going. When William said, to Mr Wolland's at Heavitree to see his daughter, the Bishop had ordered his servant to dismount and help the old man get up behind his carriage. At the end of the journey William had asked who was the gentleman he had to thank, and the servant replied that it was the Bishop of Exeter – which made him glad that he had asked, said William, else he might have thanked his Honour rather than his Lordship.

Worldly Mr Wolland, finding it hard to believe the Bishop would condescend to pick up a poor man on the road, was sure the servant had been mocking William, so to settle the matter William went to ask the turnpike what gentleman went through in his coach at that time. When he reported back that it was indeed the Bishop of Exeter, people expressed their amazement at his display of Christian charity – apparently beyond anything one might have expected from a bishop![41]

At Heavitree Joanna's father told her about another strange occurrence. On January 6 (the day she had been sealing up the King and half the nation) he had heard a voice saying loud and clear:

Southcott! Southcott! Thy name must spread far and wide: there
is a lady in Hertfordshire who hath great possessions for thee,
and wants thy family to possess it [sic].[42]

He was so excited at what he saw as the prospect of regaining his
lost inheritance that he refused to listen when Joanna patiently explained
that the words had referred not to him personally, but to the Jews. She
went on to tell him about her writings and asked him to add his signature
to the seals. In a state of some bewilderment he complied, but had no
sooner finished than he wanted to blot his name out again, suspecting a
cunning plot to get him to sign away his son's birthright in favour of
Joanna. She told him his fears were crazy. He remained unconvinced. It
took the combined voices of Mary Wolland and Sarah Minifie to persuade
him to let his name stand on the document. Later, when Joanna recounted
the incident to Squire Putt, he simply laughed and said her father was
getting senile.

Susanna, visiting her father later in the year, found herself growing
similarly impatient with him – and with her younger sister. What with
him talking so much divinity and Joanna so much philosophy, Susanna
said that living with either of them would send her mad.

Upset at hearing this, Joanna was answered by her Spirit:

Thy foolish Father shall appear
For to confound the Wise
For foolish things I now have chose
My Bible to make Good;
But those that are so worldly-wise
Will perish in the Flood.

And lest there be any mistaking that 'worldly-wise' was a dig at
Susanna, the verse continued:

Then to Divinity thou'lt come
And make My Bible clear
Thy Sister's madness all do see
Before I have ended here.[43]

Sadly for Susanna the day would come when Joanna could remind
people of these words and show how they were prophetic. At the time
they were uttered, however, it was not Susanna's worldly wisdom but
Joanna's fanaticism that was worrying her family and friends. Mr Wolland
grew so concerned that he threatened to burn her writings as the work
of the Devil – causing Joanna to spend a sleepless night, with thunder
and lightning raging overhead, before deciding to leave Heavitree and
carry her papers to the Taylors for safe-keeping.

On 11 March 1796 she sent a letter to the Venerable George Moore,
who as Archdeacon of Cornwall exercised the Bishop's power of spiritual

censure. She was warned by her Spirit that he would not reply. That same month, she dreamt she saw a large plum-tree in a garden. People were gathering a rich harvest of green and red fruit, but there were two flowers on the tree that Joanna took for plums and found to be only poppies. She threw them away.[44]

One day Mrs Taylor sent word that there was an angry gentleman wanting to speak to Joanna. She left her work and went down to find Pomeroy who explained that, having heard that Joanna had prophesied lies, he had come to warn her that, if this were so, she had sinned against the Holy Ghost and would surely go mad.

Luckily for Joanna, Mrs Taylor quickly denied the charge and Pomeroy calmed down.

'Then your prophecies were not false,' he told Joanna, still trying to warn her about the dangers involved. Finding this useless, he referred to her demand for twelve judges to examine her prophecies, adding, 'Then why don't you have your writings proved? You will wait till you bring the sword, the plague, the famine upon us. If you cannot get twelve, get six. I will meet with any.'

'Sir, it must be twelve,' Joanna insisted.

'Then let it be twelve; but do not wait till you bring the sword upon us,' Pomeroy repeated.

Even though she suspected him of hiding his true opinions, Joanna rejoiced. 'For he that can conquer his own passions is a greater hero than he who taketh a city,' she thought philosophically, and 'He must be a good man that can so condescend to convince a fool of her folly.'

The following May she went to Pomeroy's house and, handing him a letter, said, 'Sir, as you doubt what Spirit I am led by, be pleased to keep this letter till the end of the year; you will then judge of its truth.'

This Pomeroy consented to do. For him it was a fatal move, one that he would regret for the rest of his life.

Joanna's letter contained a reference to the Bishop of Exeter's death, even though at the time he was in the pink of health. Pomeroy's surprise may be imagined when, at the end of October, Bishop Buller fell ill and was dead before Christmas. Since it seemed that Joanna's prediction had come true, Pomeroy had to take notice.

'Formerly, if it were asked of a prophet, how the wars would tend, he could tell,' he declared. 'Now, if you can inform me of what will happen in Italy or England, I shall believe you.'

Happy to oblige, Joanna sent him three sheets of prophecies relating to national affairs and waited for events to prove her right.[45]

Meanwhile, having still received no reply from Archdeacon Moore, she went to the Cathedral to hear him preach and was mortified when he seemed to use his sermon to reproach her. She was all the more outraged when he refused to see her to discuss the matter. In fact, Moore's attitude left her seriously alarmed for the clergy. Joanna now realised that by taking Bishop Buller, God had cut off one of His servants to try what was in the rest, and that their only hope was to heed her warnings. Were they not all, like the late Bishop Buller, subject to divine culling? Thinking about it, she saw their fate clearly foreshadowed in the flock of sheep which Mr Wolland had bought without knowing whether they were in lamb or not. After killing one and finding it barren, he had announced that if the rest were without milk he would send them all to the butchers.[46]

But trying to persuade people to take her seriously was proving a dreadful strain; small wonder that her health began to suffer. At Heavitree on the first Sunday in June she had to take to her bed with a violent headache. Mary and Sarah brought in some flowers and fruit from the garden to cheer her up, providing just the kind of inspiration she needed. She immediately fell to drawing a full-blown rose with a cherry on either side to signify Christ close accompanied by his chosen people.[47]

Not everyone was as supportive (or tolerant) as the Channon sisters, and in the course of her travels Joanna met with more than her fair share of difficult people – unless it could have been something in her that brought out the worst in fellow passengers. On one journey from Gittisham back to Exeter that year she was almost kicked off the dicky-seat by a guard who was so drunk that the driver eventually dumped him on the road.[48]

Back in Exeter, Joanna took on the job of making a hair mattress for Mr Swales who owned a wine cellar in the city. Sitting amidst a pile of horse-hair, she was alarmed to see a three-year old running about without shoes. The hair would prick his feet, she warned. Instead of heeding her words, the little boy demanded to know why then it did not prick her hands. For once Joanna was lost for an answer.[49]

Harvest was remarkably good that year. Joanna went as usual to Plymtree to help Susanna, who wanted to know why she never visited their brother and his wife nowadays. Because they had grown too grand for her, Joanna retorted, opening herself up to the charge of having too much pride. In self-defence she added that she did, on the other hand, visit her father and those who were poor.

The discussion had revealed Joanna's sense of inadequacy beside her richer siblings, just as an envious streak had shown itself in a recent dream in which she and her late brother John had been doing the milking on their brother's farm; Joanna took a ladle of acorn mast to eat with her milk, but after tasting John's and finding it sweeter, vainly tried to filch his.[50]

Pursuing the subject of her sister's estrangement from the family, Susanna said that even their brother Joseph felt he no longer knew Joanna.

'It is true, for none of my brothers and sisters know me,' Joanna murmured.

Susanna, rapidly losing patience, asked her if she knew herself.

'No,' Joanna replied.

'O, well then!' Susanna snapped, concluding the argument with a sarcastic suggestion that in any case all things were types of something else.[51]

When she left, Joanna took her precious papers back to Mrs Taylor to keep with her other writings. After receiving so much criticism for illegibility, she had been ordered by the Spirit to have them all copied and printed, but the very day she gave them to the printer, Pomeroy returned to Exeter. The die being already cast, Joanna decided not to tell him what she had done until the book was published. The Spirit, however, instructed her otherwise.

She obeyed only to find her own caution justified by Pomeroy's reaction. He threatened to cut off all contact with her if she published his name, remaining adamant about this even when she took two friends to reason with him. He also told her she must have her 1792 writings copied out before handing them to him, as he could not expect his colleagues to read her dreadful handwriting.

Joanna accordingly had her writings broken open before witnesses, then marked, copied and a section sent to Pomeroy. A week later she saw him again. This time he complained that what she had sent was not enough to convince the clergy, so on the following day she again summoned witnesses to watch her break open the seals which she had set in 1794 and 1795. These papers she then sent to Pomeroy, giving him three weeks to consult his colleagues and with them come to some judgment as to whether her writings came from God.[52]

She spent Christmas at Heavitree, happy to join in the local custom of burning ashen faggots on Christmas Eve, despite Mary Wolland's objection that it would have been better to give the money spent on such jollities to the deserving poor.[53] As for Mr Wolland, he was preoccupied by the undeserving poor, especially the one who had been stealing his eggs. In fact, he had gone so far as to devise a plan which involved boiling his eggs and replacing them in the nest with a secret mark on them so that he could discover the culprit. Ordered by her Spirit to write this down as a parable, Joanna went upstairs to sit in the cold, wringing a piece of silk in the inkstand to get enough ink to wet her quill, while downstairs everyone else was enjoying themselves playing cards. Eventually, Mrs Minifie, worried in case her friend caught a chill, yelled: 'Fire below!' – which brought Joanna scuttling down to rejoin the company.[54]

On New Year's Day (New Style) Joanna went to see her father, whose third wife seems by then to have disappeared from the picture. Despite having thoroughly cleaned his house back in the summer, Joanna found it filthy again and had to set to, boiling up ashes to scour his pot, scrubbing the floors, and unhanging all the windows. Once good order was restored, she told him he must employ someone to keep it that way if he could not manage it himself. She might as well have saved her breath. Old William moaned that he had not the heart to clean up properly, being so depressed by the fact that all his children neglected him – all, that is, except his 'one Ewe lamb for to comfort his sorrows'. And once he started on his catalogue of woes, it took all Joanna's powers of persuasion to stop him venting his spleen by sending her brothers and sisters a furious letter he had already written.[55] Eventually, having promised to pay his debts, his 'one Ewe lamb' basked for the moment in his favour and even managed to engage him in a discussion of the Scriptures. She mentioned Susanna's notion that, since anyone can understand the Bible as it is, it needed no further revelation. Old William, master of the put-down when it came to women, dismissed Susanna with the remark that, like a ship over-masted, her topsails were too heavy for the bottom.[56]

Such petty triumphs did nothing to mask Joanna's disappointment at the fact that 1797 had dawned without any official recognition of her mission. Nevertheless she made her first task the sending of further important prophecies concerning France and Spain to Pomeroy. It was vital that she keep up the pressure, especially in the light of such bad omens as the news that her nephew John was very ill again and unlikely to survive.

On the last but one night of January Joanna, feeling very low, was kept awake by heavy rain and thunderous winds. After a fit of weeping she at last fell asleep and dreamt that Satan came to her, put his hand in her mouth and – although afterwards not absolutely sure what she had done – she rather thought she had bitten off his fingers.[57]

The following day, while writing this down, she collapsed in a faint on her bed and it was lucky that Mary Wolland was on hand to revive her with some drops.[58] When, a few nights later, in a fit of despair Joanna prayed so hard that she fainted again, instead of resorting to drops, Mary and Sarah came in and poured water over her head. It seems to have done the trick, for Joanna revived – even if she did complain of feeling poorly all next day.[59]

She was, in fact, sinking into a deep depression, which was hardly surprising when her friends blamed her for wasting so much time writing stuff that nobody wanted to read. And Pomeroy was proving difficult. Once, when she took him a prophecy, he said he could not make out her writing and when she offered to read it out loud insulted her by saying that he would not know if she was reading what was written or simply making it up! Furious, Joanna had banged her fist on his table, crying, and declared that he must judge her to be worse than the witch of Endor if he thought she would mock God and deceive man in such a way.

Startled by this violence, Pomeroy had tried to placate her by calling on her friend Miss Bird to witness that he believed Joanna to be a religious, good woman. Mary Bird agreed that was his opinion. Then Pomeroy asked Joanna to sit down while he patiently explained that her writing had to be legible, not for his sake (he believed her in any case, he said), but for others who might want to read it.[60]

Mollified and prepared to give him another chance, Joanna would have read her letter to him there and then had he not suddenly remembered that he had to go out to tea so had no time. Perhaps she could come back next week, he had added weakly. Joanna had agreed she could, but when she got home, the Spirit ordered her not to go. Instead she must write and ask Pomeroy to send her letter back.

Things were clearly not going well. After Archdeacon Moore ignored her letter, she had sent one to the Chancellor of the diocese, Nutcombe, only to have it returned by his servant with a message that his master was away. She sent it again and, although this time her letter was retained to await Nutcombe's return, she guessed he would treat it with contempt. Moreover, the fact that Pomeroy had failed to place her prophecies before a jury as promised added to her anguish.

Then came Lent and, despite feeling in need of meat, Joanna began a rigorous fast, taking nothing but one basin of broth each day and a little meat on Sundays. Her dreams began to reflect the effect of this abstinence. She dreamt she was in a cornfield hatting (stacking and covering) the wheat as it was cut down, but she grew so thirsty that she stole some cider and was then whisked away through the air to strange places.[61]

All this time she had been bottling up her troubles, fearing that nobody understood the questions which vexed her. When she asked other people whether they thought anyone could possess knowledge of God in themselves, they simply told her not to worry her head over such matters. Someone had even suggested that it was not God, but her own spirit that communed with her body.[62] Not for a moment did she believe this, but it was a disturbing notion.

STRANGE EFFECTS, 1797-1801

What man appoints, God disappoints.
Letter to Pomeroy, 23 March 1800

There is no corner that a man can drive you up in but the Spirit finds a gutterhole to creep out.
Joseph to Joanna in Bristol, 1798

May 1797 found Joanna working again for the Wollands, enjoying the company of her old friends. There is little doubt that Mary Wolland and her sister Sarah Minifie, with their down-to-earth sense of fun, were good for Joanna in her present highly strung state. Certainly, having known her since childhood, they refused to put up with anything they regarded as humbug.

Life at Heavitree clearly had its lighter moments. There was the time when a vain show-off came to the house. Knowing that he was illiterate, the sisters handed him a French book and gleefully watched as he read it, page by page. They then asked how he liked it.

'Very well, in the manner it was of,' he declared, a remark greeted by fits of laughter.[1]

But though Joanna was fond of Mary and Sarah, she was ill at ease as a servant and unable to refrain from pointing out their short-comings. After Mr Wolland rescued his prize lark from the cat but found it dead in its cage next morning, Joanna had to be sure what had happened. Ordered by her Spirit to pluck the unfortunate bird, she exposed the cat's teethmarks in two places and then solemnly pointed out that the fault was Mr Wolland's for not noticing that the cage was broken.[2]

If her employer was less than charmed by such bluntness, Joanna did not care. She might be a servant but, in her eyes, she could not be less than equal to folk who were unbelievers and Mr Wolland had shown himself sceptical of her prophecies. As for Mary and Sarah, she had never regarded them as fellow handmaids of the Lord and there were painful scenes as they showed themselves dismissive of her spiritual pretensions.[3]

One day Sarah Minifie took up a book by Richard Brothers, who claimed to be in possession of 'revealed knowledge', and started laughing at his prophecies. When Joanna did the same Sarah accused her of speaking in his favour some years before. True, Joanna agreed, but that was before she had seen his writings. Then it was wrong for Joanna to praise something she knew nothing about, sniffed Mrs Minifie.[4]

It was the kind of put-down that Joanna found increasingly difficult to tolerate. She was tired of being badly treated. People must be made to take her mission seriously. Her dilemma was solved by her Spirit's issuing a new instruction: Joanna must no longer go out to work nor call any man her master.[5]

Not work? Then how was she to earn her living?

The Spirit provided clarification: though not to receive wages, she could take work home and accept presents for any services rendered.

It may be imagined what the Wollands thought of this new command – or demand – from one to whom they had been kind enough to offer work. The friendship which had lasted half a century began to cool, especially after Mary and Sarah committed the mortal offence of refusing to testify publicly to Joanna's powers of prophecy.

Meanwhile Joanna, on a trip to Exeter, heard that the Methodists were also disputing her powers. Ordered to call at Mr Taylor's, she met there a Mr Manley who reported that Chancellor Nutcombe had discussed her letter with Archdeacon Moore, to whom she had sent a similar letter twelve months before. Neither dignitary found any fault in her words. They simply thought her crazy.[6] Joanna was furious and calmed down only after her loyal friend, Lucy Taylor, suggested that it was the Methodists who had persuaded Mr Manley that Joanna's prophecies were false.

Meanwhile at Heavitree the talk was all of war – Mr Wolland insisting there would be peace before July; Mrs Minifie arguing the opposite.[7] In mid-July Joanna met the Reverend Joseph Pomeroy and placed in his hands sealed prophecies relating to the next twelve months. If by the end of the year he remained unconvinced, she had been told she would have to wait a further two years before her writings were judged.[8]

In a fit of depression, she paced up and down Mr Wolland's garden until midnight, weeping and looking up at the sky, wanting to die. Her utter frustration was made worse by news that her nephew, John Southcott, had just died after lying 'twelve hours in greatest agonies and repeated groans unutterable.' He was buried at St David's, Exeter, on 24 July 1797.[9]

Her father's situation was also giving cause for concern. Since William Southcott, now over eighty, could barely cope with living on his own, Joanna had made it her business to return to Gittisham every summer to clean his home. Because his landlady refused to make repairs, his cob-built cottage was so dilapidated that Joanna was able to use the rags that stopped draughts from broken windows as cleaning cloths to dry the floors.[10]

As the old man entered dotage he lost all prudence in the management of money and his plight became embarrassing. Joanna resented how the rest of her family left her to shoulder the burden on her own, apparently thinking that because she was single she had nothing better to do with her time – or her money. This was a view shared by her father who, despite the many pounds she had given him that year, followed her back to Heavitree and asked for more. What should she do? It was hard to refuse, but she knew he would keep coming if he saw she had money to spare. She adopted a little subterfuge, asking Mary Wolland in front of him to lend her money. Mary obliged by giving him meat to take home as well as money, and the old man thanked her profusely, saying his cup ran over.[11]

Joanna also displayed a generous spirit when she was sent into Exeter to buy an old rug for the poor. After visiting five or six places and seeing nothing but worn-out blankets full of holes, she kindly spent her employer's money on a new one.[12]

In early August 1797 Mr Nix, a neighbouring farmer, tried to reduce the heat in his hay-rick by cutting it partly through. Unfortunately this drew up smoke like a chimney and the rick burst into flames. Though it was practically burnt through, Mr Wolland bought what remained with the idea of salvaging some hay or making a profit on the ashes. One local, however, laughed up his sleeve at Wolland, saying if the Devil looked after his own, this time he had missed the mark.[13]

There were other disasters. As a result of the wet season Mr Wolland had a wheat-field full of rust disease and canker, which he had to cut green and leave till it dried as it was too soft to thresh. Sunday, 6 August, dawned the first dry day since reaping started and Joanna spent it nursing a headache brought on by her efforts to reconcile differing opinions about the harvest. John, Mr Wolland's servant, said the corn was good. Mr Symons agreed. But Mr Wolland said it was bad, and Mr Swales declared he had never seen worse. What did Joanna think? Unable to decide, she went indoors to lie down.

She was in such a low state that even the upholstery work she had been doing for twenty years was now proving too much for her. Or perhaps it was her inner resistance to such menial tasks that brought on a crisis. Whatever the cause, the job she had undertaken for Mr Hicks, an Exeter builder, went wrong. He had commissioned her to make cushions but they finished up too short. When he asked her to lengthen them, her Spirit told her to leave them as they were. Mr Hicks expressed himself warmly on the subject, but Joanna, under higher orders, would not touch the cushions again. Deadlock was overcome only after her friends, Mrs Wolland and Mrs Minifie, agreed to do the work for her.[14]

It was a vexatious time. Even nature had a few more stings in its tail – as Mr Wolland found to his cost when attacked by a bee in his garden. Joanna spread honey on the wound and tied it up. But when he went to visit Nutcombe, the Chancellor advised him to use a vinegar and oatmeal poultice instead, with the result that Wolland spent an anguished night. Next morning Joanna persuaded him to put oil and honey on his hand, and this cured it.[15]

Meanwhile Mrs Minifie was criticising Joanna for writing about trivial things and spreading fear and despondency, for – as far as she could see – there were no great troubles ahead. But then Sarah Minifie was no prophet and could not foresee the imminent tragedy facing her brother. John Channon's mental state had been growing steadily worse. Increasingly argumentative, he had gone so far as to suggest that Joanna's calling came not from God but Satan. Referring to his remarks, Joanna wrote:

> Such ignorant men as he would come
> Like fools for to dispute
> Until their Crowns do all Come down
> And I shall make them mute. . . .[16]

It could then have come as no surprise to her when in late November John Channon, aged fifty-five, collapsed and died. His body was taken from Heavitree to Ottery to be buried near his parents – but his influence on Joanna's life lived on in a mysterious way. For it was about this time that she started to use a special seal that, according to her, she had found while clearing up after a house-sale years before. The seal bore the letters 'IC' with a star above and below. After picking it up she had, so she says, without thinking put it away in a drawer and forgotten about it. Why she did not attribute the initials to John Channon and give, or return, it to him remains a mystery. It is perhaps significant that she felt free to use it only after his death.

Nevertheless, it was a dismal end to the year. Another link with the past was severed, for she had known John Channon since childhood. Eight years her senior and a bachelor till 1775, she might once have felt romantically drawn to him. One of her later dreams suggests this might have been so. But now, approaching fifty and menopause,[17] her dreams tended to reflect less troubled times. Harking back to her brother's farm, she found herself reciting familiar field names and standing among crowds of people waiting to see the soldiers marching by.

Dreams of Sidmouth could not fail to stir up memories of Noah Bishop and former hopes of married love.[18] Such missed chances only made sense in the light of her present mission. Restless and depressed, she sought out the one man who had shown some understanding of this mission – the Reverend Joseph Pomeroy.

Since first hearing him preach in Exeter Cathedral, Joseph Pomeroy had come to assume great importance for Joanna. Born in Liskeard in 1749, the son of John Pomeroy, gentleman, Joseph had been appointed Vicar of St Kew, Bodmin, in 1777, a parish he continued to serve for the next six decades. He was married to Melloney Scobell who, after giving birth to six children in as many years, by 1797 was a chronic invalid. Not surprising then, that Pomeroy looked askance at a letter sent him earlier in the year in which Joanna had identified herself as the Bride of Revelation and Pomeroy himself as the Bridegroom, hinting at dire punishments if he refused his destiny.[19]

Now when she asked him again if he thought her prophecies came from the Devil, Pomeroy exclaimed:

> Do not mention the Devil, for there is not a word in your writings likely to come from him. But how do I know but you have this knowledge from yourself?

At which Joanna protested that she knew no more than his table what the Lord would do on earth.[20]

So why did she not publish her prophecies, Pomeroy demanded, making it clear that he wanted no more to do with her.

Joanna pondered over this snub, then, remembering her letter, wondered whether he could possibly have misunderstood her references to them as Bride and Bridegroom. Although her intentions had been pure, might he not have seen her as someone trying to rise above her station? It did not occur to her that it was an insensitive letter to write to a man with an invalid wife. Or that Pomeroy might have considered her notions blasphemous. All Joanna could see was that he had condemned her for aspiring to link her name with one whose family was far above her own.

Pomeroy's change in attitude left her embarrassed and wanting to get away. Her turgid feelings were exposed on Christmas Day, 1797, when Mr Wolland caught her in tears as the choir was singing the carol 'Arise, O Zion' – although, when asked why she was crying, she said it was for joy.[21] To Joanna it seemed that no matter how hard she tried, she met with no support in Exeter. Her friends refused to take her warnings seriously. Church dignitaries ignored her letters. Dissenting ministers had shown themselves hostile to her mission. One Methodist preacher, Sir Egerton Leigh, had even advised her to burn her writings because they came from the Devil.[22]

If Exeter was such stony ground, she might have to travel abroad to find sympathisers.

After hearing that her brother Joseph had just got married to Sarah Hall in Bristol, her Spirit ordered her thither.[23] Although Lucy Taylor urged her not to go, once Joanna proved resolute she persuaded her menfolk to lend a hand – Mr Taylor finding out the cost and his son making arrangements with a suitable landlord.[24] Then, with a last warning to Mr Wolland that there would be dearth if the clergy clung to their unbelief, Joanna set out for Bristol.[25] On the morning she left there were two almighty claps of thunder.

She must have felt strange to be travelling so far from home. It was years since she had seen Joseph, having fallen out with all her brothers and sisters after they tried to stop her writing down her prophecies.[26] After taking lodgings, she went to the market, introduced herself to his wife and, discovering that they lived at Whitehall, a mile out of town, asked her to bring Joseph along to tea that afternoon without letting on who had invited them.

Sarah, who was pregnant, played along with the joke. Thinking they were going to visit a stranger, Joseph was amazed to see Joanna and became quite emotional. He thought all his family had forsaken him, he moaned. He had written to Susanna six months previously and received no reply. And he thought Joanna had been too offended to write to him again. Now here she was and had sent for him. But staying in lodgings was not good enough. She must give them up immediately and come and live with them.

Joanna obliged and stayed for half a year, eagerly awaiting Sarah's delivery after being 'told' that the birth of a son would bring her own 'trial' on – and being disappointed when Sarah had a daughter. During her time in Bristol she sent back prophecies about the harvest to Lucy Taylor, and marvelled when people were prepared to pay half-a-crown for a newspaper to find out if a rumoured victory was true.[27]

Joseph was puzzled by his sister. Frankly sceptical of her mission, he said the Lord had not been so familiar with man since the days of His incarnation and would never be so again.[28]

'God knows from whence your prophecies are; but I shall leave them to time for I cannot tell,' he concluded, adding with more than a hint of exasperation, 'but there is no corner that a man can drive you up in but the Spirit finds a gutterhole to creep out.'

'My father had five wise children and one foolish one – or he had five foolish children and one wise one,' Joanna replied sagely.[29]

Joseph muttered that he did not think she was any wiser than Susanna, so if she prevailed it *must* be by the power of God.

One day she met up with an old friend, William Brown, son of her former employer in Honiton. Arthur Brown had transferred his bookshop to Bristol and died in 1787, leaving his son to continue the family business. Joanna told William Brown about her prophecies. He repeated them to Mr Edgar, whose mother rented Joseph his gardens. Some months later, this young man approached Joseph at Whitehall to ask if he had a sister who was a prophetess? Joseph said, No. Mr Edgar insisted that William Brown said he had. Joseph, highly embarrassed, said he must have confused them with another family in Gittisham with a similar name.

That evening Joseph repeated what had happened. Joanna was furious. He had sinned by telling a lie, she said. If he was so ashamed of her, he should have answered that he had a sister whose head was filled with strange prophecies. In 1792 she thought she had been visited by the Holy Spirit and despite all their efforts neither he nor his brothers and sisters had been able to persuade her otherwise. Or he could have repeated Susanna's words: 'I might as well persuade a tree that is falling to stand, as persuade her out of her prophecies.'[30] Then he could have added, 'If you wish to know what grounds she has for this strong belief, I will introduce you to my sister.'

If he had used words like these, said Joanna, warming to her subject, he would have made a friend of Mr Edgar, who was keen to find a prophet because some men in Bristol had recently issued a wager of £300 to £1 on there being a king on the French throne by October 1799 and he could have won that wager if he listened to her. Indeed, she was prepared to bet £3,000 herself (if she had it) that there would be no king in France by that time.

Sarah Southcott was impressed. She told her husband,

>   What sister saith is a wiser answer than what you made, and
>   had you spoken in that manner you would not have disgraced
>   yourself and Mr Edgar might judge for himself.

Cowed, Joseph mumbled something about not thinking of such a reply at the time and, although sorry for what he had done, supposed Mr Edgar too much a gentleman to take offence.

Events sadly proved otherwise.

Joseph paid £8 an acre to Mrs Edgar for gardens which were so neglected and overrun by weeds that they left him out of pocket. Having paid up to the last quarter, he relinquished his tenancy, leaving behind fruit trees and bushes valued at £30 to cover the last instalment of rent. Joanna said he should have asked Mrs Edgar first and then taken them away if she refused to accept them as rent. No, Joseph exclaimed, her son knew the value of what was left and he would act honourably.

Joanna was sceptical. He would not be able to claim anything back once he had left, she warned. Moreover, he could be arrested for the last quarter's rent.

No, young Mr Edgar would never see him hurt, Joseph protested.

Such was the situation when Joanna returned home from Bristol for Christmas.

A few weeks later she received a dramatic letter from Sarah. Mrs Edgar had had Joseph arrested and thrown in prison. When Sarah had pleaded with young Mr Edgar, he refused to listen, saying it was his mother's business and nothing to do with him. The Bristol Humane Society had pleaded on Joseph's behalf. Still Mrs Edgar remained adamant. She would make no allowance for what was left as he could not remove plants, and he would stay in prison till the debt was paid.

Since Joanna apparently had no money, Joseph's release was secured by the Humane Society paying one half of his debt and his sister Susanna Carter the other.

'He was always too proud – like the man who pruned the tree upwards till he could not come down without help,' Susanna grumbled as she sent the money. Adding more caustically that Joseph was like a child going to a fair; he spent hundreds as if he had thousands and did not consider whose substance he was wasting or whose mercies he would come to. In fact, Susanna had a great deal to say before paying up and getting her brother out of trouble.[31]

Back in Exeter old frustrations continued to vex Joanna. There was still no response from Archdeacon Moore, so she sent both him and Pomeroy a copy of the letter sent to Lucy Taylor the previous August with her predictions about the harvest. Then she sent Moore a letter saying what kind of harvest would follow in 1799, with three seals which were not to be broken before the end of the year.

On Good Friday she listened to Archdeacon Moore and the Reverend Joseph Pomeroy preaching respectively on the texts: 'His blood be on us and our children' and 'When we were without strength Christ died for us.' Such erudition – yet Joanna recognised their limitations. For, as her Spirit pointed out, 'neither of them can clearly discern from whence thy writings come.'[32]

The following month Joanna wrote to both men again, together with the Bishop, Mr Tucker (Moore's curate at Heavitree), and other clergy. They were annoyed at being pestered, but this did not signify. Joanna was beyond their reproaches. Her orders came from on high, albeit through mysterious channels. For instance, in July she was ordered to put her quill-pens into the Bible and mark where she found them – a procedure she was often to repeat when seeking direction.[33]

That same month her father, who had gone to stay with Susanna was taken ill and Joanna rushed to Plymtree to help nurse him.[34] She arrived to find him apparently dying. He was having convulsions and it was all the three wakers appointed to keep vigil at his bedside could do to keep him in bed.

Watching by his side, snatching what sleep she could, Joanna dreamt that Susanna came and said: 'Now my Father is gone, we will take a walk.'

In the dream they went on a most beautiful walk along gravel paths amid flowers into a large meadow with a straight path through it. Here they saw a dog on a long chain that took Joanna by the hand and would not let it go till they came to the edge of the field. Joanna was afraid of the dog until someone said he would not hurt her, nor could he go any further than the edge of the field.[35]

In the morning old William was still delirious, fighting with anyone who came near, shouting that he was in a tussle and begging some one to help.

He seemed to be struggling between life and death, onlookers thought. Then to their amazement he grew better and even got up for a few hours before growing faint and returning to bed. 'Just lighted up before his death,' was the verdict.

While waiting, Joanna took up her quill, hearing as she did so the words:

As I compared thy father to the nation in his life so I shall in his
death; which will not be till after many days. I shall shew thee in
a dream of his death.

She was now shown a length of chain that stretched through a large field from one gate to another before pulling her father back.

When Susanna, convinced that their father was dying, wanted to know if the chain lasted as long as a month, Joanna received the following answer:

One month thy sister doth allow, before she judged the end;
One month you'll see your destiny, what will befall your land.

Joanna took the words to mean that old William would die within the month.[36] It was Susanna who had doubts. After careful study of the words, she concluded that if the message was from the Lord it meant their father would not die then.[37]

William Southcott had been taken ill on 13 July. Now, as the days passed, his condition improved until the time came when he was well enough to return to Gittisham. Joanna was dumbfounded.

But while octogenarian William Southcott survived, on 30 August 1799 Melloney, the forty-seven year old invalid wife of the Reverend Joseph

Pomeroy, died.[38] Joanna did not record her feelings at the news.

Meanwhile, hopes of the glorious harvest confidently forecast by the Rector of St Martin's, Prebendary James Carrington, in his Exeter Cathedral sermon were washed away by the onset of torrential rain.[39] Joanna's friends told Archdeacon Moore's servant, Chapman, that this was exactly what she had foretold in her letter to his master in March.

Was it true? Chapman persuaded Moore that the only way to find out was to open the letter. The Archdeacon complied, but after struggling in vain to read Joanna's handwriting cast the missive into the fire.[40]

As if to prove Joanna right in her opinion that it was the clergy's unbelief that was responsible for every catastrophe, pouring rain continued until the end of the year, wrecking any chance of salvaging the harvest. In early December, when Joanna was working at a farmhouse in Tiverton, the fields were so flooded that the farmer feared his sheep would all be drowned. Fortunately, once the water went down, he found them safe on a steep bank where they had taken refuge.[41]

Soon afterwards Joanna found her own place of safety, when she was engaged by Mr Taylor for two years.[42] She was still supporting her father, sending him what money she could afford and, heaven knows, needed a period of stability and friends like Lucy Taylor. For she was about to meet another crisis in her life.

Joanna had already identified herself as the Bride in the Book of Revelation and named the Reverend Joseph Pomeroy as her Bridegroom. In this context, news of the death of Pomeroy's wife assumed tremendous significance. Pomeroy – the name held so many associations. She saw it as 'Pomme-roi', the royal apple sent as the antidote to Eve's.[43] It was a name she had grown up with, for in Gittisham 'Pomeroy' was the imposing house seen across the valley from the Southcotts' humble farm. When Joanna heard stories about her father's lost inheritance it was possibly a house like 'Pomeroy' that she imagined as her birthright.

Now she had met a man of that name and the flesh-and-blood Pomeroy gave promise of much more. As the Reverend Joseph Pomeroy, he represented the Established Church whose endorsement of her mission would ensure its success, for, having been rejected by the Methodists, she felt it was now up to the Church of England to confirm her message and help her awaken the nation from its slumber. And the fact that Pomeroy was a handsome widower the same age as herself may even have suggested a romantic tie.[44] After all, why should Joanna not be drawn towards Pomeroy as a man? There were sound biblical precedents for late marriage and, nearer home, neither Sarah nor Mary Channon had married till in their forties.

Whether romantically drawn towards him or not, Joanna saw Pomeroy as having a vital part to play in her mission. Seeing it as her duty to convince him of his role, she began to bombard him with letters.

And Pomeroy? He saw it as his Christian duty to counsel those in spiritual need – no matter how tiresome and opinionated they might be. He tried hard to do the right thing, only to find that there were limits to a man's patience.

A hint of his growing irritability was reflected in Joanna's letter to him on 3 December 1799:

> You asked if I judged myself so great a favourite of Heaven as to think the Lord had sent a curse over the land because men had despised my writings. To this I answer, not for my sake, but for his great name's sake, to prove the truth of what he had spoken and threatened.[45]

Finding it impossible to argue with such a woman, or ignore her, Pomeroy was being forced into a corner. It became clear that if he had any hopes of remarriage or preferment, both might be blighted by his association with Joanna.[46]

While Pomeroy took steps to distance himself, her family on the other hand drew closer again. Certainly by 1799 Joanna had been reconciled with both Joseph and Susanna. In fact she took to discussing her writings with Susanna, who took an intelligent interest in her prophecies. And because she had some respect for her religious but more pragmatic sister, she was prepared to hear her out when Susanna declared that she was being misled.

According to Susanna, Joanna's writing was too variable to be the work of the Lord – whilst some of it made sense and was consistent with the Bible, other parts were such nonsense that she could hardly believe they came from the same pen. And Sarah Minifie, she added, said the same.

It was a clever ploy. Susanna knew how much, in her younger days, Joanna had been influenced by the opinion of her friends. What she did not realise was that things had changed – Joanna now had an invisible 'ally', her Spirit. She did not argue when Susanna attacked her version of the day of judgment by saying that if the Lord was just He would consign all evil people to the Devil. She simply waited to consult her Spirit on the matter.

The reason for their conflict, she was told, was that whereas she, Joanna, was awake, Susanna, like the rest of Adam's fallen race was fast asleep and, like men asleep, they judged their Bibles as a dream, one interpreting it this way, another that.[47]

So that was it. As far as spiritual knowledge was concerned, Susanna was asleep, as was the rest of humanity. It made sense. For Joanna it explained why nobody took her seriously. They were all asleep and incapable of reading the signs of the times – despite the fact that the writing was on the wall in such very big letters. They were all asleep – even the clergy. One might say, most of all the clergy! In January Joanna noticed what appeared to be a small spot on her leg. But this spot when removed, erupted into a severe inflammation that affected both her legs. Joanna correctly interpreted her suffering as a sign that the heat of the summer would bring in food shortages.

Even so, there was no convincing the clergy. They continued to mock her writings even after all the farmers in Devon agreed that the corn would not last till Lady-day unless they brought in supplies from abroad. In fact, people were soon complaining that a guinea had gone further in 1799 than one and a half guineas a year later, for vegetables had trebled in price and butter, cheese and animal food cost double.

Seeing all this, surely nobody could doubt that affairs were approaching crisis point?

On 23 March 1800 Joanna wrote to Pomeroy:

Reverend Sir,

You may be surprised to receive a letter from me, after saying in my last letter that I meant to go abroad for two years, if my writings were not now proved. But what man appoints, God disappoints, I find I cannot go one step in myself, to do anything; I must stay to see the event of what I have written. . . .

After listing people's complaints, she asked if he thought it prudent to run the hazard of another harvest.

Pomeroy's reply was direct and to the point. He declared she was mad and wrote blasphemy.

Joanna immediately wrote back, humbly asking him to show exactly how her writings were blasphemous. She also told him not to trouble any more clergymen on her account. 'I find I must bear my own burthen,' she concluded sadly.[48]

It would surely all have seemed hopeless, had not her Spirit been there to guide her past all the obstacles placed in her path. In May she was busy penning vital prophecies about the next four years' harvests when Susanna started nagging about spoiling so much paper. Her Spirit responded with a suitably lofty defence. Far from being spoilt, the paper on which Joanna had written would be the means to awaken thousands.[49]

On 29 May Mrs Symons's children marked the day by sending Joanna some gilded oak-apples – a gesture which pleased her at a time when she needed cheering up.[50] She had been ordered to go to her father's house and stay there a month. It was something she did every year, using the time to clean his cottage and take stock of his larder, but this visit had more than usual significance. After the scare at Plymtree the year before, her Spirit told her to look on her father's life as a sign: if he died within the month, the harvest would be good; if not, it would be bad. After she had been in Gittisham a few days, the message was changed. She was told that on St Swithin's day it would rain, thunder, lightning and hail – and her father would die. She wrote this down and waited. 15 July, St Swithin's day, dawned fine and dry – and her father was better than usual.[51]

So, had her Spirit been wrong? No. For Joanna there was another, far more disturbing explanation. The message had not come from her Spirit at all, but from Satan. She had been deliberately misled. In her misery she penned,

> I thought all prayers were fruitless. O my Father you are on a Bed of Sickness and so am I also; sleep has departed from my eyes and Slumber from my Eyelids. My Sorrows are greater than I can bear; while thousands that fear not God, nor think upon His ways, sleep secure in peace, and rest. . . .[52]

In a fit of anxiety in which she figured that if Satan could deceive her in these things, he might do so in others, she decided to burn all her writings. But before she could carry this out, she was answered that what she had just experienced was another test of her faith. The Lord had permitted Satan to tell her lies, for Satan had said that if she was told lies on her own, she would never admit to anyone else what had happened. But she had confounded Satan by being determined to tell the truth. Moreover, if she had any lingering doubts, she would know that this was now the Lord speaking when she saw the next harvest.

August arrived, and she woke one morning full of despair. Her father was growing increasingly unmanageable and the harvest, despite all she had been told, looked very promising. After the heat of earlier summer, everyone was saying the corn had never looked finer and expected a bumper crop. In fact, farmers had already dropped their prices from 25s. to 16s. a bushel in anticipation that they would soon plummet to 6s.

Joanna, not knowing what to make of the situation, felt she would rather die than face further mockery. In this state of confusion she was told to return to Exeter, show her documents to her friends but not break any seals until the end of August when, if she judged her writings to be from God, she should publish them to the world.

'I have prolonged thy father's life to shame and confound thy enemy, the Devil,' declared her Spirit, 'and the harvest shall confound man.'[53]

Back in Exeter she found folk whispering that she had gone to Gittisham to kill her father in order to prove her prophecy. This slander gave her a clue as to why his life had been spared. By not dying, her father had confounded her enemies. Which still left her with the problem of the harvest. Of course there was always the possibility that, as in the previous year, it might be ruined at the last moment by rain. But the reaping of exceptionally large ears of corn commenced under clear blue skies. It was only when the grain was threshed out that the true situation was revealed: they had harvested little more than dry husks. In the catastrophic dearth that followed, the quartern (four-pound) loaf rose above 2s. in price.

Before the end of the year news came from Black Torrington that Joanna's brother-in-law, Nicholas Paige, had died – a timely reminder of mortality and the fact that time was pressing.[54] Joanna had been told to wait no longer than New Year's Day (Old Style) 1801 before having her writings printed. When the day arrived with still no word from the clergy, she went ahead and published *Strange Effects of Faith*.

In the Preface she boldly set out her feminist thesis:

The word of God is as a book that is Sealed, so that neither the learned nor unlearned can read (that is to say, understand) it; for it was sealed up in the bosom of the Father, till he thought proper to break the Seals, and reveal it to a Woman, as it is written in the Revelations.

Had these things been known or understood by man, the world would have seen many of these women in every age and century; but the Lord hath concealed it from man, as he did from the Jews the manner in which Christ should be born. . . .

Now if any twelve Ministers, who are worthy and good men, will prove these writings come from the Devil and his foreknowledge of things; and explain clearly to me those mysteries of the Bible that I shall propose to them I will refrain from further printing: But if they cannot, I shall go on, till I have made public all the mysteries of the Bible – the times which are to come – and what shall happen till Christ's Kingdom be established; sometimes from parables, sometimes from types and shadows, sometimes from dreams and visions, and also from the Bible which sheweth, by the account of the tree of knowledge that knowledge must come to *Man* from the *Woman*. As she at first plucked the fruit, and brought the knowledge of the evil fruit; so at last she must bring the knowledge of the good fruit.

If, from the publication of her book Joanna expected glory in the form of praise from her family she must have been disappointed. Her father, who had once encouraged her writing, had now turned against it. Her eldest brother and sister, who had always disapproved, thought she had taken leave of her senses. Practical Susanna feared it was a colossal waste of money and decided to take her younger sister to task before she fell into debt and ended up, like brother Joseph, in gaol.[55] After giving her a severe telling-off, she sugared the pill by offering to help her do anything else in the world if she would give up these prophecies from the Devil. Joanna was outraged. How dared Susanna speak to her like that? What did she know about spiritual matters?

Clearly getting nowhere, Susanna cast around for someone else to speak to her sister – someone with authority, someone whom Joanna respected. A clergyman, for instance. The Reverend Joseph Pomeroy came to mind as someone whose words would prevail where her own had failed. So Susanna wrote to Pomeroy, enclosing a letter which she asked him to read to her sister on the pretext that Joanna could not read her hand-writing. Pomeroy duly sent for Joanna and read out Susanna's letter which alleged that her prophecies came from the Devil.

Feeling utterly betrayed, Joanna immediately went on the attack. Susanna had no idea what she was talking about. Besides, how could anyone take her judgment seriously when, as far back as 1792, she had declared that none of Joanna's prophecies would come true? That there would be no war, no scarcities, that England was never in a more flourishing state.

Pomeroy politely agreed that Susanna was mistaken then.

And so she was now, Joanna rejoined.

However, any sympathy Pomeroy might have had evaporated when he read Joanna's book and saw his name there in print. Horrified, he sent for Joanna, Mrs Taylor and Mrs Jones and after inveighing against Joanna forbade her from the Sacrament until she promised to blot out his name and tell her friends to do likewise.[56]

Although after this some kind of peace was restored, Joanna never forgave Susanna for interfering. She might have acted out of mistaken love but, in Joanna's mind, her sister must be conceited if she thought she knew better than Joanna herself what was good for her. For this reason, she declared she could never go to stay with Susanna nor take pleasure in her company again. She concluded,

> Her persuasions would make me of all women the most wretched
> and miserable should I attend to them; for then I must begin in
> the spirit and end in the flesh.[57]

It was a sad day when Joanna fell out with Susanna whom she described as the sister 'that I once loved as my own life'. Moreover their quarrel marked another turning-point. From this moment on, Joanna looked not to family or old friends but further afield for support – and found it in most unexpected places.

TRIPLE SEALED, 1801-1802

There are thirteen sealed up, to whom I was ordered to send the three seals: for no man can be judged one of the twelve without them.   *Joanna to John Wilson*, 16 December 1801

Thomas Foley, Vicar of Oldswinford in Worcestershire had come up to London to secure a dispensation to hold two family livings. He later wrote:

> It was early in the Spring of 1801, when I was in London, that I first heard of Joanna Southcott, and from some extraordinary accounts of her which were then in circulation – and of her being about to publish some Books to the World, made me leave direction to my Booksellers to send them to me as soon as they came to London.[1]

Born in 1758 into a rich, influential family (he was cousin to Lord Foley), his handsome looks, private income and affability had enabled him to cut a fine figure at Cambridge, where he took his M.A. in 1782, and after election as Fellow of Jesus College soon obtained a college living. Later he accepted the more valuable living of Oldswinford, which was in the gift of his family, settling there with his wife and children, and trying to live within his means although his account books show that he frequently borrowed money from his friends. He took delight in country pursuits, on occasion appearing at funerals with a surplice thrown over his hunting pink.[2]

Foley probably heard about Joanna through his friend Stanhope Bruce, the elderly Vicar of Inglesham in Wiltshire and a fellow believer in the prophet Richard Brothers. Whoever heard of her first, the little coterie around Brothers must have been excitedly whispering news of Mrs Southcott, the latest prodigy in that momentous spring of the new Millennium.

Unaware of this interest, Joanna in Exeter was still vexed by her sister's lack of faith. Dreams of winning Susanna over were reflected in a Communication from her Spirit received by Joanna early in 1801. She was told that if no one took her warnings seriously, there would be three years' famine in the land and her father would die before 22 September. Susanna would then meet her at their father's grave and, seeing the judgments starting to happen, be convinced that Joanna's writings came from God. Consoled by this touching scene, Joanna put the Communication into Mr Jones's hands on 10 April and settled back to wait.[3]

On 1 May came news of English armies driving the French out of Egypt[4] and on the 26th Joanna received another communication – not this time from her Spirit but through the post. It was a letter from the Reverend Stanhope Bruce and it changed everything.

Someone – a member of the clergy – was at last taking notice, asking her to send more copies of her books and even offering to help with her writing. It was the sign she had been waiting for, confirmation that her prophecies really came from God. And above all, it meant that the condition set out in her earlier Communication had been met – there was now no need for famine or her father's death!

She quickly wrote back:

> Your generous and kind offer I shall ever acknowledge. A gentleman of your good sense and learning might be a great help to me, if you were present to direct me how to place the words without changing the sense; but what is delivered to me from the Spirit I am ordered not to add thereto nor diminish therefrom; but to put them in print as they are delivered to me from the Spirit of the Lord. . . .
>
> I have taken the earliest opportunity to send you this letter with the books by Mr Charles Taylor; and Mr Taylor, sen. will be in London in a fortnight, and will wait on you, when you may know any particular truths from him, as I worked at his house in the upholstering business in 1792, and told them then what was coming on the whole earth. . . .[5]

Four days later she was writing to Bruce again, this time identifying the ministers mentioned in her books and explaining that any typographical errors were due partly to the fact that they were copied out by a young lad but mostly to the careless printer.

After this things moved quickly. By early June Thomas Foley had received the first three parts of *Strange Effects of Faith*, which he read carefully and found perfectly consistent with the Bible and common sense, at the same time opening up an amazing new vista. He announced,

> In my opinion, there is a greater Body of Spiritual Light given to the World in these Writings than was ever given since the Bible was completed.[6]

He wrote to Joanna for some further explanations and another correspondence began.

Then came a letter from the Reverend Thomas Webster, another disciple of Brothers, enclosing details of a vision he had himself experienced. In her reply, Joanna (who had apparently never read any of Brother's prophecies)

*The Revd Thomas
Philip Foley, Vicar of
Oldswinford, was one of
Joanna's most
enthusiastic followers.
This portrait, painted
in about 1828, shows
Thomas Foley in his
gown with his bands
and academical hood.
His hand rests on the
Bible, whilst behind
him there are
bookshelves holding
what is probably a
library of Joanna's
works. The partially
withdrawn curtain may
be designed to suggest
revealed knowledge.*

cautioned: 'You may rely on some of Brothers' words, but you cannot believe all the prophet hath told you.' She then put Webster's vision carefully on one side to include in her next book.[7]

Later in June Stanhope Bruce sent Joanna a gift of money: 'the first I ever received from any man concerning my writings,' she gratefully acknowledged, adding: 'and you are the first minister from whom I ever received a letter of approbation. . . .' She explained that her first book had been printed badly because the printer was an atheist who, being convinced that he was printing nonsense, tried to make it so. Now that she had been 'ordered' to change printers, the results should be better.

This friendly exchange between Joanna and individual members of the Brothers' clique was suddenly put in jeopardy when Stanhope Bruce received an open request for money – not from Joanna herself but one of her Exeter supporters, John Symons. Joanna declared herself most embarrassed by this unauthorised approach:

> You are right about the money. I am sorry it should be mentioned:
> I did not desire any thing of you; but only to make plain the
> paths of the Lord before mankind. . . .

> May I take the liberty to say you may well call me, sister: for
> I did not think there was a man on earth so much my brother, to
> have one mind and one heart, so much alike. . . .
>
> I have but a few hours to write this letter and four more; and
> must have them all copied off, which is a disadvantage to me, as
> I have a great deal of work to do in a little time.

Being called 'sister' and suddenly finding herself the object of interest
to such worthy men – it must have been a heady experience for Joanna,
but her satisfaction was mixed with anxiety that her new admirers might
not be aware of her humble social and educational status. To avoid any
misunderstanding, she wrote to Foley on 19 July, 1801:

> I return you thanks for your kind offer to send me Mr Brothers'
> prophecies, but I never read any books at all, but write by the
> Spirit as I am directed. . . . I have no time to read. You may
> judge me a woman of higher rank than I am: but I will not deceive
> you; I have no more than I work for; and therefore I spend all
> my time in working when I am not writing. I have told you my
> station in life, that you may not judge you are writing to one
> higher than I am. I know some ministers, to whom I have been
> ordered to write, have treated my letters with contempt, and
> would not give them a hearing – to think that a person unlearned
> should instruct them that are learned. . . .

On 1 August, 1801, Joanna wrote to Stanhope Bruce, still on the
subject of Symons's request for money. To ensure this could never
happen again she asked Bruce to check that all letters purporting to
come from her bore her writing – which presumably meant her signature,
for she added, 'I wish, sir, you could read my handwriting'.

As the correspondence developed, each account Joanna gave of herself
confirmed the group's faith until their support for her took on the fervour
of fanaticism.

On 22 August 1801 Colonel Basil Bruce, Stanhope's son, wrote to
her from his home in 77 Jermyn St, St James, saying: 'I received your
first two books with rapture, before my father had seen them. . . .'
Anxious to allay her fears about her humble background, he protested
that 'the Lord can reveal himself to whom he pleases, how he pleases,
and when he pleases. . . .'[8]

Exactly her thoughts. Equally gratifying was Basil Bruce's promise
to send her 'a little purse'. Moreover, his friend, Thomas Foley, was
about to arrive in town, he said, and Joanna could be sure she would be
the chief subject of their conversation.

After so much rejection and insult, it was wonderful for Joanna to
find herself treated with such respect. Stanhope Bruce was old enough

to be her father and in the next few weeks she poured out her heart to him.

'I am sorry to wound the feelings of my friends, to say I am at present in some distress,' she told him in a letter on 23 August.

Publishing her book had plunged her into debt – just as Susanna had said it would. Ordered to print one thousand copies of each of the six volumes of *Strange Effects of Faith*, Joanna had had to sign away the profits in advance to secure a loan. Now, despite good sales of the first four volumes, she had nothing left in the kitty to print the last two.

And whose fault was this? Susanna's, of course.

'I had a sister in the country who I well knew could assist me, and I thought it unkind in her to deny me,' Joanna complained to Bruce, before reverting to her favourite theme – how the Lord had decreed that her father would die before 22 September so that Susanna, meeting her at his funeral, would be forced to admit, 'My God and sister have I both denied'.

Not that Joanna worried about money on her own behalf, Bruce should understand, for

> the short time I have to live in this world, who am but a single woman, and no one to provide for but myself after the death of my father . . . if I can get food and raiment I am content, as this is no world to me. All my hopes of happiness are in a better; and to know the will of the Lord, and obey it, hath been my daily prayer. . . .

On the other hand . . . seeing that Stanhope Bruce had written to offer his help, who was she to refuse him? Especially as he was clearly acting in obedience to the will of the Lord – for Joanna had already been 'told' this would happen. At her lowest ebb she had been warned in a dream that the Lord had friends who would help her, and it was as a sign to them that He had stopped the rain at harvest time. Moreover, if Bruce had any doubt about what she was saying, this prophecy and others like it had been sealed up on 10 April and placed in the hands of Mr Jones (who was copying out the present letter) and later passed on to Mr Pomeroy.

This brought her onto the subject of all that had taken place as a result of Susanna's letter to Pomeroy, and Joanna was still in full spate when she reached the bottom of her notepaper. She signed off, promising to continue in a letter to Stanhope's son – which she did on the following day.[9]

Joanna's excitement at the prospect of securing financial help to publish her writings was shared by her new circle of friends. In a hasty reply penned as he was setting out for Market Deeping, the home of his married sister, Basil Bruce wrote: 'Sorry I can't write proper answer now, as whole day occupied with preparing to leave town at five o'clock tomorrow morning for Lincolnshire. . . .'

But rather than delay sending the promised gift Basil had paid £14
into his banker's hands in return for a post-bill payable to Mr Taylor,
who would then pay Joanna. The money had come from the following:
William Sharp in Titchfield Street had, after reading her letters, given
him seven guineas, saying that he had long intended to present her with
such a trifle; Basil's sister, Mary Beecraft, gave two guineas; his father
a guinea; he and his wife the rest.[10] On 2 September, 1801, Joanna
wrote back:

> I received your kind letter with a bill, which you and other worthy
> friends were so kind to me with, to strengthen my hands to
> forward the works of the Lord.

Through her new friends the future smiled on Joanna. And just imagine!
– they were not local people but fine folk from as far away as London, and
they had not only heard of her but were clamouring to hear more!

The words heard by her father on (Old Style) Christmas day, 1795 were
coming true: 'Southcott, Southcott, thy name must spread far and wide.'

She related this to Basil Bruce, telling him too how she had been told
that gold would be sent to her from afar, that the Lord had friends in
London to assist her and that her father would die. All this was to happen
before 22 September so that, if her father's death followed, none but a
fool could doubt whence her prophecies came.

Ten days later she was writing to William Sharp:

> I received your kind letter, unknown and generous friend! The
> kindness of my friends I could not bear, had I not strong grounds
> to say, 'It is the Lord's doing and marvellous in my eyes'.[11]

This 'unknown and generous friend' was to play a momentous part
in Joanna's life. A year older than her, William Sharp was one of the
country's finest engravers. Son of a gunmaker, he had served an
apprenticeship to an engraver of firearms before marrying a French-
woman and opening a shop as a writing-engraver in Bartholomew Lane.
Then in 1782 he had moved to Vauxhall where he developed his own
original style and began publishing his own work.

In his younger days Sharp had been a supporter of parliamentary
reform and joined the Society for Constitutional Information as a friend
of Thomas Paine and Horne Tooke. In fact, he narrowly missed being
tried for treason alongside Horne Tooke in 1794. Summoned before the
Privy Council several times, Sharp on one occasion was supposed to
have interrupted proceedings to ask Pitt and his colleagues if they would
like to subscribe to a work which Horne Tooke intended to undertake –
with the result, according to his biographer, that 'a hearty laugh at the
singularity of the proposal ensued, and he was soon after liberated'.

Although Horne Tooke was acquitted, his trial had shown the govern-

William Sharp, the celebrated engraver and close friend of William Blake. Sharp engraved this half-length portrait of himself which had been painted by G.F. Joseph, A.R.A. The picture was published by John Smith in 1817. According to the Annual Register, *'this bold, handsome, jocular man looked as if he liked the good things of this world'. A staunch supporter of Joanna Southcott, Sharp became the First Custodian of her Box of Sealed Prophecies.*

ment's determination to crush reformers, and soon after this Sharp seems to have given up all active involvement in radical politics in favour of more spiritual concerns. After flirting with the ideas of Mesmer and Swedenborg, he fell under the spell of the man whose portrait he unveiled on 16 April 1795. The portrait, entitled 'Richard Brothers, Prince of the Hebrews', showed the recently imprisoned self-proclaimed prophet with rays of light descending on his head, and in the margin over the signature of William Sharp the words: 'Fully believing this to be the man whom God has appointed; I engrave his likeness.'

Sharp was never half-hearted in the causes he espoused. Convinced that the Millennium was at hand and Brothers about to lead the Jews back to the Holy Land, he had already prepared for his own journey to Jerusalem by ordering strong shoes and a coat with specially large pockets to carry shirts and cravats. Such was one of the passionate believers who wrote to Joanna in 1801.[12] More were to follow.

Less than a fortnight later a large box addressed to Mrs Southcott was delivered to the Taylors' home in Fore Street. In the parlour with the family gathered around, Joanna opened it up to reveal a set of expensive mourning apparel sent by Basil Bruce's wife, Maria. Such was the strength of her faith. Joanna had said that her father was about to die, and Maria Bruce accepted this as if it had already happened.

Examining the quality of the clothes, Mrs Taylor was most impressed.

'What a good family must they be,' she cried. 'What are they? I am astonished at them!'[13]

Writing to thank Maria, Joanna effused:

Doth one heart, and one soul, and one mind possess you and me? . . . I was ordered to put my mourning in order and the Lord hath inclined your heart to do it for me. . . . But your goodness, dear Madam, has so far taken my senses, and drowned my eyes in tears, that I cannot find words to express my gratitude to you. O may the heavens reward your goodness. . . .[14]

The problem was that 22 September came and, although Joanna had received money from afar and assistance from the Lord's London friends, her father had still not died. Her prediction remained only partially fulfilled. Two days later (in what may have been a displacement of unacceptable desire) she dreamt of her father's horse being killed.

Joanna spent 26 September writing letters. It was time to marshal her forces, for now that the six dissenters could not act as her judges she had to find others to fill this role.

After expressing her relief to William Sharp that she had been able to forestall his subscription on her behalf: 'to send me twenty pounds is too great a favour . . .', she explained that every man who had offered his help had been chosen to judge her writings.

Heaven hath inclined you, Sir, to forward the work; and when I warn you to appear, I trust you will not draw back. . . . As soon as my fifth book is out, in the first that is made, I am ordered to write every man's name that hath been my helper, and then to seal it up. Now, Sir, you write me of a gentleman whose name I do not know. I must deal faithfully with all men. Though unknown to me, he is not to the Lord. . . . You say he is the father of twelve children. Little does he know what lies before them. Let the father appear and judge for himself and children. If he thinks proper, he is at liberty, if he writes me a letter before that first book is sealed up, but after, it is too late. For every man's name must be found written in that book when the seals are broken.

When I send my books to the bookseller, I shall send a parcel enclosed with letters for all my friends, whose names are written, sealed up with three seals, with two stars and two letters on the seal – a deep type of Christ's second coming. . . .[15]

In a similar letter to the Reverend Thomas Webster, an Anglican clergyman from Falcon Court, Borough, she added a postscript:

Sir, you may be surprised to see my letter sealed with a black seal before I am clear my father is no more. Strange as this may appear, I am ordered thus to proceed. The shadow in all my writings comes before the substance. . . .[16]

She might have added 'though it be long in coming' for, despite all her predictions and her supporters' faith, old William Southcott was still holding fast to life.

She also wrote to the Reverend Thomas Foley: 'You, Sir, have put your hand to the plough, and I trust you will not draw back . . . .'

After describing her father's illness in 1799 and her vision of the chain signalling the length of his life, she admitted, 'I have been foiled more about my father's death than ever I have in all my writings.' An enigmatic postscript followed:

You will please to observe, that my father lived till St Swithin's day this year, and then it followed in rain – and great you see is the mystery concerning him. When the sun is behind a tree, the shadow comes before the substance. . . .[17]

All this to-ing and fro-ing of letters and the prospect of such grand people descending on Exeter, summoned by Joanna – it was immensely exciting, enough to go to her head were it not for the petty vexations which kept her feet on the ground. The people around her, for instance, treated her with no special reverence.

She was currently living with the family of Mr John Tremlett Symons, General Appraiser, Auctioneer and Undertaker of 4 Gandy's Lane, and was not best pleased when they took away her bedstead and shifted her into a spare room. On 28 September her Spirit ordered her back to her own room even if it meant sleeping there without a proper bed. Having complied, she was woken at midnight by Mrs Symons coming to ask her to give up the spare room for a friend of theirs who was in desperate need of shelter. Amazed to find Joanna already back in her own room, she asked her if she knew *everything*.

A letter from Joanna to Stanhope Bruce revealed the story behind the emergency. Parnell, a farm labourer who had always mocked her writings, had fallen out with a fellow worker called Clive. Clive hit Parnell with a bridle. Parnell struck back with a stick, dealing Clive a fatal blow on the head before fleeing to the Symons's house for refuge.

Although Clive died and Parnell went out of his mind, Joanna was able to draw some consolation for this double tragedy from the fact that it did explain why she had previously been ordered to send out her letters sealed with black! It had, after all, nothing to do with her father's imminent but ever-deferred death. It was to do with Clive. Hence the 'C' in her 'IC' seal![18]

On the following Saturday, she went to see her father in Gittisham. Since growing too old to manage his farm, he had been living in a cottage with a small garden and just enough apple-trees to make a hogshead of cider. But even this aroused the envy of his neighbours, who thought the cottage worth more than he gave for it, so they tried to get him out by breaking his windows and disturbing his peace. When he started to suffer from dizzy spells, Joanna and Susanna begged him to give up the house and go into lodgings but he refused. Gittisham people hated God and all that was good, he growled, and he would rather be shot than live with them in the suburbs of hell.

The sisters knew when they were beaten. After that, apart from periodic visits to clean his house, they had left him to his own devices until the previous summer when he had fallen down in a fit and been carried home apparently dead. This time the Rector of Gittisham, Thomas Putt, stepped in and, not wanting to hear of old Southcott dying alone, insisted that he give up his key and go into lodgings.

Joanna was happy to think of her father now living with people who would keep an eye on him, but when she visited him in his new home, she found him deeply depressed. He cheered up only after she had reassured him that he would never be left in want. This improvement, however, did not last long. When she returned on Saturday morning, 3 October, she found him in a pitiable state, his mind and eye-sight so far gone that he did not recognise her. Only after she made herself known did he weep aloud for joy and praise God for sending her, since the people in the house were making his life unbearable.

What were they doing? They were trying to stop him saying his prayers and singing a psalm before he went to bed. Joanna was horrified. These were things he had done all his life, she protested to the others. Surely they would not ask a man on the brink of the grave to give up his prayers? It was not his prayers they objected to, they explained, it was the way he said them so 'hard'. William growled that he said them as he always did and could not say them any softer.

Joanna left with a heavy heart, weeping bitterly when she thought how her father could say with Job: 'The thing which I feared hath come upon me, and that which I dreaded hath happened unto me. . . .' Only when she arrived back in Exeter and heard that peace had been made did she realise why she had been ordered to visit her father and witness his situation. It was because he stood for the nation. Just as William Southcott had been at war with his neighbours to keep possession of his house, so had the British been at war with other nations to keep possession of their land. The present peace treaty was like her father giving up his key and throwing himself on the mercy of others.[19]

On Saturday, 10 October, she wrote in feminist vein to Maria Bruce:

It was with great pleasure Mrs Taylor and myself read your intention of coming with your worthy husband and the Rev. S. Bruce, who are chosen of God to judge of his just decrees from the foundation of the world. You ask if a woman may be present? I answer, yes. There are no bounds set to woman. . . . As one and all were included in the fall of Eve; so woman has a just right to hear their cause pleaded, before an infinite and wise God. How just are his decrees! To pass on Satan the blame the woman cast on him in Paradise. No man knows what he is to sit in judgment for: such a judgment as never entered the heart or thought of man. To think he must sit in judgment against himself, and say the man was wrong to cast the blame on his Maker. He ought to have said as the woman did; 'The Serpent beguiled us and we did eat.'[20]

At three o'clock the following day she took the letter to Mr Jones for copying and while there heard him read out one of Thomas Foley's recent dreams, which to her mind had the same meaning as her letter to Maria Bruce. However, Foley's dream also contained a reference to Richard Brothers, and after praying for an explanation, Joanna received a Communication which put this rival prophet in his place.

'Tis I am the Brother that you must all crown:
And as to the bride, I named so here
I tell you your bride unto me is as dear.
When all is explained you'll find your mistake;
For all men are brothers, I died for your sake. . . .[21]

Basil Bruce's excitement at the prospect of meeting Joanna received a further fillip in mid-October when Charles Taylor, in London on business for his father, delivered some of her letters and spent the evening with Bruce's family. Impressing them as a fine, sensible youth, he would have spoken glowingly of Joanna whom he had worshipped since childhood.[22]

On about the same day Joanna was writing to Stanhope Bruce describing what was a typical dream for her at the time:

> I dreamed I was carried in the air, more than the height of the hedges above the ground. I thought I was carried for miles; and every field was ploughed and rolled, and marked in squares like a pavement of broad stones. The squares were full of prints. Every field was alike: there was not one green field to be seen: every hedge was pruned bare, and every tree the same. At last I was brought to earth to a landing-place, where there was a house. There appeared two roads; one amazing high, the other a valley which went down amazing low. I thought there was a tumult of people disputing about my writings.[23]

Although she did not admit it, her mind was troubled. There was her father stubbornly outrunning his predicted time, and she had just had another row with Pomeroy. Why, he wanted to know, did her remarks about her father's death keep shuffling forward and back and why could she not put her prophecies more plainly? By way of reply she loftily announced that there were several church ministers and gentlemen coming down to Exeter to prove her writings. Taken by surprise, Pomeroy agreed to meet and join with them.

Through her books Joanna was now attracting attention from all kinds of people writing to her with accounts of strange visions. Among these, Mrs Ann Field, wife of Elias Jameson Field of London, described dreams full of symbols connected with the Book of Revelation. It was clear to Joanna that events were hastening towards the Second Coming and in a letter to Stanhope Bruce on 17 October she identified her own role in what was happening:

> My Second coming you'll see clear.
> My Spirit is already come;
> You'll find me in the woman's form,
> With arguments that I shall plead,
> As never entered in thy head,
> Then every mystery they will see
> Of every dream that's sent to thee. . . .

And just in case any should doubt her authority, she added in her normal prose:

Whatever some men may think, I am clearly convinced the same spirit which inspired men to write the Bible, hath inspired me. . . . Whatever spirit directs me, he hath more wisdom, and more knowledge, than all the men upon Earth. . . . Call all your friends together and put in print their letters: such as you think proper, as far will fill three sheets of paper, of the same sized books as mine are: and print one thousand and send me some, that I may seal one up with my fifth book.[24]

Obeying instructions, Stanhope Bruce published Joanna's correspondence in a book containing forty-eight pages under the title *Divine and Spiritual Letters of Prophecies*. As the material was going to press he received another possible entry – a letter Joanna had sent to Mr George Turner, a merchant in Leeds. Because it was impossible to include it without exceeding the prescribed length, its omission was recorded, together with a note that Turner was nevertheless chosen to be one of her judges.[25]

Arrangements were now falling beautifully into place for the trial of Joanna's writings. With Anglican clergy such as Stanhope Bruce and Thomas Webster committed to being present, as well as distinguished men such as William Sharp and George Turner, her confidence soared. On 20 October she received an ecstatic letter from Colonel Basil Bruce, saying that he intended to come.

'I am ready to sit in judgement against myself and all mankind, to free the woman, and pray God to cast all on Satan, that arch-enemy of the human race,' he declared, adding that, through Richard Brothers' teaching, he had lived the last six years of his life fully believing that he was about to see God's glory burst on a benighted world. Referring to his happy marriage and to Joanna's 'divine' letters of 8, 10, and 11 October, he agreed that man's regeneration must start with that last best work of Creation – 'lovely woman' being reunited with man in principle, in spirit and in love.

Basil Bruce then asked Joanna to thank the Taylors for their offer of hospitality, but tell them that his wife would not be accompanying him to Exeter as she would be about seven months pregnant with their seventh child by then.

So wrote the husband – and might have added 'man proposes, woman disposes' for, having finished his letter at two in the morning, he received another from Joanna nine hours later. After devouring her words – 'language cannot express our ravished senses at the perusal of them,' he declared – and deciding to forward them to his father who was still in Lincolnshire, Basil sat down to add a postscript to his earlier letter. Maria, reading over his shoulder, burst into tears when she reached the bit about her not accompanying him and insisted she would go.[26]

Joanna's tone was also becoming more defiant.

'By the manner in which I have written to you all, if I am an impostor you must find it out: for you must deal with an honest woman as with a knave,' she wrote to Stanhope Bruce on 7 November before roundly castigating his friend, the Reverend John Mossop of Deeping St James, for drawing back after showing interest in her mission. All she wanted was for some decent, honest people to examine her writings and tell her if they were inspired by God. If not, then she would never publish more. She wrote in answer to criticism,

> As to my gains by writing, people have erred there, for I have suffered great loss thereby: but this I do not value. . . . I shall print what I am ordered to print; and no man stays my hand.[27]

Joanna's tension was clearly mounting. When a letter came from William Sharp on 14 November, she had such a violent headache that she could not hear it read till evening. In her reply she explained how it gave her pain to think she was imposing on him, yet she knew her Sixth Book had to be printed, so she hoped his friend would lend her the necessary £10 or £14 and then recoup it from the bookseller.[28]

By the end of the month Joanna had persuaded Thomas Foley to lay his parish duties aside and come with the others to judge her writings. She stressed the need for perfect obedience if the Redemption was to succeed: 'as man was drawn in by the woman to disobedience, so he is brought back by the woman to true obedience.' She justified an allusion to one of Mrs Bruce's dreams in her recent book by pointing out that it was not within anyone's power to omit what God decreed should be included.

But if anything was needed to reassure Joanna that she was on the right track, it came in a box from William Sharp on 28 November. She opened it to find two pictures – one, a framed print of the Virgin and Child; the other, a portrait of Richard Brothers which the engraver explained was not worth framing. Seizing on the former to draw attention to the very different treatment Jesus received in the arms of his mother and those of men, Joanna warned: 'Marvel not if you see mankind place all these thorns on my head if they can.'

But it was not mankind so much as one particular man, the same as ever, who vexed her. Pomeroy was now causing trouble because she had printed his name in her book and he had even gone so far as to suggest it was the Devil, not God, who inspired her to do it. Mortified by this reaction, Joanna insisted on his name being left in the first, sealed volume even if, at his insistence, it was blotted out of all subsequent copies. All this she reported to Sharp, together with details of the accommodation being arranged in Exeter for her friends, and asking them to arrive some days before Christmas.

Pomeroy was still on her mind when she wrote to Foley ten days later:

> I have felt the severest blow from Mr P – I ever did from any one in my life, as it was not temporal but spiritual. . . . But I must say, I feel for him; as I know in my writings he is spoken of as a man greatly to be blessed, if he goes through to search out the truth: but fatal are the judgments pronounced against him if he draws back through unbelief. . . . This is my fear for him, as it was said to me some years ago, 'A Judas he should be to me, if he do me deny, no comfort in this world he'll have, and tremble for to die'.

Her letter bore three seals – the sign that Foley had been chosen one of the judges in the forthcoming trial.

When on 16 December she wrote to John Wilson, the prolific father earlier recommended to her by Sharp, it was to confirm that he too was one of the twelve judges even though his inclusion brought the number of similarly sealed people to thirteen.

'But who will fall if you do come, I know not,' she added ominously.[29]

Ten days later, Colonel Basil Bruce died at midnight just as his father was setting out for Exeter where he received the tragic news.

9

JOANNA'S GREAT BOX

The cords round the box were sealed with seven seals.
William Sharp's Answer to the World, 1806

At Christmas 1801 seven men arrived in Exeter. All felt they had been sent by God to examine Joanna's writings and judge whether or no she was an impostor.[1]

First to arrive were George Turner, himself a visionary prophet, and Peter Morrison, a headstrong cotton-printer from Old Street, Liverpool. Then came Thomas Foley, Stanhope Bruce, Thomas Webster, William Sharp, and John Wilson – and for seven days the Seven were hospitably entertained by the Taylors. In the convivial atmosphere the visitors seem to have warmed to Joanna and their hosts. But, amidst the budding of what were to prove lifelong friendships, the Seven never forgot their important business. And since it had been written that Joanna's writings could not be proved unless there were twelve judges, her Spirit ordered them to invite five leading local clergy – Bishop Courtenay, Archdeacon Moore, Chancellor Nutcombe, the Curate of Heavitree, and the Reverend Joseph Pomeroy – to make up their number.[2]

Not only did they all refuse, but the Bishop candidly told Foley, Bruce and Webster that he thought Joanna utterly mad. It was not a good start. Without the twelve judges her writings could not be proved so the full investigation had to be deferred to some future date.

But it was not a wasted journey. Not only had the Seven enjoyed the privilege of meeting Joanna, they also had a chance to quiz the Taylors, Joneses, and Symonses – people who had known her for years. All agreed that Joanna was pious, honest, industrious and, above all, quite sane. They interviewed witnesses and collected ample proof that she had prophesied accurately about the war, the harvests, the weather and other extraordinary events. As for her writings, there could be no doubt about her inspiration, for the visitors were present when she received a message from the Spirit. They also watched as she opened her Bible and gave a wonderful off-the-cuff exposition of the Scriptures.[3]

By the end of the week they were convinced: Joanna Southcott's powers were genuine. She was indeed a prophet. They must arrange for her to come to London at the earliest possible date. Such discernment

*The Box of Sealed Prophecies, photographed by John Norris in 1861,
after the death of Richard Foley, Rector of North Cadbury, Somerset, who
had been its Fourth Custodian. Richard Foley's successor, Samuel
Jowett of Leeds, went with a friend to fetch it from North Cadbury, where
it was put on the scales at the railway station and found to weigh 156 lb.*

was acknowledged by her Spirit who promptly told Joanna to commit
all her writings to their care. She accordingly had the sealed box stored
at Mrs Symons's house brought round to the Guildhall.[4] The precious
papers were then distributed among the Seven, who left for London,
each carrying a sealed parcel which he had sworn to guard, unopened,
until summoned by Joanna to produce it before twelve judges.

A box holding the greater part of her writings was bound by cords,
fastened with seven seals and given to William Sharp. At Bath on his
way home, Sharp had a large case made to enclose it and a quantity of
tow put between the box and the case to preserve the seals from being
broken.[5] Thus was Joanna Southcott's famous Box launched on an
unsuspecting world.

In Exeter Joanna was left with a mixture of elation and disappointment.
To be accorded respect by such worthy men was gratifying, but how
frustrating to know that her grand trial had been wrecked by the clergy
in Exeter, and Pomeroy in particular. He held the key to her destiny, yet
he had let her down. Why? Because he had fallen foul of local gossip.

Four days out of the five which followed the departure of the Seven from Exeter, Pomeroy came round to the Taylors' to pester Joanna about removing his name from the book she had published. His friends were making his life a misery, he moaned. He could no longer go into the coffee house without being mocked and called a prophet for supposedly supporting her.

Joanna listened with a degree of sympathy. There had to be a way to help. On 10 January, 1802, she handed a long letter to Sarah Heard, proprietress of Mol's Coffee House, the club which Pomeroy frequented in the Cathedral close. Her letter carefully avoided the offence of referring to Pomeroy by name. Its gist was:

> Reverend Sirs and Gentlemen,
>
> As a prevailing report is amongst you in the coffee-house, that the Reverend Mr P——— has strengthened my hand in prophecies, I must now beg to answer for myself. . . .
>
> Had not my writings been of God Mr P———'s wisdom and prudence would have stopt my hand for years agone. . . .
>
> Had Mr P——— acted contrary to what he has done, he must have acted contrary to the Gospel of Christ. . . . I am sorry the world has blamed Mr P———. Is a Christian minister to be mocked and despised for paying respect to the laws of God and man? . . .[6]

Far from being grateful, when Pomeroy heard about Joanna's intervention, he was furious. Accusing her of trying to murder his reputation, he insisted that she ask for the letter back. She did, but even this did not satisfy. Pomeroy now took a piece of paper from his pocket which he asked her to sign so that he could send it to a newspaper and clear his name in the eyes of the world. Joanna always had difficulty with other people's handwriting. She handed it to Mr Taylor, who pointed out that Pomeroy had never said that Joanna was inspired by an evil spirit until she printed his name. Joanna, however, tired of all the fuss, agreed to sign that this was what Pomeroy was saying now.[7]

On 14 January the following letter appeared in the *Exeter Flying Post*:

> To the Public
>
> To prevent any Misrepresentation of the Reverend Mr Pomery's [sic] opinion of me, or my writings, I think it necessary thus Publicly to acknowledge that he used every argument of Reason and Religion to convince me that my Pretensions to Prophecy were false and that I was influenced by a deluded Imagination, a deranged State of Mind, or the Evil Spirit, and that my Writings were full of Blasphemy:– To contradict whatever may have been asserted to the contrary, I freely make this Public Declaration.[8]
>
>   Joanna Southcott
>
>   in the presence of me, Lucy Taylor.

What her family must have thought of this public announcement may be imagined. Susanna's husband, William Carter, arrived on her doorstep the following day. They presumably talked about more than just her father's health – although that is the only part of the conversation recorded by Joanna. So how was her father? Old William would outlive them all, Carter reckoned – if looks were anything to go by. He had called on him the previous week and found him hale and hearty.[9]

Whether or not Carter criticised her letter, it is clear that Joanna was already regretting her action. She hated the idea that others might now assume that she had completely given way to Pomeroy's judgment. Since this was not the case, she had no choice but to go on the attack. After ordering a thousand handbills to be distributed in Exeter, she demanded all her writings back from Pomeroy. She wrote to him on 17 January,

> You say you are afflicted in your family, then if my writings are from the Devil, it is he that has afflicted you, because of your unbelief of him. Now to remove that affliction I must desire you to remove the cause: so I beg you will send me back every letter I have sent you; and every book you have of mine in your possession – let not my name abide in your house. . . .
>
> My heart always trembled, my legs always shook whenever I was ordered to go to you. . . . I fear for you, that you will . . . find you have a God to deal with, and not a simple woman.[10]

There was no mistaking the threat in her words, but poor Pomeroy could have had no idea what relentless fury he was about to unleash. All he knew was that Joanna was asking him to return her letters and this was something he could not do because, as he explained to Mrs Taylor, he had thrown them all on the fire. On the fire? Joanna's precious prophecies? Lucy Taylor gazed at him in silence as he mumbled some excuse.

Meanwhile Joanna, describing the incident in a letter to Stanhope Bruce, grumbled that Pomeroy's newspaper advertisement was typical of Fallen Man, who blamed Woman, but did worse himself. Regarding her visit to London, she explained that she had something important to do in Exeter before she could set out.

Although it was the Pomeroy dispute she had in mind, it was at this juncture that she received the long-awaited, but in that moment unexpected, call. Her father had suffered a stroke the very day Carter had reported him looking so well – and he was dying. She would have to go immediately if she wished to see him alive.

So what should she do? Her Spirit intervened and forbade her to go that day. Next morning she borrowed what turned out to be a very frisky horse and, after a difficult ride to Gittisham, [11] arrived to notice that the fine row of cedar trees that had been growing next to the road had all been cut down. [12] She entered her father's house and found him barely conscious. She expected him to die before nightfall, but her Spirit told her that he would live till midnight or cock-crow and she must be sure to mark exactly what time he died.

Sitting down beside him, she clasped his hand and called him Father.

'Father? Be you my Father?' he mumbled.

'No, my dear Father. You are my Father,' she explained.

'Who are you then?'

'Joanna.'

He gripped her hand and muttered, 'My dear child, if thou art come then Christ is come.' [13]

She sat by him for the rest of the day. At eight o'clock that night he started to have convulsions and the family assumed he would die before ten o'clock. But the fit continued till dawn, during all which time they could hear a violent storm raging outside. Then, at first cock-crow, William's arms stopped flailing about and he subsided into a sweet sleep. At half past four his breath stopped, and Joanna announced that her father was gone. He had died in his sleep with her holding his hands. [14]

Naturally there was a lot to do. But Joanna, after her rush from Exeter, declared herself too ill to stay and help Susanna make the arrangements. Although the storm was still raging, she set out on horseback, several times being nearly thrown. Then, within a mile of the city, her horse took off at such a gallop that, if no one had been there to stop him and help her off, she would have been badly injured. After that she let someone else ride the beast home while she walked.

When William Southcott was buried at Gittisham on 24 January, his body was attended to the grave by Susanna but not Joanna, who had been instructed to 'let the dead bury the dead'. Poor Susanna was forced to keep company with her stepmother, whom she despised for having neglected her father and made his last days miserable – thoughts which perhaps she voiced, for Joanna hints that there was trouble between the two women at the graveside.

The funeral had a profound effect on Susanna, who must have shared her sister's psychic gifts if her own account is to be believed. When their father's body was taken from his room, Susanna said she heard beautiful music sounding like the Corinthian Anthem, 'Behold Christ is Risen'. Unaware that it was something extraordinary, she asked the woman of the house if the singers were coming. When she said no, Susanna took little notice of her reply. She heard the same music coming from the inner room where her father's body was laid out, this time sounding like the Christmas hymn, 'Behold I bring you glad tidings'. She heard it again as she walked behind his coffin to the grave.[15]

Back in Exeter, as soon as she had sufficiently recovered, Joanna went out to buy mourning accessories. Not clothes. Thanks to Maria Bruce's generosity she had no need of new clothes, but she wanted to send white gloves to friends, as was the custom among gentlefolk. Included in her list of recipients was Stanhope Bruce, to whom she wrote on 27 January 1802:

> Reverend Sir,
>
> You may be surprised to receive a parcel from me with gloves which I have sent to my friends as a token of love on account of my father's death, who departed this life the 21st day of January; soon after the death of your worthy son. . . .
>
> Last Sunday was the first time I had ever the fortitude to hear Mr Bruce's letters read since his death: and then Mr Taylor's family was obliged to take them from one to the other to read them as tears stopped the utterance of their words. . . .
>
> I was ordered to send the gloves to you as a sure sign the hand of the Lord is in the whole: and so close as a glove is to your hand, so close will the Spirit of the Lord be upon you when my writings are proved. So I have sent a pair to you, Mrs Bruce, Mr and Mrs Beecraft (your son and daughter), the Reverend Webster, Mr Sharp, and Mr Wilson as tokens of love and a sign to Mrs Bruce the hand of the Lord will protect her safe till she arrives at the resurrection of the just, seated with her happy husband in the new Jerusalem . . . arrayed in white robes, such as she sent to me.[16]

The week following her father's death was a busy one for Joanna – with letters, gloves and parcels of books to be despatched, and serious repercussions from her handbills in the form of a summons for blasphemy.

Accompanied by Mrs Jones and Mrs Symons, Joanna presented herself at the Guildhall to answer before the Mayor. After denying the charge, she proceeded to regale the court with all the details of her holy visitation in 1792. The Mayor and his friends listened politely before suggesting that she bring her writings to the Guildhall so they could all know what was about to happen. Joanna explained that they were no longer in her possession. The Mayor then asked her to give him a prophecy for some other year. She declined, saying she could trust no one but her friends. Suddenly the officials of the court lost interest. Joanna quickly explained that she only had the handbills printed as an

answer to Pomeroy's newspaper advertisement. The court had heard
enough. They dismissed the case.

Exeter people were not so easily satisfied. They were fascinated by
Joanna's dispute with Pomeroy and daily besieged the Taylors' house
wanting to know what was behind the story. Determined to correct
some of the wilder rumours, Joanna issued another handbill.

> Whereas some wicked ill-disposed persons have been mocking
> God, and trifling with eternity by saying that fire should descend
> from heaven on the four corners of the City to burn it down;
> and to add still more to their guilt, have basely asserted that I,
> Joanna Southcott, did first publish it.
>
> Now in direct contradiction thereto I thus publicly Declare
> that I never said it, thought it, nor did such Words ever come
> from my mouth, as that fire should descend from Heaven on the
> city and I shudder to find people can so boldly mock with
> judgments, though they wish to bring them on their own heads.
>
> And as a further testimony of my innocence I hereby offer a
> reward of five guineas to any person who will bring forward the
> authors of such falsehoods so that they may be punished as the
> law directs.
>
> Exeter, February 4th, 1802. Signed Joanna Southcott.
> (G. Floyde, printer, High Street, Exeter)

Joanna then settled down to wait, sure that the clergy must now
want to see her writings, that any day now they would be sending for
her. She had no doubt she would be able to convince them. All they had
to do was send. But as weeks went by with still no word from the
Bishop or the other ministers she began to despair of them.

On the first Sunday after Easter 1802 she received a communication
that reaffirmed her faith in her own, or Woman's, mission:

> The tree of knowledge must be found,
> That there the serpent's doom was placed,
> I said it was death for man to taste –
> And death to man it did appear,
> But now the mysteries I shall clear –
> As Satan did the murder bring
> And tempt the woman to the sin,
> And out of Eden she was cast,
> In grief she owned the sentence just:
> Then now in justice I'll appear –
> I died the woman's guilt to clear,
> And put the weapon in her hand,
> That she the Tree of Life might stand. . . .[17]

The trouble was, Joanna did not want to leave Exeter without the Church's blessing. Her reluctance was overcome only when her Spirit explained that the ministers would send after she had gone – just as the mayor had summoned her after she had gone to her father's. It urged,

So get thyself ready to go, as thou hast appointed. If I do not approve of thy going I shall prevent it, but if I do not, thou must not defer longer than the last journey of Jones the following week.

Obeying this instruction, Joanna accepted Mr Morrison's offer to come from Liverpool to escort her, and together on 20 May they wrapped up well against the cold and set off in Mr Jones's mail-coach for London. Two days later she arrived at the home of Mrs Basil Bruce in Jermyn Street.[18]

At fifty-two and making her first visit to the metropolis,[19] Joanna's agitation expressed itself in one of her recurrent infections and her right eye became inflamed.[20] Nothing, however, could dim her pleasure in her new surroundings. She enjoyed the company of Maria Bruce and her brood of amiable children.[21] Everyone treated her with respect and, for the first time in her life, she had no worries about money, all her expenses being paid by Thomas Foley and William Sharp.

When someone asked how long she planned to stay, she could not say. All she knew was that she had been ordered not to return home until her writings were proved.[22] Not that she was on holiday! Heaven forfend! There was no letting up from her Spirit, who had brought her to London for a further purpose. She was here to help Foley, Sharp and Bruce to obtain Richard Brothers' release from prison. So, despite her tiring journey, she immediately entered the fray.

The day after she arrived she sent John Wilson with a letter to Nathaniel Brassey Halhed, former M.P. for Lymington and one of Brothers' chief supporters,[23] to ask how she should set about petitioning the Houses of Parliament on Brothers' behalf. The reply was disappointing. Halhed, who lived as a recluse staying in his room and seeing nobody, could give no advice unless God directed.[24] Joanna saw this response as another example of the weak, vacillating nature of men. What they needed was a woman to inspire and organise them.

Her Spirit agreed.

He [Halhed] waits for My directions, and I will direct him. He said that he was like the prophet who was not to eat bread nor drink water in the place, nor turn back the way he came out. Now I give to him and to thee, and to all mankind this answer to his words.

Man never shall turn back to Paradise the way he came out, for . . . man first blamed his Creator for the woman, and sorrow

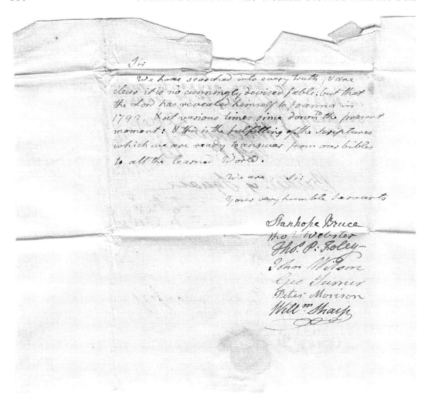

Affidavit signed by the Seven Stars in 1802, confirming that they had found Joanna Southcott's powers of prophecy to be genuine.
Sir, We have searched into every Truth, and are clear it is no cunningly devised fable; but that the Lord has revealed Himself to Joanna in 1792 and at various times since down to the present moment, and this is the fulfilling of the Scriptures which we are ready to answer from the Bible to all the Learned World. London May 29th 1802. We are Sir your very humble servants, Stanhope Bruce, Thos.Webster, Thos.P.Foley, John Wilson, Geo Turner, Peter Morison, Willm.Sharp

has followed him ever since: but I will never deliver man any other way but by the woman's hand, that he may bless and praise his Maker for the woman.

For now I shall put men to their wits' end which way to set free the imprisoned prophet [Richard Brothers], and when they have given up all, confessing that they cannot find any way to deliver him, then I will come to the purpose. This is my strict command to thee, when Bruce comes home, let the seven stars be assembled together, and then shalt thou say unto them: which way shall I get a letter to the Parliament House?[25]

By 27 May the Seven Stars – the Reverend Thomas Foley, The Reverend Stanhope Bruce, the Reverend Thomas Webster, Sharp, Morrison, Wilson and Turner – had all arrived in London.[26] Following her instructions, they set to work and printed about a thousand letters describing Joanna's life since 1792, how all her prophecies had come true and how she had now been sent to London to free Mr Brothers. These letters were sent to King George III, his sons, and each member of Parliament, together with the information that her book could be purchased from E.J. Field's, 3 Broad Court, Long Acre, where directions should be sent if Parliament wished her to appear before them.[27]

On Friday, 28 May Sharp called on Sir Richard Ford, an undersecretary of state and chief police magistrate for London, to inform him of Joanna's presence in the city. [28] In the course of a 'most agreeable interview' he told Ford about the messages from Joanna's Spirit, warning him that unless Brothers was released some calamity might fall on the government and nation. He then presented Sir Richard with all Joanna's books.

It was clear that Joanna had infused new energy into Brothers' followers. As a solemn sign of their mission, eight of them – Joanna, Maria Bruce, Elizabeth Foley, Stanhope Bruce, Thomas Webster, Thomas Foley, William Sharp and John Wilson – gathered in an upper room at 77 Jermyn Street and took the Holy Communion together. 'And the Lord, Praised be His Holy Name, was remarkably with us, from ye heavenly joy we all felt,' wrote Foley in ecstatic mood.[29]

Meantime, Maria Bruce had received a letter of despair from Richard Brothers and on Monday, 14 June, Joanna journeyed to Islington to see him in the lunatic asylum where he was incarcerated. Although she was refused entrance, she glimpsed the 'imprisoned prophet' through a window and the pair saluted each other.[30]

At the end of the month, while still awaiting some positive response to her letters, Joanna travelled northwards with Maria Bruce to stay with her late husband's sister and brother-in-law, Mr and Mrs Beecraft, who lived in Market Deeping. [31]

Was it passing through the summer countryside that filled Joanna's mind with thoughts of home, her brother's farm and the folks she used to know? Her Spirit found inspiration in those familiar scenes when giving her an answer to the Reverend John Mossop, Vicar of Deeping St James, who had warned his flock to separate the rubbish from the good in her writings.[32]

Mr Mossop, said Joanna's Spirit, was stirring up a spiritual hornets' nest by sifting through all her words. He was like young Mr Bishop who years ago ploughed up a hornets' nest and caused his infuriated bullocks to trample on an innocent boy. The boy was killed, Mr Bishop died of a broken heart, his mother never smiled again. To avoid making a similar mistake, Mr Mossop should follow the example of Joanna's brother who, when he saw wasps flying up in front of his plough, pulled back the sull [blade] and went to another part of the field. However, after dark he returned with some wood and straw to smoke the pests out.

If the moral of this story was somewhat obscured by its end, another part of its message was most revealing. Joanna's Spirit compared young Mr Bishop [possibly a brother or cousin of Noah] to Pomeroy 'who had ploughed her heart deeply and then stirred up a hornets' nest and left a wound that could not be cured by men.'

Joanna had travelled hundreds of miles from home and moved into higher social circles without escaping her obsession with Pomeroy. His name – and her feelings for him – were revealed again the following day when her Spirit answered an earlier assertion by Pomeroy that 'the Marriage of the Lamb must take place in Heaven' by explaining that 'in Heaven it must take place, but then to Earth must surely come to wed the human race.'

Joanna began with high hopes of, Mr Mossop, the Vicar of the parish seeing him as one of her potential twelve judges. Before he accepted such an honour, however, he wanted to hear what his fellow clergyman, Pomeroy, had to say, so Joanna suggested he write him a letter. Meanwhile Mossop continued to raise objections to her mission, suspecting she was led by a 'Jesting Spirit' because it spoke in a voice too familiar to come from the Lord. Joanna with the help of her 'familiar' Spirit answered all his queries, but by 9 July her patience was wearing thin. She must, she insisted, have an answer within three days: would he come to London to judge her writings or not? Mossop could not say until he received an answer from Pomeroy. Moreover he was not sure if he should leave his flock on a Sunday.

Excuses, excuses! Her Spirit replied that Mossop was simply waiting for Man, in the person of Pomeroy, to decide for him instead of God – and as for fearing to leave his flock, did he not realise he would find them fresh pasture if he followed Joanna?[33]

After days of argument Joanna eventually dismissed Mossop as being far too influenced by the writings of Emanuel Swedenborg to be open to the truth. Nor had she arrived at this judgment without burning the midnight candle and writing till she could scarcely see, trying to counter Swedenborg's description of Heaven. She must even have dipped into the Swedish philosopher's works herself before concluding that Mossop should read them 'like Arabian Nights and gather honey from them like a bee, but not rely on them. . . . [For] if I had read Swedenborg's writings some years ago, I'd have been like a tall ship over-masted,' she confessed in a phrase reminiscent of her father.[34]

As if Mossop was not enough to contend with, on 9 July Joanna received a letter which caused her great embarrassment. She asked for it to be read aloud, not realising that it was a vituperative, anonymous note taking issue with her mission. Luckily her friends rose to the occasion by politely laughing at its contents before Joanna went upstairs to pray (or collect herself). She returned with an angry answer from her Spirit: 'Now let this boasting Christian make his name known; for this is my answer concerning him; he is of his father, the Devil – and his works he does.'[35]

By this time Joanna had settled comfortably into the Beecrafts' home, making a favourable impression on the family, relaying to them her daily Communications and availing herself of Mr Beecraft's services as amanuensis. She was introduced to the Beecrafts' friends, many of whom, like themselves, were followers of Richard Brothers. So it was a good opportunity for her to get to know more about the 'Imprisoned Prophet' who had (inadvertently) done so much to prepare the way for her. Although aware of his writings as early as 1798, she insisted that she had never read any before coming to London.[36]

On Saturday, 10 July, she was sitting in the Beecrafts' parlour busily reading Brothers' books when she heard the sound of a coach and jumped up to see if it was the mail. After despatching parcels of her own writings for Jermyn Street, she drew her friends' attention to a great flock of pigeons flying before the coach as it left. That evening she was gazing out of the window with Maria Bruce when they saw a large white owl flying over the same spot, which Joanna interpreted as a portent of death to her enemies.

Simple observations when shared with Joanna took on a numinosity that partly explains her affect on people. They could not ignore Joanna's presence, for her total faith in her Spirit sent a charge through otherwise ordinary events which lent them an unforgettable glow – as witnessed on that same evening while they were sitting at supper. This time it was not a sight but a sound that had Mr and Mrs Beecraft and Maria Bruce intrigued. They thought they heard a whistling noise coming from Joanna's mouth which she was too busy talking to notice. Later the Beecrafts heard it again and this time Joanna confessed that she could hear a noise in her ears that seemed to be coming from her.[37]

Sunday evening was so pleasant that they delayed sending for candles and lingered at the table chatting after supper. Suddenly Mr Beecraft espied a ring of bright stars in the sky and they all rushed to the window to see. There were five remarkably bright stars and a sixth more faint shining in a circle amid dark clouds. The friends stood a long time staring at the heavens.

There was no such thing as coincidence. Everything had significance. The higher world reflected the lower. Joanna was led to understand that by sharing one bed she and Mrs Bruce were as close on earth as the late Colonel Bruce and Joanna's Spirit were in heaven. 'But as thou art inferior to Bruce in this world, so is Bruce inferior to Me,' explained her Spirit, easing away class distinctions. 'But as she makes thee her companion, so have I made Bruce My Companion, And . . . as thou canst do nothing without assistance; neither can I without the assistance of my Friends. . . .'[37] It was a nicely judged rallying-call for the Colonel's wealthy widow.

Soon after they arrived at Market Deeping Joanna had received news that John Wilson, one of the Seven Stars, had fallen seriously ill and it was for his sake that her Spirit ordered an immediate return to London on 19 July. Foley met her off the mail-coach and, after eating breakfast together, they set off at about ten o'clock for Wilson's home in Kentish Town.[38] They found him looking like death and suffering from a ghastly pain in the head – a condition which, according to Joanna, was entirely due to the treachery of his wife. For Mrs Wilson had been trying to turn her husband against Joanna and might have succeeded had he not, in order to preserve his faith, left home. Now the strain of abandoning his wife and twelve children had left him prostrate.

As soon as Wilson saw Joanna, his spirits rallied and he was much better during the hour she spent with him. However, Joanna had been told that he would not get well till she had visited him twice and, sure enough, at seven o'clock that evening he had a relapse that lasted two more days. At this point Foley took Joanna to see him again. Finding him almost out of his mind with pain, she stayed half an hour. Within twenty-four hours his pain had disappeared and he was perfectly well. John Wilson described his recovery as miraculous.[40]

It was not surprising that this experience as a healer on top of the effects of so much travel – her journeys to London and Lincolnshire – left Joanna drained. On Sunday, 25 July, 1802, she went to Orange Street Chapel to hear Dr Hunter preach on a text from 1 Corinthians 13: 'Charity never faileth, but whether there be prophecies, they shall fail; whether there be tongues, they shall cease; whether there be knowledge, it shall vanish away'.[41]

Prophecies to fail and tongues to cease – it was a dreary message and sent Joanna into a fit of depression made worse by a visit to Colonel Bruce's grave, where a large dog leapt up at her as if it would break its chain.[42] There was something else bothering her too. She had fallen out with Maria Bruce and the following day was commanded to leave her house and go to another that would be prepared for her for a very special purpose. Explaining this to friends, they arranged for her to occupy Stanhope Bruce's lodgings in Portman Place.[43] But having accompanied her there on 2 August, they obeyed instructions and left her entirely on her own, having been told that the special purpose for which she had come was – to confront the Devil.[44]

Joanna later described her seven day ordeal in *A Dispute between the Woman and the Powers of Darkness*. Satan did not appear immediately. Instead she met his 'friend' who tried to persuade her that Satan was a lively, cheerful spirit who had been cast out of heaven because the Lord could not stand his innocent mirth. When Joanna refused to accept this, Satan himself appeared and the fight began in earnest. As days passed, it was not her moral strength but her stamina – or more precisely her volubility – which wore Satan down. He complained:

> A woman's tongue no man can tame. God hath done something to chuse a bitch of a woman that will down-argue the Devil and scarce give him room to speak – for the sands of a glass do not run faster than thy tongue. It is better to dispute with a thousand men than with one woman.[45]

The result was a foregone conclusion. After seven days Joanna emerged victorious. However, it had been a narrow scrape, for what she did not say in her book was that at the height of her ordeal she felt something like a physical hand upon her shoulder. This terrified her. Moreover, having emerged shaken but triumphant she had immediately to face a further challenge. She was ordered to fast for forty days, touching no meat or anything that had known life.

Now, Joanna liked her food and this unaccustomed diet left her light-headed and abstracted. On Sunday, 15 August, she sat for half an hour, staring out of the window at a hot-air balloon drifting across the sky. Then night-after-night she had vivid dreams.

On 16 August she dreamt there were cocks crowing and bullocks passing her window at two in the morning; a whirlwind carried her off to her father's orchard in Gittisham where a bullock threatened her with his horns and she ran away.

On 17 August she dreamt of a large circle in heaven which enclosed herself and many friends.

On 18 August she dreamt of horses – some pulling coaches, others in carts with their heads decked with lead-coloured plumes; a hearse was pulled by eight or ten black-plumed horses which were so entangled with each other they could scarce go along.

On 19 August she dreamt of a large black horse moving through the air with a man on its back.

On 20 August she dreamt of watching her father stripping off his coat, waistcoat and shirt until his back was naked; he looked so sick that she pushed up the window and told him to go out on the lead roof; he had almost done this when Mr Wolland entered the room.

On 24 August she noticed an unusual brightness in the eastern sky at nine o'clock, as if a firework had burst into flames in the same part of the sky where she had seen the hot-air balloon a few nights before. The brightness lasted until eleven o'clock when a dense body of stars appeared.[46]

Not only did Joanna record all these dreams and experiences but she had them quickly printed by E. Spragg of Covent Garden and sold for 2s. 6d. by E.J. Field in London and William Symons in Exeter.

Now nearing the end of her fast, if she hoped for a peaceful period in which to convalesce she was to be sadly disappointed.

10

TRIAL AT HIGH HOUSE

> Every woman is commanded to appear in white in token of their
> innocence that was betrayed.
>
> *Joanna to Lucy Taylor*, 22 December 1802

On 13 September, 1802, Elias Jameson Field, Joanna's London
bookseller, called on her at Portman Place. He had come to take down
some of her writings but, finding her suffering from a violent headache,
sat listening to her latest dream instead. They were interrupted by the
landlord, Mr Newbury, who arrived to say that he had been instructed
to make up the bill as Mr Bruce would be quitting the house by 29
September. This was the first Joanna had heard of it and she was highly
indignant. Surely such behaviour was unworthy of the Reverend
Stanhope Bruce? It was. He had nothing to do with it. The instruction
had come from his daughter-in-law, Maria Bruce.

Stanhope was staying at Market Deeping. Joanna immediately dictated
a letter to Mary Beecraft, protesting at the lack of warning and offering
to pay the next quarter's rent herself so that she could stay in the house
until Christmas. She also wrote to Maria Bruce with what amounted to
a declaration of war.

It seems the two women had quarrelled over money, and in the course
of their dispute Maria demanded the return of all the mourning apparel
she had sent Joanna the year before. Loftily agreeing to pay for the
clothes, Joanna declared, 'I would not wear them for the world, [for] if
you are led by the Spirit of the Lord NOW, you must have been led by
the Spirit of the Devil THEN'. [1] Letters soon arrived from Mary Beecraft
and her father positively denying that Mrs Bruce had any right to give
notice on his lodgings – a response which gave Joanna the moral high
ground from which to launch her future attack.

For the moment, though, she had other, more important, battles to
wage. Towards the end of her fast, her Spirit warned her that she was
about to be ill – that Satan would make her suffer physically for seven
days and only then would the Lord's answer to the Powers of Darkness
be given. [2] To arm herself against her foe she penned the following and
sent it to all her friends, urging them to collect as many signatures as
possible:

Christ's Glorious and Peaceable Kingdom to be established and come upon Earth, and His Will to be done upon Earth, as it is done in Heaven: and satan's kingdom is to be destroyed, is the prayer and desire of Joanna Southcott. CHRIST'S KINGDOM ESTABLISHED – and Satan destroyed.

All who put their name to this prayer would be entitled to a paper signed and sealed by Joanna as a protection in the dangerous times that lay ahead.[3]

On 20 September she went to bed and dreamt that she was lying on a stony bank, gazing up at the planets and strange cloud formations. She awoke with a violent pain in her stomach and bones as if she had been lying as in her dream. When she fell asleep again she dreamt she arose from the same bank to follow some passing reapers; she was carrying an ox-goad which she threw over another bank, but it instantly sprang back to her hand; she threw it again and it returned as before; when she threw it gently, it came back gently.

She awoke to find herself full of pain.

Fortunately William Sharp had taken note of the warning that she was about to fall ill and sent her some special wine. After drinking this she felt a little better and lay down to rest until Mrs Field arrived and let herself in. But then her pains returned, together with a fever, and next day she was seized with a fit of choking and laughter which lasted over an hour. An apothecary was summoned, but by the time he arrived at eight o'clock that night Joanna felt better, so refused his prescription. By midnight she was so delirious she no longer knew what she was doing. She got up, was violently sick, then collapsed on the floor. Mrs Field helped her back into bed, but she was soon up and vomiting again. Mrs Field helped her back once more. But when Joanna, still delirious, sat up and began to talk and fight, Mrs Field reached the end of her tether and declared she could not stand another such night.

Seeing her friend so upset, Joanna pulled herself together and told her to undress and come to bed. Before she could sleep, however, Mrs Field had to listen to Joanna's latest dream in which she had been lying on a bed fighting with the Devil.

'I think you have been fighting with the Devil,' agreed the weary Mrs Field, 'and I shall tell you tomorrow.'

Next day Mr Sharp brought in another apothecary, who told Joanna that her fever would last twenty-one days.

'Then I shall not live so long,' she murmured.

'You may not be so bad as you are now all the time,' he reassured her.[4]

She continued to be haunted by strange dreams – involving cornfields and sheets of paper with her writing on them, flocks of pigeons and partridges which she caught and put in her apron. On the fourth day her fever subsided, and for a couple of hours she chatted to her friends and seemed quite recovered. But next day, when her pains redoubled, she began to doubt whether she could recover within the seven days. She was so ill, all her friends grew anxious too – apart from William Sharp who declared his faith as firm as ever.

Later it was revealed that on 24 September, while Joanna lay so ill, Foley also had a dream: of a coloured dove which flew through his window and settled on the washhand-basin to drink, then turned into a beautiful girl about twelve years old in a white crepe dress; he saluted her, then awoke.

On the seventh morning of her illness Joanna was told by her Spirit that she should get up at four o'clock perfectly restored to health. Mrs Field was overjoyed. Why not play a little joke on Mr Sharp, she suggested; they could put a dummy in the bed and make it look as if Joanna was still lying there sick. Joanna demurred. Surely it was their first duty to thank God for her delivery? Her Spirit, however, told her that she could return thanks and play a little joke at the same time, 'for the thing was simple, but not sinful'.

So, when William Sharp and a female friend arrived that evening they were shown into the room where a bundle of clothes had been put in the bed. Despite what he saw, Sharp declared that he still believed Joanna had recovered. Joanna then emerged from her hiding-place and every one laughed except Sharp's companion, who was offended by the prank.

Having emerged victorious from her confrontation with Satan and survived all that he could throw at her, Joanna was not going to let a puny foe like Maria Bruce trifle with her. So when, having returned the contentious mourning clothes to her, she received a complaint that there were articles missing, she was outraged. On 6 October, she replied:

> Dear Madam,
>
> I have sent back the cloathes you sent me to Exeter but was lost in wonder when the servant brought me word you demanded a pair of pockets that you never sent me, or gave me a pair in your life. You demanded two more handkerchiefs which you never sent me. I have sent back every thing you sent me, with the white cloathes, save two pair of stockings which I had worn, and thought to pay for out of the six guineas Mr Sharpe left to pay for my mourning as I had worn it, although you have put me to an unnecessary expense, having two suits of mourning of my own before. But I cannot think the mourning came to six

guineas, as I could have bought it much cheaper at Exeter.

You sent 13 yards of Bombazeen, a Pettycoat of Bombazete, two white muslin caps; not one of these articles did I want, but now I find myself compelled to pay for them. The old Gown you made up for me, as it is worn out, I shall satisfy you for that also. So I must beg you will give Mr Sharpe the bill and settle with him, but I shall now inform you, when you refused me to pay for my Washing, when you was taking the pretty Guineas of me to lay by, I put one in your hand more than you knew of, as I thought I would not impose on your goodness.

Three shillings your eldest son borrow'd of me a few days before I came away, one shilling you ordered me to give for you at the Collection beside what I gave myself. . . .

'Render unto Caesar the things that be Caesar's and unto God the things that are God's.' I have strictly obeyed to Return unto you all that was your due and now I am commanded to Demand from you all that is the Lord's, so you must return back my Sealed Writings in your hands that was sealed by me, for they are ten thousand times more worth than all you have got, and if you keep one of my sealed writings in your hands, the Lord will send a Curse upon you. . . . I must conclude by saying my soul feels for you, for your own sake, for your Husband's sake, and for your worthy Father's sake whose judgment you will find far superior to your own.

> I am with respect,
> Joanna Southcott.

P.S. The Seals I demand is the three sealed letters I sent you the end of 1791, the sealed parcel the gentleman brought you from Exeter, and the sealed parcel I sealed up in your house; all to be returned to me, as I returned the Cloathes to you, and I should also be glad if you would return me back all my letters.

Two days later Joanna was writing again.

Madam,

I am sorry a lady of your ability should let yourself down to act with principles you cannot clear; whenever Mr Sharpe goes to your house you are denied, can you say with a safe conscience you was not at home when he called last?

If you judge my writings are from the Devil, it is a sin to keep them when they are demanded, do you know how many scores of pounds my writings have stood me in? And shall I leave them in an Enemy's hands?

[N]ow I shall intreat Mr Sharpe once more to trouble you to

have a fair account, and pay for what I have had of you, and
you are to return all the writings you had of mine. . . . [A]nd
was you a man and not a woman, I should send you a letter you
would blush to read.

I am your much injured friend,

Joanna Southcott.[5]

When William Sharp called on Maria Bruce the following Monday,
she still refused to see him. He was told there was no message.

By 12 October Joanna had completed her book, *The Answer of the
Lord to the Powers of Darkness,* written by Sharp at her dictation and
sealed with her 'IC' seal. In it her Spirit revealed:

> what thou hast wrote at thy father's house shall be made known,
> before this year is ended by the Old Style. I let it stand one year,
> from the time thy friends went to Exeter to search out the truth.
> . . . If the thorn blossoms at Christmas, at Christmas my blossom
> shall appear. And every letter thou hast sent to Pomeroy, Moore,
> and Nutcombe and other ministers must be made public. . . . Let
> them be warned.[6]

This fighting talk may be partly explained by the letter Joanna had
just received from Stanhope Bruce, containing more criticism from the
Reverend Mr Mossop. In a state of some agitation Joanna opened her
Bible and wrote down the first verse marked by her quill. It fell on
Psalm 69:6: 'Let not them that wait on thee, O Lord God of hosts, be
ashamed for my sake: let not those that seek thee be confounded for my
sake, O God of Israel.' As she read on: 'Because for thy sake I have
borne reproach. . . . I am become a stranger unto my brethren, and an
alien unto my mother's children. . . .' she took comfort from the words.[7]
Her alienation from her family and the reproaches she endured merely
confirmed that she was doing the will of God.

On the other hand, having lost the friendship of Maria Bruce she had
to admit she was lonely and even homesick for Devon. On 29 October
she wrote to Mrs Lucy Taylor in Exeter, asking her to send one of her
daughters to keep her company:

> I am now in my lodgings in Paddington which belong to Mr
> Bruce – and am alone – and would like one of the Miss Taylors
> with me. . . .
>
> On January 1 (OS) my writings are to be proved so hope to
> see you and Mr Taylor at that time – if you come (or write to
> me) come or send to Mr Field in Broad Court.
>
> When my writings are proved and my business settled in
> London I am commanded to go to Leeds . . . but unless the
> Lord decrees it otherwise I intend to have the pleasure of coming

into Devonshire first because I really do so much long to see all my Dear Friends whom I so much love.[8]

It was settled then. Plans were afoot to hold a formal trial at which her writings were to be judged – and not before time! She had come to London with vital messages for the country's rulers, and what was their response? Nothing. The King, his sons, the Lords and Commons had – to a man – ignored her.

Her dreams reflected her frustration. She dreamt of a handsome youth in blue clothes who put his arm around her; she wandered through Mr Bruce's dining-room into an adjoining chamber where there were six blind men.

To her the meaning was obvious: mankind must continue blind until her writings were proved.[9]

But if those in power were blind to her message, the same was not true of humbler folk, who flocked to sign her prayer and be 'sealed'. Moreover, Joanna's endeavours on behalf of Brothers had won her the support of many of his followers, some of whom hailed her as his natural partner, the Eve to his Adam. Even Halhed had been sufficiently convinced to accept one of her seals as a sign of his faith in the prophetess.[10] She had also received some 'candid and generous' letters from churchmen such as the Reverend Nicholas Bull of Saffron Walden, whose objections she brushed aside by saying, '"I have not added to the Scriptures nor taken from them but explained their meaning.'"[11]

Among the many requests to be present at the proving of her prophecies came one from Benjamin Hadad, a Jew who insisted that he had been ordered by the Lord to attend.

'I cannot receive men from their own assertions. If I [did], I might have many impostors,' Joanna replied, before giving grudging consent. 'But as I have given liberty by Divine Command to six Jews of repute, who are permitted to be present – if you are a Jew, your calling is right and you are the best judge of your own motives.'[12]

The trouble was, there was so much misunderstanding about her mission that could be remedied only by a public examination of her writings. It was time to summon the Seven.

In his diary for Tuesday, 16 November, Thomas Foley recorded:

I reced. a letter from Joanna, saying it was the Lord's pleasure that I should be in Town early next week – as He had a work for me to do. I with the utmost Joy and humble gratitude obeyed This summons. Amen and Amen.

After packing a crate of good port wine to take with him, Foley set out from Oldswinford to join his wife in London. He had persuaded his kinsman, Lord Foley, to allow them to use High House, Edgware Road,

Paddington, for the 'trial' and they moved in on 30 November – a 'fine, clear, and sun shiny Day', an auspicious omen.

Before helping to select suitable judges and jury Foley had a small domestic matter to attend to – the baptism of his eighteen-month old son, Richard. The chosen day – Sunday, 12 December – was described as 'glorious fine' in the proud father's diary.

> Mrs Southcott favoured me with standing God-Mother to my Child – and Mr Field and Mr Carpenter (who stood in the room of Mr Sharp, because he was absent) did me the favor to stand as God-Fathers. . . . Richard Foley was registered on my List and a sealed paper was given to him from Joanna to become inheritor of Xt's [Christ's] Glorious Kingdom.[13]

Joanna was by now obsessed by her 'trial'. In pursuit of suitable judges, she sent another letter to King George III explaining why she had asked Parliament to free Richard Brothers, and pointing out that she was ready to prove her calling before any scholars or clergy His Majesty cared to appoint.[14] She received no reply.

She sent her latest book to Halhed and invited him to be present at the public examination of her writings. He declined. She sent invitations to her friends and relations in Devon – the Taylors, Mrs Symons, Mary Bird. And of course Susanna. (Let her make what she would of a letter written for Joanna by the Reverend Thomas Foley, inviting her to stay at the grand High House, Paddington.)[15]

In a long, flowery letter to Mrs Taylor on 22 December Joanna made it clear that she expected them to arrive in London no later than 10 January.

> I trust you will not suffer *anything* to prevent you and Mr Taylor coming – for then you will see what you have at long wished for – and all my friends are particularly anxious to see you.

She reminded them to bring their gloves and explained that

> every woman is commanded to appear in white in token of their innocence that was betrayed and all the ladies have white cambric muslin dresses prepared for the occasion.[16]

Christmas was spent quietly, with Joanna and her young friend, Charles Taylor, going to the parish church with the Foleys in the morning before joining them for lunch. In the afternoon Stanhope Bruce came to drink tea, and they spent a 'Heavenly' evening listening to Foley reading some of Joanna's Communications.

After Christmas, preparations for the great day continued apace. Witness the following extract from Foley's diary for Monday, 27 December:

> A glorious day. I dined at home. . . . Mrs Fy. went into London

to purchase thgs. agt. the proving of Joanna's writings on 12
January 1803 – and T.P. Foley purchased his Seal of the Lion
this day, as he was Ordered to by dear Joanna Southcott. T.P.
Foley met with it entirely by chance. He tried a vast number of
shops without success and found it at last in the shop he went
to first in the morning going from Paddington towards Oxford
St. and He rejoiced Greatly.

The following week he went again into town, this time to buy special
crockery for the 'trial'.[17]

There is a sense of mounting excitement as Foley records the arrival
in London of George Turner from Leeds, Mrs Taylor and her daughter
Fanny from Exeter, Mary Beecraft from Market Deeping. An
advertisement was placed in all the morning, evening and Sunday
newspapers asking for any twelve Anglican divines to come forward
for the 'trial'.[18]

On 9 January 1803 Joanna left Portman Street to go to High House[19]
which she had described to Mrs Taylor as 'nearly opposite Mr Bruce's
lodgings with a gravel walk to it with ranks of trees on one hand and the
garden wall on the other.' The house, high-built but almost invisible
from the road, was approached through an enclosed garden. Once inside
the visitor was confronted by a remarkable staircase, winding round
and appearing like galleries. At the top was a landing giving on to a room
overlooking a fine barberry tree in the garden. There was also a splendid
dining-room large enough to hold fifty people.[20]

Here, on 9 January, Joanna and many of her supporters gathered to
celebrate Thomas Foley's forty-fifth birthday. Foley met her at the door
when she arrived and ceremonially presented her with the Great Key of
what he called the Lord's House, explaining that it had been taken for
her. But Joanna begged him to keep the key.[21] At six o'clock that evening,
after a happy day together, the friends watched as Joanna's writings
were taken downstairs and deposited in a vault where, according to
instruction, they had to remain until eleven o'clock on 12 January.

What happened when that day came is best told in Foley's own words:

The men first went down into the Cellar where Joanna's writings
had been deposited. . . . The Ladies then went down and viewed
them in the sepulchre – and then they were taken from thence
by the Judges and Jurymen and carried up into the Large room.
. . . Joanna entered the Room with the Rev. T.P. Foley's Little
Child RICHARD in her arms, the Little Boy bearing a piece of
Cake with a Starry Crown upon it – Mrs T.P. Foley attended
Joanna into the Room. Joanna was much affected; she, however,
soon recovered, and began a very animated speech setting forth

by the Types of the Little Boy and her writings (which are the Word of God) and that had been buried for the Three Days and Three Nights – the Birth, Burial and Resurrection of our Blessed Lord. Joanna made use of these words 'Kiss the Son, lest he be angry' and Joanna said 'You must kiss the little Boy'. The Company then kissed the little Boy, who was one year and near six months old, as the Emblem of Christ's Second Birth in the Spirit, and the conduct of the Little Boy was most remarkable and extraordinary: as he received the kisses of all present with evident marks of delight and Satisfaction, that appeared to the most of those present almost equal to a Miracle or at least it was wonderful and astonishing.[22]

The twelve judges were all male: the Reverend Stanhope Bruce, the Reverend Thomas Webster, the Reverend Thomas Foley, Elias Carpenter, William Jowett, Peter Morrison, William Sharp, Charles Taylor, George Turner, William Roundell Wetherell, John Wilson, and little Richard Foley.

The jury was also composed of men: Charles Abbott, William Belk, William Coy, Elias Jameson Field, Richard Law, John Morris, Thomas Stephens, George Stocks, William Taylor, John Torin, William Layton Winter, and John Young.[23]

But women had a special part to play. 'As the woman hath borne the Pains of Hell to bring in her natural children, so now she shall bear the Joys of Heaven to bring in her spiritual children,' Joanna declared. Although most had arrived in their special white clothes, two who failed to comply were sent away. Joanna had also rejected a fine suit of clothes sent for her to wear on the day because she thought they had not been sent in good faith.

The 'trial' took seven days – during which there was open house for any one to come and pass his judgment. There was an occasional hitch in the proceedings. For instance, when the Box was opened, the papers became so mixed up that Joanna could not refer to the most interesting parts and some of her audience grew restless. It took Foley to restore confidence by pointing out that, like the Day of Creation, there was need of some darkness with the light.

On the last day Joanna entered the room in good spirits and, after shaking hands with most of the company, sat down to hear the last of the extracts which had been read daily. She then stood up, threw her glove on to the table, and challenged anyone to come forward if they thought she had been led by the Devil. . . .

No one stirred.

She went on to speak for nearly an hour, showing how her works came from the Living God.

Afterwards the fifty-eight people present joined with her in the following declaration:

> I, Joanna Southcott, am clearly convinced that my calling is of God, and my writings are indited by his Spirit: as it is impossible for any spirit but an all-wise God, that is wondrous in working – wondrous in wisdom – wondrous in power – and wondrous in truth – could have brought round such mysteries so full of truth, as in my writings; so I am clear in whom I have believed, that all my writings came from the Spirit of the most high God.

The assembled company then signed Joanna's Petition to the Lord:

> To cut off all the power of Satan from the face of the earth, as the head of John the Baptist was cut off, and bury him down, as John was buried down.

The trial ended on 18 January with all the people singing Psalms 18 and 104. Most of the documents were re-sealed and replaced in the Great Box which was handed over to William Sharp. Foley's diary entry on that day concludes with the words:

> Satan was cast, and the woman was freed. Thank God! Thank God! Thank God![24]

SEALING FOR SALVATION, 1803-1804

The object of her visit is to distribute CELESTIAL SEALS to the faithful; and as these seals, like the Agis of Minerva, will protect the possessor from all danger even at the cannon's mouth, we recommend the Volunteers to lay in a stock preparatory to the arrival of Bonaparte and his sharp-shooters.

Leeds Mercury, 22 October 1803

Joanna stayed with the Foleys in High House for nearly five months, enjoying life with no money worries. Her dreams seem to reflect a growing self-confidence. On the night of 22 February 1803 she dreamt she was perching with a great flock of people in a huge tree; when she reached the end of one branch she was held fast by a higher one which stretched like a jet of water to carry her over dangerous places; after sailing over two horses she landed on a high, clean bank.[1]

Joanna may have been living in unaccustomed luxury but she was not idle. With Foley's help she continued to publicise her mission through books. Prepared for the press by Foley from manuscripts read to him by Joanna, the first, in 1803, was entitled: *A Warning to the Whole World, from the Sealed Prophecies of Joanna Southcott*. Among the events she claimed to have foretold were the war in 1793, fever in America, rebellion in Ireland, and the French conquest of Italy.

They could produce books, but not necessarily command attention. Writing to Mrs Taylor in Exeter in April to thank her for the nice turbot she had sent, Elizabeth Foley mourned the fact that the world was ignoring Joanna's writings, despite all the handbills sent out. It was a chatty letter, showing how friendly the two women had become during Joanna's recent 'trial'. The big news was that Stanhope Bruce and Mrs Dix, whom the Taylors had met at High House, had married on Easter Tuesday. Her Spirit had instructed Joanna to keep the ceremony secret, so afterwards, when the announcement was made, Wilson and Sharp thought it was a joke, not expecting such an aged couple to wed. (Stanhope was seventy-three, his bride sixty.)

'I suppose this marriage will occasion a little ferment in Jermyn Street and that Mrs Bruce there will be greatly enraged when she hears,' wrote Elizabeth Foley.[2] Joanna's glee at Mrs Bruce's discomfiture can be imagined.

Amidst news of their son Charles and her own little Richard's first efforts to talk, Mrs Foley told the Taylors about their recent discovery of a youth who had beautiful visions which seemed to match Joanna's prophecies.

Mrs Foley was referring to eighteen-year old Henry Prescott who, besides having visions for the last ten years, had enough artistic talent to produce watercolours of what he saw – all the more surprising for one brought up in a workhouse. He had come to the attention of Elias Carpenter, a wealthy paper-maker of Neckinger House, Bermondsey and one of the judges at Joanna's 'trial', who took him from Christchurch Workhouse on 27 February and employed him in his mill. It was an act of charity characteristic of the man. Having himself come up the hard way – at fourteen working in a merchant's counting-house in Antigua – Carpenter was keen to help others who were prepared to help themselves. Not only did he provide free books, pens and slates to his workers, but spent two hours every evening teaching them to read and write.[3]

Into this caring environment came the almost illiterate Prescott. Carpenter wrote:

> His growth having been greatly checked, I strove to improve it by making him work in the garden and other employment which had air and exercise; this, with good living, soon materially altered his appearance. His temper was good, his mind cheerful, but volatile and giddy to excess; yet, while with me, free from any known vice. He was very ingenious, apt to learn, and, having musical instruments about the house, from seeing others perform, he learned to finger them, and, by the same means, to play the flute. In fact, he was always in action. When I first took him he was about fourteen years old, but so small as by some supposed not to exceed ten years.[4]

Joanna met Henry Prescott for the first time on 28 February 1803, the day after Carpenter brought him from the workhouse. He was henceforth known as Joseph, a name resonant with meaning for Joanna.

In the Bible Joseph was the son whom Jacob blessed above all his sons.[5] Joseph saved his brothers by his power of prophecy. Joseph was the name of the Virgin's helpmate. Since childhood Joanna had always been linked with a Joseph – the brother who betrayed her in Bristol. Then there was Joseph Pomeroy, from whom she still expected great things despite the way he had betrayed her in Exeter. Now, at the end of February 1803, when the stage was empty for another Joseph to enter her life, this visionary artist appeared and Carpenter presented him to Joanna as a sign that the Millennium was approaching just as she had forecast in *Strange Effects of Faith*:

The time is come, that your women shall prophesy, your young men shall dream dreams, your old men shall see visions; for the day of the Lord is at hand.[6]

On 4 March she began to interpret Joseph Prescott's dreams. Two days later he showed her a watercolour of one of his visions and soon a partnership developed with Joseph painting what he 'saw', Joanna's Spirit explaining its significance – and Foley writing it all down for the next book.[7]

A typical vision occurred at about ten o'clock on 7 March. As Joseph stood staring at a part of the paper mill everything went dark and he had a vision of the Lord riding on a huge grey horse and wearing a red cloak over a bright purple tunic. On his head was a crown of twelve stars – a star between each of four arches, one on the top of each arch, and four in a cluster on the top of the ball. He held a sword in his right hand, guiding the horse with the left. The figure was surrounded by a nimbus of clouds enclosing a crowd of angelic faces, shouting: 'Glory to thee, O Lord. Ride forth, Mighty God, conquering and to conquer.'

On 23 March Joseph was sitting beside the fire at High House when he 'saw' the figure of Christ standing with arms outstretched facing four young men – one black, another dark with whiskers, the third fair, and the fourth 'a copper colour'. Each carried a musical instrument and stood next to some sort of national flag. To this little group, apparently representing mankind, Christ announced: 'I will be known in all hearts, throughout the whole world, from the emperor on the throne, to the meanest subject on the earth.'[8]

The Foleys made the most of being in London to see old friends and proudly introduce them to Joanna. On the second Sunday in May they set out on foot to visit the surgeon, Dr William Roundell Wetherell, at his home in the Grove, Highgate. Joanna wrote,

The weather was remarkably fine. I went on my journey very pleasantly till I came to the latter end, and then my feet began to be painful when we left the green fields for the high road. When we came to ascend Highgate Hill, Mrs Foley called to her husband to assist us, as we were feeling faint and tired.[9]

There was some excuse for their tiredness. Joanna was over fifty. Elizabeth Foley was six months pregnant. Foley, who had been leading the way, turned back to give them each an arm. Still Joanna despaired of reaching the top, especially as Foley promised them they were nearly there so many times that she lost all faith in him. Eventually they reached Highgate only to find that the first lad they asked had not heard of Dr Wetherell. His mother, however, supplied directions and when they arrived at the house – with Joanna speechless with fatigue – quite a little gathering was there to greet them.

Despite her thirst after the walk, Joanna was afraid to drink much until she returned home. But she supped a little tea and fell, as usual, to lamenting the state of the nation. Someone probably mentioned the huge green snake recently discovered in an East India ship carrying sugar in its hold. The newspapers were full of the story.[10] Perhaps they also discussed the fragility of peace. For the Treaty signed the year before had settled nothing, and just over a week later Britain renewed her war against France. The outing finished pleasantly enough with John Wilson giving them a lift home in his coach – even though poor Mrs Foley felt very sick and 'left part of her dinner in the Way'.[11] Back in High House Joanna opened a letter handed to her by Mr Field that afternoon and with mixed emotions found that it contained gold and silver sent by her supporters in Leeds. 'This gave me pleasure and pain – pain for fear they had distressed themselves,' she recorded, 'and pleasure to think they had so much love and faith for the cause.'[12]

In fact, regarding Joanna as something of an icon, people were beginning to arrive at High House just to see the famous prophetess, to hear her talk and if possible take away a sample of her writing. On Tuesday, 10 May, William Belk, Mary Belk and Ann Carney came with this in mind and Joanna, unaware of the dreadful fate in store for Mrs Carney, willingly gave them one of her signed papers. One week later, she was busy sealing copies of *The Answer of the Lord to the Powers of Darkness* when Mrs Foley, Emma Carney and the maidservant heard her seal making a cracking noise. After Mrs Foley suggested something was wrong, Joanna examined the last sixteen books and found she had sealed them upside down.[13]

She had now been in London for over a year. Foley's lease on High House gave out in early June when he planned to return to Oldswinford so Joanna had decisions to make. Should she stay on in London? Go with the Foleys to Oldswinford? Return home to Exeter? Or travel further afield to visit those supporters who had showered her with corres-pondence and gifts? Finding it hard to decide, her agitation was reflected in recurring dreams in which she was swept along through the air. But she need not have worried. The decision, as usual, was made for her.

Hearing that Mrs Foley intended to visit the Carpenters before leaving town, Joanna asked her to deliver a valuable silver cup to Neckinger House for her. She was accompanied home by Carpenter's daughter in a light chaise. The evening air being chilly, Miss Carpenter lent the good lady her own greatcoat and fur tippet to wrap round herself. But somewhere on the journey the tippet went missing and was never found – a sad loss because it was particularly well-shaped. However, a week later came a parcel addressed to Mr Carpenter, containing a replacement from Mrs Southcott. The accompanying letter read:

Dear Sir,

Strange are the ways of the Lord to show us how strict we ought to be in observing all His directions; yet we are sometimes permitted to err in small things to teach us wisdom in greater. . . .

After the determination made by Mr and Mrs Foley on the Saturday night to beg Miss Carpenter to do them the favour of accepting a present to repair the loss which her kindness had occasioned, I was ordered to call to my remembrance the words spoken to me concerning Mrs Foley's going to the Neckinger, which I was told that morning to forbid, and that she would be prevented going in the coach – which she was by its being full.

But . . . knowing Mrs Foley had a desire of seeing Mrs Carpenter on a week day, and taking a last leave of her, I did not mention it, but must confess I was afraid of an accident, and therefore desired Mr Foley to accompany her part of the way till she was safe out of danger which he did. . . . But when I heard of the loss which had happened, and saw Mrs Foley hurt that she had been the cause of it, it all came to my remembrance that I had been warned and did not give the warning.[14]

To make amends for this failure, Joanna had to replace the lost tippet even if it meant staying a week longer in London than she intended – for the Lord who looked after sparrows, would also take care of a friend's lost scarf.

I leave this house on 6 June and as I am ordered to go to various parts of the kingdom, I cannot tell at present where to give directions but letters directed to me, post paid, at E.J.Field's, will be forwarded,

she wrote on 2 June. Then, as she uttered her prayer for the Foleys' departure on Sunday, 4 June, she was suddenly told by her Spirit to be ready to leave London at five the next morning. She was to go to Exeter with Elizabeth Foley and little Richard and stay with the Taylors.[15]

This time the reception Joanna met in her home county was overwhelming. With the renewal of war against France, people flocked to ask for her seals.

The number of Enquirers and Believers were daily and hourly visiting me that I had scarce time many days to eat my meat. Some came nineteen miles to see me, others thirty miles and all expressed the greatest satisfaction from everything they had seen and heard. . . .[16]

This was not quite true. She was criticised for spending too much time showing Joseph Prescott's pictures – which gave her the excuse, if such was needed, to pack them away and concentrate on her own Communications. Moreover, despite the stir caused by her visit, there was always one person who refused to accept her with uncritical acclaim – Susanna. Still sure her sister was being misled, she insisted that whereas some of her writings made sense and were consistent with the Bible, others were simply nonsense, as if written by someone else. Nor was this just her opinion, she declared. Mrs Minifie thought the same.[17]

If Susanna thought this would shake her sister's confidence, she was mistaken. Joanna was no longer the impressionable young woman she had once known. Things had changed. Nowadays she cared not a fig for the opinion of people like Mrs Minifie. On the other hand she was prepared to hear Susanna out when the latter questioned the source of her inspiration and could not understand why she had ditched her former beliefs.

In the old days, Joanna explained, she had always relied on her own judgment, but *now* she listened only to the wisdom of the Lord.[18]

Poor Susanna! She must have realised there was no arguing with that.

On her way back from Exeter Joanna stopped in Bristol to call on her brother Joseph and no doubt impress him with her new friends.[19] Then she journeyed on to Oldswinford, staying with the Foleys from 15 July till 11 October.[20] Although the war was uppermost in people's minds, Foley knew they had to speak carefully of such events and make it clear that Joanna's mission was not revolutionary in the political or social sense. Times were dangerous. Richard Brothers was imprisoned when his claim to be in possession of revealed knowledge led him into what the government saw as 'treasonable activities'. The Wordsworths had been persecuted by government spies in Somerset in 1798. During his months in London, Foley had been sending out letters and copying Joanna's writings for the press. Now that war had been resumed, he was anxious to point out that 'we totally disclaim all meddling with Politics so these [writings] are only for our own private Information and to teach us how to guard against the coming-desolating Storm.'[21]

Unfortunately he could not control the actions of Joanna's more intemperate followers and was no doubt embarrassed by the letter sent on 19 July to Prime Minister Addington by Richard Law, former flax-dresser and one of the jury at High House. After describing Joanna's mission and begging for the release of Brothers, Law wrote that only if England announced its faith in the Second Coming would Bonaparte be defeated. Moreover, if Addington supported Joanna this would 'do infinitely more to save the nation, than all the ships in the navy, or all the armies that can be raised.' Finally he declared that 'there are thousands in the land who have already signed for Christ's kingdom to come; and before another year is past there will be tens of thousands.'[22]

This could sound very threatening to the authorities, especially if in any way linked with radical politics. Part of the reason why Brothers had been sent to jail was his refusal to break the biblical injunction 'Swear not at all', a notion which, followed to its logical conclusion, could lead to the collapse of an army whose discipline relied on the oath of obedience to king and country. Joanna maintained that behind the objection to taking an oath was the biblical command not to say what one will do on the morrow, for one knows not what a day may bring forth.[23] By holding to this teaching, Joanna was in danger of being trapped in the dilemma, how can a man serve both God and Caesar?

Not that there was any doubting the patriotism of her followers. For them Bonaparte was the embodiment of Satan, the Great Beast who must be vanquished at all cost. The only question was, should they take up arms against him or rely on religious practice to bring about his downfall? It was a vexed question. Soon they were fighting each other over the issue, with Elias Carpenter championing the pacifists and Joanna coming down on the establishment side.

Reminding them of Prescott's vision of the horseman in the sky, she pointed out that the rider's sword was two-edged – a sign that believers had a temporal as well as a spiritual battle to wage against Satan. However, she had modified her views by 25 July when she wrote to William Sharp telling him that her followers should join parish associations of volunteers and fight only if England were invaded.[24]

Taking up the issue again in August she told Carpenter: 'You and I understand the words . . . "Have nothing to do with the contentions of the Nation" to mean, *you ought not to take the Sword.*' But, she explained, her recent experience in Exeter had taught her to think differently. There she had seen fine young men, all strong believers, signing up for the parish associations to keep themselves from being sent abroad, and although she wanted to dissuade them from taking up arms, something always stopped her speaking. It was only after Mr Field wrote to ask about the matter that she prayed and received this surprising answer: they should comply with the demands of king and country and breed no contention about it. As for Carpenter, his letter had caused her sleepless nights until the Spirit gave her a message for him: because he was working spiritually for the Lord, he was not required to fight physically if his conscience forbade it. On the other hand, he should not presume to judge others who had been called by the Lord to take up arms.[25]

It was, it seems, a matter of horses for courses. Elias Carpenter was called to work spiritually, whereas someone like John Wilson, who had now succumbed to his wife's doubts, might as well join the army. In a 'Letter to Believers in Yorkshire', Joanna wrote:

> I have directed him [Carpenter] not to take the sword if he can screen himself. . . . Wilson's wife prevents him using the sword of the Spirit therefore let Wilson take the sword of war: for every house that is divided must take the Sword of War. But . . . Field is not divided and I do not order him to take the sword, if he can be freed by man, but if not, let him drop contention. . . .
> I order them to enter into their parish associations to defend this country if an invasion takes place, to prevent them from being drawn to go abroad.[26]

It was a pragmatic solution and it suited well, especially as news now reached Oldswinford that there was no great danger from France and many volunteers were being rejected – a judgement borne out by a dream in which Joanna watched a dog opening its mouth to catch a cat which leapt in and worked its way right down his throat. The cat, her Spirit explained, was France; the dog, England.[27]

Amid all this talk of politics and war there were lighter moments; the urbane Mr Foley saw to that. He put in Joanna's hands a novel called *Romance in the Forest*. She enjoyed it, not for any trivial reasons, but, as she was careful to explain, for the way in which it showed up vice in its true colours.[28]

Sending congratulations to the Fields on the birth of a son, Joanna particularly approved his name (he was christened Southcott) and declared her willingness to stand godmother if he should live until her return to London.[29] By the end of August Mrs Foley had also given birth and her little girl was named Mary Joanna.[30]

Despite suffering from crippling gout in his left hand, Mr Foley was still busy writing letters and Communications for Joanna. A digest of her writings in a pamphlet entitled *A Word to the Wise* was printed at Stourbridge on 31 August. It was financed by her friends so that it could be given away to those who could not afford to buy her previous books. Or as Joanna put it: 'I now print this little Book to give the Poor, by the bounty of the Rich.'[31] In it she referred to her own mystical experiences, the part played by Satan in human suffering, the imminence of the Second Coming and the promise of the Millennium – before concluding with the astounding claim that she herself was one of the three most important women who had ever lived. There had been Eve. There had been the Virgin Mary. And now – Joanna Southcott.

Nor, having made such a claim, was she tempted to hide her light under a bushel, for she wrote to the Reverend Stanhope Bruce:

As soon as the book is out, the Rev. Thomas Foley will send
some to you, for your disposal, to give to whom you think
proper, in your own parish, or the neighbouring parishes around;
as I am ordered to have them spread as much as possible.

There were, however, many deaf ears – especially among the clergy,
one of whom apparently said 'We know enough already and want no
prophecies to teach us more.'[32] Joanna, deeply shocked, dreamt that
she heard the Reverend Thomas Foley loud in prayer, using very beautiful
words, until he suddenly stopped, out of breath.

The lesson was clear: so might the Church suffocate if it cut itself
off from prophetic inspiration.

Nor was the local response to Joanna's mission very pleasing. 'Not
one of the rich has come in here during Mrs Southcott's stay to sign for
Christ's Kingdom to be established and for Satan's to be destroyed,'
Foley wrote to a friend, 'making good what is said in the Gospel "that it
is easier for a camel to pass through the eye of a needle than for a rich
man to enter into the Kingdom of Heaven".'[33]

There also came grim news from London where Mrs Carney, the
woman who had visited Joanna with the Belks, had been murdered by
her husband. This tragedy. like all such sudden deaths among Joanna's
followers, raised the awkward question: why had the victim's seal not
protected her? Writing to Mr Field about the Carneys on 1 October
1803 Joanna – or more likely, her amanuensis – tried to lighten the
mood by joking that although Mr Foley was much better, 'still he is
very lame and cannot win a foot-race without it is given to the last
instead of the first.'[34]

By now the sale of Joanna's books had grown into a considerable
business and before she left to journey northwards Joanna wrote to Mr
Symons in Exeter, doubling her order from fifty to one hundred books
and wanting to know how many this left in his cupboard.[35] She also
received a letter from an unmarried lady in London who, having read
her books, wanted Joanna to share her home. Her name was Jane
Townley and she was a neighbour of William Sharp in Titchfield Street.[36]
The trouble was, Joanna had been told that, because of the clergy's
lack of faith, London was under threat so there was no point in taking
up the offer. However, her Spirit instructed her to return the compliment:
'so let Townley settle her affairs that she may be ready when I warn her
to come to thee, wherever thou art, for no evil shall come nigh thy
dwelling.'[37]

'Wherever thou art' were the operative words, for Joanna was about
to set out on her travels again, leaving for the north on 11 October[38] and
being accompanied as far as Birmingham by the Foleys and their children,

despite the fact that Elizabeth and the new baby were far from well.[39] After saying goodbye, Joanna went on to Chesterfield to spend a day with some supporters there before proceeding to Leeds where George Turner had taken a six month rental on a house for her.[40]

Her reception in Leeds was very different from Worcestershire.[41] In Leeds crowds flocked to see and hear 'the Prophetess from Exeter'. There were times when Joanna had difficulty in finding a quiet place to be alone. On her first Sunday in the city she told Turner that her Spirit had ordered her to stay on her own the next day to prepare for some revelation. But on Monday morning friends came to take their leave and detained her until mid-day. She eventually made her escape, only to be immediately called downstairs by Mr Turner to hear a letter he had just received from Elias Carpenter with bad news about Carpenter's dear friend, Mrs Wilmot, who was desperately ill.[42] Because the Spirit seemed to suggest that Mrs Wilmot was dying, Joanna promptly sent a Communication to Carpenter which said: 'If Wilmott now die, it is time for London to fear: for if I begin to take my Jewells, it is time for the others to fear.'[43]

At the end of the month, in the teeth of a gale, Joanna travelled to Stockton-on-Tees to a mixed reception: great kindness from believers but bitter opposition from others who began to poison the air with scandal. According to them, Joanna Southcott had given birth to several bastard children who were being brought up by the parish; she had spent time in prison; she was actually Bonaparte's brother in disguise! Of course, it was easy to laugh off such rumours, but more telling was the accusation that Joanna Southcott's prophecies came from the Devil.

'I no more believe these words come from the Devil than I believe the paper is black and the ink is white,' she wrote indignantly.[44] And describing the effect of her presence on the Methodist Society in Stockton: 'Those that believe in my writings, and of the near approach of Christ's Kingdom gave up their Chapel to me and it was thronged with many hundreds, if not a thousand.'

These people flocked to hear Joanna because she gave them the message they wanted to hear. They knew times were desperate. The proof was in their daily lives. When she pointed at recent calamities as evidence that God's judgments were in the earth, they could only say, 'Amen to that', and join the queue for one of her seals. Whereas fifty-eight had signed up for salvation in January 1803, one year later Joanna recorded that there were over eight thousand 'whose names stand for Satan's destruction'.[45] This increase reflected the success of her mission to the north.

Joanna was accompanied part of the way back from Stockton by

John Mackay whose name, according to Joanna's Spirit, was a 'shadow' for the true Messiah who was with her in all her journeys. The weather was freezing and once Mackay and his friend got out, Joanna kept up her spirits by singing out loud until more passengers boarded the coach.[46]

She was back in Leeds by early December, writing to thank Mrs Symons for sending the goose and fowls from Exeter, but asking her not to send more until she was back in London as carriage was expensive and they were comparatively cheap in Leeds. 'My neglect of writing is from lack of time not lack of love,' she assured her friend. 'Last week I was in the country eight miles from Leeds where I was visited from morning till near midnight by large companies including several ladies and gentlemen.'

Joanna undoubtedly liked meeting 'ladies and gentlemen' as opposed to the lower classes who made up the mass of her followers. The following day she was taken to another 'lady's' house and introduced to a clergyman who turned out to be an old college friend of Foley's. Declaring himself interested in her mission, he promised to visit Leeds when the Foleys arrived after Christmas. Joanna took lunch with her new friends before standing on a table to speak to a hundred or more people who had crowded into the kitchen to hear the famous prophetess. Then, being told that there were three times as many people in the yard, she went outside and, standing on the steps, addressed them. Later in the day she spoke to a crowd of people at Mr Ordsley's, where she spent the night before travelling five more miles to speak to another group at Mr Dixon's before returning to Leeds.[47]

Soon the weather closed in and Joanna felt so cold that she despaired of getting warm, even after piling so many clothes on her bed that she could scarce turn under their weight. Her Spirit's mood began to reflect the miserable weather by grumbling about the New Style calendar: 'they have changed My Bible, and the time, as they have changed the Style: so My birthday is kept wrong; and as wrong do they keep My Gospel.' On the other hand, the Spirit reassured Joanna about two precious rings – one with a diamond, the other a ruby – which had been given to her as presents. Although these rings were causing jealousy, this was because some could not stand the dazzling light that came from her hand. Joanna should ignore such people, 'for all men shall know that the light of the Lord is on thy handwritings, a much more dazzling light than the rings that are on thy fingers.'[48]

On 2 January 1804 Joanna was still waiting for the Foleys to arrive in Leeds when she wrote to Mrs Taylor. Too busy to write a long letter, she explained that, with the help of Mr Hirst and Mr Turner, she was signing and sealing thousands of new believers. She enclosed the letter in a parcel being sent to Mrs Symons, who had asked her for hundreds of seals, and she wanted Mrs Taylor to tell the Miss Eveleighs that they should seal up their list by the end of year (Old Style) with the Seal of the Lion.[49]

Mrs Taylor would not have been surprised by the Foleys' delay in leaving home, for she had been in regular contact with Elizabeth Foley over the previous month and knew they had problems. Their baby, Mary Joanna, had died in November, leaving them devastated. 'Our poor little girl suffered ten days more than tongue can express and then departed this life, causing us much grief,' Mrs Foley wrote to Fanny Taylor on 8 December, mentioning that they had both found some comfort in Communications received by Joanna, and that their misery was compounded by the fact that Foley was still suffering from gout.[50]

The death of the child named for her must have shaken Joanna. If it was a case of the shadow coming before the substance, what did it portend? After sending a letter to Foley early in the new year, Joanna was sitting writing when there came a rap on her table, loud and shrill. Seeing it as a token of her death, she felt sufficiently resigned to declare, 'I do not wish to live one day longer if I should be writing from any Spirit that is not of God.'[51] This pessimistic mood prevailed when, on 12 January 1804, Joanna learnt that enemy ships had been sighted off the coast and the French were expected to land any day. Her worst fears were confirmed by a spate of terrific storms. Everything pointed to the fact that the judgments of God were in the earth. Her Spirit warned: 'Nine parts of the Inhabitants of London will perish, as the streets will be filled with dead Bodies, French as well as English.' She wrote immediately to William Sharp to ask if there was enough money in stock to pay for the printing of her latest book. Not for nothing was it to be called *Sound An Alarm*, for the day of judgment was nigh and the sealed people should be prepared to leave London at one week's notice.

Sharp read her letter with dismay. Although it had to be taken seriously, he did not want to cause general panic so, before circulating her message, he added a footnote: 'The brethren cannot be too cautious in keeping this from those who are not sealed, in order to prevent Evil and false Reports going out into the World.'

Joanna possibly had the same thought when she wrote to Elias Carpenter on 23 January: 'Prepare yourselves to be ready when the evils come on the City for the decree of the Lord hath gone forth.' However, after mentioning that disaster would strike in February (Old Style), she told him not to leave London until the Lord commanded.[52]

By the end of January the Foleys had arrived. At last. Although he had recovered enough from his lameness to make the twenty-four hour coach

journey north, Foley had been left with such a painful cough that he
was unable to read any of Joanna's Communications at public meetings.[53]
He was present, however, when Joanna herself read one on the origin
of evil and asked a dissenting minister in the audience to name the source
of her writing. When the minister replied that he thought the Reverend
Mr Foley had helped her, Foley solemnly assured him to the contrary,
insisting that in the two years he had known Joanna all her
Communications had been given to her by the Spirit without the aid of
books or men. Next morning the dissenting minister returned to tell
Joanna that, after saying that her writings had come from the Devil, his
bed had been shaken violently all night.

After this, Foley helped Joanna prepare her book for the press from
manuscripts that she read to him, and *Sound an Alarm in My Holy
Mountain* was printed in Leeds by E. Baines, price one shilling. In it,
Joanna repeated: 'I should rejoice at the summons of death to stop my
hand and leave this world, if I am deceived and deceiving mankind.'[54]

Out of the blue John Wilson and Elias Carpenter arrived from London,
seeking instruction on how to hold meetings once the final judgments
began. Caught on the spot, the Spirit still stressed that time was short,
but commanded: '[L]et him meet in his own house all the friends he can
depend on . . . and read to them . . . and let them consult together as
men if they can form a plan free from danger to meet in public.'[55]

As days went by . . . and weeks . . . without the world ending, Joanna
seemed less sure of herself, even grew a little careless. On 10 March,
while making some water gruel for Foley, she poured it over her hand,
scalding it badly. She immediately plastered it with wet mud, changing
it when it became hot. Then she made up an apothecary's prescription
of strong soap lather on a flannel and applied that to her hand. And
before she went to bed, she used one of Mrs Foley's remedies, placing
a thick layer of salt on the wound and sewing it up in linen. By next
morning these three applications had brought about a perfect cure.

What was sauce for the goose should work similar wonders for the
gander! On 13 March, the day before the Foleys left for home, Joanna
received a Communication about Foley's illness: he needed three things.
He should take pills made up of powdered rhubarb and best soap, the
Daffy's Elixir which her sister Susanna said had saved her life, and
some medicine from an apothecary which had been blessed by Joanna.
In addition to this, because tea on its own was too 'fretting', he should
continue putting an egg in it. Foley obeyed her instructions and by the
end of March was reporting to Mr Taylor, 'blessed, blessed be God, I
have the happiness to say my tightness is quite gone, my cough almost
gone and I am gaining health and strength every day.'[56]

Belfield Hall – where Jane Townley was born in 1761. One of the oldest houses in Rochdale, Belfield Hall was owned by the Townley family from 1728 to 1851. Jane's father, Colonel Richard Townley, refronted the house in 1752 when he was High Sheriff of Lancashire. A man of literary tastes, Colonel Townley was a friend of William Wordsworth, patron of John Collier, and one of the earliest supporters of Sunday Schools. After Belfield Hall was sold by Jane's nephew, Richard Greaves Townley, M.P. for Cambridgeshire, it gradually declined and was demolished in 1914.

Whether Joanna missed her friends or found it hard to cope with the blunt attacks she was receiving (latest rumours suggested that she had borne a child in Leeds by a married man),[57] by early April she had had enough. Although the house had been rented for her till June, she wrote to Carpenter on 10 April: 'I'm ordered to leave Leeds intirely and not to return.'[58]

Meanwhile she had heard again from Jane Townley, the lady in London who had invited her to stay. Full of enthusiasm for Joanna's books, she had sent off copies to her relatives and friends only to find that they did not even bother to acknowledge them. Joanna reassured her that since she had done all that was required she should set her heart at rest and leave her friends and relations to the Lord.[59]

It is not clear how much Joanna knew about Townley before they met. If she had mentioned her name to friends in the north they might well have explained that, as a daughter of the late Colonel Richard Townley of Belfield Hall, near Rochdale, she was rich and very well-connected. She was, in fact, the kind of supporter Joanna needed; someone worth encouraging.

In a letter to William Sharp on 27 March 1804 Joanna praised Jane Townley for having built her faith 'on the Rock that cannot fall because she hath built her faith on the truth of the words that are delivered by me . . . and so with steady prudence she will reach her happy shore.'[60] These reassuring words, if passed on to the wealthy spinster, would leave her all the more eager to welcome Joanna to her home.

When Joanna arrived back in London she must have felt relieved, if not abashed, to find the city in much the same state as she had left it, the streets – as yet! – not filled with dead bodies. She went to stay with William Sharp and his wife Ann in Titchfield Street, and it was there that she received a visit from Miss Townley on Friday, 20 April.[61] They immediately recognised each other as kindred souls and formed a partnership which transformed Joanna's mission.

SISTER, BRIDE AND MOTHER, 1804

Thou art thy mother's daughter that loatheth her husband and
her children; and thou art the sister of thy sisters which loatheth
their husbands and their children.   *Ezekiel* 16:45

At one o'clock in the morning of 3 May 1804 William Coy, one of the
jury at Joanna's 'trial' at High House, 'broke a blood vessel in coughing
and died cover'd with blood.' His death once more called into question
the efficacy of Joanna's seals, because one who had signed 'for the
destruction of Satan' was supposed to have gained eternal life in the
flesh as well as the spirit. The Spirit reassured them: the friends

> must not put their hearts so strong upon this world, to judge all
> happiness is in living in this world. . . . [T]rue happiness lieth
> . . . in the mind and heart being resigned to the will of God . . .
> and let them copy after Coy: be faithful unto death, and I will
> give them Crowns of Life.

Coy's funeral was arranged by his son-in-law, John Hows, a visitor
at Joanna's 'trial' who, having come as a hostile critic, had by the end
of the day been won over. Hows arranged for Coy to be buried at Bunhill
Fields on Thursday, 10 May, but on the morning before the funeral
Joanna heard that many friends were afraid to attend because Mrs
Carpenter had had a dream warning them of danger. The question was,
should Joanna risk going herself? Her Spirit put her mind at rest: 'Let
no one's fear alarm thee, thou shalt go and I will be with thee, and
nothing shall harm thee.'[1]

Before setting out, she took off all her rings except one which Mr
Abbott had given her. Then, accompanied by Townley, Sharp and Wilson,
she made her way to Coy's house, 95 Moorfields, and joined the
procession. As they approached the burial ground, a great wind got up
and, according to Mr Field, 'almost blew the cloaths over the ladies
heads so that it was with difficulty they could prevent themselves from
being exposed.'

There suddenly came a blast of cannon. Joanna, battling with her
skirts and emotions, was shocked rigid. Her legs began to tremble. Was
Mrs Carpenter's dream about to come true? Had the Day of Judgment
begun? Mr Hows put her mind at rest. The firing, which continued

throughout the service, came from over the wall between the cemetery and the Artillery Ground attached to the barracks.

After the interment the friends left in a stately procession only to find themselves caught up in a crowd chasing pigs and then had to hurry back to the house to avoid a violent rain storm.[2] It was only afterwards that Joanna realised that Mr Abbott had been absent from the proceedings and that was why she had been told to wear his ring that morning – the ring had stood for Abbott at Coy's funeral.

The following day Joanna and Jane Townley left London by coach for Inglesham to stay as guests of the Reverend Stanhope Bruce. They whiled away the hours of the journey by reading the manuscript of Joanna's latest book, which was then at the printers, and reached the very same point at which they had been interrupted previously when they found themselves interrupted again by a stop to change horses. Amazed at this coincidence, Joanna and Townley entered the Inn and found it crowded for a meeting of the Justices.

On their first Sunday in Inglesham Jane Townley woke up at three o'clock in the morning to hear a cock crowing seven times. After repeating this to Joanna, she was told that this signified that Townley must be her witness – just as Peter bore witness to Christ.[3]

Overwhelmed by this glimpse of her destiny – or perhaps simply tired after a disturbed night – Townley stayed in her room that afternoon and thus missed hearing Joanna speak to the forty or so people who declared themselves 'very much pleased and gratified' by the experience. Whatever the reason for her staying away, Townley's absence was the subject of a Communication given to Joanna the following morning:

> Now I tell thee why I ordered Townley to be alone, as a shadow
> of thee; for the time is at hand when thou shalt be shut up, as
> she was shut up, and SHE MUST APPEAR IN THY STEAD;
> then will men hear with as much silence as they heard thee on
> the day that is past and say of her, as Bruce said of thee, 'She
> hath spoken wisely and to the purpose'.[4]

From this moment on, any doubts Townley had disappeared. Nothing was too much for her – or her maid – to do if it helped their 'dear Joanna'. After all, they knew their labours would not be needed for long, for Joanna's followers were frequently told that her life had been set to run no more than fifteen years from 1792. Moreover, Joanna constantly repeated that her time was short – a fact that must have been easy to believe in 1804 when she was clearly approaching some kind of spiritual (or emotional) crisis.

After Inglesham, Joanna and Townley were commanded to go on to Bristol to publicise Joanna's mission in that part of the world. Joanna's mounting tension was expressed on 14 May in a command from her Spirit to let Townley take over all her public activities when they arrived in the city, while she herself lived incognita and used her mother's maiden name for letters.[5] Townley was also to send for Ann Underwood, her servant who had been left behind in London, to join them in Bristol for 'ends afterwards to be made known'.[6] She agreed without demur. With little idea what was going to happen, Townley must have been swept along by the sense that her life was suddenly primed with significance – and very exciting.

Even the elements heightened the drama as they approached Bristol at seven o'clock on the evening of 16 May. Thunder cracked the skies, reminding Joanna of her journey to the city from Exeter in 1798 when she met her new sister-in-law and found her pregnant. She had been so disappointed when Sarah Southcott had given birth to a daughter. Now, six years later, Sarah had given birth to a son who was unlikely to live,[7] and Joanna's circumstances had changed in that she was returning to Bristol, not as a poor relation, but with a rich patron.

Sending Mrs Taylor the latest news on 21 May, Townley said she had written to Joseph Southcott asking if he had any vacant apartments in his house, 9 Trinity Street, and he had. On Wednesday they had arrived to find Joseph's five-week old son dying of convulsions. Townley and Underwood sat up with the infant all Thursday night, watching over him until he died peacefully on Friday afternoon at five o'clock.

What is clear from her letter is how Jane Townley had completely integrated herself with Joanna's circle of friends. She had never met Mrs Taylor and had known Joanna for less than a month, yet here she was writing as if she had known them for years. She said, referring to Charles Taylor, who quickly became a favourite of hers,

> I saw your son the night before I left Town and his health was better. [I]t is very flattering to me to hear that he laments my absence very much but I hope we are not parted for long, and I shall have great pleasure in being acquainted with you and all the rest of your family.

What is not clear is the whereabouts of Joanna:

> If you have anything particular and private to say to Joanna you must send it to the Reverend Stanhope Bruce's, Inglesham, near Lechlade – but if you have anything of a public nature I shall be obliged to you to send it to me and I will forward it to her, as Mr Bruce desired her to stay with him till her Trial is over.[8]

From this it would seem that Joanna had stayed behind at Inglesham, but other evidence suggests that Townley's words were no more than a smokescreen to protect Joanna's privacy. Indeed for the next few months there are countless references to Joanna's secret lodgings, some times hinting that she is living at some distance from Trinity Street, or possibly outside the city. It is likely that she was, at least part of the time, secretly occupying an upper chamber in her brother's large house in Trinity Street.

The reason she invented this elaborate charade was partly histrionic, partly because she sensed she was about to undergo some tremendous ordeal and did not want her frailties to be exposed. 'My Visitation there [in Bristol] was stronger than I ever experienced before or since,' she later wrote,[9] and the effects of her 'visitation' proved as devastating as a nervous breakdown. Yet from the lofty heights of her spiritual experience, the tragedy in her brother's family could be viewed philosophically – her tiny nephew identified as a 'type' of the nation, his sufferings a 'shadow' of what would happen to all.

In a Communication on 17 May 1804, Joanna was told:

> The year is come that I told thee thy Trial will come on. [Joseph]
> hath a son that appears dying in convulsion fits
>> So let thy Brother not complain
>> Because the Child must suffer pain
>> That for a time he doth endure
>> But soon his sufferings will be o'er
>> It's but a shadow of your land
>> How in convulsions all will stand
>> As I from Types and Shadows go
>> For Foley's daughter thou dost know
>> I placed a shadow then of thee
>> How thy convulsions they would see
>> And then they all would see the star
>> That is of Glory to appear
>> Because that child bore then thy name
>> And now behold thy brother's son
>> He bears the name of John before
>> And now the shadows you see clear
>> For in convulsions 'twill come on.[10]

The child's death was but another sign that Joanna's trial was upon her. Since the hurricanes of January there had been a host of signs and wonders: a dreadful thunderstorm hit Manchester on 8 May, two earthquakes shook Scotland in March and another hit Malta in May. But none of these matched the tremor felt by Joanna when Napoleon Bonaparte, the Adversary incarnate, declared himself Emperor of the French on 20 May.[11] She knew this desperate event must call forth some desperate remedy.

On 21 May the Spirit sent Joanna a 'wonderful Communication' which she immediately passed on to Townley:

> I have brought thee hither with these two (Jane Townley and her maid), whom I call my Mother and my Sister; for I said they that did My will, the same were My mother and My sister; and by them My will is done.
>
> Now I shall give directions to thee, and tell thee what is meant by My mother and My sister. As a mother wishes to support the honour of her son, and the happiness of a son, so does she wish to spend her time and money like a mother, for My honour and glory, and for the good of My brethren; and as a sister that loveth her brother joins with her mother, just so is her servant now joined with her mistress; here is the shadow of My Bible fulfilled. . . .
>
> Here I have placed you three, as true helpmates for man; and as such let men receive you, if they wish to be made alive in ME, as they died in Adam . . . by the hands of you three my wondrous working shall go on, till your light shall break forth as the morning, and the truth be made clear as the noonday's sun, that the woman is the true and perfect helpmate for man; for by the woman I will now complete his happiness, but no other way will I ever accomplish it.[12]

Convinced of her own high calling, Townley wrote a letter to the Bishop of London, Beilby Porteous, a personal friend,[13] trying to convey the awesome significance of little John Southcott's death.

> My Lord,
>
> . . . Myself and maid being strong believers, the Lord through Joanna Southcott ordered us to come to her brother's in Bristol on 16 of this month for ends we should know hereafter. On my arrival I found Mrs Southcott had an infant son (who was born 9 April and called John) to all appearance dying in convulsions. They told me the child was suddenly seized with convulsion fits a little before one o'clock on Tuesday morning and continued to have fits till three-thirty on Friday afternoon, when it laid in peace till after the clock struck five when it expired in sleep.
>
> I sent these particulars to Joanna and she immediately returned an answer, which is copied for your Lordship's perusal and I think, after reading it, your Lordship must be convinced fatal would be my end if I concealed its contents from the world, and trusting the Lord will protect me if I am obedient, I fear no man nor any ridicule I may meet with from the world.
>
> I am your Lordship's humble servant
>
>   Jane Townley.[14]

The burden of Joanna's accompanying letter was that she had been urged to bring Townley down from London in order to witness the death of her brother's innocent child because his suffering was a type for mankind. And although unbelievers would deny that there was anything unusual in his death, she wished to point out that what made it uncommon was that she had been told in 1798 that her brother would have a son when her prophecies were about to be fulfilled. Everything, she stressed, was now falling into place:

> [A]s the clouds gathered in and the heavens were filled with clouds after the child's death, so the clouds will follow the nation. . . .
>
> Now you will see how the death of my brother's son is perfect like the Warning given me at midnight, with the Rolling Stone three stairs down at Christmas – oh! how doth the Lord condescend to give sign upon sign, and warning upon warning, to prove his calling clear to man – and yet they are blind and will not see. But we must be clear from the blood of all men, and I am ordered to write to you, for you to warn the Bishops and Clergy, of the fatal Judgments pronounced on them, if they are now careless and do not search into every truth, to warn their flock of approaching danger.

These letters were ready for posting on 22 May, the day of the baby's funeral. Joanna did not attend so did not see the violent fit of trembling that came over poor Townley as she entered the churchyard with Underwood. Afterwards Townley's nerves, already frazzled, snapped when her letters were returned, having missed that day's post. She and Underwood hurled recriminations at each other and peace was only restored after Joanna's Spirit explained that the Bishop's letter would have been sent on the same day as the funeral had this not been brought forward a day after a nurse judged the little body would not keep.

The lesson was clear. Joanna's trial would come on sooner than she thought, because men would fear the putrefaction in her.

Hearing this, Townley and Underwood immediately had three thousand copies of Joanna's letter printed and circulated among the bishops and clergy.[15] Although the Bishop of Peterborough, Dr Parsons, was the only bishop who bishops deigned to send a polite reply, the two women refused to be discouraged. During the next six months they slaved away, twice being ordered to get up at two or three in the morning to send warnings by express post. Told always to take note of the weather, they noticed that each occasion was marked by a sudden storm of wind and rain. It all seemed to signify.[16]

What was important to Joanna was that Townley was settling nicely into her role as set out in *On the Prayers for the Fast Day*, published that month:

> Townley hath wisely discerned to weigh the past with the present . . . therefore I HAVE CHOSEN HER TO WARN THE SHEPHERDS, and if they take not the warning, they shall find the floods to come upon them.

Joanna could not have found a better partner than Jane Townley – someone of rank, wealth, undoubted moral virtue and unquestioning faith in Joanna. Townley later wrote,

> I neither flattered nor exalted Joanna. . . . As she was placed the standard, and knowing this to be a spiritual warfare, I obeyed her in all things, as anyone must have obeyed the Duke of Wellington, who was an officer in his army, without taking in question the duty assigned to him.[17]

Having appointed the perfect adjutant, the superior officer now withdrew herself behind the lines and lived as a recluse:

> Here my dear Miss Townley, you see what a strict charge is given to you, not to discover my abode: neither must you let my friends in London know what place you have taken for me, or where my abode is. I am very comfortable and hope to have the happiness of seeing you soon. I am sure of the pleasure of seeing Underwood every day to bring me all the news and to receive the directions. I have another communication to write to you tomorrow; but you know I must have my secretary. The Lord bless you, and strengthen you to stand the fiery trial with men. The people in this house are very quiet and civil. Accept my kind love, and am yours sincerely in heart and mind
>
> Joanna Southcott.[18]

Whether these 'very quiet and civil' people referred to Joseph, Sarah and their daughter Susan, or whether Joanna was staying somewhere else in Bristol is unclear. What is clear is that, renewing contact with her brother in 1804, she met a warmer reception than before. Since she had last seen him, Joseph had suffered several hard knocks – the post at the Customs House did not last long and he had fallen back on his old trade of umbrella-making to support his family.[19] It also appears that of several children born to Sarah, only Susan survived childhood. Amid such gloom Joseph seemed delighted to greet his sister again, especially when she turned up in such grand company.

Circumstances clearly made the woman. Joseph now accepted Joanna as a true prophetess and was happy to bear testimony to the virtues of her early life.

Joanna welcomed his support, especially at a time when she was planning another assault on Pomeroy. But there were many others who refused to take her seriously. In Leeds, for instance, she had received a sarcastic letter from an anonymous man in London who wrote:

Dear Madam,

. . . a gentleman and myself would gladly become converts to your doctrine if you can convince us by some extraordinary proof of your mission from God to us, by answering this letter without the gentleman or myself giving you any directions of our names or places of abode. A letter to either of us will be received with thanks. Speedy answer will be esteemed a favour.

Such a challenge could not be ignored. Joanna's Spirit tartly replied: 'these men, whose hearts are not mine, must go to their masters for their names. . . . My answer is, I know them not.'[20]

Well pleased with this response, Joanna asked Townley to have the correspondence printed.

After this she suffered a string of insults. At the end of May Townley sent her a newspaper advertisement requesting the Religious Society for the Suppression of Vice to examine Joanna Southcott's books, and there came word that some men at Stourbridge were printing a book against her writings.[21] A clergyman named Booth was turned out of his living for believing in Joanna's Visitation[22] and, when William Sharp sent a print of Christ and another of the Blessed Holy Virgin to a bishop, they were returned with the rebuke that his Lordship wished Sharp's religious sense was as fine as his engraving. Nor did Jane Townley enjoy any greater success when she wrote to the bishops on Joanna's behalf.

Although Joanna was furious at these rebuffs, her letter to Jane Townley on 2 June contained a whiff of satisfaction at the thought that not even social rank had ensured a kinder reception:

Knowing I was so much their inferior in rank and fortune I bowed in submission with a broken heart to their silent contempt: but now I find that you a lady of family and fortune not inferior to them, and Mr Sharp an artist of no low profession and well known in the world, to be treated with this contempt hath raised my spirits with indignation – so I shall thank you, or Mr Sharp, to write to the bishop in my name, or your own, what is the duty of a bishop, if he judge the calling not of God. To try and prove it by his arguments, and showing his strong reasons, is the command of the Lord unto man. I must conclude with saying, I wish the bishop was as good a judge of his duty as a bishop, as Mr Sharp is of his engraving as an artist.[23]

Joanna might well consider Mr Sharp an excellent *engraver*, but as an *editor*, or more precisely *her* editor, he left much to be desired. When first copies of *On the Prayers for the Fast Day* arrived from London, she found that Sharp had seen fit to alter one or two Letters before the book went through the press. In other words, he had used his human intelligence to interfere in something dictated by her Spirit! She was outraged.

> There is no pen can paint, nor heart conceive, the horror and misery I have felt, ever since the book, that is now printing in London, has come to my view; when I saw it was placed wrong it went as a dagger to my heart . . . the horror of the Devil was upon me, I felt I could not bear my existence.[24]

Poor Ann Underwood described how she bore the brunt of Joanna's fury:

> She begged me to leave her to herself, and to take with me all the knives and everything she could hurt herself with. . . . Oh! what a day! and how the house has shook.

She tried to divert Joanna's attention by showing her a letter from Mrs Foley saying her husband was very ill. In her reply Joanna omitted the usual commiserations in favour of reasons why she rejoiced at the news – after all, the illness was from God, was it not? And if not, then it was better that Foley, and she herself for that matter, should die.

That point being settled, Joanna returned to the fray. On Wednesday, 13 June, Townley wrote to Sharp that she had that morning been to see 'our dear Joanna' for directions about the book in which the Letters had been placed wrongly. 'It has been a day indeed,' she sighed, 'a day of everlasting remembrance to me.' She described how she and Underwood had joined Joanna in swearing on the Bible that in future they would follow no directions but the Lord's 'for we are determined to be taught of God and not of man'. After this, Joanna had asked Townley and Underwood to leave her and return to their own lodgings, which they did.[25]

Joanna was left to consider her situation. She had come a long way from the days when she worked on farms or cooked and did housework for tradesmen in Exeter. Here she was, in a cosy retreat with two women, one a lady of rank, to wait on her and see that all her daily needs were met. Such a change in her position must have given her pause for thought, just as it provoked questions from other people who were anxious to know more about her origins and early history. Surely there had been something special about her birth and upbringing, something worth recording for posterity? It was unfortunate that her script, despite costing her so much effort, was almost illegible and everything she wrote had to be copied before it could be read. There had to be an easier way to put her message across.

Sunday, 17 June, started strangely. Joanna came downstairs dressed all in white, and seeing Ann Underwood look puzzled, explained that she had tried on two coloured gowns before being told by the Spirit that she must wear white for the next three days. After this announcement, Joanna withdrew to her secret room upstairs and started to write until she was overcome by a fit of trembling. She was then ordered to put down her pen and never take it up again except for signing seals.[26]

Not that this meant there would be no more writing; it simply meant that someone else would have to do it for her. So it was decided that Ann Underwood, as one of the few able to read Joanna's handwriting, would in future act as her amanuensis, and they set about devising a method of working that would answer those people who accused Joanna of copying from books or being helped by men. Every day Underwood wrote as Joanna spoke, then sent everything she had written to Townley, who kept these originals, while sending off copies to Sharp, Foley and others.[27]

But that first Sunday, soon after starting to dictate a letter to Foley, Joanna grew very agitated and could not go on. Her mood verged on paranoia as she told Underwood to stop what she was doing, take her keys, lock up all her papers and deliver them to her brother, making sure that they were packed up and signed and sealed by him, Townley and herself.

Underwood immediately obeyed.

Once these things were done, Joanna carried on dictating, and remained quite calm until the Spirit ordered her to recount the history of her lovers and her father. She did, but as the sessions progressed she grew more and more agitated, especially when mentioning anything to do with her father.

By suppertime she seemed to have regained her spirits but when she went to bed, no matter how she struggled, she could not remove her gown. Underwood, trying to help, found Joanna's arms red with trying to tug it off.[28] It was a lesson they both had to learn. Henceforth, said the Spirit, Joanna should dress herself but have help in undressing.

At eleven o'clock that night, Underwood heard a thumping noise from Joanna's room. She rushed upstairs and listened outside her door. Joanna was wailing about the miserable state mankind was in through the arts of the Devil. Underwood stayed there and listened until Joanna subsided.

Next morning Joanna asked both Townley and Underwood to come and copy something down about her father. Taking it in turns, the two women wrote for hours. But the more Joanna said, the more upset she became, pacing up and down the room until she collapsed in hysteria. Townley had to support her in a chair while Underwood fetched pillows to put on her lap to stop her beating herself black and blue. Still her fury seemed to lend her strength as she stamped the floor until she made the house shake – all this time continuing to expatiate on her father and lovers and the Bible.

Eventually drawing to a close, she announced she would lie down on her bed while Townley and Underwood went away to finish her letters for the post. They had not been downstairs more than ten minutes before more noise brought them rushing up again to find Joanna flat on her back on the floor. Here she lay for an hour, despite all Underwood's pleas for her to lie on a mattress.

'Our Saviour was on the ground,' Joanna declared, 'and so must I [be]. Remember this is the sixth day. My labour must be done.'

No sooner had she stopped writhing on the floor when she announced that she was sick to death and started to vomit. Underwood ran downstairs for warm water; this Joanna refused. Underwood offered her some wine; this she accepted and drank, saying that it was now time for the vats to run over with new wine.

'Poor soul,' remarked the patient Underwood, 'to see how she has bruised herself with the thumping on the floor.'

Nor were her ministrations complete. Joanna now asked her friends to wash her feet and put her on clean linen; all of which they did. She then wanted to go on with her history but was too ill, so Townley and Underwood brought in a bed and made it up on the floor. Whereupon Joanna insisted that she would sleep there while they took her bed.

Not surprisingly after all this, Joanna passed a fitful night, tormented by dark dreams. In one she dreamt she was going to some place with little Richard Foley, now nearly three years old, but she left him behind in a field where she could hear him calling after her like a mad child, 'My Janny, my Janny!'

The following morning she felt weak and was off her food, eating only a small piece of tart and imbibing nothing but camomile tea, a drink she cordially disliked. Although she kept to her bed, she somehow found the strength to carry on talking about her life, labouring over every detail of her affair with Noah Bishop.

Then on Thursday night, just as things were settling down, came word from Exeter that a letter sent by Robert Portbury to Pomeroy on Joanna's behalf had been returned without comment.[29] Nothing could have been designed to send Joanna into further frenzy. At midnight she was so moved by the Spirit of the Lord that she banged her hands about hard enough to knock one of the blue stones from the gold ring that Mr Abbott had given her.[30] Very upset, she fell into a sleep haunted by confused dreams about marrying her brother-in-law Paige and being told to kill her nephew.[31]

On Saturday morning she woke with the distinct impression that she heard someone calling, 'Tom!' Underwood said no one had, and Joanna was mystified until later that day a letter came from Foley – *Thomas* Foley. He mentioned how Mr and Mrs Hirst had recently come from Leeds to take their sick daughter to Mrs Hughes in Kingsland, after he had recommended her as a healer. They had been terribly disappointed, however, and thought the woman was an abominable impostor.

News that Mrs Hughes, a potential rival, had been found wanting cheered Joanna up and new Communications came through so fast and furiously that the room shook and Townley and Underwood had to clear things off the dresser. In a state of utter amazement Townley lay down and listened to all Joanna said, while Underwood stood spellbound, gazing at her from the foot of the bed. Joanna declared,

> All of a sudden, the Spirit entered me with such power and fury, that my senses seemed lost; I felt as though I had power to shake the house down, and yet I felt as though I could walk in air, but did not remember any words I said.

Next morning she woke in similar high spirits, ready to continue her story, thrilling the women with stories of her grandmother's maids being murdered after they had ignored warning dreams and how it paid to take heed of such signs, even if obscure. Like Joanna's garters, for instance. When, towards the end of the day, Joanna casually placed her garters across a fan she was reminded of some words of Mr Wolland about throwing villains either side of the gallows. Horrified, she immediately grabbed them back and flung them on the floor. Refusing to touch the wretched garters again, she got Underwood to pick them up and throw them on the fire.[32]

Townley had by now taken to sleeping with Joanna, only returning to her own lodgings at odd times during the day. She must have missed much sleep, for on Monday night Joanna got up soon after ten o'clock and started pacing the floor. When Underwood came up to see why she was upset, Joanna explained that she was not upset but filled with joy. Up and down, up and down she paced, waving a fan which was sometimes open, sometimes shut, inveighing against the Devil and making so much noise that the master of the house said he could hear it from the street. When asked why she was still in her bed-clothes, Joanna said she had been told not to get up again until she heard the Lord call her name.[33]

The women could not go on much longer like this. Townley, whose health had never been robust, was losing too much sleep and there was a limit to how much even the patient Underwood could manage. They clearly needed more help. But, who? It was not as simple as hiring another servant. It had to be someone specially designated by the Spirit.

On 22 June Townley wrote to Mrs Taylor explaining that from now on everything that Joanna communicated had to go into print. Moreover,

> as all her words must be penned by two women, and my health not permitting me to sit from morning till night, and by writing so much am prevented giving Information to any one that may call, the Lord has permitted me to have an assistant, and Miss Frances Taylor were proposed to me, which I was very happy to accept, and now I hope you will do me the favour to let Miss Fanny come as soon as possible . . . for me the sooner the better, but I do not mean to keep Miss Fanny to writing all the day long, as Underwood and I am obliged to, but I find the task is too hard for one – and I shall thank you for Miss Fanny's assistance as there is no man permitted to come into Joanna's room, nor no woman but they who are appointed to assist in labour for she is ordered to be shut up intirely from the world. . . .

There is no escaping the tone of desperation. In case Fanny had doubts about travelling on her own, Townley arranged for Mr Southcott to meet her at the inn if he knew what time to expect her, but if she arrived in Bristol unannounced she should ask the ostler to get a coach to drive her to 9 Trinity Street. Townley wrote,

> Joanna says she longs to see her as we visit Joanna every day and are compelled to abide in her lodgings though we have not give up our own, we are bound not to tell where her lodgings is (you must conceal where Miss Fanny's gone lest Joanna's friends want to come and see her).

After stressing the urgency of the situation: 'I was so ill yesterday that I feared I should have fainted with the pen in my hands. . .' Townley added a postscript saying that Joanna felt nothing but pity for Pomeroy:

> We received your letters and they throw'd Joanna into the greatest agonies for Pomeroy to think the Devil has such Power over him, but call'd to her remembrance the letter that was sent to him –
>
>> A Judas he shall be to me
>> If he do me deny
>> No comfort in this world he'll have
>> And tremble for to die.[34]

On Sunday morning, 1 July, Joanna dictated a letter to Foley complaining about the trouble she was having with John Symons in Exeter, who owed her money for books. As Underwood wrote, Joanna grew so agitated that she became quite faint and 'squammy'. The cause

of her weakness was partly the Symons's situation and partly the fact
that she was not eating properly. She had eaten no breakfast for a
fortnight, Underwood told Foley, and been unable

> to put a bit of bread in her mouth, cake or bun, for more than a
> week. She drinks a cup of tea in the morning, which makes her
> faint, she desired me just before eleven to give her a tumbler of
> beer, which I did, she drink'd part of the beer, and held the
> rummer in her hand, leaning it upon her knee with one hand, and
> flicking her thumb against the rummer with the other which she
> did for some time; of which we took notice of the particular
> noise it made, it sounded like the tolling of a Bell, but we said
> nothing.

Having kept up this flicking with her thumbnail for about ten minutes,
Joanna found herself unable to stop and had to keep on flicking the
glass faster and faster, while at the same time telling her friends exactly
what to write to John Symons. This went on for fifty-five minutes;
whereupon she stopped flicking the glass with her thumb and started to
twirl it around in her fingers until every drop of beer had been spilt on
the bed.

At this point, (blessed relief!) the post arrived. Townley and
Underwood fell to reading a letter from William Sharp that required an
immediate answer, while Joanna broke open two letters from Foley.
Starting with the smaller one, she took comfort from what appeared to
be some sort of apology from Mrs Foley for the present coolness
between them. Quick to respond, Joanna announced that she utterly
forgave Mrs Foley as she realised she was as much to blame herself.
Townley and Underwood rejoiced to hear it.

They then read out the longer letter in which Mrs Foley – like sister
Susanna – dared to suggest that Joanna was being led by a wrong spirit.

Misled? Joanna, scarce believing her ears, could only conclude that
the Devil must have drowned Mrs Foley's senses for her to suggest
such a thing! And to fancy, just moments before she had been prepared
to forgive her erstwhile friend!

She went to bed still very agitated and woke next day with the
realisation that she had no right to forgive because Mrs Foley had sinned,
not against her, but against God. In fact, by announcing her forgiveness
she had herself sinned and by way of expiation for 'acting like a Pope'
Joanna proceeded to beat herself for three hours on end. Then she paced
up and down, kicked off her shoes and told someone to take them from
the room when she remembered that she had been ordered to walk only
in new footwear. Eventually persuaded to drink a little port wine, she
promptly brought it all up.[35]

There was nothing to do except wait for her to calm down. Even then, it was unclear how long the peace would last. Her companions realised there was a hurricane brewing, of which this was but a preliminary squall.

On Monday, 2 July, after eating supper and assuring Underwood that she would go to sleep, Joanna was just settling down for the night when Townley came upstairs with a new worry. Her two false teeth had fallen out and poor Townley feared lest their loss (they were probably porcelain ones supplied by Monsieur de Chemant) would alter her voice. Quickly reassuring her, Joanna said she was glad the teeth had gone and she should not put them in again. Townley agreed and went to bed.

Heaven knows, Townley had need of sleep if she was to cope with the next crisis, for that night Joanna experienced what she called 'a Visitation from the Holy Ghost'. It seems she was just composing herself for sleep, hovering in the twilight zone, when she felt the hand of the Lord touch her, just as a woman might feel the hand of her husband.

What happened next is best told by Joanna:

I was surprised with seeing a most beautiful and heavenly figure, that arose from the bed, between Townley and me. He arose, and turned himself backwards towards the feet of the bed, and his head almost reached the tester of the bed; but his face was towards me, which appeared with beauty and majesty, but pale as death. His hair was a flaxen colour, all in disorder around his face. His face was covered with strong perspiration; and his locks were wet like the dew of night, as though they had been taken out of a river. The collar of his shirt appeared unbuttoned, and the skin of his bosom appeared white as the driven snow. Such was the beauty of the heavenly figure, that appeared before me in a disordered state; but the robe he had on was like a surplice, down to his knees. He put out one of his legs to me, that was perfectly like mine, no larger; but with purple spots at the top, as mine are with beating myself, which Townley, Underwood and Taylor are witnesses of. Methought, in my dream, he got himself into that perspiration by being pressed to sleep between Townley and me.

I said to him, 'Are you my dear dying Saviour, that is come to destroy all the works of the Devil?' He answered me, 'Yes!' I thought I called Underwood and waked Townley to look at him, which they did with wonder and amaze. I then thought I would go out of my bed and fall down on my knees before him, to return him thanks for his mercy and goodness: but, as soon as these thoughts entered my head, he disappeared, and a woman appeared in his stead, which gave me pain to see he was gone, but the woman told me many wonderful things, that were coming upon the earth, and what was coming upon the Devil; yet I grieved at the loss of my dear Redeemer, for I saw no beauty in the woman, and, though the woman would reason strong with me, her reasons I did not like. In this confusion I awoke, and heard the bell tolling for the dead, and the drums beating at the same time: which I remarked to Townley.[36]

The sweat, the moist, ruffled, flaxen hair and shirt unbuttoned – the strong young body, like a corn god, rising up in the bed after being pressed between her and Townley are all images suggestive of lost life and lost loves from her past. They are images redolent of sex and sensuality, but in this context (Joanna was aged fifty-four), was it a hymn for lost youth or a paean for spiritual rebirth? Small wonder Joanna woke confused.

Meanwhile, her latest onslaught against Pomeroy was getting under way. On 5 July, 1804, her brother, as one putative gentleman to another, wrote Pomeroy a letter containing a string of indictments.

Reverend Sir,

Conscience and honour as a Christian and a Brother to Joanna Southcott, demands me to take her part: for I may say with David, is there not cause enough, when I see my Sister, in everything she has laid before me, appear clear and innocent. . . .

I understand you took an unfair advantage of what you wheedled her to sign. . . . Now to clear my Sister's injured honour, I must demand all the letters she has sent you; as she tells me you promised her to keep the letters faithfully, that she put in your hands year after year. . . .

As a gentleman of honour, I trust you will act with honour in this; for, as she has no Husband or Father on earth to protect her, therefore it is my duty, as a Brother, to stand in their stead.

He ended by threatening to call in the law if Joanna's letters were not returned.[37]

BREAKDOWN IN BRISTOL

> She was split in two and life gone out of her so she could not
> speak to anyone.
>> *Joanna to Reverend Thomas Foley*, 6 July, 1804

Renewed contact with Pomeroy stirred Joanna's feelings into a whirlpool of disturbed dreams.

She dreamt she stood with a crowd of people in her father's house in Gittisham looking over a gate at the sky; then she was on horseback, naked apart from pocket handkerchiefs tied about her neck and over her lap, and she tried to hold them on as the horse galloped along a lane, through water and towards a gate and open fields. She woke confused to find herself staring at the wall where there was a beautiful little boy, no higher than a new-born babe, smiling and dancing. She noticed a heap of dry peas such as her brothers used in pop-guns and was afraid they would stop the child dancing.

She fell asleep again and this time dreamt that the master of the house had upset his wife by providing a banquet for the crowds coming to see Joanna. Joanna shook hands with the company, who expressed great joy at seeing her, but then wandered off by herself when she saw the mistress so angry.

Eventually she felt herself split in two, and life come out of her like a child which she wrapped in her petticoats and carried along. She said to a woman who was with her, 'I shall lose my pocket handkerchiefs. Do take care of them, for I am parted in two parts and must take care of the child in my lap.'

She returned to the house to tell the mistress she could get rid of the company, for she was split in two and life gone out of her so she could not speak to anyone. The mistress then grew more civil and said, 'Don't keep the child in your lap. Put it upon a bed, and my daughter will shew you where.'

Joanna placed what appeared to be a dead child on the bed, thinking that by being parted, they would both die. But she had not gone twenty yards before hearing the child cry aloud, 'Janny! Janny! Janny!'

Then she cried aloud for joy, 'The child is alive, and life will return in me again.'[1]

It is hard to know what twenty-five year old Fanny Taylor made of such dreams, but she picked her way through Joanna's 'scenes' with an air of common sense and sweet reasonableness. On 12 July she wrote home to ask her parents whether Mr Jones had been to Pomeroy yet, mentioning that Foley and Sharp were both writing books and would put everything concerning him in print if he did not return Joanna's letters.

Joanna had not dressed and had scarcely been out of bed since Fanny arrived. 'Townley and Underwood have been through a great deal,' she wrote, going on to describe Joanna's latest dietary requirements.

> It was fix'd by the Lord what she should eat this Week which is as follows: Green Pease, Cherries and Cream with them if she like, Tea, and Port Wine, and not anything else whatever. She has not eat any bread since I came to Miss Townley. . . . Satan wanted to tempt her to break this command and sent her a longing for French beans – and pork with the pease – but it was of no use – for she said she would sooner go without meat for the whole week than to disobey the Commands of the Lord.

It cannot have been easy for Fanny to enter such a rarefied environment, but Joanna and Townley did their motherly best to look after her:

> Mrs Southcott and Miss Townley make me walk evenings for my health. They are very kind indeed. Miss Townley has given me a very handsome white gown and I have bought myself a small Chip Hat very much like Sisters that she had of Mrs Hull and Mrs Southcott has given me a ribbon for it.

Despite their kindness, Fanny obviously missed home and wanted to know if anything had happened at the Assizes and was there any one staying in their lodgings at the moment: 'I hope you will send me some news as we have none where I am. One would suppose we were in the Deserts of Arabia for we hear nothing about worldly concerns.' Although she had been up to Clifton – 'I think it is a beautiful place' – Fanny accepted that she had come to Bristol to work and quickly set about clearing the backlog of letters that needed copying. Once that had been done, the women saved time by all three sitting together to write 'from Joanna's mouth'.[2]

Fanny's letter included a request from Townley for Mrs Taylor to take an enclosed letter to the Misses Eveleighs, who were to pass it on to Mrs Symons after asking her to come and speak with them, without explaining why – a Machiavellian strategy to circumvent John Symons, who refused to let his mother see any letters sent to the house. And what was in the letter? A full indictment of John Symons's misconduct.

Townley, visiting Joanna on Sunday, 15 July, found her very depressed and calling for some beer.[3] This she was given. But having emptied the glass, Joanna flung it from her, screaming that thus would God smash to smithereens all those who betrayed their faith. The glass flew through the air so fast that Townley, standing by the bed, only realised what was happening when it smashed on the floor.

When Fanny returned from church she was amazed to see the glass in such tiny pieces, so Joanna asked for another – to show her how she did it. Taking hold of the glass without meaning to break it, she suddenly found herself lifting her arm and flinging it exactly as before. Result? Two smashed glasses!

On Monday morning there was a letter from Exeter telling Joanna to expect Mr Jones's reply about Pomeroy that evening. Her every nerve on edge, she immediately felt sick and faint. Unable to stay in bed, she writhed on the floor, groaning that she did not know whether to pity or condemn Pomeroy. Then her rage settled on the clergy, and she got back into bed and asked for a glass of wine. She drank it and immediately fetched up. Next she dashed a basin violently across the room, smashing it to pieces. After that she tried to swallow a mouthful of lamb which had been brought up for her dinner. When she could not, she spat it into another basin and promptly dashed that on the floor.

Suddenly she felt happier – and had a realisation: just as she had broken both basins, so would the Lord in his anger break the clergy. It was as simple as that!

Her equanimity, however, failed to survive Mr Jones's letter when it arrived that evening. Not only would Pomeroy not listen to him, Mr Jones wrote, but he had called Joanna *a liar* and said she was as mad as a March hare![4]

Joanna's fury at hearing this lasted an hour. Not surprisingly, she could not sleep and after a restless night felt sick and unable to eat, retching so violently that she thought she would die. In fact she only regained composure when the Lord explained that sick as she was, He was as sick of the clergy, and He would not remove her sickness until she had promised to publicise their conduct to the world and her brother had written to Pomeroy.

At one o'clock she asked for some wine, was sick again and continued so for the rest of the day. At about eight o'clock she was seized by a violent shivering. Her friends covered her up and sent for some warm mulled wine, while Joanna sat staring at the floor, saying that she was seeing the most beautiful vision she had ever seen – a circle of fire with a rim of gold and candles burning in its midst, whilst a large candle burnt with sparkling light at the door.

After this vision came another shivering fit, then Joanna took a little mulled wine which left her sweating. Lying beside her in bed, Townley scarcely dared move until Joanna announced that she was not asleep but happily communing with the Spirit.[5] At midnight the watchman sprang his rattle under their window and they heard the fire-bell. Underwood got up to see what was happening and from the back window saw the glow of flames from Bushell & McAdam's turpentine factory in Little George Street. Then they heard the alarm-drum beating to summon up the garrison and the Royal Bristol Volunteers who brought the blaze under control.[6]

After Pomeroy's insulting reply, Joseph Southcott wrote again, accusing him of being a disgrace to the cloth for calling Joanna a liar. On Saturday evening at eight o'clock, Joanna received another disturbing letter from Exeter, which she felt all the more because she had just been recounting the episode involving William Wills and all the injustice she had suffered at his hands. What could it mean, she wondered, to be going through the same kind of ordeal again? She had been told that her sufferings were a 'type' for the nation, so there had to be tremendous significance in these events.

And what could be more significant than the Day of Judgment?

On Wednesday, 25 July, Joanna was told that this Day had begun and it was time for the Saints to judge the Earth, to decide between the Devil and Joanna. The following morning she fell asleep and dreamt she was in a most beautiful street where the light sparkled like diamonds; there was a hail storm, and Joanna was lifted and swept along to a hut where she got dirt on her breast and found herself in the lap of a uniformed soldier who clasped her in his arms and held her fast; she could not see his face, but woke up feeling happy and safe.[7]

In a mood of sublime resignation she wrote to Fanny's mother on the last day of July:

Dear Mrs Taylor,

As the hours of my departure draweth near, for I have no idea I shall live long after My Trial, I wish to give my near and dear friends something to keep in remembrance of me, and I have sent a Chambre Muslin, as I know you do not like white gowns. . . . I hope you will be pleas'd with the colour as it was the choice of every on[e] of us, and they look neat for young or old. I thought to have the fellow muslin for Miss Taylor and Miss Lucy of the same kind as Miss Townley have been so kind to give to Miss Fanny, but the shopkeeper had sold them all, but expect more in a few days which I then shall purchase for them.

I have wrote this in a separate letter . . . as I wish no one to know it at present but yourselfs that no envy nor jealousy may arise in the hearts of believers, though they cannot expect me to give presents because they are believers, but you are both believers and friends yet I know it would cause jealousy and give pain if it was made known for I find their is a great deal of jealousy at Exeter, about our friendship, judging I love your Family better than I do any in Exeter, and I should think myself ungrateful if I did not.

The letter (directed to Mr Eastlake) you may read it yourself and put a wafer in it and get Molly Bird to take it. Miss Townley thought it her duty to give a new suit of clothes to each of the Jurymen – and as my Brother was to be call'd forward as a Witness she made him a present the same, and now as Mr Jones will be call'd forward as a Witness he will have a handsome dark broadcloth coat, waistcoat and breeeches, of what he please, but the coat must be blue, and send her the bill and she will send the money by Miss Fanny.

We all unite in kind Christian love to you and family,

Joanna Southcott.[8]

On the same day Fanny was writing to Sarah and Lucy Taylor:

Dear Sisters,

Miss Townley desires your acceptance of these vails and sends her kind love to you both, as old friends of her dear friend Joanna. I think they are very handsom. I have finished one to show you how they are worn in Bristol.

I told you in a former letter that Miss Townley was going to give me a white gowne. I have inclosed the piece of it for you to see as Mrs Southcott is going to give you both one of the same kind to keep for her sake. I have had more made up and it looks very handsom. Indeed I think Mother will like the gown that Mrs Southcott has sent her in this parcel. Miss Townley has one like it. . . .

I think the Bristol air agrees with me as thank God I am very well. I hope you will write me soon. . . . I have received a letter from Charles and have answered it – tells me Mrs Gill is going into Devonshire to see her Daughter and she enquired of him where I was. He told her he believed I was in Birmingham with some friends but he did not know exactly where I was. I suppose by this time she has come down.

Do pray let me know who is married, buried or run away for I hear nothing upon Earth of Exeter. Give my kind love to Miss Rowe and ask her when she is going to break the ice.

Love to Father, Mother, Brother, Mr & Miss Rowe, Susan
Isop Thomas and all enquiring friends

Frances Taylor.

P.S. to prevent envy Joanna desires that the contents of this
letter may not be known.[9]

For weeks Joanna had been lying in bed in obedience to her Spirit's
instructions not to get up until she heard her name called aloud. On
Wednesday, 1 August, the call came.

'Joanna!' – she distinctly heard the name and asked Underwood to
see if there was anyone in her brother's room. It was empty. She asked
her to shout from his room to see if a voice could be heard from there.
It could not. Joanna then realised that she had been called by the same
voice that she had heard so often in the past.

Next morning she woke feeling faint and had to be revived with a
little wine after another disturbing dream. This time she dreamt that she
slipped while scrambling in a hedge and fell into a flooded lane where
she feared she would drown. Then Mr Channon asked her to marry him
but she refused; another man did the same and she refused him too.[10]

Her dreams, mirroring her preoccupation with an earlier life, were
full of allusions to Gittisham, its flooded lanes, her father's farm, and
young men like John Channon who lived in the neighbourhood. Perhaps
their vivid quality owed something to the fact that Joanna had been
fasting for the last seven weeks. However, now that she had heard her
name called she had to go back into the world and prepare herself for a
new 'trial' of her writings being organised by her friends.

In a letter to Mr Hirst in Leeds on 15 August she described a dream in
which she was placing a large cloth full of eggs in a cart but, when she
let the cloth go, some eggs broke as they rolled about. The eggs, she
explained, were the sealed people: the faithful remained whole, others
were irretrievable.

After the dream she had woken up feeling faint and began fretting
about the forthcoming 'trial' until Townley brought her a little port wine
in a tea-cup.

'May I drink deep into the Spirit of Christ!' Joanna murmured as she
supped. Whether or not she noticed that Townley's precious tumblers
were being withheld, she was immediately answered:

'Wilt thou break that tea-cup as thou didst the glasses? Then I will
take thy Trial from thee, for thou wilt break thyself off from me.' This
remark made her very careful indeed not to drop the cup![11]

A week later Joanna woke up depressed because her Spirit seemed to
have deserted her. Whilst never doubting that her visitation had been
from the Lord, she had received no Communications for days and could

not understand His silence. After tearful prayers and meditation, she was ordered to get up, dress, put on her rings, then summon Underwood to come and write.

No sooner had she started a letter to Foley than she realised the reason for the silence. She had not been deserted. The Lord had only hidden His face for a moment in order to show how useless she was without Him. As for William Brown, her Bristol bookseller friend who insisted that he needed no spiritual guidance other than the Bible, he could not interpret the Scriptures properly. In fact, the Spirit said: 'I tell thee this . . . there is not a novel in his shop more false than he makes my Bible.'[12]

Suddenly everything was on the move again and the crisis was past. Joanna was up and about and in touch with her Spirit. It was time to call her champions into battle. Stanhope Bruce, Thomas Foley, Charles Taylor, Elias Carpenter, William Sharp and a new recruit – Colonel William Tooke Harwood – came to Bristol for several days to examine the letters which the clergy had returned to Townley with such contempt.[13]

Colonel Harwood was the owner of large estates in Norfolk who, like Sharp, had been deeply committed to the radical movement for political reform in the 1790s. He was an intimate friend of Horne Tooke, and through him William Godwin and Thomas Holcroft, who had possibly inspired his millenarian beliefs (even if their ideas of utopia were political and social rather than religious). In 1796 Harwood married Holcroft's eldest daughter, Ann. By 1804 he was running into financial problems, but had adopted a braggadocio attitude to money which young Fanny (and doubtless Joanna) found most impressive. 'I think he is equal to any of the gentlemen who came to Exeter,' Fanny wrote enthusiastically to her parents on 26 August. She described how, although a lawsuit demanded his immediate presence in London, he had declared himself prepared to lose £4,000 to stay in Bristol with Joanna and said he would not appear in London if it meant disobeying the Lord's commands. Such dedication was rewarded by his being chosen as a judge in the next 'trial'. Meanwhile, though, since there was no point in throwing away money, Joanna told him to go to London and confound his enemies.

The arrival of such convivial friends proved a temptation to Joseph, who never needed much encouragement to take time off work. 'Mr Southcott says that he never was so happy in any company in his life as these gentlemen,' Fanny wrote. 'He had a very convenient pain in his arm which kept him at home the whole time they were here.' For Joanna's female companions the visitors also provided a welcome break after their stressful confinement with Joanna.

'We have had nothing but crying and laughing this last week. . . .' wrote Fanny. 'The Reverend Mr Bruce is the life of all the company and says no one ever had such a helpmate as his. Mr Wilson, Sharp, Foley are the same good creatures they ever were. Mr Carpenter appears to me a very worthy man. . . . They are all so good I cannot find fault with any of them.'

And, of course, there was her twenty-one year old brother whom she, like every woman, wanted to mother. 'You'd be pleased at the change in Charles . . . he is so much steadier. . . .' Fanny remarked, referring to her brother's nervous stammer. 'We have had some long conversations and I'm happy to see him so improved. I do not think anything could shake his faith in Joanna's writings. . . .' Fanny was right. Nothing would ever shake Charles Taylor's faith in his beloved Joanna. To people who said that her followers were mad he simply replied that he never wished to be cured of such madness.

This was the kind of fervour that impressed another young man who suddenly appeared in Joanna's circle. The Reverend Samuel Eyre, born in Wylye, Wiltshire, in 1776, son of the Reverend John and Susanna Eyre, had recently come to Bristol for his health. Hearing about Joanna's mission, he had written to Mr Foley, who then called on him in Bristol and, as he was not at home, left an invitation to come to tea. Eyre came and, after listening attentively to everything Foley had to say, borrowed some books from Miss Townley to make a study of the matter himself.

And so the week passed with much coming and going. Fanny went with Charles to visit Mr Hare, an old family friend who had a carpet-making business in Bristol. Naturally they mentioned Joanna's writings, and Mr Hare accepted Miss Townley's invitation to come and meet the gentlemen so that he could hear more about them. The matter, however, went no further, because Hare was beset by problems involving a wild son who had suddenly left home to go to the East Indies.

On Friday afternoon, Harwood set out for London to sort out his affairs, and the rest left on Saturday – Bruce for Inglesham, Foley for Oldswinford, Wilson, Carpenter and Taylor for London. Life must have seemed dull after their departure as the women returned to their former preoccupations – Fanny to her sisters' new clothes: 'Our dear Joanna has got the muslin gowns – one of them is perfectly like mine and the other as near as possible, I think equally handsome if not prettier'; Joanna to her dispute with John Symons. The trouble was, the money Symons owed her for books was to have been passed on to Mr Jones and Mr Portbury for them to buy themselves new suits of clothes for her 'trial.' Without it, Joanna was in danger of upsetting these two gentlemen. Fanny told her parents:

> Joanna wants Mr Jones to write when he has been to Mrs
> Symons. She would have sent a £20 bank note in this letter for

you to give Mr Jones the £10 and have paid for a suit of clothes, and the £5 for Mr Portbury but she waits to know what Mrs Symons says because Mr Jones was ordered to try her once more. She [Joanna] hath the £20 bank note by her that will be sent as soon as she has Mr Jones's answer. . . . Joanna says she can not help being sorry for Mrs Symons to have such a son that is always stirring up strife and keeping his mother at variance with her neighbours.

Trying desperately hard to be businesslike, Townley added to Fanny's letter a postscript intended for her father:

Upon second thoughts I shall enclose the £20 note in case Jones should be in any distress for the money. I shall be obliged to you to lend him £10 as from yourself till he has got Mrs Symons's answer and then if Mrs Symons does not pay him, you will be so good as to tell him to keep the money, but if she does, you will be so good as to return it. . . .

'With the rest to pay for Jones's clothes and possibly (if enough) Mr Portbury,' she wrote, adding that she would put her name on the note and take down the numbers – and would like a receipt, please.[14]

With the dispute still unresolved, Joanna and the three women left Bristol in the first week of September to stay with the Foleys at Oldswinford. She knew it was almost forty days since being warned that the Day of Judgment had begun (25 July, 1804). Examining her journal, Townley confirmed this was so. Since nothing fatal had happened, it must have been a dream, Joanna said, but Townley pointed out that something could have happened elsewhere in the world and the news not reached them yet.

Hardly reassured, Joanna woke feeling sick after dreaming of a butcher's shambles all night. Instead of getting up, she asked them to draw the curtains at the foot of her bed and let her go back to sleep.[15]

Next night she dreamt of falling into a kettle of scalding water at Susanna's house after her sister had refused to help her. The meaning was clear. If only Susanna had helped her in the past, Joanna would not have fallen into the clutches of the Symons family, whose tongues were heated like scalding water against her.[16] Townley, disturbing Joanna's sleep as she came up to bed, was surprised to hear her murmur that she could smell roses and carnations in the room.[17]

During the course of another restless night, Joanna fell asleep after four o'clock in the morning and dreamt that little Richard Foley had fallen into some muddy water from which she had difficulty rescuing him. As she carried the boy along in her arms, he seemed almost dead and Joanna felt she was dying herself. She found herself on a cart in the midst of the sea, her only escape a hayloft that had faggots tied to it with ropes on which to swing to a protruding shelf. Risking her life, she sprang to catch hold of the faggots, but, afraid the sticks might break, grabbed the rope instead and was carried safely across. When the faggots broke, just as she had foreseen, she descended from the rope on to dry land, declaring, 'Now I can go down and walk'.

As she woke she heard her name being called aloud, although Townley, who was already up heard nothing.

Her Spirit explained what her dream meant: the faggot she distrusted was Pomeroy, for had she relied on his judgment he and she would have fallen together.[18]

Which reminded her. . . .

On Tuesday, 4 September, Townley penned a letter from Joanna to Mrs Taylor to ask what Pomeroy had said to Jones. She also sent new instructions about Mrs Symons who seems to have threatened to go on the streets to find the necessary money to pay Joanna:

> Please send to Mr Jones and pay him the £10 and tell him that Mrs Symonds [sic] is not to pick up money out of the streets for me, neither is she to pay him money if she oweth me none, but I cannot tell what she has done with my books for she had 2900 when I left Exeter last summer unless she sold them before and did not know it, but there was that no. due to me and the hundred I sent from Stourbridge, 270 from Leeds, which makes 3270. . . . But I do not believe Mrs Symonds will designedly cheat me, so let her act according to her own conscience. . . . (Field says the £10 Mrs Symonds sent me in London was for books that he had sent so Mrs Symonds has never paid me for none she sold at Exeter. . . . I should thank her to send me a fair account. . . . about 1000 unaccounted for!)

And just to remind people in Exeter how desperate the times were, Joanna included Turner's latest news – that the corn all around Stockton and York had got rust and mildew; the storm on Malton Moor had caused £2,000 worth of damage, with hailstones falling the size of chestnuts; bread was dear, and the poor man and his family were suffering so that the rich could profit from large rents.[19]

The letter reflected Joanna's mounting anxiety as she grew desperate to convince people that Judgment Day had begun. After a spate of restless nights, fits of shivering and violent sickness, she awoke one morning feeling, not faint, but furious. How could men deny there were judgments when they only had to look around to see the suffering poor, huge price rises, and all the deprivations of war? Joanna complained,

> I must say they are like one of my brothers, that when he was

doing a thing that he knew would offend his father, we told him his father would beat him, and so he did. But my brother said, though his father had beat him, he did not feel it. My father heard him speak these words and immediately took hold of him and said now you shall feel it, and beat him severely. . . .[20]

Once they were back in Bristol, Townley wrote to Mrs Taylor who had been asking when Fanny would be coming home: 'Joanna says not till three months are up . . . as she is wanted for a witness as well as a writer.'

After living without wheat products for the past twelve weeks Joanna had now given up meat. Her nervy state was not helped when a letter came from Mrs Symons saying that she had paid Mr Jones £10 but not a word about whether she owed Joanna money or not.[21] But her quarrel with the Symons family came to a head when John Symons heard that Joanna had invited his mother, but not him, to go to London as a witness at her 'trial'. Sensing an opportunity to visit the capital and live it up at some one else's expense, he wrote Joanna an insolent letter suggesting terms on which he too would be prepared to testify on her behalf. Joanna replied with a very sharp reprimand.

The following night she groaned so loudly in her sleep that Townley woke her up before seven. She had been dreaming of her father's farm, Joanna said. In one of his fields the corn had been crushed into the earth and Joanna's dead aunt was walking round it. In another pigs were eating up the wheat. Although the third was full of beautiful standing corn, the gates were open and, despite Joanna's attempts to turn him back, her father's white horse rushed in. She caught him by the mane to lead him out, but her strength failed and she fell to the ground. The horse stood very quiet leaning his head over her. When she called her sister to help, she heard Townley's voice asking what was the matter – and she had woken up![22]

For Joanna this dream was not about something as personal as Townley taking over her sister Susanna's role in her life. It was a sign to the nation, and she promptly wrote to warn Pomeroy that there would be famine in the land if he and his brother clergy continued to ignore her mission. At the same time Robert Portbury, one of her supporters in Exeter, gathered together samples of corn, barley and beans eaten out with mildew and rust, and sent them to Archdeacon Moore in an effort to convince him of the truth of Joanna's prophecies.[23]

Joanna found it encouraging to hear that some at least were taking the judgments seriously. She was at her best when dealing with gentle souls like Miss Eddison of Billericay who, having recently received a seal, wrote in some distress to confess that she felt unworthy of the honour. Joanna reassured her that she was only unworthy if she requested the seal as a means of self-preservation and not because she genuinely wanted Christ's Kingdom to be established.

On Thursday morning, 13 September, Joanna and Townley each regaled the other with their dreams.

Townley had dreamt of being in a large room of a country mansion full of people. There came a loud flourish of trumpets and drums, and a gentleman called from upstairs that there was a judgment coming on. Townley wanted to go up and see for herself but could not. Instead, after struggling to a window she saw an oblong of stars and men in the air with guns and smoke. She called others to come and see.

Joanna had dreamt again of Gittisham. She was in her father's orchard among flourishing appletrees with red and white blossom shining in the sunlight. An old man and boy were there, selling cucumbers. Joanna bought one from the man for a penny, but it felt soft and rotten. After she bought a good cucumber from the boy, the old man horse-whipped him for breaking the rule of the market which was: anyone who refused to buy from the first trader, should not be offered goods by a second.

Just as Joanna finished telling this dream a letter arrived from George Turner to say that Mr Senior had been ejected from the Methodist Society for believing in her mission. She immediately saw the significance. The cucumbers in her dream stood for the Methodists and their rotten wisdom! She wrote explaining this to Turner, asking at the same time if he knew of any lawyer who could suggest a way of legally holding Pomeroy to his promise to act as a judge at her 'trial'. Turner replied that if Pomeroy could not return her letters then he should be made to appear in person to say what they contained. Joanna quickly sent this message to Sharp.[24]

By now Joanna had developed her art of dictation. Finding that she could best receive a Communication when her mind was otherwise occupied, she took to cutting scraps of folded paper into patterns of holes, then standing them on a table to form a kind of 'mis-maze' such as she had seen at Lord Rolle's house in Bicton. However, according to Townley, even this simple amusement was turned into an improving exercise:

> When we were writing about Solomon, she had placed a large pincushion in the middle and made a mis-maze all round it. Ann Underwood and I were ordered to take a pencil and work round all her scraps of paper . . . so as to bring them into a straight line in the middle, but thinking we were to bring everyone to the middle we brought them all crooked, which were twenty-four in number. Then Joanna took the pencil and worked round the

outward ones first and when she came to the bottom she brought them up in a straight line to the middle, and the same at the top – and so she worked the table round and brought them into four straight lines, that we brought into twenty-four crooked ones. . . .[25]

While Joanna took things more easily, her followers busied themselves on her behalf. Robert Portbury used a business trip to Cornwall to call twice on Pomeroy's house in Bodmin, but when he tried to argue with him about Joanna's prophecies, the reverend gentleman turned pale and went upstairs.[26] Furious at this harassment, Pomeroy wrote to Stanhope Bruce on 1 October, castigating Joanna's behaviour and repeating that he had none of her papers.[27]

The following day Joanna, pursuing a course of daily readings from the Scriptures, reached the end of Psalms and explained exactly how she differed from David:

I never could feel that anger and indignation against the greatest enemy I had in this world, but always felt in my heart to pray for my enemies, that the Lord would turn them from the evil of their ways.

Could she possibly have had Pomeroy in mind when she delivered this passage to Townley? Presumably not, for he certainly felt the effects of her 'anger and indignation' and his life was made wretched by persecution from her friends. Towards the end of September William Sharp had written to him demanding the letters which Joanna had left with him as a 'sacred deposit'. Pomeroy angrily repeated that he had none of her papers and ventured to criticise her in no uncertain terms.

Joanna heard about his insults one Saturday morning when she was in the middle of a long explanation of Ecclesiastes and Proverbs. No way could she or her Spirit let Pomeroy get away with insulting her when he himself was the villain of the piece! The Spirit stormed:

Now thou has gotten new paper, I shall relieve thee for the present from the Bible, and come to ******* [Pomeroy] – there my anger is kindled by his calling thy writings a farrago of nonsense.

A barrage of letters ensued. Joanna wrote to remind Pomeroy of all the letters he had received from her via her Exeter friends Elizabeth Boucher, Mary Bird, Mrs Taylor and Mrs Symons's children. Then Townley sent an imperious demand that Pomeroy come forward to justify his charges against Joanna's 'upright and just' character, instructing him to send his reply to Inglesham where Joanna was now staying with the Reverend Stanhope Bruce. As all her supporters mobilised against him, Joanna felt sure Pomeroy would see the error of his ways and, if he could not produce her letters, do the next best thing

– add his name to those prepared to vouch for the truth of her prophecies. She declared,

> The wisdom of the Lord is so powerful that he [Pomeroy] can in no way shun his destiny now; neither could I shun mine; neither can the nation shun theirs.

Her conviction was backed up by William Sharp, who sent a further letter to Pomeroy making it clear that Joanna no longer stood alone, that he and all her friends had good names to lose, that by accusing Joanna, he was accusing them all. Foley underlined this threat by sending Pomeroy his personal testimonial. He had known Joanna for nearly three years, living much of that time in the same house, and had never met anyone of a clearer and more sound understanding. A list of her virtues – piety, charity, honesty, honour – then dripped from his pen before he concluded by begging Pomeroy to come with twenty-three others to meet her friends and decide the matter.

At about the same time as receiving this letter, Pomeroy would have opened a vindication of Joanna Southcott sent to him from London containing the signatures of twenty-four men: S. Bruce, T.P. Foley, T. Webster, G. Turner, W. Jowett, W. Harwood, E. Carpenter, J. Wilson, P. Morrison, W.R. Wetherell, W. Sharp, C. Taylor, W. Belk, C. Abbott, J. Torin, T. Stephens, J. Young, J. Morris, R. Law, G. Stocks, E.J. Field, W. Layton Winter, W. Owen, J. Hows. It was a formidable list.[28]

Townley, left with just Underwood to help her, had so much writing to do that she could send Fanny Taylor in Exeter only a few lines about Joanna, whose health was deteriorating as she again grew agitated about Pomeroy. After her three months' fast, she had regained her appetite for five weeks, then suddenly lost it again on 24 October – since when she had eaten but one meal a day and become so weak that she could not stay up more than four or five hours, and even then had to lie down every so often.[29] Nothing, however, was allowed to interrupt the flow of Communications which were sometimes still being penned by her faithful amanuenses well after candle-light.[30]

On 27 October the Spirit assured Joanna that Pomeroy would eventually come round and state the truth. The words failed to soothe her, for that night she dreamt she saw a book on her bed, full of fire with sparks flying out so fast she was afraid they would burn the bedclothes. She woke up feeling desperately ill and unable to get Pomeroy out of her mind.[31]

In mid-November Townley wrote to Mrs Taylor telling her that all Joanna's friends were asked to leave home on Monday, 26 November, to go to London for her 'trial' concerning Pomeroy. Among her Exeter friends being summoned were Mary Bird, Mrs Taylor and Fanny, and

Mr Jones. Realising that some might find it difficult to drop everything and come, Townley wished to assure them that all their expenses would be met, including what it might cost Mary Bird to provide a friend to stay with her invalid sister, Patty, in her absence. On the other hand, if Mary Bird found it impossible to leave her sister, she should write down everything she could remember about Pomeroy and give it to Mrs Taylor before witnesses.

In a separate note to Fanny, Townley reminded her to bring her 'blanch'd' gown, and make sure that someone like her brother Robert, whose handwriting would not be known, addressed the enclosed letter to Pomeroy and put it immediately in the Exeter post office.

Townley then confided a more personal worry to her young friend. Her family had obviously heard about her connection with Joanna and, after sending in a spy to discover the true situation, were now trying to wean her away from what they considered a dangerous influence.

> About a fortnight ago a man came to ask a great many impertinent questions and wanted all the Books but after staying near two hours went away without buying one. After he had been gone about 1° hours came one of my sisters and a sister of Sir Charles Cottens to take me to Bath, and I was obliged to be very warm and resolute to get rid of them for they would not take a civil refusal. They told me more friends were coming from Bath, but I fancy the reception I gave them has deterred the others.

It was a nerve-racking time for Townley – warding off the enemy within her own family whilst rallying Joanna's troops to make sure they duly appeared in London. She was exasperated when even loyal Mrs Taylor hesitated to make the trip because she did not want Jane Townley to be burdened with the expense. Townley replied,

> Expense has nothing to do with it, as an unknown gentleman has thrown into the treasury enough for to provide a House in London and bear the expense so you are not to fear that all shall come from me. . . .

Mary Bird was a different category. Instead of pressure being put on her, words were put in her mouth. Joanna declared,

> I do not wish her to run the hazard of leaving her Sister, but wish her to recollect if she can the words Mr Pomeroy said to her when he came to her House, the first time he spoke to me.

And just in case this should prove difficult, Joanna prompted:

> When I told him that Mr Leach said it was from the Devil, his answer was their is not a word that I have heard liken to come from the Devil, beg her to recollect the end of '97 when she went with me to Mr Pomeroy to read the Writing I had put in his

hands, how he first disputed (I might read anything) as he could not read it himself, till he threw me in a passion, and I said he must judge me to be worse than the Witch of Endor, if he judg'd I would put Writings in his hands to deceive him, how he immediately appealed to her . . . that he had always said he believed me to be a Religious Good Woman . . . ask if she can recollect afterwards that I was ordered to send for the writings . . . of the events of 1797 and that Mr Pomeroy was to write upon every leaf and send them to me to be copied off. . . .

So she went on, supplying in minute detail all that Mary Bird was to send in her written affidavit for the 'trial'. Her evidence was to be witnessed by the Misses Eveleigh, and, just in case writing it down proved an obstacle, she would be amply compensated for any time lost from work.

Similar promptings were sent to Mr Jones, who was urged to recollect that four years ago, when discussing Joanna's foreknowledge of the bad harvest, Pomeroy had said she was a shrewd woman whom he had tested every way and that he had been surprised at her answers.

Joanna, Townley and Underwood left Bristol for London on 22 November. The day before leaving, Joanna had received a humble letter from John Symons asking if he could still appear as a witness on her behalf. This time there was nothing offensive in his tone – not even overt mention of expenses – so it was agreed he could come. In London William Sharp had already found them lodgings about six doors down from his own house in Titchfield Street. To avoid any unpleasant accusations from Townley's family that Joanna was living off Jane's money, it had been taken in Joanna's name and her friends were asked to direct all letters not to Townley but to Mr Sharp at 50 Titchfield Street.

The lodgings were above a grocery business owned by Mr Scales, and writing last instructions to Mrs Taylor and Fanny, Townley told them:

You will see the shop and we shall be looking out for you . . . and we hope you will have as pleasant a journey as the time will permit and we shall be glad to see you and you must not disappoint us. God bless you all.[32]

'JOSEPH OR ME!', December 1804-1805

He must rely wholly upon one or the other, Joseph or me.
The Controversy between Joanna Southcott
& Elias Carpenter, 1805

Joanna's last 'trial' had taken place before an assembly of her own faithful followers. Hopes for a more distinguished jury in her third 'trial' were disappointed when the bishops and Pomeroy refused to appear and she had to settle for lesser mortals. Even some of these were less than forthcoming. The Reverend Edward Robson, Curate of Whitechapel, for instance, rejected Foley's invitation in no uncertain terms, telling him he was no Christian and should 'go home and get some water gruel'. Eventually some fifty men were assembled, including Stanhope Bruce, Webster, Foley and Eyre – all clergymen; and William Sharp, George Turner, Elias Carpenter, Peter Morrison, and William Tooke Harwood; also William Jowett and John Scott, a lawyer; and Jedediah Holland, Abel Peplow Sharp, and the three-year old Richard Foley. Also present were a number of dissenters, including a Mr Fischer with his Moravian Brethren,[1] Baptists, Wesleyans, Whitefieldites, and one Quakeress, and one American Indian.

Arrangements were elaborate. The 'trial' was to be held at Neckinger House, Bermondsey – the home of Elias Carpenter, who provided an altar-like table spread with a white cloth and bearing six silver candlesticks, decanters of red wine, two silver cups and a silver urn. All these, together with the tea provided for teetotallers, were paid for by Carpenter. However, a German supporter called Shomer baked one thousand small loaves scored with crosses so that they could be pulled into quarters – a contribution so generous that two baskets full of leftovers were later distributed to the poor.[2]

The 'trial' opened on 5 December 1804 with a jury consisting of twelve 'First Believers', together with twelve other men and little Richard Foley – making altogether twenty-five 'Witnesses of the Truth'. The first hearing began at eleven o'clock with the replies of the clergy to Joanna's invitation being read aloud. Since some of these were highly offensive, the tone was then raised by calling forward witnesses to Joanna's good character.[3]

Enter John Tremlett Symons, Exeter shopkeeper, to testify that he had known Joanna for ten years and been employed to copy her letters. He declared that Pomeroy had supported Joanna's work in 1801 but changed his opinion around November 1803. And Symons himself? He had been convinced of Joanna's prophetic powers after she predicted a calamity in his family shortly before two of his sisters died.

Next, Joseph stepped forward to describe how, as a child his sister was of 'a mild, placid disposition and, as she grew up, of a religious turn.' Then he launched into a catalogue of her virtues – she was honest, well-balanced, competent and reliable. As for her prophecies . . . well, when she stayed with him at Whitehall in 1798 she predicted that he would settle in Bristol even though he tried to fool her into believing that he was off to the West Indies. Nevertheless, it was only when she turned up with Foley in 1803 that he became convinced her mission was real, being especially impressed by 'the very respectable characters engaged in the work with her.' Before this he had refused to copy out one of her letters, dismissing her as 'too insignificant a character to send such a letter to Mr Pomeroy.'

John Jones, the Exeter coach-driver who had known her for five years, came forward next and was able to remember exactly what Pomeroy had told him years ago: that Joanna 'had a great deal of shrewd sense.' He contrasted this with the very different response he met when he later accosted Pomeroy in a Bodmin street and told him he had a letter for him.

'What? Is it from that mad woman at Exeter?' Pomeroy shouted, in a voice so loud that people stopped to listen. He then declared that Joanna was as mad as a March hare. When Jones objected that there were many respectable people who supported her, Pomeroy had replied, 'They are all mad.'

William Sharp, when examined, named all the books he had published for Joanna since 1802 and described their method of working together: 'she read them to me from her own manuscripts, and I wrote from her reading.' Foley gave a similar account when he was called as the last witness on that first day.

Next morning the assembly met near the house at ten o'clock and, after receiving a message that Joanna was 'agitated', went immediately to the room where she and her women friends were sitting. She spoke to them all until mid-day, at which time her Box was placed on the table and various parcels of sealed writings taken out. It was a dramatic moment – enhanced by the fact that Joanna suddenly came over faint and had to be helped from the room.

Afternoon proceedings began at three o'clock with the first female witness – Mrs Lucy Taylor – being called. Having known Joanna for over twenty years, she could testify to her honesty, sobriety and cheerfulness. She reported how, in 1796, Joanna said that she had been ordered to write to the Reverend Joseph Pomeroy, telling him about her mission and warning him of future calamities; how her children had written letters for Joanna which were taken to Pomeroy by Miss Bird or their two apprentices. And what was Pomeroy's attitude to Joanna's mission? Mrs Taylor had often heard him say, 'My dear Joanna, do whatever you like, but leave my name out of the question.'

The examination of Mrs Taylor was followed by Mary Bird's deposition, which had been witnessed in Exeter by John Jones, Sarah Dewdney, Frances Taylor, Robert Taylor (junior), Edward Laskey, and Mrs Taylor. She had happily 'remembered' all that Joanna required.

Fanny Taylor, the next witness, confirmed that she had copied letters from Joanna to Pomeroy and been impressed by the accuracy of Joanna's prophecy of the French conquest of Italy.

Then Mrs Symons confirmed that her son had copied letters for Joanna; that when she asked Pomeroy if Joanna's writings came from the Devil, he said 'No'; that she had kept Joanna's sealed writings in her house from the end of 1800 till January, 1802.

Jane Townley testified to the fact that she had written from Joanna's manuscripts until 17 June, 1803, and after that from dictation.

Esther Elizabeth Bruce gave evidence that she had known Joanna since 1802, slept in the same room from 10 January to 12 April 1803, and had nothing but good to say of her.

Finally from Mary Beecraft it was heard that, when Joanna stayed at Market Deeping in July 1802, she had predicted the renewal of war in 1803. She had also described how she would be in a trance when her enemies appeared at her 'trial', so Mary had bought oil and flannel to anoint and wrap round her feet.

The day ended with the assembly passing five Resolutions – all exonerating Joanna – a deed which affected her so much that her heart 'beat and seemed to swell too big for her body.' She cried out, collapsed in tears and had to be helped upstairs by Mr Brandon.

The third morning began soon after ten with the calling out of the forty-eight names of the assembly, who were then told that Joanna was – at that very moment – receiving an important Communication that she would bring in as soon as it was finished. They waited with mounting excitement. An hour later she appeared and it was read. The Spirit had told her,

> All that will happen, till my Kingdom is established, is in thy writings; but not to be known at the present, 'Nothing shall be concealed from thee that I will do upon the earth'.

The announcement whetted their appetites for that moment when, at half past eleven, Joanna cut open the sealed bundles of her writings. What would happen next no one knew. Some expected her to go into a trance. Indeed, before the 'trial' a woman belonging to Orange Street Chapel had told all and sundry that Joanna's friends would 'give her a dose in order to put her to sleep and deceive the public.'[2] To avoid any such scandal, Joanna made it clear that had the assembly asked her to go into a trance, that would have been a sign of their lack of faith. Instead she explained at great length the nature of the 'trial' before retiring at four o'clock to receive another Communication, which she duly presented at five o'clock. The day's proceedings concluded at quarter past eight when Joanna retired in good spirits for the night.

At eleven o'clock on Saturday, the fourth day, Joanna attended a public meeting-house where a crowd of seven hundred had gathered to hear her. After singing and prayers, she gave them an account of her mission, but in the afternoon was so tired and depressed she had to take to her bed and leave the 'trial' to continue without her.

That evening at seven o'clock she entered the assembly and read the following Communication: Joanna had felt 'faint and dying' when she met the public, but as soon as Mr Carpenter came to the Lord's Prayer she had been revived by the Spirit of the Lord. However, when the Spirit left her to rely on her own strength, she had had to lie down. The meeting took the hint and decided on a later start for the morrow. They would gather at three o'clock in the afternoon, giving Joanna enough time to select those writings which should be sealed up till after her death.

On the sixth day they met in the morning without Joanna, whose absence needed no further explanation when she appeared at half past three, clutching a melancholic Communication she had just received.

Thou sayest the kindness and attention of thy friends come too
late; when thy appetite is gone thou canst not enjoy it; perfectly
so, I tell thee, by mankind, thousands will become thy friends,
when thy life is gone, and thou canst not enjoy them; for I know
I told thee in '93, thy death would convince more than thy life.

Because the seventh and last morning dawned so fine and clear, the assembly met in a field where they were joined by Joanna and her women friends at eleven o'clock. Joanna launched into a stirring address along the lines: Beware, the Kingdom of Christ is nigh!

Any fears of being ignored by the wider world were suddenly dispelled by a mob of protesters who came storming into Carpenter's property across a canal and threatened the assembly. The situation seemed about to turn nasty and Joanna almost lost a shoe in the scramble to get back into Carpenter's garden. Mr Goldsmith, following behind, called out to

Foley: 'Stop, let me pull my mother's shoe up at heel.'[4]

The day was saved by the weather. Dark clouds obscured the sun and rain began to fall – only a few drops, but enough to disperse the mob.

Safely back in Neckinger House, Joanna left the room at quarter past five to seek advice on how to enter names on the Resolutions. The judges were: Stanhope Bruce, Thomas Webster, T.P. Foley, William Sharp, George Turner, John Wilson, Peter Morrison, Elias Carpenter, William Wetherell, Charles Taylor, William Jowett, and little Richard Foley, whose name was to be associated with William Tooke Harwood, so that the number still came to twelve.

The jury were: Charles Abbott, Richard Law, Elias Jameson Field, George Stocks, John Morris, John Hows (on behalf of William Coy, deceased), William Belk, William Owen (for William Taylor, absent) John Young, William Layton Winter, John Torin, and Thomas Stephens.

Because twenty-four clergymen would not come forward to witness to the truth, the following were chosen instead: Reverend Samuel Eyre, John Nisbet, Samuel Hirst, Thomas Senior, John Grimshaw, John Chanter, Edward Laskey, J. Ingall, J.Middleton, Wheldon Jones, Abel Peplow Sharp, J. Cook, Jedediah Holland, James Spring, William Rea, J. Bedford, Richard Goldsmith, William Brandon, J. Bullen Pritchard, J. Mackay, Robert Eyre, Abraham Crouch, William Booth, and Richard Messenger. John Scott was present as attorney when the papers were signed.

At seven o'clock wine and cakes were brought in and Joanna said:

Let the wine be poured into one cup and let it be handed round by the ministers; but let the words be repeated by everyone that drinketh.

These words were:

May I drink deep into the Spirit of Christ;
And may his Blood cleanse me from all sin.

Making it clear that, even though this should not be regarded as a sacrament, they should let their words and actions be the desire of their hearts, Joanna supped first then passed the cup to one of the women. 'Then follow with all the women, as I am come to redeem the Fall of women,' she instructed. The cup was then passed to the twelve judges, then to the jury, then to the twenty-four 'Elders'; then to other witnesses. After everyone had supped, Joanna pronounced:

As we all have drank in one cup, may we drink into one faith,
and may that faith be in Christ!

At nine o'clock she sealed up those writings which were to be kept until after her death before returning the Box to William Sharp for safe-keeping. Then she handed her women friends cakes which they shared among themselves in token of love and friendship. The men followed suit, and amidst what had now become a joyful party atmosphere Joanna retired, leaving the rest of the assembly, about seventy people, to sign the Resolutions and go home.

In its limited way the 'trial' had been a success. Although the Church had, as usual, refused her any support, Joanna had drawn together a significant group of supporters. It now remained for her to rail in those others who were still hanging back. Chief among these was Nathaniel Brassey Halhed, who had received one of her seals as acknowledgement of his faith in her mission in November 1802. Since then, however, he had done less for her than for Brothers, who still commanded his first allegiance. It was time for Joanna to clarify her position, to make it clear that she could not go along with people who, like the late Colonel Bruce, had hailed her as Brothers's coadjutor, the new Eve to his new Adam. Joanna's connection with the Spirit was personal, her mission unique; she could not share her influence with anyone.

Carefully – anxious to wean people from Brothers without alienating them in the process – she began to marshall her case. Since coming to London she had been loud in support of Brothers' release. Because he had been jailed for insisting that God disapproved of the war with France, Joanna also warned that current food shortages were a sign of divine displeasure and would worsen if Brothers was not freed. Her statements confirmed his followers in their new loyalty to her, but she had to be careful not to contradict herself when she started openly to attack him.

Her main charge against the imprisoned prophet was that he had nurtured an ambition that was scarcely distinguishable from that of Bonaparte, 'who judges all power is given to him as Brothers thought it was given to him.'[5] Such overweening ambition coupled with spiritual pride had cost him God's favour.

Halhed, aware of these criticisms, was still reluctant to abandon Brothers, so on 16 December 1804, Joseph Southcott and James Spring paid him a visit to try and win him over. They apparently had little success, for the Spirit was soon ordering Joanna to go herself, if 'not this Week, go the following Week.' Wasting no time, she went three days later accompanied by Townley, Foley, and Sharp and reported that 'Mr and Mrs Halhed seemed very glad to see them.'[6] The meeting went well – with Joanna listening patiently to Halhed's interpretation of the Creation, and Halhed claiming that Joanna had liberated him from his house where he had felt himself a prisoner for the last ten years.[7]

Factors other than philosophical were causing some of Brothers' followers to lose faith. Foley, for instance, on the strength of Brothers' prophecies had bet twenty guineas that there would be no more monarchy in France and now came news of the coronation of Napoleon Bonaparte. The day after his visit to Halhed saw him at Wilson's house, bitterly complaining about his lost wager.[8]

Joanna had other reasons to bemoan Bonaparte's elevation. Having identified him as the Beast described in Revelation, it was another clear sign that the last days had come. So thought many of her followers, including Mr Grimshaw's friends in Leeds who asked if they should come immediately to London. After giving it some thought, Joanna advised them to stay where they were and establish themselves in business while awaiting further instruction.[9]

Meanwhile Jane Townley's sisters had remained concerned about her attachment to Joanna and their anxiety grew as her enthusiasm showed no sign of waning. They perhaps regretted not taking more notice when she had sent them copies of Joanna's books. Then, in that first year after their father died, Jane might have been prepared to listen to them, but not now.

On Wednesday, 2 January, 1805, Jane's older sister, Catherine, widow of the Reverend Charles Wager Allix, descended on Titchfield Street and created a scene. Insisting that she was only telling Jane 'something for her good', she tried to persuade her to leave Joanna.[10] Listening to their raised voices from the next room, Joanna could not contain herself. In she rushed and haughtily told Mrs Allix that she would not allow Jane to be thus ill-treated in *her* house.[11] The reaction of Mrs Allix, daughter of a former High Sheriff of Lancashire, at being spoken to like this by a woman with thick Devon accent may be imagined. '[I]t was with some difficulty I got her away,' reported Jane Townley. Still, it did the trick. Mrs Allix bowed out and no one in the Townley family made any further attempt to dissuade Jane from the cause.[12]

The confrontation had unsettled Jane's nerves though, and left her unequal to a row which broke out the following day between Joanna and the owner of the house when he tried to charge her half a guinea more than they had agreed for the rent. At ten o'clock that night Joanna received a Communication telling them to leave their lodging next day without giving notice. So Joanna and Townley did a midnight flit, taking refuge a few doors up at Mr Sharp's house while he and Underwood were left to pack up their things and pick up the tab. Hearing that Joanna had left for good, the owners grew 'pale with passion and a noise and great anger ensued.' While Underwood tried to pack, the row spread from Sharp and the owners to their servant, who railed against her mistress for forcing Joanna away and so depriving her of her livelihood. At which stage, fearing for the servant's safety, Underwood was forced to intervene. After this, the mood became so violent that Sharp and Mrs

Eyre, who had come to invite Joanna to her house, had to stay and protect Underwood until she was ready to come away.

Two days later, on Old Christmas Day, Townley wrote an agitated letter to Fanny Taylor describing her sister's visit and the subsequent bother with their landlord:

> [W]hen you write you must to Mr Sharp and put a 'T' in the corner, for as my Family are disposed to persecute I am order'd to be in concealment. Thank God, Joanna and I are both vastly well and very comfortable.
>
> I really hope Joanna is quite free'd from Satan, and I am thank God much more good humour'd.[13]

On the morning of 28 January, 1805, Joanna was dreaming one of her typical dreams – of swimming in a river, then being carried over roof-tops – when she was woken by Underwood taking down the shutters. Through the window she saw a black cloud all over London and a fog which grew so thick that it was too dark to write. This omen presaged the arrival of Elias Carpenter carrying two newly published books, both attacking Joanna. The darkness continued so intense that at midday they had to call for candles and keep them lit until nearly two o'clock, when the mist eventually cleared.[14]

This experience foreshadowed dark times ahead, for Joanna's followers were about to experience a painful split in their ranks.

Towards the end of the previous year William Tozer, lath-render by trade and Devonian by birth, had hurried up from Exeter when he heard of Joanna's prophecies. On his arrival in town he paid his respects to Elias Carpenter at his chapel, the House of God, in Bermondsey and tried to ingratiate himself by proclaiming Carpenter as that 'Elias' referred to in Chapter 4 of Malachi: 'Behold, I will send you Elijah the prophet before the coming of the great and dreadful day of the Lord.'

Meeting with little success in this quarter, Tozer next solicited an introduction to Joanna, which was granted in December 1804. What she made of her fellow Devonian at their first meeting is not known, but the emotional, wild-looking fellow with a voice like thunder soon won her confidence and in the spring of 1805 was given the wherewithal to build and open for her followers a new chapel in Duke Street, St George's Fields.[15]

Meanwhile, trouble with Carpenter was already brewing. He claimed that Joanna had approved his plans for what amounted to a Communion service on New Year's Day, 1805, when the faithful were invited to Bermondsey 'to commemorate the Lord's dying love together.' However, when the day came, Foley, Bruce, and Webster, the three Anglican clergymen associated with Joanna, would have nothing to do with this service. Although 'some hundreds partook with me', said Carpenter, there is no evidence to suggest that Joanna was among this number, and the occasion provoked a rift between them.

What further diminished Carpenter in Joanna's view was his poor financial situation. A man of 'warm and rash temper' whose home was always open to friends, Carpenter took no money collection at his services, but asked for contributions from some of Joanna's richer patrons.

'We sent our subscriptions and I was in hopes all would have passed away in silence,' Joanna said with little sympathy for one who lavished his money on a religion which extended beyond her own mission. Her Spirit informed her that Carpenter 'was filling his house, feeding men at his table, consuming his substance, not to my honour and glory, but to his own hurt.'

Joanna and her Spirit were especially censorious when it came to the various protégés for whom Carpenter had provided a home. Not only was there young 'Joseph' Prescott, but there had been a poor elderly man, Thomas Dowland, known as Jerusha. 'A man of a timid nature, feeble in body, and equally so in mind; but the fear of God was uniformly before his eyes.' When Carpenter first met him in September 1803 Dowland was sixty-three and had been experiencing visions for over ten years. Once Dowland turned up at a Southcottian meeting, only to be turned away at the door by a woman he had seen in his dreams ten years previously. Although refused admittance because the room was too full, Dowland felt it was a judgment on him for having condemned Prescott's paintings and Joanna's writings as blasphemous, and decided to kill himself if he were turned away again. Next time, however, he was allowed in and at the meeting declared his faith in Joanna's mission and received a seal. Soon afterwards he began to communicate with a spirit who confirmed his new faith in verse and, despite the fact that Dowland was barely literate, the words were dictated as fast as he could write them down:

> Come, see Joanna, see the saint arise!
> Burst earthly prison, soar above the skies,
> To that bright world where joys immortal grow,
> And life's unfathom'd pleasures ever flow;
> There rob'd in white, she'll join the heav'nly train,
> The ransom'd throng for whom the lamb was slain:
> She'll share the glory of the sealed race,
> And bask, and triumph, in the God of Grace.[16]

If 'bask, and triumph,' sounded well, 'share the glory' chimed ill with Joanna's notion of her mission, and although Prescott and Dowland championed Joanna, she grew increasingly critical of the way they had both battened on Carpenter, demanding maintenance from him when she herself had managed to serve the Spirit for ten years whilst at the same time supporting herself and her father. But it was not Joanna's criticism of the two visionaries that caused trouble, it was her insistence on being their sole interpreter.

Shortly before Christmas 1804, after leaving Carpenter's house, Dowland was found dead. Carpenter was deeply distressed until reassured by Joanna that the death was merely a type for her own (which was imminent – again!) and that it had been timed so that Dowland's prophetic warnings could now go into print without being tarnished by his dismal character.[17] With regard to Joseph Prescott's visions, Joanna reiterated that Carpenter must not presume to place his own meanings on them.

'He must rely wholly upon one or the other,' Joanna declared in May, 1805, 'Joseph or me.'[18]

When Carpenter proved obstinate in this respect, she suggested that they should meet, each accompanied by one friend, any day after two o'clock to resolve the matter. Carpenter refused.[19] The boil was left to fester.

It was ironical that on 2 June, soon after the difficulty caused by Carpenter's sacramental pretensions, Joanna herself received a command from her Spirit to administer the bread and wine in Holy Communion to Jane Townley and Ann Underwood and she complied with apparently little reflection on the significance of her action.[20]

Then came a letter from Yorkshire with news that both Mr Senior and Mr Hirst had been expelled from the Methodist society for declaring their belief in Joanna's mission. In fact, Thomas Senior, a class leader at Leeds, had been turned out before anyone had even read her books to see what he was talking about. Not that it mattered. Since leaving the Methodists he had attracted a congregation of thousands, come to hear him preach about Joanna. The same went for Mr Hirst who had become a Southcottian preacher with similar success. So, far from stamping out her mission, the Methodists had poured oil on the flames. Indeed many other preachers now came over to her cause, including 'a Mr Slake, in Yorkshire, the finest preacher I ever heard,' as Joanna declared, 'and in conversation the most humble and becoming Christian, but rejected for his faith in my Visitation; and they have established Meetings to themselves on account of the Methodists rejecting them.' Not that this had been their intention, she explained, they were simply 'acting like the deer, that as soon as they see one wounded, all the rest will thrust him out of their company.'

The figure of speech was possibly prompted by memories of her own problems with the Methodists in Exeter. Her Spirit added,

Thou sayest that these men were once thy familiar friends in
religious duties, . . . and once they showed thee respect and
love: but now it is turned to anger against thee, which wounds
thy heart and grieves thy spirit to see thy friends become thy
foes in the cause of religion.[21]

There were any number of things to grieve her Spirit that spring,
including continued slurs about her making a fortune from the sale of
seals. Mr Field received an insolent letter asking him to send 'one half a
hundred of yr seals. . . . Direct to Robert Currier, post office, Salisbury.'
But the unkindest cut came from the man who cast aspersions on her
poetry, saying that it was no more than doggerel verse(!) – a remark
which sent her straight to her Spirit for reassurance. She was told to go
away and write verses by herself, using some theme from the Creation,
or a text from the Bible or her own wisdom – and to make her style as
'high' as she could. She hid herself away and wrote twelve grandiloquent
verses before the Spirit interrupted her by saying that it was not the
high-flown language but the simple innocence of her heart that was
beautiful in His sight.[22]

When Mr Robert Taylor came to London on business towards the
end of April, Underwood took advantage of his visit to send a letter
back to Fanny enclosing a recent Communication about Atheists 'as
Joanna says there is enough of them in Exeter as well as at other places.'
Underwood was a widow with just one child – Ann, who was of a
similar age to Fanny and frequently ill. Her mother wrote,

I am obliged to you for your kind enquiries. . . . Ann is got
vastly well and looks quite healthy, and is quite full of Spirits
she say she should much like to see you, if she had the wishing
cap we so often used to talk of, excuse this scrawl, I am writing
this the time your Papa and the Ladies are at chit-chat.

Underwood also mentioned that there had been remarkable lights seen
in the sky at Doncaster and an earthquake in the Birmingham area.[23]

There were also problems connected with Peter Morrison, whose
boastful behaviour caused trouble everywhere he went. Finally losing
patience, Joanna ordered him to return to his family in Liverpool. He
did, only to find that his wife had other ideas and refused to take him
back. After some heated exchanges, Morrison rented lodgings elsewhere.
So when in June 1805 Joanna received a request from Thomas Hopkinson
at Harpstoft for Morrison to come and speak to the friends in Nottingham,
she was happy to let him go.[24]

Foley, while hearing of all these disputes, was enjoying a period of
quiet family life in Oldswinford, turning down an invitation to visit the
Taylors in Exeter on the grounds that he could make no move until

Joanna sent him orders. Until that happened he seemed happy to stay 'quietly in his tent' with Elizabeth, who had just given birth to another child, privately baptised Noah Philip, and four-year old Richard, who was 'in the hay-field being very active and as it is holiday time, we endulge him in this amusement'.[25]

Foley was not alone in awaiting further instructions. For many who had been keyed up by the excitements of the 'trial', bought Joanna's books and applied for her seals in anticipation of the Final Days, the summer of 1805 proved something of an anticlimax. Joanna was failing to fulfil all her followers' expectations. When on Saturday, 13 July, the Spirit told her to write down her feelings, she was depressed by the thought that so many believers were expecting to be freed immediately of their troubles. Her depression grew when she remembered how in 1792 she had been given signs that she would die within fifteen years.[26]

When William Sharp took Charles Taylor along with him to see Joanna on Friday evening, 20 July, Joanna took her usual motherly interest in the young man who had worshipped her since childhood. She recalled how, as a boy, Charles had promised to be good if he could go to heaven and be a trumpeter there.

> He said a trumpeter to heaven he'd go
> A trumpeter on earth he'll surely be
> And after that he triumph shall with me

– these words were among the Communications sealed up in 1794 when Joanna had left the Taylors. Later Charles told her how much he wanted her words to come true, even though his parents had sent him off to do an apprenticeship after he refused to follow his brother into the upholstery trade. Joanna disapproved of this move, being convinced that he should stay with his parents until her writings were published and she could introduce him to a wider circle. Fate intervened when Mr Taylor bought a plot of land in Castle Street, Exeter, on which to build a warehouse at a time when Charles had just been sent home by his master, who was in dispute with the Taylors. Rather than kick his heels, he joined the men working on his father's house and picked up the building trade. Naturally he came in for quite a bit of teasing and even blows when talking about Joanna, but his loyalty was rewarded when, once the building was finished, Joanna was able to supply him with useful introductions to friends in London. Thus he had been able to stand in for his father as one of the twelve judges at High House and, in the following year, substitute for no less than Archdeacon Moore. Joanna, to forestall criticism of her young friend, explained that, though humble and prone to stammer, he was to be judged 'from inside'. More to the point, she added that as Mrs Taylor had given her food, entertained her friends, and got her children to write for Joanna over the years, she deserved some sort of reward.[27]

So Charles Taylor became an intimate of Joanna's circle, developing a warm, lifelong friendship with Townley, Underwood and Foley. As Joanna sat talking to him that July evening in 1805 she heard that he was thinking of going to Windsor where they were building large cavalry barracks. As she listened she looked carefully at his face, checking on the skin complaint that affected his eyes. She was pleased to see his face clear of spots and wanted to know if he was still rubbing ointment on his eyes which, though red, looked much better.

'You've heard that Mr Charles' face and eyes are in miserable condition,' she wrote to his anxious mother, before reporting the vast improvements she had noted. 'We remarked how well he looked – health a great deal better – not so nervous as he used to be, but quite solid and steady.' When she sealed up her letter she gave instructions for it to be left at Miss Eveleigh's shop, opposite the Old London Inn in St Sidwells, together with a letter and parcel for her brother. If Miss Eveleigh could not send the parcel on to Sidbury, Mrs Taylor was asked to post the letter on to William so that he would know where to collect his parcel. In a postscript she added: 'I have sent my brother's letter unsealed for you or Miss Eveleigh to take out the Scriptures that alludes to Prophecy and you will see explained in answer to the Book printed against me at Halifax.'[28] Clearly, William and her friends at Exeter were kept well informed about Joanna's career as prophetess.

On the first day of August Joanna had been woken up by the sound of fluttering. She got up, put down the shutters, and seeing a bird trapped between the wood and the glass, pushed up the window and let it fly away.

It was an omen. Joanna, feeling trapped between two sections of her supporters, flew away for a while and was out of town with Ann Underwood when the dispute erupted between Webster, Sharp and Townley on one hand and Carpenter, Prescott, and Fischer on the other. The trouble had again arisen over where they should take communion – Carpenter keen for all the friends to receive it at Neckinger House; Mr Webster insisting on people coming to his home so that his sick mother-in-law could be included. In the end there were two ceremonies.

When she heard, Joanna was furious. Immediately siding with Webster, Sharp and Townley, she accused Carpenter of acting out of pride and vain-glory. William Tozer, who still regarded himself as Carpenter's friend, argued on his behalf to no avail.

'I made no answer to the praises he gave Mr Carpenter,' Joanna recorded, 'and as I was silent, my friends were likewise, as they are

always afraid to introduce a subject they see me silent upon.'[29] Her
friends had learnt fast!

In the midst of the dispute Joanna accepted an offer from Mr Wilson
to drive her and Underwood to Tottenham Court Road on Sunday
morning, 18 August, to hear Mr Huntingdon preach. They arrived to
find the famous preacher out of town and heard the Reverend Mr Groves
instead. Sitting up in the gallery, Joanna gazed around, impressed by the
chapel's beauty and then more impressed by the preacher's text: 'Thou
shalt see greater things then these' (1 John 50). She listened intently to
a sermon, clearly aimed at her, which said Christ would call His own
from no matter how wicked a place. Just as *she* had been called – yet,
she could not help thinking, it was men like this preacher who would
not accept her calling. 'Therefore I thought to myself, man was an
Inconsistent creature at best.'

They drove home to find Townley with two more friends come to
see Joanna. Wherever she was, people flocked to see her and, Townley
– especially after the battering she had recently endured from her family
– was suffering from self-doubt and even self-pity. This was reflected
in her reaction to Joanna's dream about a flock of sheep and a basket
containing a few lambs. Townley immediately identified with the sheep
whose blessings were not so great as those who were inside the basket
with Joanna. No, Joanna quickly explained. The dream actually showed
the opposite. She herself had seen the basket from the outside and so it
must be showing who were the lambs gathered around her.[30]

In fact, her mind was preoccupied not by the need to sort lambs
from sheep, but sheep from goats. New arrangements were made for
the two sides of her followers to come together. Carpenter's friends –
Winter, Tozer, Brandon and Pritchard – were to meet Joanna's friends –
Wilson, Owen and Hows – on Monday, 9 September. Suspecting a
strategy of 'divide and rule', the seven dissidents sent a letter on the
Sunday evening saying that unless all were invited, none would come
next day.[31]

There was no way Joanna would allow such terms to be dictated.
She tried another tack to split the enemy. She wrote to Tozer warning
him that Carpenter, by styling himself Joseph before whom the eleven
tribes bowed down, was doing the work of the Devil. At the same time
she issued a handbill making it clear that Carpenter had disobeyed her
commands since 13 August and so they had parted ways.[32] Tozer, left
with a straight choice of loyalty, sided with Joanna and, according to
Carpenter, began

> to publicly tell the inhabitants of the metropolis, that nothing
> was to be received but through this woman. . . . And,

notwithstanding his illiterateness, his gross language, and repulsive manners, he prejudiced two-thirds of the people's minds against what, if understood, they would have firmly held as the pearl of great price, and made a breach which has never yet been healed.

While Carpenter and his friends went round blackening Tozer's name, Joanna quoted an anonymous person in Exeter, who had lived in the same parish and known Tozer from a child, as saying that he was honest, good-tempered and generous.[33] At the same time she gave him great support in setting up her chapel in Duke Street, writing to him at the end of October with practical advice drawn from her connection with the Methodists.

I think it will prevent great confusion amongst the people if . . . every one had a ticket for their seats, then the people who may come out of curiosity, or to make any disturbance, will be prevented from filling the place. . . . It will prevent a riotous people from assembling to interrupt those who wish to meet seriously together, and assemble themselves together to hear and judge for themselves, the Scripture pointed out for the coming of the Lord.[34]

With Tozer won over, Joanna turned her attention to Pritchard and Brandon, telling them that although Carpenter and Winter were cut off from the faithful, their own cases were not hopeless and they should go at once to Mr Tozer, listen to his advice and then choose. Her magnanimity was lost on them. 'Undivided Union is our aim', they declared, refusing to desert Carpenter.

Trying another tack, she ordered Pritchard and Brandon to come with the others at two o'clock on Wednesday, 20 November, to Mr Field's house where Underwood would read the actual words contained in the sealed letter they had quoted as giving them leave to stay united. Their reply was sniffy: 'We presume not to judge the Spirit that now communes with you. Your three books do not shew it hath worked either love or spirituality in your mind.'[35]

Clearly she was getting nowhere with them – and suffering as a result. Her friends must have felt worried about her mental state when one evening at table, confused and almost too weak to move her hand, Joanna looked around for a candle which she thought Underwood had removed, only to be told by Townley that it had not been moved and that there were two burning on the table. After staring at these, Joanna went into another room and started to complain of seeing two rims of fire before her eyes wherever she looked.[36]

The trouble was, Joanna was never one to back down, especially over an affair which called her honour into question. In the case of Carpenter versus Southcott it was her honesty and that of her chief supporters that was challenged. If Carpenter and his friends could prove them all guilty of lying, then the moral high ground was theirs – and in their minds Joanna and Foley had lied in their description of how Joanna had left the field when threatened by the mob at Neckinger on 11 December, 1804. It might seem trivial, but establishing exactly what happened that day assumed as much importance for Joanna's opponents as the precise number of angels dancing on a pinhead had for certain medieval theologians.

Carpenter insisted that it was he, not Foley, who had taken hold of Joanna's arm and assisted her from the field. Joanna insisted that Foley had taken hold of her right arm, and Major Eyre her left, and could not recall whether Carpenter or Brandon came up once she had reached the safety of Carpenter's garden.[37] Foley bore out Joanna's version by saying that, as soon as the rain came on, Joanna had taken his left arm while his wife took hold of his right; then, after going a little way and being pressed by the crowd, his wife had said, 'Go on with Joanna and set her in a place of safety – and I will get out of the crowd, and then come back for me;' which he did.

Using language in which actuality and allegory overlapped, Foley denied seeing Carpenter do anything to clear the way for Joanna. But beyond writing such letters, Foley was kept out of the dispute by problems of his own that summer and autumn. All his family had been ill. He himself was suffering from an ulcerated throat and the usual gout.[38] Four-year old Richard had plunged twenty feet from his bedroom window in August to end up with – mercifully – little more than a scratch.[39] Later the lad had a nasty attack of whooping cough. Then little Noah Philip was innoculated against smallpox which, caused Mrs Foley's breast to become very sore round the nipple where he sucked. All in all, the family were left so low that Foley packed them off for a holiday – sending them four miles away from the rectory to stay on the edge of a fine, dry common where the air was much better.

In November, Foley catalogued all these woes in a letter to Mr Taylor to excuse himself for not writing more often and his wife for failing to 'execute a little commission in the China way at Worcester.' They seldom or ever went to Worcester which was twenty miles away, Foley explained,

> but if you are not in any great hurry I will embrace the first
> opportunity and give you all the particulars. I know for about 6
> Guineas a very handsome tea set of white & gold may be obtained
> because i had some thoughts of purchasing a set myself. But

what a dinner set will come to, I do not know – but you wish to
have a blue & white set for tea – and also for Dinner.[40]

Whether the Taylors took the hint and settled for what Foley
considered more handsome china is not known.

Foley had recently met Sharp in Oxford and heard that Charles Taylor
had undergone 'a great operation in the eye'. It was clearly a success,
for when Townley wrote to Mrs Taylor a few weeks later – to thank her
for the goose and fine fowls – she remarked that Charles was in a great
good spirits when he drank tea with them the previous Sunday. And the
reason? '[I]n London he is fully employed and we are of opinion that
not being so . . . at Exeter makes him more nervous and think of every
trifling complaint.' Charles, possibly engaged in building Joanna's chapel
in Duke Street, was delighted with his new situation and more relaxed
than Mr Tozer had ever seen him.

As 1805 drew to a close, if Joanna looked back over a year of triumphs
and reverses, she would no doubt have placed among the former her
meeting with the Recorder of London – although that gentleman might
have seen the interview in a very different light. Informed of Joanna's
presence in the capital and needing to assess whether her influence might
cause civil unrest, he and Mr Valliant, a lawyer, came on 18 October
together with Sharp, Wilson and Tozer. They listened attentively as Joanna
described – in detail – her Visitation in 1792 and all that had happened to
her since then.

Coming rather abruptly to the point, Mr Valliant asked whether she
was the Woman mentioned in the Book of Revelation, Chapter 12. Joanna
said yes.

The interview descended abruptly into farce. If she was the Woman
of Revelation, then she must have the sun upon her back, Mr Valliant
declared. And, warming to his subject: when was she in heaven? how
had she got there? when had she given birth to the Man Child?

By way of reply, Joanna asked him to explain the relevant chapter
himself.

The 'Woman' referred to in Revelation was the Church, he averred.

Then was the Church in heaven? Joanna asked, proceeding with her
innocent logic to expose his position.

Mr Valliant conceded that the 'Woman' was not actually the Church,
or the People, but the ecclesiastical law. . . . He then, according to
Joanna, proceeded to argue 'like a Councillor at the Bar trying to
confound the Witnesses.'[41]

The contest resulted in a draw. Although no action was taken against
her, Joanna had failed to convince the authorities that she was the 'woman
clothed with the sun' who would deliver her people.

'I AM WHAT I AM', 1806-1807

It is your long letters, your tedious compositions; your artful
insolence and craftiness; and the complete jumble of nonsense,
so conspicuous in your writings, that have hitherto sheltered
you from controversy.

Letter to Joanna from Lewis Mayer, 22 March, 1806

Although Jane Townley's family had given up overt attempts to prise
her away from Joanna, she still had other hostile influences to overcome.
Jane had always been delicate in the opinion of her doctors a 'hopeless
case', until 1798 when she felt suddenly convinced that she would live
to see the Millennium. She put herself under the care of Dr Moseley,[1] a
physician to the Royal Hospital at Chelsea, whose 'skill and penetration'
she claimed brought about her recovery.[2] When soon afterwards she
met and was won over by Joanna, she longed for the good doctor to be
similarly convinced and was very disappointed when he not only
disapproved of her new association but refused to meet Joanna for fear
of damaging his professional reputation. Because Moseley was a man
she respected, his scepticism shook Townley's own faith – until the
Spirit issued a special Communication:

> Townley hath ascribed to the man the honour and glory due
> unto Me. Now let Townley do by Moseley, as thou didst by
> Pomeroy, and resign the man unto My care. . . . If you weary
> yourselves about your friends, you may go mourning all the day
> long. . . . Know the Lord loveth a cheerful giver: therefore,
> whether you give with your hands in writing in love to Me; let it
> be done with cheerfulness and a willing mind. And he that giveth
> gold to support My Cause, let him do it with a cheerful mind
> also . . . and My Eye shall be to make you perfectly happy in
> time or in Eternity.[3]

After this rallying call, the idealistic Townley returned to her cheerful
and willing giving, and Joanna to her happy acceptance.

Charles Taylor, joining in the vast crowd which attended Lord Nelson's
funeral in January 1806, was lucky to escape injury with so many being
hurt in the crush.[4] It was a sad start to a bleak year. On 23 January
came news of the Prime Minister's death: Bonaparte's great victory at

Austerlitz having, people said, sent Pitt into an early grave. Against this grim backdrop, Joanna published *The Full Assurance that the Kingdom of Christ is at Hand from the Signs of the Times*.

Nor was she alone in her prognostication. A Leeds woman named Mary Bateman, former disciple of Swedenborg and of Brothers, was claiming that her hen had started to lay eggs with the message 'CHRIST IS COMING' written on them lengthways – a phenomenon witnessed by Mr Hirst.[5] Joanna was unsure what to make of this until she remembered something her father had told her. According to old William Southcott, a master once got his servant-girl pregnant and then denied all responsibility only to find, when the baby was born, it had his name written on its thigh for all to see. Bearing this in mind, Joanna gave credit to Mary Bateman's story, declaring later:

> If the thing were real, I thought the warning was striking to all,
> as the crowing of the cock reproved the denial of Peter. And so
> I thought from the hen – it reproved an unbelieving world that
> denied the coming of their Lord.[6]

If Joanna imagined that such warnings would inspire solidarity, she was mistaken. A new row had erupted in Yorkshire, where her followers were split between the competing claims of Grimshaw, one of the twenty-four witnesses at her 'trial', and Fischer, the immigrant Moravian preacher. Both men needed money: Grimshaw because he was old and sick; Fischer because he wanted to be employed as a preacher. Joanna sided with Grimshaw, castigating Fischer as being too idle to make a living for himself among his German Brethren. After all, had she not had to support herself and her aged father, she reminded his supporters, and did people not realise how humbly she and her friends lived now? Sharp had offered to provide Fischer with work carrying parcels for shops, but this was rejected because some people thought a former preacher should not 'sink so low'. Well, 'before Honor, cometh Humility' Joanna insisted, just as Christ sank low when He came down to redeem mankind.[7]

Joanna was not the only person upset by Fischer. Another prophet had predicted that Christ's kingdom would be established by the destruction of Bonaparte. This was Lewis Mayer, who lived at 9 Coleman Street, Bunhill Row and he wrote to Joanna in March, taking her to task for statements made by 'Mr Fisher, the German preacher, one of your sealed people' who had referred to Joanna as the Woman in Revelation. If she confirmed this, Mayer declared, he would condemn her publicly as an impostor.

Joanna's reply came the very next day.

'I received your friendly letter,' she began drily, before explaining in what respects Fischer was wrong about her and – at great length –

putting her case. Not only had her prophecies been fulfilled, but she claimed that she had, before publishing them, applied to the clergy, an action which should clear her of any charge of imposture.

Back bounced a second letter from Mayer.

'Madam – I received your long, laborious and complimentary letter but could wish it was more to the purpose,' he wrote, accusing her of 'artful evasions' and demanding to know whether she claimed 'the appellation of the Bride, the Lamb's wife'? Joanna's indignant riposte was,

> You ask me what I am? I answer, with St Paul, by the grace of God, I am what I am, and to men of sense I can answer for myself in every thing I have published to the world.

Mayer wrote again, in a tone even ruder than before:

> It is your long letters, your tedious compositions; your artful insolence and craftiness; and the complete jumble of nonsense, so conspicuous in your writings, that have hitherto sheltered you from controversy.[8]

No wonder Joanna was furious with Fischer for leaving her open to such abuse. She wrote to Fischer,

> [A] feigned friend is worse than an open foe. I have a long time born with your wild random ideas that you have drawn from my writings . . . and have advised you to get some employment that you might not impose on the labour of others and go about doing hurt . . . from a letter I received from Mr Mayer I am condemned for an impostor and my friends as a Deluded People by the Erroneous assertions that you made to him . . . you said that Bonaparte is not to fall by the hands of a man, but by the Bursting of my Seals in October next . . . and that I should ascend into Heaven in the month of November. . . . How such things came into your head I know not. . . .

In future, Joanna stormed, she would thank Fischer to keep away from her friends – and in case he should fail to take the hint, had already written to Abbott and Field telling them to take up no more collections for him.

Not everyone, Joanna must have thanked God, was as cantankerous as Lewis Mayer. In general, her followers clung to her every word, relying on her guidance in both their spiritual and worldly concerns. On 2 April, 1806, Joanna encouraged them to believe that, although none would enjoy supreme power, those believers who were alive at the Second Coming would be made 'rulers over many places as priests unto the Lord.'[9]

With regard to practical matters, however, she warned people not to assume that all would suddenly be wonderful:

> [I] wish no one to think that trade and business will cease in our land after the deliverance comes of the clouds that now hang over us; all kinds of trades will go on the same. It was a wrong spirit that advised Brothers to tell the people to give up their business, as they were all going to Jerusalem, and many people have been ruined thereby.[10]

When one of her supporters asked whether in view of the imminence of Christ's Kingdom being established in England he should sell his estate, Joanna replied with sound common sense:

> The Lord never directs any man's property what he shall do. In these things we are left to judge for ourselves, and you must be the best judge whether you can sell the estate to an advantage to do you good; but as you ask my advice, I shall tell you what I should do myself, unless I was distressed, and obliged to sell my estate, I must say I should not sell it if it was land, for come what will, that will stand; but if it be in houses, or the greater value of it be in a house, I should sell it as soon as I could get its worth. . . .
>
> Do not act with any imprudence, expecting wonders to change in the following year concerning worldly affairs. As to that, I must conclude with the advice the Reverend Mr Stedding gave my father, to live today as though he was to die tomorrow. . . . This is the advice I give my friends, and then they are prepared for every event.[11]

Writing to the Taylors on 25 March Joanna has a favour to ask. There was a young lady, a relation of Colonel Harwood, and her mother had just died. She did not need to earn her living but wanted to go into the upholstery business and the Colonel was prepared to accept this, so long as she lived with Believers. She was an innocent, good-tempered girl and, having already made a gown and greatcoat since coming to London, was quite competent. If the Colonel paid her board and expenses, would the Taylors take her on?

The Taylors did not like training up new workers, but, as a favour for a friend, and possibly realising that Joanna was referring to the Colonel's own daughter – they agreed. So Miss Harwood arrived in Exeter to take up her new employment, her father having agreed to pay £30 per annum for her clothes and pocket money – 'Joanna said she was sure you would advise her how to lay it out so she does not lay it out foolishly', Townley told Mrs Taylor – plus fifty guineas for her board and washing. 'Joanna thought you would be pleased with that and would treat Miss Harwood as your own Child. . . .'

And well might the Taylors have been pleased – had they ever received the money! But as the months wore on, to Joanna's embarrassment and chagrin, not a penny of the promised settlement was forthcoming from the Colonel, and the Taylors were left to feed, clothe and support the young lady entirely from their own pockets.[12]

On Maundy Thursday, 1806, Joanna had a strange dream: the Bible she always read had to be boiled before it was fulfilled so she tied it up with a cord and put it in a pot. After it had boiled some time she saw the Bible curl up and rise out of the water on to the edge of the pot. 'Now the Bible will be fulfilled, for all is finished,' she said, taking the Bible to a table where she cut the cord and opened it at the Psalms. Townley went to take a closer look, but as it was wet it began to break. Joanna said, 'Oh, Miss Townley, you must not open the Bible before it begins to get dry. We must mark the places and look into another Bible.'

Townley immediately stopped and looked only at the page opened by Joanna.[13]

Pitt's death had led directly to changes in the administration and indirectly to the release of Brothers. When he came out of the madhouse after Easter, Joanna wrote to thank Lord Erskine and Sir Richard Ford, chief police magistrate for London. She also wrote to Brothers to say that, if he repented his sin of spiritual pride, and accepted her leadership, everyone could unite happily together. Her letter was returned unanswered.

After his release, Brothers fell under the sway of a new supporter, John Finlayson,[14] a Scottish lawyer, and neglected his former friends. As a result Foley, Sharp and Halhed transferred their entire allegiance to Joanna and in bitter mood, Sharp announced that he was going to destroy all his prints of Richard Brothers. Joanna persuaded him otherwise. He should simply blot out Brothers' name and the title 'Prince of the Hebrews', she suggested, preparing to lend a hand.

'I sent for one of the Prints and I painted his name over in three Red Streaks and compleatly blotted out his name with the Red paint,' she told Foley by letter in August.[15] In fact she had gone much further and on 17 and 18 July supposedly defaced as many as one thousand copies of the portrait.[16]

Joanna, rarely in the best of health, was by now dependent on spectacles and suffering from such weakness in her legs that she could scarcely walk more than a hundred yards. But one day that summer, after walking round and round the garden plucking a leaf every time she completed a circuit, she was amazed, when she counted them up, to see how far she had walked. Owen Pughe,[17] a renowned Welsh lexicographer and friend of William Blake, cunningly assured her that it

Published at No. 8, Charles Street, Midd.ᵗ Hospital London, April 16, 1795, by W. Sharp.

*Richard Brothers, as engraved by William Sharp in 1795, with
the inscription: 'Fully believing this to be the Man whom GOD
has appointed – I engrave his likeness.' This print shows the
inscription after it had been vehemently blotted out by Joanna's
'three Red Streaks' on 18 July 1806.*

was the same distance as Pentonville Chapel, so next day she walked thither and back. Again she amazed herself: 'I could not bear to walk round the Garden once in the heat of the day,' she marvelled, 'and could scarce speak only in coming upstairs.'[18]

And was her effort worthwhile? Apparently not, as far as the preacher was concerned. Preaching on the relative merits of prophecy and charity, he came down on the side of charity. Whereas prophecy showed God's love for man, he argued, charity was evidence of man's love for his fellow man and was therefore superior. Joanna heartily disagreed. But then she had little faith left in the wisdom of the clergy, Anglican or dissenting, as her letter to William Beet on 5 July 1806 showed.

Mr Beet had approached two clergymen to ask their opinion about the Second Coming of Christ. The first told him that it was of no concern to either of them; that if he led a good life according to the Scriptures, he would be safe. When Beet asked what he thought about the further Redemption (of the body) mentioned by St Paul (Romans 8:22-23), the clergyman replied that churchmen knew no more than he did about such mysteries.

Mr Beet then quizzed a dissenting minister and found his answers no more satisfactory.

'It is marvellous in my eyes,' wrote Joanna, 'how men professing the Gospel, can be so ignorant.'[19]

She was speaking from strength, being herself engaged in a course of strenuous study. 'I have been reading over the books of Josephus,' she announced later that month, 'where he writes of the destruction of Jerusalem . . .' and she was quick to draw parellels between disasters which befell the Jews and Europe's defeats at the hands of Bonaparte. Moreover she agreed with Josephus when he said: 'it will be evident to mankind in general, that our Destruction arises from our Misconduct, our ruin is certainly to be attributed to ourselves, after being premonish'd of future Events.'[20]

At the beginning of August an old scandal erupted again: signed seals were being sold for profit. Joanna knew immediately who to blame. A woman calling herself Bennett (but probably Downs) had recently come to see her, saying she knew her brother and the Reverend Eyre in Bristol and wanted seals for many people she had brought into the cause. Knowing that Eyre had run out of seals, Joanna sent the woman along to Field to have her names put on his list. The woman then returned to Bristol and sold the seals to people who merely wanted to break them open to see what was in them.[21] In response, Joanna issued new regulations about the distribution of seals: they must only be given to people who could show they had bought a copy of her book (*Sound an*

Alarm) and who would sign that they believed her calling was from God.[22] These measures, designed to stop scams, did not put an end to criticism.

Joseph Cockin, Independent Minister in Halifax, preached a sermon in which he castigated Joanna's followers as 'bantering, hectoring, brazen infidels, slaves, and fools', referring to the sealing as 'a shame to Bedlam'.[23] Moreover, on 13 August she received a book entitled *Satan's Power Extraordinary Detected, or the Strong Delusions of Joanna Southcott discovered, by the Author of an Awful Visitation of Satan and the Powers of Darkness*. Joanna's Spirit ordered her to reply to its author, 'a man in London', demanding to know what spirit inspired him. Instead of being posted, her letter was carried to him by a deputation consisting of Ann Underwood, John Wilson, Colonel Harwood, and William Tozer.

Ann Underwood, describing their visit, remarked how 'the countenance of the man appeared to us to be envious, subtile, and crafty; easily irritated to passion at the least contradiction: positive in his assertions, though when asked how he would prove them, he evaded any explanation.' As for what spirit inspired him, he said that he was frequently in touch with the departed spirit of a woman he had known in the West Indies as well as with an angel of light and an angel of darkness.

> Formerly he said the evil spirits stood before him as well as the good, with a thin veil of light between them, of late the spirit of darkness hath moved behind him. . . . He said he had seen the Devil, and conversed with him. . . . He received his communications from the spirit of light, which he calleth divine.

Mr Wilson demanded to know which spirit inspired him to write against Joanna. The man hesitated a long time before admitting that he had never read her writings, but had heard others talking about her doctrine and then had written against her 'by the Revelation of his Divine Attendant Spirit'. He denied the Millennium and Christ's Second Coming, insisting that Satan's power over the inner man had already been destroyed.

When he then started to complain of his dreadful affliction by evil spirits, Ann Underwood seized the opportunity to ask why he was not joyful if Satan's evil power had already been destroyed. He made no answer. She read out Joanna's letter, ignoring his frequent interruptions of 'Stuff! Stuff!' Then they left.[24]

Joanna wrote on 8 September,

> This morning about 8 o'clock I was turning in my bed, seized with a nightmare. I was perfectly sensible that Townley was up and saw the light in the room as plain as though I had been awake and heard them in the next room. I groaned aloud to

make them hear me and heard someone walk across the Dining
Room and open the door . . . looked and saw a young man in
Regimentals of a pleasing countenance, who smiled, came to
my bedside, awakened me and then vanished.'

Joanna had no trouble in identifying the pleasing young man.[25] She decided
it was the Lord, come to wake her out of a bad dream, such was the
nature of their cosy relationship.

On 28 September and 5 October Joanna went to hear Mr Huntingdon,
the popular, if eccentric, Calvinist preacher whom she had wanted to
hear the previous year. Having arrived at his chapel and paid for a seat,
she found that the place was already full and she was unable to sit
down. Far from being impressed by this show of popularity, she
afterwards sent him an indignant rebuke – for selling excess tickets,
and also for preaching election for some and exclusion from salvation
for the rest; his reply to be directed to her c/o William Sharp, 50 Titchfield
Street, Marylebone.[26] Her letter was returned with contempt on Friday
morning, 10 October, just as she was setting out to watch the funeral of
Charles James Fox.

The body was being taken from Chiswick House to Westminster Abbey
and Joanna had been invited to watch the procession from the windows
of Mr Halhed's house in Pall Mall. She went accompanied by Underwood,
Wilson and Sharp who, together with Halhed, his wife and one other
visitor, watched as soldiers with drawn swords led the stately cortège,
followed by a horseman carrying a crest shaped like a fox, and then
what should have been a stately line of noblemen's carriages – except
that two carts for the poor and another full of sand somehow got in
their way.

Afterwards, especially once the other guest, the only 'Unbeliever' in
the party, had left, Joanna's friends spent a delightful day talking to the
Halheds.[27]

Nevertheless Fox's death was another sad blow for a nation already
facing crisis as Bonaparte proceeded to pick off their allies one by one.
Mr Field wrote from London, full of anxiety, to Peter Morrison in
Mansfield the day after Fox's funeral: 'we have received News that the
WAR is likely to break out with more fury than ever. Our Ambassador is
suddenly called home – and we are in Daily Expectation of hearing of a
battle between the French and Prussians – and all the powers on the
Continent seem arming in a more dreadful manner than ever, and the
flames of war is now lighted up in Europe – Asia – Africa and America.'[28]
If they were searching for signs of Armageddon, they had not to look
far.

Meanwhile, poor Carpenter was in a sorry state. His home life had disintegrated when, because of a Mrs Wilmott, his wife went to live with their newly-married daughter, Mrs Winter. Then Joseph Prescott, to save his own soul, abandoned him to the company of Mrs Wilmott, the only one to stay by him as he gradually lost his grip on reality.[29] Much criticised after Dowland's death, Carpenter tried to restore his credibility by printing two handbills. The first announced that he had been asked to open a place to distribute Joanna's books near the Elephant and Castle. The second was a confirmation by Joanna that he had carried out all the orders she had given him at Leeds.[30] However, this official seal of approval was withdrawn after a year-long dispute over money and on 30 October Joanna publicly declared that Carpenter had renounced his faith, as she failed to see how anyone who refused to sell or return her books could possibly believe in her mission.[31]

In response to a query from a follower in Derbyshire about this time, Joanna explained the vague nature of prophecy like this: if her words were uttered with such clarity that they required no interpretation, then unscrupulous people might simply repeat them as their own and take all the credit![32] Her words did nothing to comfort poor Foley, still struggling with the repercussions of his bungled interpretation of one of Brothers' prophecies which had led him into wagering twenty guineas against Major Pidcock that there would be no more monarchy in France. As far as Major Pidcock was concerned, when Bonaparte was crowned by the Pope on 2 December, 1804, he had won his bet. Foley disagreed.

Their dispute rumbled on until August 1806 when Pidcock and Mr Justice Homfray, a fellow magistrate, descended on Foley's rectory and, after an exchange of insults, challenged him to a duel. Fortunately Mrs Foley was away at the time, staying with the Taylors in Exeter, and so was spared the worst of what followed.

Under the guise of 'holding out an olive branch' Foley sent a haughty rebuke to Pidcock and Homfray. Then, after delivering his sermon in Oldswinford church on Sunday 31 August, proceeded to regale the congregation with his side of the story: how the two magistrates had insulted him in the course of some trivial dispute and challenged him to a duel. And he concluded with the ringing declaration that he would defend his honour!

Soon afterwards he was writing a long, chatty letter to his wife with details of how he had been to the Bishop to forestall his enemies' latest move – they had raised a petition against him. And he had sent a letter to Scott who was prepared to act for him if he took Pidcock to court. And he had written to his newly married cousin, Lord Foley, who was a mighty power to be reckoned with in the locality.

Although the Pidcock affair obviously dominated his thoughts, Foley knew there would be other things on his wife's mind, for Elizabeth had gone to Devon leaving a fifteen-month old baby at home and a five-year old at boarding school, as well as her dairy animals and garden to be tended by others.

Lucky for her that Foley was a practical man with a special interest in medicine that enabled him to apply a poultice when little Noah Philip developed a whitlow on his toe.

'Let me have soon a long letter and full of news,' Foley begged, 'see I set you a good example – God bless you!'

Two days later he was writing again with answers to her questions about domestic matters.

> Betty returned home from Bromsgrove between 8 & 9 o'clock and told me you had got a place in the coach. . . . Sally goes on very well and I have no fault to find. . . . Your cow for the last two weeks has made rather more than 9lb of Butter each week. . . . We have sold 7°lb each week at 16° and 15° – and the Milk woman paid me for the milk last week 3 shillings and for 1lb Butter. Mrs West has had 2lb each week & Mrs Foxall 1lb each week and the settlement with them is to remain till you return. . . .

Noah Philip's whitlow was getting better and 'I do not forget to give him the kisses you send him.'

A week later Foley, the perfect husband, was not only providing Elizabeth with more details of how much milk and butter her cow had produced, but declaring 'I am gathering great Riches for you. Do you want any money, for if you do, with great pleasure I will transmit you some. . . .'

What followed paints a picture of what life was like in the Oldswinford rectory as autumn approached.

> The Damsons are done by Sally, one Peck, and I hope they will prove good. . . . Nelly Dillard was here on Friday and brought me a fowl which she would not have anything for and because she would not take money I gave her a piece of black silk, about half yard, to make her a bonnet of – she says the Elderberries begin to be ripe, but the late ones may not be ready till the first week in October, by when I hope you will be back.

As a fond father he had also sent Mrs Morgan over to Richard's school at Chaddesley, about seven miles away, 'with a cake and some apples and pears, with which our dear Dick was greatly delighted.' The little boy had asked if he might come home two or three days before Christmas – a request which Foley was inclined to 'endulge him in'. Meanwhile, Foley pressed his wife to bring Miss Taylor back to

Oldswinford with her, stating (as if that settled the matter) that he had already written to Joanna telling her that she was coming for the winter.[33]

So it transpired that the Taylors' eldest daughter, Sarah, accompanied Elizabeth Foley home and stayed at the Rectory over Christmas. Although no one was prepared to let the dispute with Pidcock ruin the festive season, still it refused to go away. Towards the end of January Foley wrote to declare that he would never acknowledge Bonaparte King but, as a compromise, would pay the wager money to Major Pidcock if – and when – the British government made such a public acknowledgment.[34] This did not please Pidcock, who replied:

> Sir,
>
> Your letter is by no means satisfactory to me. I will not allow that the beast – Joanna Southcott – Religion – the Scriptures – or Revelations have anything to do with our Bet – and I am sorry you oblige me to say, that I shall never rest satisfied until this unpleasant business is settled in a proper and gentlemanlike manner. . . .

A blistering series of letters ensued, with both sides insisting that it was not money that was at stake, but principle; each was refusing to accept that the other was acting like a gentleman.[35]

All this time, Joanna could do no more than support Foley from afar. She was busy with her own affairs as she, Townley and Underwood moved into a new home at 17 Weston Place, Paddington, where, together with Mr Abbott, they set up a business distributing her books. Her following had increased so rapidly that by the end of 1806 the 'sealed' numbered nearly fourteen thousand. Not that all were of equal virtue, many of the first sealed had fallen away and known impostors were now expunged from the list. For, as Joanna said: 'They are not all of Israel that are in Israel.'[36]

Nor did everyone behave as she, their 'Mother', wished. Whereas some, such as those in Leeds, worked together in harmony, others seemed always at each others' throats. Exeter was notorious in this respect. On 6 December 1806 Joanna had written to G. Woolcott in Exeter giving her approval of the meetings which were taking place:

> For as knife sharpens knife, so does a man his friend; and by these meetings in different places many have been strengthened and established. Therefore as you have began, I wish you to continue.

She was not, however, in favour of their setting up a Southcottian chapel. 'As to establishing a place of worship with any alterations to the Prayers of the Church, it is not approved of by God or man. . . .' Besides, there was always the difficulty of finding a suitable minister. 'Ye know in Exeter how deeply a man's character would be scrutinised who began to be a preacher to the people', she said with the wisdom (and pain) of hindsight. In order to survive he would need 'every Christian patience and fortitude.'

The man being nominated for the post was Robert Portbury, son of a bookbinder who had worked for the Browns at Honiton. Joanna had misgivings about him. She wrote,

> I am sorry to say . . . though he appears zealous in the cause, yet the rashness of his passions is such, as I fear would do more hurt than good to be at the head of a people, I do not think establishing a church for the present in such a place as Exeter would be of any kind of good. And yet, by your meeting together, you may, in time, get an united Church to join together.[37]

The question as to whether her followers should continue to attend their normal church or set up chapels of their own was frequently raised. '[N]o one was ever ordered by me to leave his Church,' Joanna declared, before pointing out that that there was very little benefit to Believers in listening to preachers because they rarely explained the Scriptures satisfactorily. On the other hand, they could learn from them the difference between the wisdom of men and the revelation of the Lord. 'I have been ordered to go to many churches in London,' Joanna explained, 'and from going to the churches and the ministers that I have heard clearly showed me that if the Scriptures were not explained by a Revelation from the Lord, they would never be explained from the wisdom of man, as none of the ministers that I have heard explained the Scriptures or preached as though they thought they would ever be fulfilled.'[38]

Joanna's low estimation of preachers was not helped by her association with William Tozer who, having been put in charge of her chapel in Duke Street, for a while did little but moan how he wished he had never been called into the work. Joanna felt very hurt by this kind of remark until the Spirit, revealing himself as a brilliant psychologist, instructed her to tell Tozer that he should grieve no more because by the end of the year (1806) he would be released from his calling and left to his own devices. After that, if he wished to go on with the Meeting, it would be purely voluntary. Moreover, because Joanna would no longer subsidise the Meeting, it would survive only by his own efforts. So, let him reflect – and if he decided to go on, think twice before complaining again!

Tozer did not need long to reflect. He never questioned his role in Joanna's mission again.[39]

PIPING TO DEAF ADDERS

One would almost think that Satan meant to destroy us by
accidents; but thanks be to God, he can go no further than his
chain. *Field to Morrison*, 5 May, 1807

Never did such a chapter of disasters befall Joanna's followers as in the
early months of 1807. The Fields were not alone in thinking that Satan
was out to destroy them. Not one of their inner circle seemed immune.
While Foley was caught up in his endless Pidcock affair, Joanna and the
London friends – Sharp, Wilson and Major Eyre – had tumbled into the
clutches of John King, a money-lender of 76 Norton Street, who was
demanding enormous sums from them. To finance the printing of Joanna's
books the three men had given King signed bills to the value of over
£2,000 but received less than half that sum back. When it came to
honouring the bills, they disputed the amount owed, and the money-
lender brought an action in the court of King's Bench to recover his
debt. The question was, should they pay up, or mount a defence? Joanna
had no doubt. They must fight.

Taking up the cudgels on her friends' behalf, she sent King a long
letter reproving his conduct, backed up by many passages from
Scripture. King immediately sent a polite reply. 'I admire your character
and revere your doctrine,' he avowed, 'and believe most devoutedly the
divine authority you quoted.' But he was not prepared to give up his
suit.

At the trial King, because he was Jewish, took his oath on the Old
Testament but admitted having been sworn on the Gospels on a previous
occasion. In presenting his case, he blamed Sharp's failure to honour
debts on his apocalyptic views, declaring that Sharp had said the country
would be in such a state of confusion by May, that there was no point in
paying anybody.

When Joanna appeared as a witness, one of the counsel remarked
that 'a new person had been presented to the court, who, under pretence
of prophecy, had presumed to blaspheme the name of God; that which
she stated was, however, true.' It seems that the defence benefited from
her testimony, even though her friends still had to pay back a substantial
amount of money. Moreover, Sharp never ceased to grieve at how he

had been made to sit for five hours hearing his character traduced without being permitted to clear himself, and even when the trial was over he remained depressed by all the lies about him in the newspapers.[1]

In March Joanna, Townley and Underwood had moved into 17 Weston Place, their home for the rest of their lives. Downstairs was a shop managed by Charles Abbott who, finding Joanna's books bringing in insufficient profit – especially during the dispute with King when funds ran too low to fund a new title – fell back on the sale of cotton goods such as gowns, handkerchiefs, and cravats.[2] For Townley, reared far from the stress of trade, it was a sad comedown, and all three women suffered in mind and body during the next few months.

Then the Reverend Stanhope Bruce slipped on some flag-stones, gashed his hip, and was left lying on the ground for three hours before help came. It took three men to carry him upstairs to bed, where the seventy-seven year old lay for a fortnight, unable to help his poor wife who was also dangerously ill.[3]

Colonel Harwood fell from his horse, broke two fingers 'and almost forced the joints up to his wrist.'

Turner and Hirst were forced to take to their beds with fever.

John Torin, a witness at Joanna's trial who professed 'full confidence in our Mother's Mission to the last', died almost three years to the day after William Coy.

Richard Goldsmith was loading a dung cart which rolled back down a slope and would have crushed him to death had he not been strong enough to leap out of the way.

'One would almost think that Satan meant to destroy us by accidents; but thanks be to God, he can go no further than his chain,' wrote Mr Field to Peter Morrison in May, recounting these disasters. Nor had his own family been exempt. His wife having suffered a miscarriage, then dropped a saucepan of boiling water over her foot. Their children had such bad attacks of whooping cough that they feared the two boys, Southcott and Elias, were going to choke. Worst of all, Field's youngest son, 'a fine little boy', had died in his arms.

It must have been some small compensation to know that Joanna's enemies were suffering as well. Fox's death meant the return to office of the pro-war administration which had persecuted Brothers and so, rather than risk causing new offence, he postponed issuing his latest prints of the *Building of Jerusalem*. This move alienated his chief supporter, Captain Finlayson, with disastrous results for Maria Bruce.

After her bitter wrangle with Joanna, Maria Bruce had returned to the Brothers' camp. However, as a widowed mother of a large family her finances were in such parlous state that she was arrested several times for debt. Nor was this the worst of her troubles for, unbeknown to her, her daughter had become emotionally entangled with Captain Finlayson who, when he deserted Brothers, persuaded young Miss Bruce to elope with him to Scotland. Before she went she raided her mother's boxes, taking what she pleased, leaving an insolent note pointing out that 'she was now of age to think and act for herself.' Soon after reading this, Maria collapsed with a fever from which she never fully recovered.[4]

In the weeks leading up to the trial over the money bills Joanna received letters from all over the country relaying this kind of news. None affected her so much as the letter from Foley intimating that Stanhope Bruce's wife (the erstwhile Mrs Dix) was dying. Joanna sent back a Communication for Foley to show Stanhope Bruce if he thought fit. Her Spirit's message was a simple one: Bruce should not grieve if he loses his partner because 'his loss will be her gain.' On Thursday, 28 May, Mrs Bruce 'gently glided away without a groan,' wrote Foley; 'I never witnessed a more easy and happy death.' A few hours before, he had read Joanna's

> truly comfortable and heart chearing Communication to Mr Bruce who, dear Man, received it with all thankfulness and gratitude from the Lord. After the first of his grief had subsided, he became perfectly resigned, composed and comfortable; and blessed be God, he has continued so ever since. . . .

Joanna, taking the news less well, kept remembering 'all her kindness and love to me' which led to 'feelings of sorrow, feeling for his loss and thinking I should never see her more in this world, though my faith was strong in meeting her in a better.'[5]

Amidst the general malaise, only the Taylors in Exeter seemed to thrive as they deserved, their business escaping almost unscathed when a tremendous fire broke out in the vicinity in April.[6] Perhaps they were being rewarded for their continuing kindness to Miss Harwood – for the Colonel's affairs had still not permitted him to make them any payment for his daughter's keep. On 25 June – the day after the trial involving King had ended, – Joanna wrote:

> [B]ut as he is now getting out of his difficulties we hope he will very shortly send Mr Taylor a remittance to the full amount and had it been in our powers we should have done it for him, but it really was not, as it has caused us a great deal of sorrow.[7]

Joanna's relief was palpable. The dark clouds of the last six months had cleared and she could see the way forward. Foley had been in town and no doubt encouraged her to write another book: *An Account of the Trials on Bills of Exchange, wherein the deceit of Mr John King and his Confederates . . . is exposed.*

Moreover she must have been relieved when May came and went with no announcement of a miraculous birth in Chesterfield, Derbyshire. For during the early part of the summer rumours had spread of a strange woman in that town who claimed that some time in May she would give birth to a boy with the name of Jesus on his right breast, who would do wonders. Since her excited followers gave out that this Child would convince more people than Joanna,[8] the claim could not be seen as anything other than a challenge. In the event there was no miraculous birth and the story might have died a quick death – had not Joanna taken the idea and pondered it in her heart.

Although Joanna soon recovered her spirits after the trial, Townley felt so poorly that a letter she started to John Hows in mid-June was not finished till August.[9] So when, on the first Sunday of July, Joanna was ordered to Mr Tozer's chapel to return thanks for the outcome of the court case she was accompanied by Underwood. Instead of making themselves known, the two women sat in a private room until the service was over. Then, after those not staying for the Sacrament had left, Tozer came and fetched Joanna. Emerging into the main body of the chapel, she was amazed to see a mass of people waiting to receive the Sacrament. '[M]y heart seem'd too full to bear my own feelings of love, joy and happiness,' she later exclaimed. After taking communion she spoke to all the others. Then there was a moment of silence before they brought the meeting to close with a hymn. For Joanna the experience was crowned by being driven home 'in peace and safety' by a coachman who was a believer.

Next morning Tozer arrived drunk with joy – as if with wine – and unable to do anything except walk about. For Joanna it seemed an irony of fate that this roughcast fellow from Devon had welcomed her to the Sacrament whereas her other fellow countryman, Pomeroy, refused her.[10] Not that there was time to brood about Pomeroy. The split with Carpenter had left a problem and, if every problem is an opportunity, then Joanna was the one to exploit it.

Her followers were known by their names appearing on her lists of sealed people. The trouble was, some seals had been spoilt by being carried around in people's bosoms, their owners being afraid to leave them at home in case unbelievers destroyed them.[11] These seals were now being sent to Joanna to be stamped again. Another problem was that the original lists had been made on paper manufactured by Carpenter. Because Carpenter was now the enemy, could it have been a mistake for Joanna to allow this to happen? The Spirit reassured her: it was right for her to use paper made in the place where the furnace of her vision stood and where Satan would be cast out. On the other hand, now that Carpenter had changed, it was right for the paper to be changed too. So, if anyone wanted to sign again, they should produce their seals and add the words 'sealed before' to their signature.[12]

On 25 September, 1807, Mr Field, chief distributor of Joanna's books, sent twenty-five seals to John Bedford of Stockport, enclosing strict instructions for the compilation of his new list. Second seals were to be given only to those whose first seals were still whole and who possessed their own copies of *Sound An Alarm* and *Caution to the Sealed*. Their names were to be entered on the right of the list followed by the letters 'S.B.' (Sealed Before). The paper was to be pasted 'one half sheet at the bottom of another' so that it could be made as long as required and then rolled up. Field wrote, doubtless rubbing his hands together in anticipation of new book sales:

> Remember one *Sound an Alarm* and one *Caution to the Sealed*
> serves a man and his wife – but if 20 in a family all want seals,
> all must comply with these conditions. . . .

And in case any one should doubt the urgency of the times, he concluded with alarming bits of gossip. From France had come news that Bonaparte was assembling a great army at Antwerp for the invasion of England. Much closer to home there had been a riot in Holborn when the Irish from Whitechapel had descended on the Irish in St Giles's armed with bludgeons and sticks. A desperate battle ensued until soldiers were sent for and seized nine ringleaders. The following week the Whitechapel Irish returned in double force and another fierce battle ended only when twenty more were seized and packed on board a ship.[13]

Lawlessness and fear of crime were natural concomitants of living in the capital. No one – not even those under special spiritual protection – were immune. One wet, dark night towards the end of September Joanna went to bed early with a headache and stomach pains only to be woken up at half past two in the morning by Jane Townley sitting up in bed, saying she had heard a violent crash. Townley threw up the sash window to shout, 'Who's there?' and was relieved to hear Mr Abbott, who had gone down into the shop, yell back, 'All's safe.'

After checking all the other rooms, Abbott returned to the shop and noticed that the shutter had been forced open and the frame and wainscot were all broken. Hearing this, Joanna and everyone else got up and, while praising the Lord for His protection, set about checking all the other windows in the house. Then they went back to bed, leaving Mr Abbott to sit up and keep watch in the shop. Next morning they heard that a new chapel had been burnt down at Holloway.

This attempted break-in confirmed Joanna's worst fears. Knowing how many burglaries there were in London, she had suggested fitting

One of Joanna's Seals (open). Dated 28 December 1806, this had been issued to John Wilson, one the Seven Stars. After the recipient's name was written, the paper was folded like an envelope, closed and sealed on the back. A number of unused papers survive, showing that Joanna's signature and red 'IC' seal were used to authenticate the document before it was allocated, and then a second and different seal would have been pressed in wax to close the paper securely.

alarm bells on the doors and windows when they moved into the house in March. Her fears had increased after Abbott opened his shop on the premises, but Townley had managed to convince her that, because they were in a public place with coaches and wagons passing all night, there was no risk.[14]

A few days before this unpleasant incident, Townley had written to her young protégé, Charles Taylor, who was working at Ilmington, near Shipston-on-Stour, and complaining that he had not heard from his London friends. She told him how much better they were all feeling since the court case was settled.

'Mr Wilson has been very happy and looked himself again since 24

June . . . but Mr Sharp was so much affected by the lies and mockery that he stayed depressed.' Although the dispute had taken its toll, Joanna's book did much to raise her friends' spirits. Even Dr Moseley professed himself delighted with it, judging Joanna to be 'a wonderful clever woman, for his friend Fox could not have brought forward clearer arguments.' Moreover, a clergyman who came to drink tea asked for one of Joanna's seals and declared that, although he had studied Scriptures all his life, after reading her book he felt he had everything still to learn.[15]

On about the same day that Charles was opening Miss Townley's letter came one from Foley mentioning that he had written a long letter to his father which he feared might have been lost as he had received no reply. 'It had a £1 note in it to buy lace for our little girl Ann Elizabeth now about one month old.'

Not much was happening in London, Foley reported – priding himself in the fact that his own meetings on Thursday evenings and Sunday afternoons were well-attended.

Foley had a wealthy uncle living some twenty miles from Oldswinford whom he thought of visiting because he was unwell. However, when his curate went off shooting, leaving him to look after the parish himself, Foley changed his mind.[16] His failure to go proved a costly mistake.

Joanna, reared on a daily diet of the Scriptures, must have been gratified when the Spirit told her that one day her Visitation would be regarded as a New Testament. Soon after receiving this message she heard a fluttering at her window, and looked up to see a swallow with an ear of corn in its beak. She carefully opened the window but, before flying away, the bird dropped the corn which, although apparently plump and healthy, turned out to have nothing but blackened grains. She found herself writing:

> Like blind flies
> Err with their wings
> For want of eyes
> Mankind will not see.[17]

And there was the rub. Although for fifteen years Joanna had been publicising her Visitation, the vast majority of people remained blind to her message and even those whose eyes had been opened were rarely of sufficient calibre to further her mission. In fact, she was often criticised for not attracting men of true learning and piety to her cause.[18] Such criticism could not apply to the Reverend Robert Hoadley Ashe D.D., son of a prebendary of Winchester and perpetual curate of Crewkerne and Misterton since 1775.[19]

Having visited Joanna for the first time on Wednesday, 23 September, 1807, Ashe sent her a letter accompanied by 146 lines of verse to express the effect she had on him:

> After I left your company, your spriritual Communications still vibrated in my ears, I thought you still speaking – still stood fixed to hear. I have taken the liberty of enclosing the verses for your approbation; they are expressive of the real feelings of my soul.

His poem included lines such as:

> When Simeon first the infant Jesus saw,
> That promised substance of the Jewish law,
> His aged eyes o'erflowed with tears of joy,
> As in his arms he clasped the wondrous Boy.

He continued,

> You will, I hope consider them as the production of a new disciple of Christ, who has been only a month in your school; but who was fully convinced by the perusal of the Second Volume, that the hand of God, the Divine Spirit, inspired every page of it.

Whatever happened at their meeting had served only to confirm for this scholarly man that he was in the presence of a genuine prophet. Next day he rushed out to buy two more of her books and found them even more convincing. He wrote:

> For more than 37 years I have diligently searched the Scriptures in seven different languages; I have consulted all the commentators with the hope of finding the truth. I have also tried to make classical learning the handmaid of religion, only to find, however, that God is now giving us the True Bread from Heaven in your Writings. The Wisdom of Man will soon be found Foolishness with God.

Nevertheless, even he could not fail to see the dichotomy involved in finding such pearls in a common oyster:

> Because this spiritual information hath not been communicated to the world through the Bishops and Pastors of His Church, but through a weak, low, simple and illiterate woman, they say of you: 'From whence hath this Prophetess learning?' I leave them to answer themselves. But first let them answer thy Writings – they cannot answer them. I defy those boasted champions, those defenders of the Christian Church, to confute a single interpretation of the Scriptures which you have revealed to us. . . .[20]

Praise indeed! And all the more surprising when for Joanna everything was so simple. Indeed, the only thing she could not understand was why others failed to see things as she did.

She wrote to Richard Warren, a young man who worked for a wool-dyer in Exeter and also claimed to have visions,

> I am astonished to hear the ignorance there is in mankind, when they see the heavy affliction that our nation is now under, and our commerce and trading so much stopped that thousands are complaining . . . they are almost starving for want of labour, and yet they are inquiring where are the judgments.[21]

There is no doubt that people found Joanna's divine utterances impressive, yet on occasions when the Spirit remained silent, leaving her to speak from her own common sense, she was equally convincing. When asked how to deal with evil spirits, she suggested rebuking them in strong words from the Scriptures.[22] Someone once asked what she thought about astrology. Making it clear that she had no Communication on the subject and so was merely voicing her own opinion, she warned them against it.[23] Whilst suggesting that many undiagnosed illnesses were wrongly attributed to witchcraft, she admitted that she had once advised a neighbour who was losing cattle to fix 'Holiness to the Lord' on parchment inside the animals' bridles, and this had worked![24]

If the Devil found work for idle hands, from October 1807 he had little chance with Joanna. Resurrecting her old upholstery skills, she had taken up patchwork to make quilts for her best friends. The first was designed for Daniel Roberts of Painswick and, because he was a Quaker, Joanna thought of doing the middle in plain colours like their dress. Only when she ran out of plain stuff and was forced to use other colours did she decide that her quilt signified that Roberts would not remain with the Quakers but find himself joined with different kinds of friends later.

In fact, the longer she sat doing her neat running stitches and thinking, the more symbolic her quilt became. She concluded that the reason for her using so many different materials was that there was no existing Christian sect large and united enough to cover mankind – which was why the Lord would cut them all up and rejoin them in Joanna's mission. She had also put an 'hour-glass' shape at each corner – and they were to remind people that the sands of time were running out![25]

Writing to describe her quilt to Owen Pughe, a doctor of law as well as a distinguished Welsh scholar, Joanna also made him privy to some news she had just received from her sister. Susanna's husband, William Carter, had deserted her – sold off all his stock, given up the farm at Plymtree and, taking all the money, run off with a younger woman. Poor Susanna was devastated; at fifty-eight years of age, after nearly thirty years of marriage and a lifetime of hard toil, left destitute. But,

A sampler worked by Joanna Southcott in 1807 which her followers regarded as prophetic. A later disciple wrote: 'The centre of the sampler, if viewed from an acute angle, takes the form of the Altar of Incense in the Tabernacle. Four continents are named at the corners and curious symbols can be seen on the design, which is worked as seven squares, the centre forming the eighth. It has a worked border of one hundred and thirty-one hour-glasses, which we think imply that that period of years should see all fulfilled.' (Rachel Fox: How We Built Jerusalem in England's Green and Pleasant Land, *Vol.1, p.129.)*

being a Southcott, she did not give up easily. She discovered that Carter was in South Molton, thirty miles away. When she went to confront him she found that, passing himself off as a widower, he had gone through a marriage ceremony with Eleanor Mylard,[26] who was expecting his child.[27] Susanna promptly secured a warrant for his arrest – to avoid which Carter fled to Germany.[28]

It is not hard to imagine Joanna's feelings when she heard this tale of woe, especially when Susanna ended up by asking her if she could send her one of her seals. Susanna – of all people – requesting a seal! Moreover she assured Joanna that she had read all her books and was now truly convinced that her Visitation was from the Lord. She even said how glad she was that Joanna had never heeded her advice about giving it up.

Surely no letter, unless from Pomeroy, could have pleased Joanna more. Dear Susanna joining her flock at last. Just as Joanna had foretold. On receiving the news, she immediately got William Sharp to extract the relevant paper from the writings sealed at High House and check what she had said eleven years before. And there it was, in black and white, the prophecy that one day Susanna would be convinced!

For Joanna it was most gratifying.

She passed on the news to Mrs Mary Symons on 31 December 1807:

Dear Friend,

I am happy to inform you that my sister Carter is at last come in a strong believer and writes me she is glad I never took her advice, she desireth me to put down her name and send her a seal. This fulfils a Communication in 1796. . . .

She shall know who is thy Master
Here Philosophy goes Deep
And mazed at thee, she'll wish to be
And never from thee part. . . .
For when thy writings fly abroad
Thousands like her will cry,
That they their senses all shall loose
To find the Mystery.[29]

Joanna's Spirit, never one to waste good copy, drew endless lessons from Susanna's plight:

Now discern from her Husband what hath made him flee and brought shame and reproach on himself for forsaking the wife of his espousals, breaking the Vows he made at the alter, and binding himself to a Harlot, these are the evils that he hath done, for which thy Sister hath told thee he is forced to flee . . . like the state of man . . . for thousands like him hath forsaken Me and broke every Covenant I made with man . . . and My Just Warrant is out against THEM![30]

There was more news to add to Joanna's satisfaction. Once the second sealing had been launched, John Symons reported that people in Exeter had streamed in to sign again and there were many new enquirers.

'*Signs of the Times* makes many mockers pause, they hardly know what to make of us, and we are men wondered at,' wrote Field in a letter to Morrison; 'But "the Woman Cloathed with the Sun will make all Nations fear'.'[31]

It seems that Field's confidence in Joanna rested on the misfortunes of her enemies, for he described with scarcely disguised enthusiasm how Carpenter had fallen out with Brandon and Pritchard over the money which was to be spent on refurbishing his chapel; how Carpenter's son-in-law, Captain Winter, who had set up a printing office and bookshop had just gone bankrupt; how Joseph Prescott now denied his visions, saying he had made them all up to please Carpenter. There was also Captain Jones (alias Baynes), a former supporter of Carpenter, who was at present in Cardiff Castle awaiting trial for witchcraft. And, of course, the sad case of Maria Bruce, whose recent death led Field to observe: 'It's wonderful how Joanna's enemies are falling.'

The strange thing is, Field saw no such connection between divine justice and the misfortunes which dogged Joanna's loyal followers. John Wilson, for instance, having emerged bloody and somewhat bowed from the King affair, was then arraigned by Miles, the late Sheriff of London, for a debt of £1,500 which, when added to nearly £3,000 worth of goods destroyed by fire, cost him his factory and caused him financial ruin. In April 1808, at the height of Wilson's difficulties, Field wrote to the Foleys to ask a favour for his friend, being very careful to include Mrs Foley in the request. Could they possibly offer Wilson asylum to prevent him going to prison? And, although it seems unlikely that Field would be acting without Joanna's approval, he asked Foley not to tell Joanna or Sharp that he had written. Warm-hearted Foley wrote back immediately. He would afford Wilson asylum 'with great joy' until the storm had blown over – the only condition being that Field acquaint 'dear Joanna' with the whole business, as it went like a dagger to his heart to conceal anything from her.[32]

In their personal lives 1807 drew to a quiet close for Joanna, Townley and Underwood. Although they had lots of letters to write, it was a silent time with regard to Communications and some of the friends were growing anxious. Thinking to further the cause, Foley wrote a letter to the queen, the bishops and the clergy, and Turner prepared an advertisement for the press – projects which Joanna quashed on the grounds that the Lord said it would be 'piping to deaf adders'.[33]

But what was a silent time for Joanna was not respected by her opponents. 'Joanna, why feignest thou thyself to be another? for I am sent to thee with heavy tidings', wrote a Calvinist preacher called Smith in March 1808, misquoting 1 Kings 14:6. Smith had published a book called *The Lying Prophetess Detected,* in which he judged the sealing to be unnecessary because 'God from eternity hath predestined certain men unto life, certain men He hath reprobated unto death.' He further vilified Joanna in verse such as:

> Thou mother of witchcraft and teacher of lies,
> Subverter of truth and deep in disguise,
> I dread not thy curse, nor fear thee to tell
> The whole of thy system proceedeth from hell.

Joanna through her amanuensis quickly took up pen in her own defence. *An Answer to a Sermon Published and Preached by Mr Smith . . . at Beersheba Chapel, Prospect Place, St George's Fields* asked Mr Smith the pertinent question, 'Who sent thee with heavy tidings to me?' and pointed out that he was 'feigning himself to be a prophet.'[34]

The Taylors had sent their usual tribute of a goose, chickens and a hare to their London friends for Christmas – largesse which left Townley feeling uncomfortable, as they had still not received a penny from Colonel Harwood for his daughter's keep. On 17 January 1808, she wrote to Mrs Taylor explaining that the Colonel was still financially embarrassed, having fallen among a den of thieves and seeing his stock sold for a third of its value. She added,

> If the Colonel does not send money I feel myself responsible to pay Mr Taylor as soon as it is in my power, but I beg you will not let her [Miss Harwood] have more money to spend than is absolutely necessary. . . . We were ignorant of the Colonel's circumstances when we requested you to take her as a boarder.[35]

It is not clear whether her father ever settled up with the Taylors, but by August Miss Harwood was back in London, sending love to her Exeter friends.

Meanwhile, the crime situation in London continued to trouble Joanna. She was particularly shocked to hear of the death of Mr Joachim who was shot through the heart as he was going home to Camden Town at midnight on 1 June, 1808. As a sealed person, his violent death had double impact. Not only was it dreadful to lose a friend, it raised the old question: why had not his seal kept him safe? Joanna was told that it was folly for her followers to think this way. There was no security in a piece of paper, only in faith in her mission.[36]

By this time Joanna had established an efficient network for the distribution of her books. They were sold by: E.J. Field, 3 Broad Court, Long Acre; C. Abbott, East End of Old Street, near Shoreditch Church; William Tozer, Lambeth Road, St George's Fields; T.P. Foley at Oldswinford; S. Hirst in Leeds; Joseph Southcott, 69 Broad Quay, Bristol; Mr Symons, Gandy Lane, Exeter and Miss Eveleigh, St Sidwells, Exeter. Prices varied, but the normal arrangement was for booksellers to buy copies from her at something like 1s.9d and resell them for 2s.3d each. According to Foley's accounts, on 20 August, 1808, he had in stock £792.15s. worth of Joanna's books.

The author's own profits were supposed to be ploughed back into further publications. Not that these profits were huge. Field, writing to Peter Morrison in 1807, had said, 'I think it will be a long time before they are about to Print another Book. The printing of so many thousand has already cost them such a sum of Money. . . .'[37] From Exeter in August 1808 Miss Eveleigh wrote offering to forego her commission if it would help the cause, but Joanna assured her old friend that she had done enough and was not required to make any further sacrifices. Instead, she encouraged her to order fifty copies of her most recent book 'as it is not worth while to send a smaller parcel on account of the Carriage' – besides, it was sure to sell briskly, for (even if she did say it herself) it was a book 'much sought after as it is greatly liked everywhere & fills the believer's mouths with arguments to confound gainsayers.'[38]

Meanwhile, the war on the Continent had taken a hopeful turn in 1808 when the Portuguese copied the Spanish by revolting against the French. To support their old allies, Britain sent an expeditionary force under Arthur Wellesley who managed to force Marshal Junot to withdraw his army from the Peninsula under the terms of the Convention of Cintra, signed in August.

This settlement was the subject of conversation between Joanna and John Wilson as they walked towards Tozer's chapel in Duke Street on Friday, 2 September. Even the pouring rain failed to dampen their spirits as they passed ships on the river festooned with flags and heard guns being fired in token of victory. They arrived at the chapel to find a service in progress, after which all unbelievers were asked to leave. Despite the storm and the fact that nobody had been expecting Joanna, the meeting was very full and included seventy-four believers hoping to receive their seals. Those who had not previously signed were questioned at the altar by Mr Tozer. The seals were then closed and the bread and wine distributed. Afterwards, Mr Tozer called out the names, and friends handed the seals to their respective owners.

Then Joanna spoke. Comparing the grain of mustard seed with her Visitation, she urged all believers to join hand and heart to clamour for Satan's destruction, just as man had clamoured for Christ's blood.[39] After the last hymn, 'Crown Him Lord of All', she said she hoped the words would strike deep in every heart, for her earnest prayer was for them all to be as one sheep under one shepherd and for Christ to keep them in the hollow of his hand. Not that the storm was over, she warned.

They must remain steadfast in faith, waiting like the Wise Virgins to enter with the Bridegroom. Joanna then took leave of a congregation which had apparently hung on her every word.

Nevertheless, things seemed not to be going well. When the new lists of the sealed were returned from around the country they showed a marked falling away. 14,000 people had signed before. Now, instead of the 7,000 she had predicted in her latest book, there were only 5,971 – and these included 4,673 people signing for a second time. Joanna might have been depressed had she not recalled an earlier vision of a prolific tree which, after shedding its first fruits, produced new berries which she knew would come good.[40]

If what counted was quality, not quantity, how was that quality to be assessed? Although Joanna respected people like Hoadley Ashe, William Sharp, and Owen Pughe for their erudition, others were valued for more worldly reasons. When Foley, travelling home with his wife from Exeter after staying with the Taylors, stopped off at Bristol in October 1808 he was most impressed by the Reverend Samuel Eyre's meeting. Not only did he find 'love, union and harmony' among the hundred or so regular members but was proudly told that one family was worth £9,000 a year and was generous with it!

Foley must have been envious, being somewhat in need of a hand-out himself. Nine years previously he had backed a note for a friend who swore on everything sacred that he would never suffer for it, but now he was facing a demand for payment of the principal plus interest on the sum. In fact, money was so tight that he even had to borrow £5 from Mr Taylor before setting out from Exeter and it seemed that only his rich uncle's will stood between him and financial ruin.

Small wonder then that the Foleys made the most of their trip, knowing what pressures awaited them at home. After their prolonged stop in Bristol, where they called on Joseph Southcott and the Joneses as well as the Eyres, they spent 'four heavenly days' with Daniel Roberts and his family in Painswick before setting out on the last, eventful leg of their journey. After a long wait in Bromsgrove, they got a chaise driven by a coachman who kept dozing off because he had not slept for six nights, and the experience proved so nerve-racking that, when a wheel came off at Hagley, they left their two large boxes with friends and walked the last mile home to Oldswinford.[41]

JOANNA'S LIKENESS

You acknowledged to two gentlemen that . . . being a prophetess,
she was fair game for any one to shoot at.
                                        Townley to Hewson Clarke, 6 July, 1812

Towards the end of January, 1809, there was a heavy fall of snow
which, as it melted, caused unprecedented flooding in Weston Place.
The first intimation of trouble came on Tuesday, 24 January, when the
women were busily occupied in their room upstairs and melting snow
began to leak through the ceiling. Next morning, Charles Abbott being
first downstairs discovered the kitchen half full of water. He raised the
alarm, but there was little anyone could do except shift their possessions,
watch the flood level rise and hope it would not reach the books. At
eight o'clock, the stream pouring along either side of Battlebridge Road,
had reached the point where the road forked to Hampstead and Highgate
and the water was up so high that people were trapped in their houses.
By midday it was flowing like a rapid river. Only at four in the afternoon
did it begin to subside. By nine o'clock, although it had ebbed and all
but gone in the street, there were still several inches covering the kitchen.

A man who had lived fifty years in Weston Place declared he had never
seen such a flood in his life. Nevertheless, the fact that the occupants of
number 17 had been caught off guard raised the question: why was Joanna
not forewarned so that more could have been saved from the kitchen? The
Spirit replied that if he warned her of every trifle, believers would expect
directions for everything and develop no wisdom of their own.

On Thursday morning at eight o'clock the floods rose exactly as the
day before, rising to within six inches of the same height by midday and
beginning to abate at the same time. That evening there was anxious
debate. Townley thought the floods would not reappear on the third
day; Harwood, Abbott and Underwood thought they would only come
outside. Happily Townley proved right.[1]

Financial stringency meant fewer books being produced. Nevertheless
Joanna managed to publish *A True Picture of the World and A Looking-
Glass for All Men* in 1809, the main purpose of which was to deny all
connection with Mary Bateman, owner of the chicken whose eggs had
announced the Second Coming and who had recently been found guilty

of the murder of Mrs Perigo of Bramley. When, in their report of its trial, the *York Herald* alleged that the accused was a 'follower of Joanna's principles', many other newspapers repeated the statement together with details suggesting that Bateman had been a thief and impostor from the age of five. Joanna acted fast to dissociate herself from the woman, declaring that Mary Bateman's only connection with her mission stemmed from the fact that she had briefly lodged with one of her supporters in 1808 – and then robbed them. There was no evidence to back her claim that she had received a 'seal' from Joanna. But if she had, it did nothing to protect her from the rigours of the law. She appeared for her execution in York dressed in white and surrounded by twenty thousand spectators, many watching out for the angel they felt sure would come and rescue her.[2]

A True Picture of the World also contained a rebuttal of recent allegations printed in Trewman's newspaper at Exeter accusing Joanna of drunkenness, making a fortune from selling seals, and ruining Bath's Easter trade by predicting that the city would be destroyed on Good Friday (as a result of which visitors reputedly stayed away in droves).[3]

Selling her seals was a charge frequently levelled at Joanna and her friends. The 'seal' – a folded, sealed paper – was viewed by some as having magical powers. Although Joanna herself often referred to it as a 'seal of safety', in 1808 she had warned her followers not to 'Suppose the Seals were made as a wall about them that no Dangers could come near them' – words which did nothing to diminish the seals' popularity.[4]

Troubled by any suggestion of trafficking, Joanna dreamt that she was challenged by a woman who said: 'I see yours is a money business, and I will give you half a guinea.' In the dream she fiercely denied selling the seals and told the woman that she despised her money.[5] In real life, however, people's suspicions were not so easily dispelled, so on 5 May, 1809, Foley placed an advertisement in the *Worcester Herald* denying that the seals were ever sold and for a while after Mary Bateman's execution Joanna halted their distribution altogether.

On the first Sunday after the flood, Charles Taylor, who was in London working on the construction of the Grand Theatre, came to Weston Place to drink tea with Joanna and Townley. In their usual motherly way, the two women remarked on his health but kept from him the news that his father was having to go to court to get money from Mr Mills after a disputed bill. It was ironic that the Taylors, always so generous to Joanna's friends in the past, were suffering financial problems of their own. Writing to them the following week to explain that Colonel Harwood's affairs were still not settled, Townley felt obliged to enclose a small sum of money from herself, warning Mrs Taylor not to tell the Colonel if he should send them something in the future.

It was the start of a difficult year for the Taylors who, despite being influential tradespeople, found themselves persecuted by a new young curate, the Reverend William Cowlard, because of their connection with Joanna. By early summer the dispute reached a point where he refused the Sacrament to the whole family. Mr Robert Taylor wrote indignantly to the Bishop, who happened to be on a visit to London at the time, so in his stead came two priests to ask the Taylors what had happened.[6] After hearing what they had to say, the clergymen declared that, if left to them, they would have turned Cowlard out there and then, but they were powerless to interfere with someone who had been licensed by the Bishop. At which point, Joanna waded in with a letter to Cowlard, defending the Taylors by stressing how at the start they had been just like him, reluctant to accept her prophecies, that it was only after events had proved her right that they had both come to believe.[7] Cowlard responded in a violent sermon against Joanna at a time when there was a veritable hate campaign being waged against her in the *Exeter Flying Post*. One of their correspondents wrote,

> Johanna,
>
> I have seen yr letter in Mr Woolmer's Paper address'd to Mr Trewman demanding of him the author of the character he gave you in his paper. I boldly declare I am he and am ready to prove to the whole world that you are what he there describes and worse the word Whore being left out which should have been in.

Such vilification had greater effect coming, as it did, over the signature of William Searle, Exeter's public hangman. Joanna wrote to Mrs Taylor, taking his words literally,

> I am not ashamed to make public his infamous assertions, as the people in Exeter know I was so far from ever keeping company with any man after I came to Exeter that I lived as much retired as possible to myself.

At the same time one of Joanna's friends wrote to Mr Trewman, the newspaper's proprietor:

> Sir,
>
> Whether your paper *The Flying Post* actually merits that title by its wide circulation I know not, for I have seldom seen it; but it was shewn to me this week because it contained a most foul and infamous slander on a virtuous woman, whose shoes (judging by thy specimen in yr paper) I am persuaded, you are not worthy to clean.
>
> A few years since the Monster by the name of Ryan Williams, who went about the streets of London, stabbing with a knife every unprotected woman he met excited . . . universal

abhorrence. . . . Will you be pleased to favour the Public with a statement of yr opinion, what degrees of moral turpitude there are between the midnight assassin . . . and the dastardly calumniator that with the serpent's venom wounds the honest character of a good and virtuous woman?[8]

And as if this 'good and virtuous woman' was not suffering enough hostility from outside, she was at the same time waging an internal battle against Peter Morrison, the cotton printer from Liverpool who had been one of the original Seven to visit her in Exeter. Headstrong and passionate, he had been preaching that, come the Millennium, all land and property would be taken away from the rich and given to the 'sealed people'. For some it was a persuasive message, for others a threat – and the two categories met within the domain of Sir Thomas White, who promptly discharged all those workers who believed in Joanna, 'because they had been laying out who was to have this part of his Estate, and that part, as the Rich were to be taken out of the way.'

Joanna attacked Morrison, pointing out that by raising people's material expectations he distracted their attention from the Second Coming, that believers must seek first the Kingdom of God and only then would all be added unto them. After all, why should God condemn the rich for enjoying the very things that he, Morrison, was teaching others to crave?

After this admonition, Morrison toed the line for a while. By early 1809, however, he had begun publishing his own prophecies and Joanna had to write again, determined to put a stop to such nonsense:

I have nothing to do with those that go on by a Spirit of their own, in opposition to the directions given to Me. . . . I have been often ordered to reprove the violence of your temper, the wrongness of your judgment and the harshness of your Words.

Again Morrison's conduct improved. But when fresh criticisms of his conduct started to pour in, Joanna decided enough was enough: 'My heart is wounded with the complaints I hear, which is more concerning you than I hear from all the others.' She urged him to clear his name by returning to his critics and proving that their allegations were false or convincing them that he was a reformed character. When he failed to do this, she forbade him to preach.[9]

By now Joanna, with the help of her copyists and trusty amanuenses, had published more than fifty books and pamphlets. She had also kept herself busy doing needlework, particularly making samplers and patchwork. Sometimes, not knowing how to go on with her writing or needlework, she found guidance in her dreams. On 10 June, 1809, for example, she dreamt that she opened her workbag and together with Underwood looked over her patchwork pieces, regretting that, though pretty, they were too small to make anything. Later her Spirit explained that the dream was telling her she must print *all* her writings and not select only those which seemed to be significant.[10]

Joanna was in happy mood when she visited John Hows on Monday, 19 June, despite the fact that his mother-in-law lay desperately ill in the house. In the evening they strolled together in Kensington Gardens with Joanna waxing lyrical about the beauty of the walks, the groves, the grass and all the works of Creation which she could see with perfect clarity through the small round lenses of her iron-framed spectacles. The only pity, groaned Mr Hows, trying to share her enthusiasm, was that one could not take pleasure in anything while there was still sin in the world. Although Joanna agreed, they passed the rest of the evening contentedly enough until it was time for her to go home. However, just as she reached the gardens that they had earlier admired, she remembered her glasses and had to go back and fetch them from Mr Hows'.

She arrived back in Weston Place with her spectacles safely stowed in their tortoiseshell case, and went to bed without being told the dreadful news that Underwood had received in her absence.

At breakfast next morning Joanna was so full of the delights of the day that Underwood let her prattle on until the moment when she could withhold the news no longer. Joanna's brother, Joseph, had died in Bristol on the Saturday. Although she had known he was very ill, Joanna was shocked and went upstairs in a state of collapse. But remembering Mrs Hows' mother and all her suffering, she had no wish for poor Joseph to linger in such pain. She also took comfort in the thought that, just as she and Mr Hows had been admiring Kensington Gardens, so Joseph, now freed from the world's sin, would be admiring much greater beauty.

Joanna decided to attend the funeral, having a great desire to see his wife and children and pay her last respects to her brother in his coffin. Accompanied by Underwood, she set out on Wednesday to arrive in Bristol on Thursday and the funeral took place the following day, conducted by the Reverend Samuel Eyre. While Underwood made herself known, Joanna kept herself concealed from most of the congregation,[11] following the procession incognita to the grave to witness the tiny coffin of Joseph's infant son, who had died three months previously, being lifted out and replaced on that of his father.

Susanna Carter was there, come to mourn her brother and renew contact with the sister for whom she now had great respect. Since being deserted by William, she had returned to live in Ottery St Mary where, she reported, many folk reckoned Joanna had made a fortune and was worth more than £10,000.[12]

By Sunday morning Joanna was feeling strong enough to face her public, so she went along to the large room in Colston's House, Small Street, which her followers rented for £25 a year, and introduced herself to Mr Eyre's congregation. Amazed by her sudden appearance, they were overwhelmed by the speech she made.

Joanna, much affected by the enthusiasm she met in Bristol, must have felt grateful for her brother's service to the cause. Since 1805 her 'inspired writings' had been advertised for sale at 'Mr Southcott's, 69 Broad Quay' and were publicly read and explained by the Reverend Samuel Eyre in the room in Small Street which opened every Sunday evening at six o'clock and every Friday at seven.[13] After Joseph died there would have been anxious discussion about how things would continue, and relief when his widow, Sarah, took on his role as bookseller.

On the following Thursday evening Joanna broke bread and took wine with many friends who called on her, and again the next morning before she left Bristol at about midday for the first stage of her journey back to London. At first she took the travelling well, but by midnight felt faint and started trembling. Underwood wanted to stop on the road, but by the time the coach reached the next staging post, Joanna had sufficiently recovered to take a glass of port wine and continue. They arrived safely in London at about eight o'clock on Saturday morning, 1 July.

Mr Hows called on them a couple of days later and, seeing Joanna, declared the Bride was in mourning. He had been meditating on how she had left her spectacles in his house and returned for them, concluding that the incident was 'a temporal artificial light'. Her Spirit concurred, explaining that the whole episode leading up to Joseph's funeral was like her spectacles, there to provide a temporary light to man so that he might increase his understanding: 'Now in that perfect likeness of thy glasses, all these types and shadows will be discerned by man to give a clearer light to their understanding.' On the other hand, such types and shadows were wasted on those who did not believe, for

> he that is blinded in unbelief, that no visitation can come from Me . . . will no more discern by the instrument I have chosen to give light to man . . . than a man that is naturally blind would see by the light of thy Glasses. . . . Let thy Glasses be applied to one that is blind, would he see the better for them?[14]

In August 1809 Foley journeyed to Tutbury in Staffordshire to visit Ann Moore, a woman whose claim to fame rested on being able to live apparently without food. He excitedly described her to Joanna. She was about fifty and looked well in the face. Her arms were thin but healthy, unlike the rest of her body which, as far as he could see, was dried up and dead. Two years and five months she had gone without food, she told him. And although she had drunk some small drops of fluid after giving up solids, since October 1808 she had not even moistened her mouth.

Her remarks left Foley mystified as to how she still had sufficient saliva, let alone strength, to talk.[15]

Accepting his testimony, Joanna agreed that Ann Moore was genuine but relegated her to the lower ranks of spiritual phenomena. 'She is no fulfillment but a SIGN,' was her verdict.

When in October 1809 George III entered the fiftieth year of his reign, Joanna received a Communication that the Jubilee should be celebrated as a shadow of something greater; just as people were now collecting money for the poor, so would the Lord come soon to feed them.[16] The anniversary reminded her that in the previous April she had entered her own sixtieth year, an event commemorated by John Pye's presentation to her of two magnificent glass communion beakers. The inscription on one: 'In the year of our Lord, 1809, to Joanna Southcott, aged 60' suggests some confusion about the date of her birth. Joanna herself knew only that it had been in April, 1750, but was unsure of the exact day. If she hoped it had been recorded in the church register at Ottery, that would explain why in May the following year she asked someone, presumably Susanna, to send her the baptismal entry.

John Pye's beakers, probably engraved by himself, featured many of the symbols most significant to Joanna. One was decorated with motifs like the beehive and vine. The other had a representation of the tree of life bearing twelve kinds of fruits, 'the Lamb' in the midst of the foliage, a man and woman gathering the leaves for the healing of nations; on the opposite side a copy of Joanna's seal surrounded by twelve stars. At the bottom of the glass was written, with a diamond: 'The gift of John and Ann Pye to Joanna Southcott, our spiritual mother, Amen.'[17]

With such devoted friends, who needed to be polite to enemies? Joanna had by this time developed a nice way with critics. Gone was the courtesy with which she treated Lewis Mayer: in its place a curt summary of how she saw the situation. Witness the following letter from Mr R. Walker of 90 High Holborn in March 1810:

Madam,

Having published a book in refutation of your prophecies, and another being now nearly ready for the same purpose, [I] should be happy to wait on you any time you may appoint, if you have any wish to stop the publication.

I remain, Madam, your most obedient servant,

R. Walker.

Joanna's reply?

Two glass communion beakers engraved with scenes from Joanna's prophecies. They are decorated with images of the Tree of Life bearing twelve kinds of fruit, with the Lamb at its centre, and a man and woman gathering leaves for the healing of the nations. On the opposite side of one is a copy of Joanna's seal (JC with a star above and below) and the words: IN THE YEAR OF OUR LORD, 1809, AGED 60. TO JOANNA SOUTHCOTT. *On its base is written:* The Gift of John and Anne Pye to Joanna Southcott, Our Spiritual Mother, Amen. *The other beaker shows a radiant sun with an eye at its centre. Above it are the words:* IS NOT THINE EYE EVERYWHERE PRESENT, *and below:* DESPISE NOT PROPHECIES. *On its base is written:* The Gift of John and Anne Pye to W. Tozer,

'What is of God cannot fail, and what is of man's wisdom must come to nothing.'[18] There was simply nothing to add.

She was more forthcoming to the gentleman who wrote to tell her the corn was looking poor.

'I fear the harvest will be short,' she replied, seeing this as a sign of the times on a par with recent disturbances in London caused by the arrest of Sir Francis Burdett. 'This is only the beginning of sorrows, the end is not yet,' she wrote; adding regretfully, 'I have no Communications given me at present.'[19]

On a particularly fine patchwork made by Joanna in 1808, using the American 'running stitch' method and designed around a central panel bearing her name worked in her own hair, someone tacked a note which read: 'Frances Taylor. June 18, 1810'.[20] The note possibly meant that Joanna had put this patchwork aside as a wedding gift for thirty-year old Fanny, formerly one of her chief help-mates, who was about to marry John Wills Luscombe in Exeter.[21] If so, it is also possible that the gift was not sent once it became clear that Fanny Luscombe had turned her back on old loyalties in the face of her new husband's disapproval of Joanna.

Even if privately bemoaning this betrayal, Joanna had to be careful when writing to Fanny's mother, for Mrs Lucy Taylor was a close friend of the Fields, around whom a damaging scandal was fast developing. Field had long been one of Joanna's most successful booksellers, distributing from his London address in Broad Court, Long Acre. In fact, Joanna found his services so valuable that she agreed to pay Field, alone among her booksellers, a regular salary. For a while this arrangement worked well. Foley reported to the Taylors that Field's time was 'most delightfully employed in answering questions upon the Prophecies & Visions – and about ten days ago he had *one order* for *fifty whole sets* of Joanna's Divine Works.'

Early in 1810 Joanna became aware of accounting errors and asked the Fields to report future book sales to her on a monthly basis. Field argued about the new system and a bitter dispute ensued.

Joanna wrote to John Hows on 25 May asking him to judge between her and Field 'face to face', and putting her side of the case.

> (Y)ou was here on the Sunday night, on the Monday Mr Turner told me he called on Field on Saturday, and they said to clear themselves the account of the stock was not taken right in September 1809 and the Five Books of the Seventh Explanation of the Bible that was wanting, they had recollected to whom they were sold, but forgot to enter them – but still said they had never knowingly cheated me of a book or a shilling.

She had written to Field about the missing books and been told that he had gone over the stock three times on 3 and 4 September, found it just over four hundred, but had forgotten to enter three books for which he had already been paid.

So why, Joanna demanded, had he then given a wrong account to Colonel Harwood and Underwood?

After a further unsatisfactory reply, Joanna had asked Hows and Owen to see Field and judge the matter. There followed a painful meeting at which Field, upset and agitated, tried in vain to clear himself from the charge of dishonesty. What he could not deny was that Joanna's friend, Mr Smith (either John Smith, steward to the Earl of Darnley, or his nephew, Samuel, who shared the same address in Princes Street) had bought three books, but Field had entered only one in the accounts. Why? According to Field, it was just a mistake. But Joanna revealed that both the Mr Smiths had come to her house and told her what books they had bought. Field, it seems, had fallen into a trap set for him after Joanna had received complaints from Daniel Roberts that he no longer liked sending her chickens and other gifts because he thought Field was defrauding her of postage money and charging for parcels which she never had.

By the end of June 1810 Field had absconded with the assets he had in hand, leaving behind him debts amounting to more than £20 owed to Edmund Baker and the milkwoman. When Joanna next received word, he admitted he had done wrong, but not intentionally.

If Field thought this would get him off the hook, he was very mistaken. A letter soon arrived from Colonel Harwood, William Owen and John Hows demanding a full confession. Poor Field was now backed into a corner. Not only was his livelihood under threat, he could face imprisonment if the friends produced evidence of embezzlement against him. Nevertheless, he fought on, rounding on his accusers for condemning him on all counts on the evidence of just one – the Smith incident, which again he tried to explain.

What, according to Field, had actually happened was that a Mr Bretton had called on Mrs Field on 22 March to buy a copy of the Seventh Part of *True Explanations of the Bible*. When she heard that he was going to Mr Smith's, she asked him to take a further two books for Mr Smith and Mr Troup. Mr Bretton paid for his own, but took the three books. A week later Mr Smith paid Field for the other two copies and these were entered in the accounts.

This version did nothing to explain why so many books had gone missing. Moreover Field's situation was not helped by the fact that his wife had been bamboozling people out of money by pretending she had lost a £5 note put by to pay creditors. Richard Goldsmith said he had given her £1 after hearing this sob story – a fact that Ann Field denied. What she could not disown was that her family's financial affairs were in a mess.

So, with books missing and the accounts wrong, what was to be done? The Fields were both contrite and at their wits' end to know how to remedy the situation. Joanna was implacable. She would not accept that Field had acted unintentionally. He had to confess that what he had done was by design and not carelessness. Nothing short of a full confession would suffice. She commanded him to appear in person to settle the issue. He refused, saying he felt it fruitless to see her face to face when he had now said all he could on the subject. She gave him an ultimatum: come in person or consider himself fired.

Arriving to drink tea with Joanna one Sunday evening, Colonel and Mrs Harwood and the Owens found her very agitated, insisting that Field's departure was proof that he had been filching money; otherwise he would never have jettisoned his job. The Colonel, knowing what financial troubles felt like, said he hoped Field did have some savings, as he did not wish to see his young family become beggars.

The following Wednesday Mr Carder called to say that he had been to Field's and was surprised to hear him say that he might not be having any more books. When pressed for a reason, Field blamed, not Joanna, but the three men who had written to him, wanting him to sign something against his own conscience. That same evening Mrs Lewis also visited Joanna to ask what exactly Field was required to sign. Nothing, said Joanna, but he had to admit he had been lying and cheating by design, or prove otherwise.

From these visits it quickly became clear that Joanna had to act if she was to stop this issue from dividing her supporters. On Thursday evening, Ann Underwood took a letter to Field telling him that Joanna would dismiss him at the end of the month but continue his pay of one and a half guineas a week until the end of August, a year from when the accounts were first taken.

On 27 July, 1810, Joanna wrote to Hows:

Dear Friend,

It is highly necessary from what I have heard concerning Field that you three should meet together again before I finally close with him. Colonel Harwood will come tomorrow night, therefore if Monday afternoon will be convenient to you, to come and meet him and Owen I shall thank you to be here about 4 o'clock. If Monday do not suit you, Tuesday, as I shall not send to him before you have met. . . .[22]

Joanna was now into damage limitation – all references to Field being accompanied by a challenge of personal loyalty. 'I could not see how any one could love me, without being angry with him,' she wrote in a long letter to Hows on 17 September, using the same words in a letter to her friend, Lucy Taylor. In the same week she wrote to thank loyal Miss Eveleigh for sending a 'perfectly right' account, showing that there was £35.0s.5d. now due to Joanna. With regard to her latest order for books, Underwood's daughter Ann was taking the parcel that afternoon to Bryon & Brandon, because Joanna had 'entirely done with Field as he dismissed himself at last.' Joanna was also sending '4 hymn books unbound as I had none by me bound and would not keep the parcel back for them.' She also thanked Miss Eveleigh for sending her a blue damask gown that she found especially delightful for its beautiful colour and the fact that it had belonged to her sister.[23] The letter shows Joanna at her charming best, giving a clue as to how she won and kept the hearts of such an extraordinary range of friends over the years.

Her thoughts at this time strayed often towards Exeter and the life she had led there in younger days. After her old friend Mary Wolland died in 1805, Mr Wolland had remarried within a few months. Now came news that he had died suddenly at the Warren, Dawlish, where he had gone for his health.[24] This meant that his sister-in-law, Sarah Minifie, living in Ottery, had to add a codicil to her will and called on Susanna Carter to sign as witness.[25]

By the end of 1810 some of Joanna's followers were beginning to murmur that things were not coming to pass as quickly as she had prophesied. Luckily she had an answer:

> [I]t was like taking a journey; suppose I was going into Devonshire to see my sister Carter, and wrote to my sister Southcott at Bristol saying, if I went that way I should be at her house on such a day, But if I went into Devonshire the other way, I should see her on my Return home to Bristol – from such a letter she would expect to see me the day I had mentioned, but when that day came, and she was disappointed, she would not know then what time I should be there . . . and she would expect my return, according to my promise, though she would not know the time without I informed her again by letter.[26]

Nevertheless, defeats in the Peninsula, unrest in Ireland, and the prospect of war with America all coming at a time when King George III was suffering mental collapse and a Regency being established confirmed for people like Foley that 'the great drama of human misery is rapidly drawing to a conclusion.'

No such gloom overshadowed Charles Taylor writing home to his father on 29 March, 1811:

> I am happy to say I have some hopes of having the patronage of
> the Marquess of Buckingham to Mr Fellows. I made the
> application through Major Brown of the Bucks Militia who once
> was a private secretary to him when Lord Lieutenant of Ireland
> and whose opinion he holds very high at present . . . if this should
> not take place with Mr Fellows it will be the means of making
> me known to Lords Fortesque and Clifford, as Lord E. is a
> brother-in-law to the Marquess Daughter through marrying a
> Mr Arundell who we are now fitting up a house for 2 miles from
> Aylesbury.

The letter throws interesting light on how influence worked in
business, how a young man without connections had to exploit every
contact if he was to make his way in the world. For Charles, who was
prone to stammer and suffered from nerves, it proved a hard lesson to
learn. Starting from the bottom, he had mastered every aspect of the
building trade, yet now had to go cap in hand to solicit business. 'If I
could obtain a good connection with the higher class of People in
Devonshire it will be a very fortunate thing,' he told his father, declaring
his intention to start up a business in Exeter after the summer.

If his tone was upbeat and his interest in his father's affairs more than
usually solicitous (he complimented him on opening a new Sale Room in
Exeter), it may have been because Charles was leading up to a confession.
He too had fallen prey to the demon of the time – debt – having the
previous winter purchased a suit of black clothes on credit from someone
who was very rude when he did not pay on time. As a result he had
drawn a bill for £20 on his father's name, payable on 20 April at Hankey
& Co. Charles hoped his father would bail him out until he received the
£100 he expected to be paid on completion of his current project.

'I am very glad to hear they are going to pave St Sidwells,' he concluded
and, no doubt with an eye to future business, added that it would be a
'great acquisition to the Street and will raise the price of land. I think
John Luscombe's house was cheap and in time it will be the best part of
Exeter.'[27]

The day before Charles Taylor sent his letter, Joanna was writing to
thank his mother for her gift of 'a beautiful quarter of lamb – very fine
and quite sweet' and she mentioned that Charles Taylor had not been in
London recently but would probably be coming at Easter when she
would remind him to write home. With regard to Fanny: 'We're happy
to hear that Mrs Luscombe has recovered,' she wrote, adding with a
degree of condescension that she would like to hear from her after her
long silence:

Tell her to take a pen in her hand and begin her letter as usual, we will excuse the past if she promise not to forget us for the future. I know she have had many things upon her hands and am sorry she have been so ill . . . and hope she is happy in her marriage; as to the family not being in the same faith in the Visitation we must leave them to time.

Joanna, aware how much tradesmen were suffering throughout the country, was glad that the Taylors had escaped so far. 'I think it is almost a miracle, considering the extent of your business,' she said, managing to imply that their good fortune owed something to their loyalty to her. On the same premise, she had not been at all surprised to hear that Mr Mills, after trying to cheat Mr Taylor in a business deal, had just lost £4,000 in a disastrous fire.

'I am sorry to hear that Law is on his way to London,' Joanna concluded, 'as he is always stirring up strife and contention wherever he go. . . . I am glad you spoke to him as you did. He is a troublesome fellow. . . .'[28]

Troublesome indeed! Richard Law – he who had formerly written to Prime Minister Addington on her behalf – had been making a thorough nuisance of himself in the pursuance of some imagined slight from Major Eyre, writing him the following hysterical letter:

To Robert Eyre esq.,

Sir, whereas I have been annoyed, disturbed, perplexed and troubled with a certain, mysterious, dangerous and pestilent report whereof I have wrote to you before, namely, that you was ordered to refuse to me the accustomed formalities of friendship, I wish to be satisfied from you, whether this embargo upon friendship, this aggressive and Hostile Rumour did, or did not, proceed, emanate, originate and issue forth from you etc. . . .

Yours in sublime revenge to the Prince of Anarchy,

Richard Law.

He had also shown himself dangerously at odds with Joanna's mission by daring to pay court to Jane Townley. For one who had been employed as a serge-maker in Exeter, marriage to such a wealthy spinster presented a dazzling prospect. For Joanna the loss of her devoted benefactress would seem disastrous, so – according to Law – she told Townley not to write to him, and managed to put a stop to the courtship.[29]

Easter came with Charles Taylor making his usual visit to London and calling on 17 Weston Place, where the ladies entertained him to dinner, clucking all the while that they had never seen him look so well. He in turn told them about his present life – how he was up every morning by five and went to bed tired out between nine and ten; the number of men he had to supervise; his hopes of securing the patronage of the Marquess of Buckingham, especially now that he had been asked by his private secretary to take him the plan of the house he was working on and been told that the Marquess was planning to inspect the building for himself.[30]

In the event, Charles was doomed to disappointment. After months of hearing nothing, he decided to beard the Marquis in his den at Stowe – only to be told that His Lordship was ill and unable to see him. Instead, Charles, who had a way with older women, was granted an audience with the Marchioness, to whom he poured out his heart, stressing how much a good word from the Marquis would help him and how he had done his utmost to serve him. That the Marchioness listened sympathetically consoled Charles at the time, but did nothing for his prospects beyond strengthening him in his decision to return to Exeter.[31]

In London, the early months of 1811 had been taken up by Joanna's controversy with Hann whose latest book, *The Remarkable Life, Entertaining History, and Surprising Adventures of Joanna Southcott*, was full of mockery. On 21 January, and again two days later, Joanna wrote demanding that Hann prove his allegations. She then published two books herself answering specific objections to her doctrine with regard to the fall of man, the Law given to Moses, the 'sealing' and redemption of the body. She loftily pointed out that Hann had exposed his ignorance right from the start by stating that she had been born at 'Getsham' in '1753'. Moreover, far from putting people off, his pamphlets had attracted many new believers anxious to judge her prophecies for themselves.[32]

Thus she put up a good defence for her doctrine, but she found it difficult to remain philosophical when the attack was personal. In August 1811 Hewson Clarke, editor of a scurrilous magazine called *The Scourge*, described how Joanna had attended Carpenter's chapel, the House of God, dressed in diamonds and there fallen in love with a candle-snuffer, a comely youth, with whom she had an affair. When these scandalous allegations were challenged by her supporters, Clarke simply shrugged and confessed that as a prophetess, Joanna Southcott was 'fair game for any one to shoot at'.[33]

With such a reputation, it was surprising to find so many would-be impersonators, yet on 29 August Joanna expressed a wish to have her likeness engraved 'as there are women of Bad Character going about London, calling themselves Joanna Southcott, by which means I have been represented as being a Strange looking woman.' She was lucky to have on hand the man whom many regarded as the greatest engraver of

Joanna Southcott as 'drawn and engraved from life'
by William Sharp, 7 January 1812.
Ann Underwood, who was present when the original sketch was
made, fetched three volumes of Joanna's own writings to support the
Bible when it was found 'not high enough'. Once the Bible was
placed in Joanna's hands, it fell open at the last two chapters of
Isaiah. A print from this engraving is held by the National Portrait

his age – William Sharp, who etched her portrait from life on a copper plate measuring thirteen by eleven inches and weighing 5° pounds.[34] The picture had to be carefully composed: Joanna with the Bible lying open before her as a sign that her Visitation was to throw open the Bible to mankind. But once they placed a Bible on the table, Mr Sharp said it was not high enough, and Underwood had to fetch three more books to prop it up. Joanna opened it at random and was delighted to land at the last two chapters of Isaiah: 'of the New Heavens and the New Earth'. She looked to see what books had been placed underneath and found the first three volumes of her own publications.[35] It all signified.

Although Joanna herself was pleased with the result – 'Mr Sharp have succeeded very well in taking it as they all say it is a Striking Likeness' – some objected to the project on the grounds that such a portrait could lead to idolatry.[36] But what mattered was what Joanna's Spirit thought. It would be sinful 'if men look at thy Likeness only as an Idol to worship,' it warned, before deciding that 'If men Judged aright it would draw their hearts to long for My Kingdom to Rejoice in My People that Sorrow and Sighing must be done away.' Such endorsement spiked all opposition.

Joanna's followers lived through 1811 full of anticipation and dread. George Turner received a Communication that convinced many that the end was so nigh that they cancelled all social engagements, thinking they would have to leave London at any moment. What they did not realise, Joanna explained, was that years were nothing to the Lord who had existed from all eternity.[37] Nevertheless, she herself had done much to stoke up their fears by emphasising that something of terrible import would happen 'when the four figures came in', i.e. 1811.[38] The King's madness was seen as one of the first signs of the nation's impending doom. Further corroboration appeared in September in the form of a huge and ominous comet in the night skies. At the same time people began to notice an unusual number of storms and floods, fires and volcanic eruptions all around. But then, what else should they expect in the wake of such a portent?

By the time the comet disappeared through the tail of the Great Bear, many had resigned themselves to expect the worst.

SHATTERED FAITH, 1811-1813

I have now given a brighter light to men to warn them the end is
at hand & the brightness of my coming than they understood
before.

Communication on the Blazing Star, 10 December 1811

Not only did Charles Taylor fail to obtain the long-anticipated patronage
of the Marquis of Buckingham but he had a difficult time in Aylesbury
over religion. He wrote to his father:

I am more partial to the Church of England than ever I was
because since I have been with Mr Arundell all his servants are
Catholic, and I dislike the appearance of them. I have nearly as
bad an opinion of them as I have of Methodists. . . . I have been
very careful what I said with them because if they had known I
was a believer in Joanna, I am certain they would do what they
could to injure me.[1]

His sentiments echoed those of Joanna, who had always hoped that
the Established Church would one day acknowledge her mission. Indeed,
with this in mind, she continued to circularise its bishops and clergy
until at the end of 1811, after years of being ignored, she bowed to the
inevitable and sanctioned independent worship among her followers.
There were, however, potential legal problems. In a letter to a friend on
2 December 1811 she warned:

I have heard of late that many have been *fined for Speaking or
Preaching Without being Licensed.* I must lay the cause before
you. If there is anyone amongst the Believers that would like to
take it upon himself to be *Licensed as a Preacher* he must be
licensed as a Protestant Dissenter, and the place where he Speak
must be Licensed also. And then it is a place of worship but if
there is no one Licensed as a Preacher I do not see any occasion
to License the room for so small a number as attend at present
and if you meet together to read the writings and compare them
with the Scriptures and neither use Prayer or Hymns they cannot
hurt you for that. [B]ut using Prayer or Hymns makes it a Place
of Worship for which if you have not a License they can fine
you.[2]

But if Joanna was concerned about the law she was equally bothered by lawlessness, fearing for her own and her followers' safety in the current climate. From Nottingham came news of rioting Luddites attacking stocking and lace frames. In London there were daily reports of robberies and violent deaths, including the ghastly murder of Mr Marr and his family, which left folk frightened to be out after nine o'clock. There were so many bloodthirsty gangs roaming the streets that the watchmen were often afraid to call the hour, especially after one of their number was shot at Richmond. For Joanna the worst shock came shortly before Christmas 1811, when she heard about the gruesome murder committed at 'The Sign of the King's Arms' public house in Gravel Lane, Bethnal Green. This was behind the home of Mr Hows who, appearing almost immediately on the scene, was able to supply an eye-witness account. 'The master, mistress and servant girl all lay weltering in their blood with their heads nearly severed from their bodies.'

Small wonder that Joanna was still shaken when she wrote to Foley in the closing days of the year: 'The people here are panic-stricken.' She told him they had just had an extra shutter fitted to their kitchen window. For no one, it seemed, was safe. Poor Miss Harwood, returning from town at dusk after fetching medicine for her step-mother, was set upon by a man who knocked her unconscious to the ground. Fortunately an elderly man came to her rescue and she suffered no more than a bruised face. Foley had also had a recent break-in – happily foiled by his sister.

And as if all this violent crime was not enough, Joanna had been receiving offensive letters from Richard Law, who was clearly unbalanced. First he would appear penitent, then really abusive, so that she was at her wit's end to know how to deal with him and the stress was making Townley ill.

Amidst all this doom and gloom there were lighter moments. Celebrations of New Year (Old Style) at 17 Weston Place were enriched by the gifts from Joanna's friends in the country, especially Foley's dressed turkey and tongue. Little Noah Philip Foley, aged six, had sent 'Janny' a design for a quilt which she would make for him when she had enough pieces. In February Foley sent Joanna a nice hare – a gift she appreciated all the more knowing that, when his hopes of a legacy were disappointed, some blamed his late uncle's attitude on Foley's belief in her mission.[3]

After leaving Aylesbury the previous November, Charles Taylor had sent his tool-chest home by water, then spent a few weeks in London before returning to Exeter to set up his own business. On 23 February, 1812, Joanna, forced to take up her own pen because Townley was suffering from a bilious fever, wrote to tell him how he could obtain one of her portraits.

> Mr Sharp thought best to leave the Prints, as your Brother is coming to Town, for him to choose for himself. I have not sent you one of mine as Mrs T. had subscribed for two – but if you wish, you can have one of Mrs Symons['s] as I have sent more than was bespoke.

She gave him the latest news about her quarrel with *The Scourge*, having decided not to sue for libel as that would only give the magazine more publicity. Instead she was going to publish another book to defend herself. After all, she added, few had seen *The Scourge* – apart from the minister at Lympstone who was spreading copies around his part of Devon.

After the usual lament about high prices and poor trade, Joanna mentioned the recent death of Mrs Merode, one of her followers. She had died intestate, leaving only a memorandum naming executors who had destroyed her former will three weeks before her death because of some offence she had taken at her cousin. It is possible that Joanna had received hints or promises from Mrs Merode herself, for she sadly observed, 'How little dependence there is in these human affairs'.[4] But if she had been disappointed in certain expectations, the lesson was not lost on her.

Some of her friends were not doing well either. Foley, still struggling with debtors, was having trouble with Mr Palmer, to whom he owed £40, and would have asked Colonel Harwood for advice had not that gentleman himself been reeling from an adverse verdict in his lawsuit against Horne Tooke.[5]

On 19 May, 1812, Joanna wrote to thank Elizabeth Foley for sending her some yellow striped linen for a gown – which 'as soon as Underwood have a day to spare she is to make it up for me' – and at the same time to mention that she had already made two sides of Noah's quilt and would finish it off with the new pieces and send it to him with a lock of her hair. She could not, however, accept their invitation to visit Oldswinford because she had to stay in Weston Place in view of the dramatic events now unfolding: the massacre at Badajoz and recent earthquake in South America, which had cost more than 14,000 lives. Even as she was writing, someone brought news that the Tower guns were firing, although they knew not why. According to Joanna, everything that was happening had been foretold in her writings and confirmed that they were living in the last days – the only wonder was how others could fail to see it![6]

Reading a newspaper on 31 May, Joanna was struck by two very different articles – one the usual lament over poor trade and high prices, the other describing the crowds' reaction at the recent pillorying of Daniel Eaton when

> [i]nstead of pelting, as is usual in similar cases . . . every individual appeared more eager than another to cheer and encourage the unfortunate sufferer. At intervals he addressed the multitude, who huzzaed him, as if he had been complimenting a candidate at a popular election.

Daniel Eaton had been sentenced to stand in the pillory between twelve and one o'clock for publishing the third part of Paine's *Age of Reason* a book which, by attacking the Bible, had shocked many when it first appeared in 1795. Even William Sharp, a former friend of Paine, had reacted strongly against Paine's deism and in his pamphlet *An Answer to the World* pointed out the contradiction implied in denying Christ's divinity yet worshipping Him for his unequalled moral virtue, when to do so was to worship someone who could then be condemned by His own utterance as an impostor.

Even after Paine's death in 1809 his message was still welcomed by many English people, hence their championing of Daniel Eaton. It was up to Joanna to point out the error of their ways. She saw, if others did not, a connection between the two newspaper articles: poor trade, high prices meant that England was being punished for the people's lack of religious faith.

In *An Answer to Thomas Paine's Third Part of the Age of Reason* she expressed surprise at the clergy for not tackling him, then waded in herself:

> I shall point out his folly, and the darkness of his understanding concerning the scriptures, knowing that his former publications hurt many weak minds, and have made many become atheists; because his reasoning is so artful, and wickedly contrived to make a mock of the scriptures.

Joanna's book also contained a letter from Townley to Hewson Clarke, editor of *The Scourge,* in which, having testified to that fact that Joanna had not stirred a foot without being accompanied by herself or Underwood since the day she had first come to live with them, their reputation stood or fell with hers. Moreover, since Clarke had admitted that being a prophetess made Joanna 'fair game for anyone to shoot at', Townley and Underwood wished to know what excuse he made for injuring their characters:

> for were there the least foundation for your charges against her, we must stand condemned for sanctioning her in infamy, and deceiving the public. And as I faithfully promised, if I discovered

the least deception in Mrs Southcott, I would announce it to the world, therefore it is not only a duty I owe to Mrs Southcott but to myself, my family and friends, to declare that her conduct has been exemplary, and that she has in every respect invariably acted upon the most strict and upright principles.[7]

At about the time this letter was written James Cosins, one of Joanna's disciples, promised to leave her part of his property when he died. Mindful of Mrs Merode, Joanna might not have placed much dependence on 'these human affairs', especially as Cosins had made no will by the time he fell so dangerously ill that he seemed unlikely to survive the night of 15 November, when Ann Underwood visited him. She realised that his friends would have to move quickly if his last wishes were to be carried out.

Next day, Joanna, Colonel Harwood, and William Owen went with Underwood to see Cosins and found him – amazingly – able to sit up in bed and write his will. After which, having handed the document to Joanna, he was said to have sighed: 'I die happy in this faith; but should not in any other.'

The deed was done just in time. Within twenty-four hours he was dead.[8]

Apart from some small bequests, Cosins had left the bulk of his property to Joanna, Townley and Underwood 'for their sole use'; Underwood had been appointed sole executrix and the will was witnessed by Harwood and Owen.[9] Although Cosins left no vast estate, it meant that Joanna received something like £250 a year for life, a sum large enough to give her a degree of independence. It meant that she need not worry about the future – and what was more, she saw the legacy as confirmation that the Lord was with her, a kind of divine recognition that she was doing everything right.

In this mood of vindication, her mind flew back, as it often did, to the man who had figured so strongly from the start. The Reverend Joseph Pomeroy was, as far as she knew, still living as a lonely widower in his parish in distant Bodmin. What would he think if he could see her now? The humble, ill-educated farmer's daughter living in London surrounded by rich and devoted followers? In the month that Cosins died, Joanna dreamt that she was with Pomeroy, talking about her Visitation, and he said that he was convinced it was from the Lord. He asked her to take hold of his arm, which she did, and he led her into a house, along a passage to the foot of the stairs where, placing her hand on the bannister, he said, 'Keep it there till I come, for I am going upstairs, to take off my dirty clothes, and put on clean ones.'[10]

In other words, the Pomeroy of Joanna's dreams had now recognised

I. *A facsimile of Joanna Southcott's handwriting, showing how difficult it was to read. The writing is oddly angular and at first appears illegible. Sceptics declared that Joanna deliberately wrote down her prophecies in a way that no one else could read, so that the words might later be amended. Nevertheless, with a little patience, it is possible to decipher her scrawl.*

II. *Emblematical needlework binding on a manuscript completed by*
'Joseph' Prescott in 1795. Pasted on the title page is an explanation by
Joanna Southcott of the symbols on the book's cover: 'The Lord Jesus
Holds the True Light. The Three Stars which is on his arm is the true
light, he holds the Fulness, for his Saints is as Stars in his hands, they fall
down at his feet, singing in his Glory, & they are not compleat without the
key of Knowledge to open their Understanding, & . . . the Star of his Love
to wear on their Breast, & . . . the Anker, believing that it will stand fast
upon Firm Land, saying, upon this Rock I Build my Church, and the Gates
of hell shall not prevail against it.'

III. *Above:* Patchwork (unquilted) made by Joanna Southcott in 1808, with **(Right)** her name and the year worked in her own hair on a small panel near its centre. There is also a note, written on laid paper, tacked near the patchwork's outer edge, which reads: 'Frances Taylors Quilt, June 18th 1810'.

Joanna refers in her writings to several patchworks that she was making for friends. At least two of these remain in conservation and the illustration shows one composed of a variety of coloured cotton chintz. Joanna's followers regarded her needlework as prophetic: her patchwork was said to represent the multitude of Christian sects which, at the Second Coming, would unite into a single, perfect and entire Church.

IV. Caricature by George Cruickshank, published by Thomas Tegg in September, 1814 – The Imposter, or Obstetric Dispute – vide - Johanna Southcote and the Public Disputations. Joanna is seen trying to brush off her enemies while Tozer, her loyal cur, emerges from beneath her skirts to bark at them. Meanwhile, a group of eminent doctors stand gossiping about her condition, unable to agree whether her symptoms suggest pregnancy or cancer.

V. *Cot presented to Joanna Southcott by believers for the birth of Shiloh. Commissioned from Seddons, Aldersgate Street, London, it is made of satinwood ornamented with gold and hung with blue satin drapes. At its head is an embroidered gold crown with the word Shiloh in Hebrew. The canopy is surmounted by a golden dove carrying the olive branch of peace, around the canopy are the words (covered by ribbon):* 'A Free Will offering to the promised seed – The Prince of Peace will now be born – To raise on Earth a David's Throne.' *The crib, donated by W.A.Howes to Salford Museum in 1860, is now in the care of the Panacea Society.*

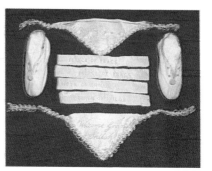

A selection of gifts for Shiloh, showing: a tiny pair of of white fine leather shoes; four ribbons embroidered in silver with 'Prince of Peace' *and* 'Birth of Shiloh'; *two triangular headpieces edged with lace and embroidered with* 'Welcome Grand Shiloh' *to show beneath the baby's bonnet.*

VI. *Satin cape, trimmed with swansdown, was presented to Joanna for her lying-in. Had a child been born, she would have expected to receive visits from the highest in the realm.*

Satin coverlet, bordered with swansdown, silver fringe and tassels, presented for Shiloh. Embroidered in silver thread: 'What good news the Angels bring, What glad tidings of our King, Christ descending from his throne, Brings his Father's glory down', *and in silver, at the top, symbols (crown, sceptre, staff, dove, stars and rays of glory). Along the bottom:* Maher shalal hash baz. *(Speed to the spoil. Isaiah 8:1)*

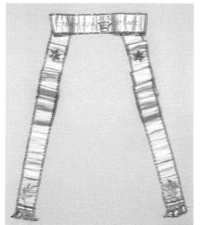

VII. *Rattle, sash, slippers, and ladle – some of the magnificent gifts prepared for Shiloh. Morocco case containing a finely chased silver rattle and whistle engraved with a dove, olive branch and crown, given by Mrs Dentham. The rattle's coral handle could be used as a baby's teether.*

A white satin sash with embroidered silver crown, stars and the inscription Crown him Lord of all, *given by Mrs Troup. Tiny satin slippers with silver-embroidered inscriptions:* King of Salem *and* Priest of God *were given by Miss Kent, a relative of Ann Troup.*

A silver ladle with which to serve Shiloh's food, presented to Joanna by Mr Hows' Choir.

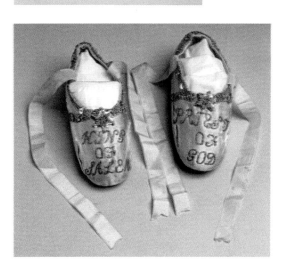

VIII. *Banner depicting Joanna Southcott as* The Woman Clothed With the Sun *(Rev 12:1). In her left hand she holds a scroll bound by her beribboned 'IC' seal. The banner was made at the Royal School of Needlework in 1917 from a design by Mabel Barltrop. Its cost was met by followers of Joanna, some of whom gave jewellery and gold to be used in the embroidery of the girdle. The rays of the sun are of gold thread and the crown of solid gold. In 1917 there seemed to be some possibility of the bishops agreeing to open Joanna's Box and the banner was intended for use on this occasion. However, the moment passed and the banner was placed in storage together with other relics of her mission.*

how he had been at fault and even declared himself ready to change his 'dirty clothes'. All Joanna had to do was wait for him to come to her with this new attitude and then they could ascend together. It must have been an enchanting prospect.

By October Joanna had not only finished Noah's quilt but also made a cradle-quilt for the next 'little stranger' that Mrs Foley was expecting the following March. Colonel Harwood had already made one visit to advise Foley on his debts, but his help was being urgently sought again over a dispute with Mr Else which had been rumbling on for ten years. Else was trying to reclaim a debt from Foley – who thought Else owed him money. From Norfolk, where he was busy letting out his farms and settling with his tenants, Harwood sent word that Foley should look back over his correspondence and work out what to do. William Owen, who was a doctor of law, offered subtler advice: Foley should simply stall by saying that he had sent his accounts to a friend in London and so could not settle anything himself, while at the same time stressing that he expected to be paid money, not to pay it.

That winter there was small comfort to be had anywhere. Stocks tumbled every time Wellington fell back before the enemy, and Bonaparte's apparent success in Russia made things worse. '[T]he number of Bankrupts is far beyond whatever were known before, people out of employment with their families starving in the streets that we cannot wonder there are so many robberies committed,' Joanna complained to Foley in December. Even in Bristol, where the Reverend Samuel Eyre's meeting had previously been a model of cooperation and harmony, affairs were falling apart – a situation Joanna blamed on the Methodist connection of many friends, which led them to demand hymns and prayers. When Eyre as an Anglican would not oblige, some formed a breakaway group under the more evangelical Philip Pullen, who had just arrived from Somerset, so that in the end Bristol became just like Exeter where the friends were always criticising each other and falling out.[11]

Foley, while full of sympathy with Eyre, who had become a close friend, did not get involved. In the face of so many problems he was retreating from social life to find refuge within the bosom of his family and from the beginning of October gave up all visiting.[12] Furthermore, with debts and a growing family – five children and another on the way – he had to watch his resources. This was not easy when there were so many scroungers keen to take advantage of another's generosity. Joanna, once she recognised this problem, gave any hangers-on short shrift and wrote to warn Foley if she saw them heading in his direction. For instance, earlier in the year, she reported that Perrin had just called to ask if she wanted to send anything to Foley, as he was going to

Oldswinford. Joanna sat silent, not wanting to encourage him. Afterwards she wrote to tell Foley that there were very few people she would sanction to call on him and he should never entertain people just because they said they were believers.

Her warning did not prevent the kindly Foleys from taking in deaf old Mr Bowman. Writing before Christmas to ask Foley to send his seasonal gift of turkey and tongue before 9 January, Joanna said,

> I find Bowman has found his way to you. . . . [S]orry he is so close as Foley may have more of his company than is agreeable . . . he called here so often that I was obliged to be engaged very often when he came, or I should have been wearied out with him being so deaf and full of trifling conversation that I found it troublesome to converse with him.

Poor Foley, it may imagined what kind of Christmas he had – grieving over his friend John Wilson who had just died, and coping simultaneously with Mr Bowman and a troublesome man-servant who became so drunk and abusive that he was sacked with one hour's notice.[13]

The new year saw happier tidings. 'We have heard that our dear and beloved wilderness friends have had a fortune left them,' Foley wrote, passing on news of Cosins' will to Charles Taylor in March. 'May they long enjoy it in health, peace and happiness. . . . [We] expect Colonel Harwood for a few days, then will know more.' But his main news was home-produced: 'Last Saturday morning at five oclock my wife had a fine and lovely Boy.' He would be called John, David, or Samuel – they had yet to decide. That they were delighted was never in doubt. Beyond that, Foley had little news except that he had received visits from George Turner, John Roberts, and Mr Jowett of Yorkshire and his son from Birmingham, where the cause was spreading fast.[14]

If Foley was disappointed at the lack of interest in his own backyard, where only a few of the very poor had joined the cause, his spirits revived with the receipt of a letter from George and Elizabeth Rea of Lea Castle on 6 March. Apologising for writing to him as a stranger, George Rea described how he had been made aware of Joanna's mission by one of his relatives who attended the 'trial at Neckinger House' but that he had taken little notice until a year ago when he started to read her books. The more he read, the stronger his faith had grown until now he firmly believed that Joanna was inspired by the Spirit of God.[15]

George and Elizabeth Rea thus joined the ranks of Joanna's wealthy supporters alongside people like Hugh Carder of Leicester Square, George Troup, a favourite valet of the Prince Regent, John Smith, steward to the Earl of Darnley, William Sharp, Colonel Harwood, Foley himself and others. They were the people of property whom Richard Law, now fallen from grace, saw being cultivated by Joanna in preference to poorer folk like himself. Law later complained to Townley,

> You being a person of property she coaxed you on to the end as she did Hows and others possessing property, but the useful and upright poor she scattered from her, though at first she was glad to profit from their labours, but as she grew stronger she would not suffer them to remain among the Prelates and Dignitaries of her new Church, but she pushed them out to put gentlemen in their room, in this you and she perfectly accorded, she was the most ungrateful woman that ever was befriended by man.[16]

Whether Law was right or merely pursuing a personal grudge, the fact that Joanna had gained such a prestigious circle of friends – there were even hints of royal interest in her cause – opened up a prospect of unlimited patronage. When John Hows bought a new house in April 1813, for instance, he immediately offered accommodation to anyone Joanna liked to recommend and she suggested her old friend, Mrs Burg, a poor mantua-maker from Exeter – 'a genteel-looking woman who lived with a lady in one of Mr Taylor's houses.'[17]

Although fortune continued to smile on her finances in 1813, Joanna was not blessed by good health. In June she wrote to George Turner that she had been very ill 'with spasms in my stomach which I am subject to. . . .'[18] Her illness possibly triggered thoughts of mortality which, now that she was a person of property, prompted her to settle her worldly affairs. She called together some friends to witness a will in which she left annuities of £10 to her brother William and sister Susanna, as well as £10 each for mourning at her death; sums of £10 each to her brother Joseph's widow, Sarah, and his daughter, Susanna, who was to receive a further £15 when she came of age; the rest of her income from James Cosins' legacy to go to Jane Townley and Ann Underwood, with the latter to act as sole executrix. This will was witnessed by William Owen Pughe, Theodore Turpin, Mary Pilbrough, and Ellen Tolhurst.[19]

After her recent experience of deathbed bequests it must have been a relief for Joanna to settle her affairs and still find the future stretching before her. But then, that was only to be expected while there was work to be done, her mission still to accomplish.

Suddenly, through the post came a copy of the *West Briton or Truro Advertiser*. She opened it and read a dramatic account of how, on 17 August 1813, the Reverend J. Pomeroy had collapsed and died in the pulpit of Bodmin church just as he was about to preach the Assize Sermon.

Pomeroy dead. It simply could not be true. Pomeroy, the first clergyman to take her seriously; the man who, despite himself, was destined to make the Church listen to her. Pomeroy, the man she had predicted would be her heavenly Bridegroom. 'In vain may Pomeroy try to flee, He ne'er shall shun his call,' she had written confidently the year before. And now he was dead? If so, then her prophecies were flawed, her faith shattered.[20]

Amidst this overwhelming catastrophe, her inner Voice urged that it was all a mistake, that Pomeroy was alive. Joanna clung to the words, desperately wanting to believe. But the common sense of her friends prevailed. It was no mistake, they said. How could it be, when there it was in the newspaper for all to read in black and white? To say that Joanna was devastated was to understate her grief. In the depth of her despair she wrote *The Book of Wonders*, a justification of her attitude to Pomeroy and a confession that she had been misled.[21]

THE VISITATION, 1813

> I told thee that I should work on Pomeroy's heart, to come in
> my Spirit, though not in my person, to propose a Marriage Union
> with thee.   *Sixth Book of Wonders*, published 1852

Joanna's first *Book of Wonders* was printed and distributed throughout
the country. Soon after the parcels had been despatched, she received
further news from Cornwall. There had, after all, been a mistake. Two
clergymen with the name of Pomeroy had been living in the parish of
Bodmin and of these it was the Reverend JOHN Pomeroy, Vicar of
Bodmin, who had died so dramatically in the pulpit. Her Voice had been
right all along – if only she had cared to listen. Joseph Pomeroy, her
Pomeroy, was still very much alive.

Joanna's ecstatic reaction to this news brought on another 'visitation'.
Sleep deserted her as she awoke soon after three o'clock each morning to
sit up in bed and commune with her Spirit. At daybreak, when she went to
the dining-room by herself, she felt as if she were surrounded by angels.
She could not eat. What need had she of food when feasting on heavenly
sustenance? She lost all appetite for breakfast, dinner or supper; could not
even drink tea in the afternoon.[1] Perhaps she would never eat again, for she
was told: 'The time of thy departure draweth nigh, for thy sands are nearly
run.' She welcomed this intimation of mortality: 'as I am as weary of the
world as the world is of me.' But what caused her great joy was the revelation
that the Lord would now convince Pomeroy of the truth of her mission.

On Sunday, 19 September she wrote Pomeroy a letter, saying: '[T]hese
words came powerfully to me; he shall say: "I yield, I yield, I can hold
out no more".'

Next morning she continued the letter after waking up with the memory
of her prophecies and the part Pomeroy had played in them.

On Monday night she had not been long in bed before feeling the
Lord's anger burst out against the clergy for neglecting their duty. At
three o'clock next morning she awoke with the words:

> So if she's high, then let her fly,
> And take your charge away;
> But if she pass too proudly here,
> Her shotsman I will be. . . .[2]

After Joanna had finished *The Second Book of Wonders,* her Spririt ordered her to have seven respectable friends meet together at four o'clock in the afternoon of Thursday, 23 September, to hear what had been revealed and what she was being directed to do.[3] She accordingly summoned William Sharp, Theodore and Thomas Turpin, Benjamin Carder, William Tolhurst, William Owen Pughe, and John Hows to hear three letters to Pomeroy read.

They heard how Pomeroy, after first encouraging Joanna, had suddenly, at the end of 1801, lost his faith in her mission. Then, when her writings were proved at Paddington in 1803, Pomeroy had been invited as a judge and when he did not come, Foley's little son had stood in Pomeroy's place, 'as no man was permitted to be chosen in his room. . . .' This action had signified Pomeroy's childish behaviour, for Joanna demanded,

> What has Pomeroy been more than a child these twelve years?
> For though he is a man, yet he hath acted like a child that is
> afraid of his mother. . . . But now his fears shall be over, because
> the mother shall free the son, and let them see the Spiritual Birth
> in what manner he is now brought forth.

Having verified the contents of the three letters, these, together with some of Joanna's books and her engraved portrait, were placed in a box which the Seven were directed to send to Pomeroy as soon as her latest publication was ready and could be included as well.[4] They were then directed to meet again at the same time on the following Monday. Meanwhile Joanna was ordered to have twelve new gowns purchased – for a mysterious purpose that would be revealed on that day.

Monday came. The Seven assembled to receive Joanna's latest revelation. That very morning it had been revealed to her that she was to be married. Not in purely spiritual union, she was to wed an earthly husband – a prospect which, in view of her age and happy single life, filled her with dread, she told them.[5]

And who was to be the bridegroom?

On Friday, 24 September, she had dictated another letter to Pomeroy, which included the phrase: '[F]atal now shall my judgments come, if Pomeroy should refuse thy hand. . . .'

Pomeroy? After all his backsliding and treachery? Surely not Pomeroy.

Going over past events in her mind, Joanna grew very angry with him. But resentment gave way to misery once she recognised that by hardening her heart against Pomeroy, she was hardening it against the Lord. She also remembered the six years of kindness and attention when he had visited her at the Taylors and Wollands. Moreover, in the last resort, she had to acknowledge that it mattered not how she felt. Her part was simply to obey the Voice of the Lord. The following morning her Spirit commanded,

> Thou must be perfect in obedience to all my commands, and therefore I told thee that I should work on Pomeroy's heart, to come in my Spirit, though not in my person, to propose a Marriage Union with thee, . . . and so I tell thee thou must go through the office of Marriage as a Bride, to fulfil all righteousness here upon earth, before the heavens are opened for thou to enter in to know my Spirit and the mysteries that will be revealed.

The Seven must have listened stunned as Joanna conveyed to them her grief at hearing of Pomeroy's death, how that gloom had been entirely dispelled on the day she heard that he was alive, since when she had been daily visited by the Spirit and filled with joy. Moreover she had been told that the Lord would work on Pomeroy's heart feelings similar to her own so that he would come forward as a strong believer in her mission.[6]

In the normal way of things, Joanna might have had doubts about Pomeroy's response, for she had not written or heard from him for nine years,[7] but having received divine assurance she proceeded with sublime confidence. In a carefully worded letter to the bishops, much edited before she got the tone right,[8] she told them that in 1792 the clergy had persecuted Pomeroy for encouraging her Mission, so they must now make amends by convincing him of her cause.

All that was needed – for the sake of Joanna, the nation and the whole world – was for Pomeroy to come forward and grasp his destiny. On Tuesday night, 28 September, the Spirit told Joanna:

> My visitation to thee is to shew thee what shall take place upon earth, and how men shall love their wives, and the wives their husbands – then I tell thee, men may judge how near the time is at hand from what they will see in Pomeroy and thee; for as thou sayest in thy heart, this is a match commanded on both sides by the Lord, because I ordered thee to write to him that he must bear all my office; and know the letter I ordered thee to send him, that could not come to the fulness till the bride was found: and if thou wast not the right one, I told him to bring one that was right.[9]

Again on 6 October Joanna was assured that she would soon be united with the one 'whom the Lord had kept her for'.

> So now thy youthful days I'll call them back,
> Thou knowest how Noah did thy heart affect:
> When that in anger thou stood'st with the man,
> Thou heardst his sorrows, how in love he mourned,

> And thou repent'dst; thy folly thou dost know,
> But still no power hadst thou thy will to do. . . .
> Mark all thy lovers, I hedg'd up the way
> So much with thorns, thou never could'st go through
> To gain a husband. . . .

Now, at long last, this earthly union was to be brought about so that 'the truth of what had been nailed up, signed and sealed by seven men and three women' with a three-fold cord and Joanna's IC seal upon it, would be fulfilled. All she had to do was contain her impatience and wait for Pomeroy's response.

The following morning found her sitting up in bed at five o'clock while lightning flashed and thunder crashed about the house, and it came as a merciful distraction from the storm when she was ordered to write up the history of her father's family. The task kept her busy for the next few days and when she finished she congratulated herself:

> My mother used to say I had a proud heart to be humbled and a
> hard heart to be softened on account of my resenting spirit, but
> since the Lord's visitation I have acted contrary to my own will
> and conquered my besetting sin by obedience to the Lord's ways.[10]

That obedience was now put to an even more stringent test when, on 11 October, Joanna announced that she had been commanded by the Spirit to shut herself up with Townley and Underwood and remain incommunicado, writing no letters and seeing no man other than a bishop or Pomeroy until her Spirit delivered her into the hands of her protector.[11]

It marked the start of something extraordinary, for from that day onward Joanna felt a powerful 'visitation' working upon her body. It was such a physical sensation that it filled her with fear. She wondered, could it be the work of the Devil? But she was soon reassured that her sensations came, not from the Devil, but from the Lord acting not in anger but in love, to show her His power.[12]

At the same time Joanna began to experience strange visions. Around midnight on 14 October, having been ordered to sit up by herself, she was staring at the candle when there appeared a large bowl behind it. Then, as the candle flared bright, there appeared a scarlet ring around the middle of the flame and a hand as white as snow came out between the bowl and the candle and pointed towards her. She trembled and was answered: 'Fear not, it is I.'

She was ordered to put on her glasses and the hand appeared a second time, more brilliant than before. Then the flame, still very bright, parted in two and the snow-white hand with a red cuff around its wrist re-appeared and pointed straight at her.[13]

The exalted mood engendered by this vision did not outlive her perusal two days later of a note from Foley, which avoided any reference to her latest book and letter to the bishops. After hearing it read, Joanna banged her hands on the table and paced up and down in fury, muttering that if the bishops took no more notice of her book than Foley had done, then she might find herself shut up in her room for a twelvemonth and fatal ruin come on the land. She answered Foley by assuring him that Pomeroy would come round to his duty once the bishops applied to him, and mentioning that there was another book printed but not allowed to go out until Pomeroy had come to see her. The letter was signed: 'Yr friend & fellow labourer in the Lord's Vineyard, A. Underwood.'

A postcript informed Foley that all letters were now being answered by Jane Townley and that, as there were no directions with regard to meetings, the friends should act as they thought best.[14]

A fortnight later Joanna's 'Letter to the Nation' was published in *The Times* newspaper. For twelve years, she declared, she had been warning people about what the Lord would do. Now, after promising five more *Books of Wonders*, Joanna defied all the bishops, M.P.s, and judges in the land to prove that her two previous books had come from the Devil or an impostor. She followed up this challenge by publishing in the *Morning Herald* her 'Warning to the Bishops', apparently threatening them with death if they refused to pronounce on her visitation. (Ever the business woman, she added a careful little postscript: 'The book alluded to is sold at M. Jones's, No.5, Newgate Street.')

There followed another barrage of letters to the press. In one to the *Morning Herald* on 15 November Joanna referred to the 'Day of Salvation' the nation could expect in April 1814. A few days later she issued a similar prophecy: 'the ensuing year will be such a year as never was seen in England, since it was a nation.'[15]

If many of her missives went wide of their mark, some clearly pierced the skin of the Church hierarchy. Her friend, Robert Portbury, waiting on Bishop Pelham in Exeter to ask if it was right for the clergy to ridicule individuals from the pulpit, met the weary reply: 'Joanna had done more mischief than ever an individual had done before.'[16] Eventually, after publishing a Methodist's reply to Joanna, the editor of the *Morning Herald* brought the correspondence to a close.[17]

When Christmas arrived with still no word from Pomeroy, Joanna was beside herself. She knew she had to alert the nation to the momentous events in store. But what could she do if the most important people refused to listen? Boxing Day dawned fine with remarkable sunshine, but the following day the weather deteriorated until by evening there was frost and such thick fog that people could not get about even with torches. In this state of outer and inner darkness Joanna began to reevaluate her more faithful friends. On Thursday, 30 December, 1813, she woke up and, in her own words:

> I began to meditate on what I would put in the newspaper, how I had been forty years wearied with the perverse hearts of men because I thought upon none but my enemies and had forgotten my friends . . . but . . . I can by no means condemn the conduct of men in general, because my enemies in mankind against me have proved the friendship in others the greater. . . . [T]he true and sincere friendship I have met with in my friends made me say that I could die a martyr for their sakes. . . .[18]

It was one thing to die a martyr, another to live without making demands. The fact was, Joanna's turbulent moods were wreaking havoc among her friends in Weston Place where, while Underwood was in bed with a high temperature and stomach cramps, the other servants knew little rest from coping with Joanna. One morning, for instance, she got out of bed at two o'clock still asleep, knocked down a chair, wandered over to a table, threw everything off, and only woke up when startled by all the noise she was making. Then, unable to find her way back to bed in the dark, she went to the window and opened the shutter to let in the moonlight. By this time Mr and Mrs Tolhurst, the couple who had replaced the Abbotts living downstairs, were wide awake but did not come up once things quietened down again. It was only when Mrs Pilborough entered to light the fire in the morning that anyone realised how close to disaster Joanna had been, for the floor was littered with slivers of glass from two rummers, a wine glass, a mug and a plate. Seeing this, Joanna declared it was a miracle that she had escaped without getting her feet cut to pieces.[19]

Outside the thick London fog persisted until 3 January, causing several fatal accidents. But on 12 January, Old New Year's Eve, there was a sparkling sunset and the next day dawned fine and clear, leading Joanna to conclude that the Old Style calendar was right.

However, not festive season nor sickness nor weather could distract Joanna from her central concern – what was happening to Pomeroy? Why had he not replied? As days and weeks passed with still no word, she grew exasperated, chewing over in her mind Pomeroy's words – that 'she was born for his ruin'. Were this so, she was now answered, then God was to blame, not her. Furthermore, if Pomeroy remained silent until the Spirit ordered her to send again, she was told her enquiry must then be: 'Will he resign that thou shalt look for another, who can bear to draw the SPIRITUAL SWORD for me, and to maintain the SPIRITUAL FIGHT?' In other words, Pomeroy must eventually resign the calling or draw the sword; 'he must bear the cross if he will wear the crown.'

Surprisingly enough, there were others besides the faithful who expected Pomeroy to come forward and stand by Joanna's side, for it was rumoured that the pair had been in collusion all along. Determined to put a stop to such rumours, Joanna repeated that she had not set eyes on Pomeroy since she had signed his declaration in Mrs Taylor's house.[20]

The truth was that, far from being in collusion, Joanna had completely lost touch with Joseph Pomeroy over the years and it seems never to have entered her head that he might have subsequently remarried and thus have rendered himself, even with the best will in the world, ineligible to appear as her bridegroom. Nevertheless, this was the devastating news that reached her some time between Christmas and New Year. Although her marital hopes had been blasted, few would glimpse her humiliation under the smokescreen she put up. When in future she referred to Pomeroy, it was only in connection with the prophecies handed to him at Exeter.

Her thinking seems to have been that, if Pomeroy could not come forward to marry her, the least he could do was confirm that she had entrusted to him certain prophecies, which events later proved true. After all, it was incontrovertible that she had handed some papers to him, and it was definitely his fault if he had destroyed them and thus made it impossible for her to prove what prophecies she had made. If there was any justice in the world, it was up to Pomeroy to redeem the situation he had created – or so thought Joanna; and this he could do only by verifying what she said was in her writings.[21] The corollary was that if he failed to do this, she and her followers would pursue him to the grave.

'SHE IS WITH CHILD'

> I am now going to lay before you one of the most important and
> delicate cases that ever a Woman had to lay before Mankind.
>
> *Joanna to George Turner*, 25 February 1814

> And in old age I gave a son
> To shew what I for FAITH had done.
>
> *Copies of Letters Sent to the Clergy of Exeter . . .*
> *Book 59* (71)

Joanna's hopes of marriage may have evaporated, but rather than sit around and mope she busied herself with the publication of the next book: *Wisdom Excelleth the Weapons of War* appeared in January 1814. In it she acknowledged her mistake over Pomeroy's death and then eclipsed the more recent news of his marriage by making a portentous announcement of her own. Something would happen that year, she declared, 'such as was never seen in England since it was a nation.'[1]

For years Joanna had been identifying herself with the woman in Revelation, chapter 12: 'And there appeared a great wonder in heaven, a woman clothed with the sun, and the moon under her feet, and upon her head a crown of twelve stars: and she being with child cried, travailling in birth, and pained to be delivered . . . and she brought forth a man child, who was to rule all nations with a rod of iron.' These words took on an awesome significance when, early in 1814, her Voice declared: 'This year in the sixty-fifth year of thy age thou shalt have a Son by the power of the Most High.'[2]

At sixty-four to be a mother? Surely this was impossible! Joanna would scarcely have been human had she not had doubts. But then, had she not doubted her Voice when it said Pomeroy was alive? And the Voice had proved right. Besides, there were precedents in the Bible. Had not Sarah and Elizabeth conceived in old age? Joanna had always believed that the God who had wrought miracles in ancient times could do the same today. Indeed the possibility of miraculous births had always been present in her mind, for there was a local tradition at Honiton, enshrined in its borough seal, that a night spent in St Margaret's Chapel would make any woman a mother.

Nevertheless she was cautious when spreading the news.

> Dear Friend, I am now going to lay before you one of the most important and delicate cases that ever a Woman had to lay before Mankind, and to which I must entreat your serious attention in this weighty affair,

she wrote on 25 February to George Turner at Leeds in a letter informing him of the conception and mentioning the seven men – Hallard (probably Halhed was meant), Spring, Goldsmith, Coles, Harwood, Tozer and Hirst – who had already met twice to make the necessary arrangements.[3] Three days later Joanna herself was put more clearly in the picture when her Spirit gave her an explanation of the conception. 'It is now four months since I felt the powerful visitation working upon my body,' she wrote. 'It began 11th October.'

She was with child – of that she had no doubt. She was also sure that her Child had an exceptional destiny. For if she was the second Virgin Mary, it followed that her son must be the second Messiah.

What, then, was his name? Apart from the Book of Revelation, another text which seemed to throw light on the Second Coming was Genesis 49:10 which, in the Authorized Version, read:

> The sceptre shall not depart from Judah, nor a lawgiver from between his feet, until Shiloh come; and unto him shall the gathering of the people be.

It was a verse based, in fact, on a misreading. Shiloh was not a person but a place – a town north of Jerusalem where the Ark of the Covenant was kept before Solomon built the Temple. But Joanna, reading her Authorized Version of the Bible, could not have known this. Whilst rejecting the current idea that Shiloh was a name for Christ, on the grounds that Judah had not surrendered the sceptre to Him, she accepted that Shiloh was someone who would arise in the Last Days.[4] And thinking along these lines brought her to the inevitable conclusion – Shiloh was her unborn son!

On 10 March, 1814, she proclaimed this glorious news in her *Third Book of Wonders, Announcing the Coming of Shiloh; With a Call to the Hebrews, etc.* She declared,

> If the visitation of the Lord to me now does not produce a Son this year, then Jesus Christ was not the Son of God born in the manner spoken by the Virgin Mary.[5]

Moreover, this time deeds would speak louder than words, for she was promised:

> Thy public trial will not appear for thee to be called forward in a solemn assembly, to testify the truth of the Child, before thou canst go with the Child in thy arms, while the milk is in thy

breasts, that men may know thou hast not been deceived.

And her book ended with the injunction:

> Let thy friends, wherever thy books are sold, send this book to
> the principal person of the Jews in the place where they reside;
> and let the Jews assemble together and pass their judgment on it;
> and tell thy friends who may write down their answer for thee –
> for no letters must be sent to thee from any one but thy friends.[6]

Her announcement was bound to have repercussions so it was as
well to take precautions. Besides, it was important to protect Joanna in
her present delicate state, for on 17 March she fell ill and during the
next five months was never entirely free of pain and nausea.[7] Despite
this discomfort, however, she redoubled her efforts to pin down Pomeroy.

Mr Walker, one of her supporters, had written asking Pomeroy to say
exactly when Joanna had put certain prophecies in his hands, but his
letter had been returned. Joanna then wrote to Walker herself, asking
him to send off a letter which she herself had written to Pomeroy on 23
March and warn him that copies of it were going to be sent, together
with one of her books and her portrait, to the Prince Regent, the
Archbishops of Canterbury and York, the Bishop of Worcester, the Duke
of Gloucester, Lord Grosvenor, Lord Ellenborough, the Recorder of
London and other dignitaries.

'Now,' Joanna demanded, 'what if all these decided to burn the
evidence and deny receiving it? How would you feel in my place?' In
other words, 'My innocence should stand condemned if they should
act as Mr P. hath done,' she explained (carefully avoiding any use of the
Reverend Joseph Pomeroy's full name so that no offence could be caused
on that score!), and adding with sweet reasonableness:

> I do not want Mr P. to believe in the prophecies; I only want him
> to send a satisfactory answer to acknowledge the truth I put
> into his hands, of what I enumerated in the letter I sent to him in
> 1804, and if he had acknowledged at that time that he did receive
> them from me, he would never have been troubled with any
> more letters on my account. And I now only want a satisfactory
> answer from him, as he is not required to come forward himself
> now.

Her letter was to no avail. Everything sent to Pomeroy came back to
Walker with an unsigned note, presumably penned by Mrs Pomeroy,
who complained that such letters caused him great uneasiness of mind
and concluded: 'Mr P. will have nothing to say or do on the subject.'

Not that any blame attached to the lady who wrote the note, for
Joanna acknowledged that it was natural for a wife to protect her
husband's feelings. On the other hand, she could not forebear to point

out that Mrs Pomeroy should realise that the real cause had to be removed before the effects she complained of could cease. Joanna also threatened that, if she received no proper reply by 11 June, she would publish the whole correspondence.[8]

Before that date she fired off another salvo to the Press, sending a letter to *The Observer* on 3 April, entitled: Questions put to the professors of religion who have condemned Joanna Southcott's last Book. She spent the whole of Good Friday, 8 April, meditating on the Gospel, coming to see how the preachers' attempts to prove it was true were doomed because they were treating it as product rather than process, acting just as she did as a child when she pinched the tips of her carnation buds and ruined all their blossoms.

She had just finished the *Fourth Book of Wonders* and sent it to the printers when she heard that Napoleon had abdicated at Fontainebleau earlier that week, and so she quickly added a reference to this apt destruction of the Beast at a time when the Lord was preparing his King to sit upon Holy Sion.

By now Joanna's claims had spread throughout the country and met a very mixed reception.[9] In Ilminster, Somerset, where Edmund Baker led an active group of believers, celebrations of Napoleon's defeat had been combined with an obscene ceremony in which effigies of Joanna and her child were paraded through the streets before being hanged, shot and finally burnt in front of the Southcottians' chapel.[10] Elsewhere similar scenes had taken place: 'Great is the mockery in Yorkshire,' wrote one of the friends. 'At Horbury they carried the effigy of Joanna through the village; then they shot at it 17 shots, then placed it with the head downwards, and burnt it in a large fire, saying she ought to be burnt; and the next day they carried another effigy, with two children, and repeated it the third day.'[11]

On Monday evening, 10 May, while Joanna lay in great pain she dreamt of going somewhere to be examined. Pomeroy was to be there, and Mrs Pomeroy came to Joanna and, putting her arm around her neck, said: 'We will go together.' Pomeroy looked at them both but did not speak. Then Mrs Pomeroy was standing in the midst of a group of men, one of whom stared at Joanna and said, 'How many Gods do you make?' She replied, 'Only one God, the Creator of the Universe.' But he said, 'He has contrived to rock the cradle.' Joanna wondered whether he meant this in mockery or not. Afterwards everyone was silent.

When she woke up, Joanna repeated the dream to Underwood, who laughed at it. Next day, although her pains returned, Joanna felt better[12] and she was soon to take comfort in a new sensation – a sensation greeted with joy by all those who knew what it was to feel a baby's 'quickening'.

I have felt life increasing more and more, from the 16th day of May . . . but never having had a child in my life, I leave it to the judgment of mothers of children who attend me, who give their decided opinion that it is perfectly like a woman that is pregnant. Then now I say, it remains to be proved whether my feelings and their judgment be right or wrong; whether it is a child or not; which a few months must decide; or the grave must decide for me; for I could not live to the end of this year, with the increasing growth I have felt within so short a space, without a deliverance.[13]

Some believers had received news of their dear Mother's 'indisposition' with similar foreboding and written to Miss Townley for reassurance. One of these was Edmund Baker who had recently suffered such outrage at Ilminster. Replying to him on 19 May, Charles Barnard, Underwood's son-in-law, wrote:

Dear Friend

Your letter with its contents I received safe, and have delivered it [to] Miss Townley. I have to beg you will not say or think anything of the Postage of letters to and from me, as it is all refunded to me quarterly. . . .

I do not understand what you mean by Mother leaving us here below as we believe now the Death spoken of [in *Strange Effects of Faith*] is only a death of Sin, so that we hope the Lord will bless us with the company of our Dear Mother for many centuries yet to come! But now I have to communicate to you marvellous News which I must entreat of you to keep in confidence till it becomes more public. Our dear Mother yesterday felt the life very strong. . . .

Your information is correct with respect to Mr Pomeroy – the Books are returned that were sent him by Mr Walker but whether by Mr P. himself is a mystery. There was a short letter enclosed addressed to Mr Walker which appeared to be written by some one for Mr P. saying – if he (Mr W.) knew the *anxiety of mind* the subject gave to Mr Pomeroy, Mr W. would not trouble him any more to which there was *no name* signed – this is all very strange – what *anxiety of mind* should it be to him if he is conscious he has done what is right? Why should the Person have any fear about signing [her] name if Mr P's conduct was justifiable? The whole affair is beyond our depth. I think there are more wonders connected with this subject.

Mrs Underwood is much better, but very busy and which will continue till the 5th Book is out, the rest are well and in high spirits.

There are now many serious enquirers – a lady in her carriage yesterday stopped at Jones's in Newgate St and bought one Book of each that she could have – this looks well – and it is singular that the Emperors and Kings should be coming to England at the time the life of the Child of Peace will be announced. . . . By the newspapers all does not seem easy in France, the French officers and the officers of the Allies quarrelling and duelling. . . .

Mrs B. unites with me in best Christian love to you and Mrs Baker. Mr Turpin and Mr and Mrs Carder often enquire very friendly after you

I remain my dear friend, yours very sincerely in the Cause of Truth

Chas. V. Barnard.[14]

Aware that they should not keep such earth-shaking news as Joanna's pregnancy to themselves, her friends sent an advertisement (which the editor refused to insert) to *Bell's Weekly Messenger* on Sunday, 29 May. It announced that 'Joanna Southcott would have a Son this year in the sixty-fifth year of her age, by the power of the Most High', and continued:

Whatever mockery the announcing of such an event may cause amongst mankind, or however wonderful it may appear, there is the most satisfactory evidence that it will be realised. This proof is established upon the testimony of the three women, being mothers of children, who have all along attended her; and upon their examination by two medical gentlemen, as to the symptoms which have taken place in Joanna Southcott from 17 March to 26 May, whose decided opinion thereon is, that, if such symptoms were in a young woman, she must be pregnant of a living child.

Of course they were right in foreseeing much mockery. Besley, a printer in South Street, Exeter, issued two handbills deriding the Millennium and attacking Joanna: 'I am told her followers are become numerous, that she has a genteel establishment, and a chapel built solely for the use of her disciples.' In her *Fifth Book of Wonders*, published in mid-June, Joanna acknowledged the truth of this information, proudly announcing, 'I am very comfortably situated; I have a number of respectable and worthy friends; and there is not only one chapel built in Duke Street, Westminster Road, but another at Greenwich, and another at Twickenham.' After answering the Reverend James Hearn, the Curate of Brixham who had preached against her mission and refused the Sacrament to her followers, Joanna turned to the practical question now vexing both her and the friends: what would be the legal status of her son if born to an unmarried mother?

> It is no reproach to a woman never to be married. But now look
> to what thy friends have said already, that thy son cannot stand
> to be an heir established by law, with God and man in one likeness,
> without the marriage union, to have a reputed Father, to adopt
> him as a son, when he is born. . . . [W]ithout marriage taken
> place, before the Child is born . . . thou wouldst be looked upon
> as an adulterous woman having a base child, and there is no
> way men could clear thy honour and innocence.

In view of her inheritance from Cosins and the very many valuable
gifts pouring in for the nativity, this was a real poser. So Joanna was
ordered by the Spirit to call together the same seven friends who had
met the year before and ask them:

> How can the Son who is to be born of her inherit as an Heir,
> after the manner of men, without having an adopted Father,
> before he shall be born?

The Seven met on Saturday, 4 June, and gave as their considered
opinion:

> According to the laws of the land, the Son so announced cannot
> be a legitimate child to inherit as an heir, after the manner of
> men, without a marriage union having taken place between her
> and some man, previously to the birth of such a Son.

The implications were so momentous that they immediately called on
other influential friends to add their agreement before sending the question
on to Halhed for his written opinion. Halhed returned an answer, signed
by himself and James Spring, explaining the situation thus:

> The laws of entail, indeed, prescribe that the Heir to real property
> must be lawfully begotten: but where there is a marriage the law
> presumes this fact, on the principle that 'Pater est quem nuptiae
> demonstrant' viz: the existence of the marriage is the proof of
> the personality of the father. And in this sense we say that our
> Lord Jesus Christ was the legitimate son of Joseph, his Mother's
> husband, and rightful heir to both Father and Mother. . . .

Thus it was agreed that Joanna should be married. But to whom?
Joseph Pomeroy was apparently out of the running, and should she
marry the wrong man, someone unscrupulous, he might make away
with the money or cause more dreadful problems. There was also a
danger that her marriage might be seized upon to give a more mundane
explanation of her pregnancy – Joanna being hailed as the oldest woman
to give birth was not the kind of acclaim she wanted. What Joanna had
to do was marry, but not live with her husband until after the birth.
Moreover, the marriage must take place in a way that was public yet
known to be conditional; the contract would not be binding unless a son

was born. In the words of her Spirit:

> [W]ithout the Son, thou hast no Father; and without the Father,
> the Son is not made a perfect heir, after the manner of men, and
> so thou canst not have the one without the other.

Joanna's friends tried in vain to secure the bishops' authority for such a conditional marriage.

The lady herself had meanwhile settled down to live as quietly as her public image would allow. Once her *Fifth Book of Wonders* was published, it was announced that no strangers were to come to the house unless invited. As for the multitude of friends arriving daily to make enquiries, they were to stay away until after the Child was born. Even postal enquiries were discouraged as there was no time to answer everybody. Instead, her followers were to study the Five Books and wait patiently for the Sixth to appear, telling them that the marriage had taken place. The Seventh would proclaim the birth of the Child. Then all wonders would cease, for there could be no more doubt that it was God in heaven who had produced all these miracles on earth.

At home in 17 Weston Place, Joanna was being tended by Ann Underwood, Mrs Pilborough and Mrs Tolhurst – all of whom were married women who had experienced childbirth.[15] No doubt they combed lists of their acqaintances in search of a suitable bridegroom. Apparently Noah Spring had already been considered, his Christian name, if nothing else, fitting him for the honour, but for some reason he was rejected as a candidate.

The trouble was, Pomeroy still represented unfinished business. Fearing that some might think she was about to marry someone (nay, anyone) else as a reaction to her disappointment in that quarter, Joanna determined to set the record straight. Going back over their correspondence, she decided that it was Pomeroy's interpretation of a letter she sent him in 1797 that was to blame for all subsequent misunderstandings. Re-reading this letter, she saw how he could well have thought that she was threatening him with dire punishment if he refused to become the Bridegroom. She now strenuously denied that this was ever her intention, admitting that since his family was a cut above hers, she could understand his reaction to such a suggestion. This being so, she decided to send John Hows, who was 'a respectable gentleman living independent of the world and therefore feareth no man',[16] to Bodmin to ask Pomeroy if it was true that he had misinterpreted her letter in this way.

Before he left, she received a Communication from her Spirit which contained a carefully contrived strategy. Hows must 'put it close' to Pomeroy that there had to be some explanation for his past conduct towards Joanna and if it stemmed from something as simple as misinterpreting her letter, then the situation could be immediately resolved. For what Joanna had really meant by saying that Pomeroy should marry her was that Pomeroy *as a priest* should carry out his priestly office and marry her to the man destined to be her groom – just as he had, no doubt, married countless other couples.

It was such a simple strategy. Pomeroy comes to Joanna and confesses his mistake. Joanna magnanimously forgives. The long persecution is ended.

But what if Pomeroy proved obstinate – failed to confess and refused to come immediately to see her? Then the next stage of the plan would operate. Hows should proceed subtly to warn Pomeroy – as a friend, mark you – that a letter was already printed, but not yet sent to the bishops, which must condemn him in their eyes if he did not take this last chance to clear himself by acknowledging that it was his misinterpretation of Joanna's letter in 1797 that had led to all subsequent trouble between them.

And if this did not work? Then Hows was to return to Exeter and speak to the person who had copied her letter in 1797, treating it as if this was evidence enough in the face of Pomeroy's denial.

Whatever happened, Hows was *not* to return to Joanna without some satisfactory answer!

On the following Tuesday evening William Sharp took the *Fifth Book of Wonders* and a letter from Joanna to the Recorder of London who, having read her letter aloud, said he admired the manner in which the marriage directions were given and, if she was married only one day before the birth, her child would be legitimate and able to inherit the property of both father and mother by the laws of the land and common sense. Well pleased, Sharp left the Recorder at nine o'clock to go and tell Joanna what had been said.[17]

Hows arrived in Bodmin on Saturday, 26 June, and made his way straight to Pomeroy's house where he was received most politely until he explained his errand. Upon this, Pomeroy became extremely agitated, refusing to listen or even to read Joanna's letter. Undaunted, Hows went away to write a note explaining why he had come and stating that he would stay in Bodmin until the following Tuesday, awaiting Pomeroy's reply. When no reply came, he sent a second letter – still to no avail. Eventually he returned to Exeter and showed Joanna's letter to Mrs Taylor, who remembered it well, as did her daughter Fanny Luscombe, who had originally copied it for Mr Pomeroy.[18]

Back in London, excitement, though not always expressed in the most

Caricature published by W.N.Jones, 1 July 1814 – Spirits at Work.
Joanna Concieveing, ie Blowing up Shiloh. *A startled bespectacled*
Joanna sits near a fire while a black demon blows into her skirts,
inflating her like a balloon. On the floor is a chamber pot of 'virgin
water'. On the other side of the room a disembodied hand ladles out
punch while a voice utters: 'FEAR NOT IT IS I. Drink this and quicken
your Conceptions.' On the wall are portraits of Tozer, Carpenter (upside
down) and Brothers, and a sack of 'Passports to Heaven five shillings
each, or two for Seven.' A clock standing on the mantelpiece between
statuettes of Moses and Aaron registers twelve o'clock.

respectful fashion, was mounting. On 1 July, W. N. Jones of 5 Newgate
Street published a lurid caricature entitled:'Spirits at Work – Joanna
Concieveing [sic] i.e. Blowing up Shiloh.'[19]

Happily Joanna and her friends could ignore such productions, busy as
they were with their own preparations. Mrs Goddard wrote on 7 July:

> The believers here (a many of them) are sending gifts to our
> Mother against the birth of the Child, of costly robes, of 80
> guineas worth some worked with gold and real pearls. There is
> not a small article that a child wants, but that it is sent by dozens,
> in deed there is more sent than can be used but the most costly
> present is a State Bed, which is what they call here a fashionable
> cot. Our blessed Lord at his first Coming had not where to lay
> his head but our little Prince of Peace will have a bed of down.

There are 20 subscribers of which I am one. The bed will cost £1400. I will endeavour to give you some description of it.

The frame is satinwood embroidered with Gold, the Bed and Pillows real down, the curtains sky-blue sarsnet with gold fringe, the Canopy or Head is ornamented with the Morning and evening Stars, at each corner the form of a small Globe, in the middle a Gold Dove with the olive branch of peace. On the front and on each side in Gold letters, Welcome the Heavenly Stranger. On the back of the Bed a Crown of Gold with word SHILO (in Hebrew), the sheets and pillow-cases fine cambric with lace, the Quilt white satin with the Tree of Life in Gold with emblematical figures of the Millenium [sic], and the motto of the woman claiming the promise – bringing the leaves for the healing of the Nations. It is likewise to be fringed round with Gold. Such is the Bed now nearly finished for the reception of the blessed Prince.[20]

In the midst of these fabulous gifts, being clucked over by anxious friends and examined by doctors, the centre of everyone's attention, Joanna continued busy as ever with her writings. It is not known whether anyone told her that her old friend, Sarah Minifie, had just died at Ottery St Mary.[21] Had they mentioned it, would she have cared to remember former times when she had worked for the Channon sisters and been snubbed in her efforts to share with them her visions? Probably not. She would have been much too caught up with the excitements of the moment.

EXPECTING SHILOH, 1814

Joanna (thank God) was large and far gone in pregnancy, and she gave me all the particulars, and also the opinions of the medical gentlemen who had attended her.

Foley's Diary, 18 August 1814

On Wednesday, 17 August, 1814, Foley set out for London to verify the miracle of Joanna for himself. His diary for that day reads:

A fine and glorious morning, and so continued. I start early for Broomsgrove, etc., and may it please the Lord to bless my expedition, and to keep me and be with me that I may do His righteous, holy and blessed will. I humbly commit my dear wife, our dear children, our household, and all that belongs to us to the care of the Lord, and may it please Him to keep them in health, peace and safety and happiness, till my return again to Old Swinford.

I arrived at Broomsgrove with my things just two minutes before the Birmingham Coach, and I took a place in it, and reached Worcester about half-past nine o'clock. I then tried the Mail for London, which was full. I then went to the other coach at The Bell, and found no one had taken a place, and I immediately engaged one for London, and at a little before twelve we started. Seven or eight soon came to the office after I had been there, and some were disappointed going till the next day. There was a pleasant party of us, and we had a very agreeable journey to Town, and we arrived safe and well there a little before ten on Thursday morning.

Foley was put down at the Worcester Coffee House in Oxford Street. After booking a room at the Kentish Arms in New Road, he made his way to Weston Place, where 'dear Joanna' and the friends gave him a warm welcome. All were in high spirits.

Joanna (thank God) was large and far gone in pregnancy, and she gave me all the particulars, and also the opinions of the medical gentlemen who had attended her, and how six of them were decidedly of opinion she was in a state of pregnancy, and that I must wait upon them separately to have their opinion from their own mouths.

He dined there and, after drinking tea with Colonel Harwood and Owen Pughe, left with them at about nine o'clock to return to the Kentish Arms for a good night's sleep.

The following morning, he rose early, breakfasted and wrote a long letter to his wife before setting out for the Smallpox Hospital (near Weston Place) and an interview with one of its resident physicians, Dr Joseph Adams.[1] Declaring himself happy to discuss the case with a 'gentleman', Adams said that from his external examination of Joanna, from her physical appearance and state of her breasts, he would have no hesitation in pronouncing her pregnant – if she was a woman of twenty-five who had been married for at least seven months. On the other hand, he knew of precedents for apparently pregnant women whose symptoms suddenly disappeared.

Hearing this, Foley agreed that in any case time must soon tell. He then dropped in again on Joanna and was delighted to find two more friends with her – John Roberts from Painswick and Edmund Baker from Ilminster, who had come to London on the same errand as himself. John Hows was also there together with a surgeon, Mr Hopgay, and Owen Pughe. After Foley, Roberts and Baker had a good talk with Joanna, they returned to the Kentish Arms where Roberts took over Foley's lodgings while Foley went to stay with Colonel Harwood. Later he was joined at the Harwoods' house by Roberts and Mr and Mrs Phillips, who stayed for dinner and then accompanied him back to Joanna's to drink tea and spend a few pleasant hours with her before going home at nine o'clock.

On Saturday morning, the four – Foley, Harwood, Roberts and Baker – collected first Mr Phillips, a surgeon who lived in Warren Street, Fitzroy Square, and then the Reverend Samuel Eyre from his lodgings at the Gloucester Coffee House before proceeding to interview the next doctor on their list: Mr Forster. They asked him whether he thought Joanna Southcott was pregnant. From his personal examination of her, he said he had no doubt whatever, for she had all the symptoms of a pregnant woman.

The six friends then called on William Tozer, staying half an hour with him before going on to the eminent Dr Richard Reece,[2] author of *The Medical Guide* and other learned treatises, who had been taken to see Joanna by one of his former patients, Mr Carder, on 7 August. Arriving in Weston Place at eleven o'clock that morning, Reece had been impressed by the simplicity of Joanna's surroundings, for instead of the pretentious luxury which newspapers had led him to expect, he was shown into a humble room where her supporters were busy folding up pamphlets. Here he had been greeted by Jane Townley, who spent some time discussing the weather before moving on to the purpose of his visit. Mrs Southcott's pregnancy was of divine origin, she declared, before elaborating on Joanna's situation and making it clear that her life had been spared only because the Almighty looked on her with special favour. Reece had listened patiently until it was announced that Mrs Southcott was ready to see him, whereupon, in his own words:

I was ushered into a small front room, where she sat, and on my entering rose, and politely received me, with that air of unaffected simplicity which forcibly struck me at the moment. On my being seated she commenced the history of her sufferings from the period of her pregnancy – stating that from the time of her quickening (which was in May) she had been subject to the usual complaints of the stomach incident to that situation, as nausea, sickness, and a disordered state of digestion. I allowed her to proceed in the whole of her statement without interruption, and after noticing her internal complaints, she came to mention the changes that had taken place in her breasts, which from being flat and sunk, had expanded, and become considerably enlarged and plump; that the same alteration had occurred in her abdomen, which had grown to a prodigious size, and that she had become thin about her loins; that her regular monthly appearance had left her for at least fifteen years. Having stated these circumstances, she then put to me the following pointed question, 'Sir,' says she, 'were I a young woman, and had been married seven or eight months, would you suppose, from the symptoms I have related, I was in the family way?' I immediately replied, from her statement, 'I could have no doubt of it'.

In every examination she acquiesced, except one, which the delicacy of her feelings as a virgin rejected, observing that had she been a married woman, even to this she would have readily agreed. This examination had been proposed to her by Dr. Walshman, the bare idea of which had shocked her, and made her very ill, and her warning spirit had desired her not to submit to such a proceeding, for the Lord would not impose on her more than she could bear.

After this explanation Mrs Underwood, her attendant, who was present, arose, and assisted her to remove the coverings from her breasts. The appearance of her breasts on inspection astonished me. They exhibited the picture of a young woman in the seventh month of pregnancy, being equally full, plump, and expanded. This fulness, on a close examination, consisted also of a real enlargement of the mammary glands, that part peculiarly destined for the secretion of milk. There was no appearance of disease or tendency to irregular enlargement, morbid hardness, or scirrhosity. All was apparently healthy. The nipples also were elongated, but the skin round the areola or disk was not so red or so clearly marked as in common cases of pregnancy, circumstances which I considered as connected with her age, and with that scaly surface which is apt to cover it at an advanced period of life. The left breast appeared somewhat larger than the right one, a fact noticed by herself.

Having thus satisfied myself of the change in her breasts, I was next permitted to examine her abdomen. Here I discovered an alteration equally conspicuous and striking. In that part occupied by the womb, where its expansion equals what takes place in the seventh month of pregnancy, I felt a hard circumscribed tumour, not less than the size of a man's head, bearing the shape of the womb, and on tracing its edges round, I had no doubt of its being really the enlargement of that organ. It was peculiarly hard to the feel, and, she declared, acutely painful on the slightest pressure. This circumstance I attributed to the rigidity of fibre necessarily attendant on age. Having finished my examination, she then asked me if I thought she was pregnant. My reply to her was in these words, 'That the fulness of the abdomen appeared to be produced by an enlargement of the womb; but whether it was the effect of pregnancy could only be established by the motion of the child'.

Dr Reece had then rested his right hand on her abdomen for ten minutes, but felt no movement. Joanna explained that it was always quiet in the presence of a stranger, but particularly active when she took food. To prove the point, Ann Underwood put a slice of peach in her mouth and, as soon as Joanna began to chew, Reece felt a foetus-like undulating motion under his hand.[3]

He was convinced.

Ten days later, when Reece was asked by Foley and his friends whether he thought Joanna Southcott was with child, he replied without hesitation that he fully believed she was, and for three reasons. First, he had examined her breasts and found the nipple protruding from the aureole which was greatly expanded to receive the termination of the lacteal vessels. Secondly, her womb was much enlarged. Thirdly, he had distinctly felt the living child within the womb. He also assured the men that he would be happy to attend the birth and act as a witness for Joanna whenever called upon, either in a public or private capacity.

The friends, except for Mr Eyre who felt ill and wanted to be on his own, then went to Colonel Harwood's for dinner. Afterwards Harwood, Roberts, Phillips and Baker went to drink tea with Joanna while Owen Pughe took Foley to meet the Reverend Mr King of Kentish Town, who for the next hour tried in vain to shake his fellow churchman's faith in Joanna and her mission. He stood no chance.

The next doctor on the list was Mr Meallin, of 2 Devonshire Street – whom Owen Pughe and Foley met at Joanna's and asked directly, was she in a pregnant state? Meallin said that he fully believed she was. Moreover, although he knew nothing about miracles, he was sure that the united efforts of all the men in London could not have got her with child. Like Reece, he wished to attend at the birth for, if Joanna had a child at sixty-five years of age, he would happily embrace this as proof of divine power.

Delighted to hear this, Foley went upstairs to Joanna but, finding her exhausted after so much company and talking, he and Colonel Harwood soon took their leave and returned home to entertain Mr and Mrs Phillips again to supper.

Sunday morning was spent by Foley, Harwood and Roberts writing up the opinions of the doctors already consulted. Later they were joined by Turner, Senior, Baker, Owen Pughe, Coles, Barnard, Wetherell, and Mr and Mrs Phillips for dinner at Harwood's and the friends passed what Foley termed 'the most delightful and heavenly day . . . together.' Mr Hirst, looking 'vastly well' made a brief visit in the afternoon on his way to Weston Place, where he found 'dear Joanna was too ill all this day to receive any of her friends, being very sick and full of pain for many hours.'

Meanwhile Foley continued to collect evidence, interviewing next his medical friends, William Roundell Wetherell and Mr Phillips, who were definitely of the opinion that Joanna was pregnant, adducing the same reasons as Reece: the state of her breasts; her womb being enlarged to the extent of rising two inches above the navel; and that they had often felt the living child. Both were ready to testify to these facts at any time or place.

One of the few dissentient voices was that of Dr John Sims of Upper Guildford Steet, who had been taken by Mr Phillips to examined Joanna on 18 August and later described what he found:

> The feel of the abdomen through her linen was not unlike that of a woman in the eighth month of pregnancy, but, as it seemed to me, less hard, except at the lower part, where there appeared to be a solid tumour, reaching not far above the pubes. I proposed to put my finger upon the navel, without any covering , which was permitted. This part I found sunk in, not at all protruded as

in pregnancy. In making this examination I was not sensible of any motion, which she insisted upon being so strong, that she could not only feel it herself, but that it had been seen by others who were sitting near her.

In enumerating the symptoms, she mentioned sickness at stomach, violent pain about the period of quickening, and great increase of the sickness, with bilious vomitings at that time; nor did she omit a sort of longing or extraordinary craving for asparagus, when she had otherwise a total loss of appetite.

Sims suggested that Joanna was not pregnant but suffering from some disease of the uterus. He was very polite and friendly, however, and having some doubts, offered to be present at the birth so that he could prove himself wrong.

Similarly, when Mr Hopgay, surgeon, was brought to Weston Place by Mr Hows to examine Joanna, he concluded that she was not pregnant, whilst observing that his opinion was not worth tuppence anyway and that he would be happy to be a witness against himself if he was present at the birth. He then stared hard at Foley for several minutes without saying a word.

More dramatic was the reaction of Mr Matthias, surgeon, who was quite horror-struck when he saw Joanna: 'his lips quivered, and his mouth opened wide, and he could not speak for several minutes, till Joanna drew him by kindness and mildness.' Joanna, he said, was suffering from a kidney disorder, for which he would send her some medicine. However, when two draughts composed of a strong preparation of mercury and bitters arrived, Joanna was warned that such a drug could make her miscarry, so she agreed to take it only if she had not given birth before November (Old Style).

Dr Walshman, of Lambeth, had also presented himself at Weston Place and sent up word to Joanna that he had his instruments with him and wanted to examine her *alone,* externally and internally. Joanna refused to see him. In fact, weary and agitated by all these examinations, she was only too glad when her Spirit ordered her not to see any more doctors for the present.

Now it was just a matter of waiting. Some friends left town to carry news back home. Mr Hirst, Mr Roberts and the Reverend Samuel Eyre departed on Monday morning, Mr Senior and Mr Turner returning to Leeds early on Tuesday. Sadly, their departure did not signal a period of rest for Joanna, for the mob, excited by a recent exchange of letters in the press, had attacked her house on Monday evening, hurling stones and brickbats at the doors. No windows were smashed, but poor Joanna

and her companions must have been terrified, and it could have come as
no surprise when the Spirit told her that it was no longer safe for her to
remain in Weston Place.

Nor was this hostility confined to London. Back home in Exeter, when
her friend Robert Portbury lent one of her books to a dissenting preacher
at George's Chapel in South Street, it was returned with this bold
inscription:

> Joanna Southcott (Counterpart of Brothers)
> Stabs sacred Truth & Sense & Reason smothers;
> 'Thus saith the Lord' (the frantic Female cries
> And propagates her dev'lish Dreams & Lies)
> 'Thus saith the Lord' What Lord? Lord Lucifer
> For He hath long *familiar* been with Her;
> Pregnant (by Baalzebub) with Pro and Con: Sense
> She travails – and brings forth blasphemous nonsense.
> All things consider'd right, we reason well,
> She's fit for Bedlam, and just ripe for Hell.

Outraged, Portbury sent the book on to Joanna, who declared that
the verse should not be erased, but stand for all time as evidence against
the preacher.[4]

Colonel Harwood and Foley heard about the riot outside 17 Weston
Place when they visited Joanna on Tuesday morning. Taking immediate
action, they went with Mr Pilborough, Mr Tolhurst junior and Mr
Barnard to the police office in Hatton Gardens, where, after relating all
the circumstances, they were readily promised assistance for as long as
it was required.

Mission accomplished, Harwood, Foley, Owen Pughe, and Baker dined
with 'dear Joanna' and passed another 'most happy and heavenly day'
before Edmund Baker left for Ilminster at four o'clock. In the evening
Colonel Harwood went again to the police station to confirm arrangements
with Wood, the officer in charge of protecting Joanna's house, alerting
him to the threatening attitude of her neighbours, the Ransoms, who
had taken to muttering insults at all her visitors. Harwood's intervention
apparently did the trick, for that night all remained quiet and he and
Foley were able to leave Joanna at about nine o'clock easy in their minds.

After taking supper with Mr and Mrs Phillips, Foley sat down to
record his delight at being shown earlier that day some of the gifts
pouring in for Shiloh and the book in which the names of all the donors
were being entered – just in case (heaven forbid!) she had no child and
everything had to be returned. Such actions were hardly the mark of an
impostor, Foley insisted, before going on to divulge various proofs of
Joanna's virtue. In the first place, she had been strictly confined to

female company between 11 October 1813 and 1 August 1814, when Dr Adams of Hatton Gardens was the first man to see her. The Reverend Mr King of Kentish Town was the first clergyman to see Joanna, on 11 August, exactly ten months from the beginning of her confinement. In the same month, Lady Mackintosh was the first woman to see Joanna apart from the four women – Miss Townley, Mrs Underwood, Mrs Pilborough and Mrs Tolhurst – who had been looking after her in the house since the previous August.

Foley also recorded that, in the face of such violent persecution, malice and lies, Joanna had been told by her Spirit that all preaching, readings and printing should now cease until after the was Child was born, unless her followers received orders through Mrs Tolhurst of Weston Place to print anything in vindication of the cause.

The following morning, Wednesday 24 August, Foley wrote two letters for Joanna, one to Mr Turner in Leeds and the following to Eyre in Bristol:

> My Dear Friends,
>
> Joanna has had a Communication from the Spirit of the Lord – That no more preaching or meetings of the Friends, after Sunday next, are to be holden, till after the Birth of SHILOH, the PRINCE OF PEACE. And she desires me to communicate this to you – and she wishes you will stop them all at Bristol, Bath, and wherever you know they are holden.
>
> Nothing now is to be published or printed in the Papers, by the Friends, without orders and permission from the Friends at Weston Place.

The letter was signed by Ann Underwood, and as a postscript carried a text from Isaiah 26, to be used at the closure of the meetings:

> Come my people, enter thou into thy chambers, and shut thy doors about thee; hide thyself as it were, for a little moment, until the indignation be overpast.[5]

After writing these letters Foley travelled through the wet streets to the Worcester Coffee House, where he deposited his luggage and booked a room. 'My coach, etc., cost me near one pound,' he complained. He dined with the Colonel, and in the evening went to take leave of 'dear Joanna' and his other friends. He wrote,

> Nothing, could exceed the kindness and attention and friendship which I experienced from my dear beloved friends in Weston Place, and in Camden Town. The Colonel made me quite happy in being with him. I supped early and retired to bed.

Foley journeyed home next day, Thursday, 25 August, through some heavy showers, taking Bohart's Coach as far as Oxford, where he arrived just after four o'clock. He put up at the Star Inn, asking to be called at twelve o'clock, when he had to take his place in the Birmingham Old Post Coach. Having arrived safely in that city, he was put down at the Dog Inn at about ten o'clock and went immediately to the Bradleys' to pass on Joanna's instructions about not reading or preaching any more until after the Child was born. Then he took the Stourbridge coach and arrived home in Oldswinford at about eight o'clock. He wrote:

> [A]nd blessed, blessed be God! I found my dear wife greatly better, the children all well, and everything gone all smoothly and comfortably during my absence, and praised be the Lord for His goodness who had kept and preserved me *safe* and *well* during my excursion to London and back again. For ever blessed be His Holy, Holy Name. Amen.[6]

Although happy to be home, Foley's thoughts must often have returned to Joanna and the troubled atmosphere of Weston Place, and he might have been relieved to know that by the time he arrived back in Oldswinford on Friday, Joanna had already left St Pancras and found sanctuary at Mr Carder's house in Leicester Square. More relaxed here, she was able to enjoy herself more than at any time since her sickness began on 17 March.

'I felt happy and cheerful and experienced a much stronger working and moving of life within than I ever felt before, and in a different manner. I staid up till nine o'clock,' Joanna confided. If anything made her uneasy it was the thought of Townley being left to cope at Weston Place, and so she wrote the following day to warn her not to answer the door herself but have all enquirers vetted by Mr Tolhurst, suggesting that it might prove necessary for Townley to leave the house too.[7]

The improvement in Joanna's spirits had been noticeable that morning when she sat up in bed just after six and found herself staring at a candle guttering low in its socket. She was just going to put it out when it re-kindled and began to burn brightly with a double flame. As it fell back into the socket again, the light took on the form of a man or woman, in great agitation as though struggling for life. This struggle continued for some time until, just as she thought it was going out, to her surprise it flared up in two bright flames above the socket, competing with each other as to which would last. It fell back again, rose for a third time, then died down for the last time. Waiting to see how it would go out, Joanna saw the flames, after struggling for some time, open and close like a mouth before the light disappeared.

Whatever the significance, Joanna remained in good spirits throughout her stay, especially as Carder's own doctor had endorsed the positive verdict of his colleagues about her pregnancy. Any misgivings she had about leaving Weston Place disappeared and she settled down to enjoy her temporary abode while others busied themselves fixing up the special lodgings required for her confinement. Although she stayed with the Carders only one week, it was a week of glorious respite after all the strain and exhausting medical examinations, and in this more relaxed atmosphere she found to her own relief – and that of her friends – her strength returning enough for her to indulge her current fad for eating asparagus.[8]

Naturally she still worried about her symptoms and the fact that there were some doctors who disputed that she was pregnant. Matthias, for instance, with his talk of kidney disorders must have disturbed her, for she fell to arguing the case in her own mind before concluding that had her swollen stomach been caused by kidney bile, her pains and nausea would not have disappeared by themselves – so Dr Matthias was wrong and her Spirit was wise to order her not to take his medicines. Her Spirit warned her to refuse any further medical examinations:

> Hadst thou gone on by his directions, the child must have
> perished in the womb and thy life soon brought to the grave,
> . . . because I know that men, through malice, would injure thee
> in their examination, if permission were now granted.[9]

If the message sounded a little paranoid, this was hardly surprising in view of the abuse being meted out to Joanna in the press.

On 25 August *The Times* carried a letter calling on any of the professional people who had visited Mrs Southcott to state their opinions as to her medical condition. Dr Reece took up the challenge and declared her pregnant.[10] When other doctors followed suit by supplying Ann Underwood with signed declarations, public interest was expressed in a series of antagonistic letters. Mr Hopgay of 130 Ratcliffe Highway, wrote to the *Morning Advertiser* on 26 August that, having visited Joanna, he had seen through the imposture which she had tried to practise on him. In similar vein, 'JW' wrote to *The Times* on 30 August, appalled at the huge mass of believers crowding into the capital:

> It is a fact, that, in consequence of what the newspapers have
> for some time been relating about this woman, shoals of
> enthusiasts, with more money in their pockets than brains in
> their skulls, are now pouring into London and its vicinity, to
> behold this chosen vessel![11]

Another newspaper accused her of being hounded out of Bath by police officers when she lived there.

'I never spent a day or night in Bath in my life,' Joanna riposted, adding that the only time she had been to that city was when passing through on her way to Bristol, when she stopped just long enough for

Caricature by Thomas Rowlandson, published by Tegg, 8 September 1814 – A Medical Inspection or Miracles Will Never Cease. *A crude image of Joanna exhibiting her swollen belly to three suspicious doctors, while her buttocks are stamped with the words: 'Aged 64. Bladders, Blasphemy and Corruption.' William Tozer ('Parson Towser') is portrayed as the devil of the piece as he sits supping in Shiloh's cradle, with donations of 'Child Bed Linen for young Beelzebub' stacked nearby.*

the coach-horses to be changed. And, of course, there were the usual allegations about misappropriation of funds, some newspapers alleging that Joanna had received as much as £30,000 worth of gifts for her unborn child and was about to skip the country, taking all these with her to France.[12]

Joanna's indignant rebuttal of these charges was contained in her sixty-fifth book, dictated to Ann Underwood while both were staying with the Carders. The book was finished on 7 September, the same day that Ann Underwood's first grandchild, Charles William Barnard, was christened in St Pancras Church.[13] It included Joanna's desperate statement:

> I am now compelled to flee, not only from the face of my enemies,
> but from my friends likewise, to conceal myself in a place of
> safety, where I am not known by any person, and my name I
> am obliged to conceal, to preserve my life from malicious and
> inveterate enemies, who threatened to set the house on fire where
> I lived, and to take my life if they by any means could get me in
> their power. . . .[14]

In the same week she sent a reproof to those believers who, by turning up to gaze at the house out of idle curiosity, hoping to recognise her or Underwood at a window, had obliged her to leave Mr Carder's. She utterly forbade them to linger outside her next abode. Furthermore, if they did not know the address, they should avoid any discussion of her possible whereabouts lest they inadvertently give it away. Her tone, as the letter progressed, became increasingly hysterical.[15]

Realising the dreadful effect all this trouble was having on Joanna's health, her friends did their best to find her a suitable house. Newspaper advertisements had produced some offers, but they were either too expensive or Joanna did not like their situation. When in late September Hows proposed forming a committee to pay for renting a large house, this again was vetoed by Joanna, who now knew exactly what she wanted, even if she had to pay for it herself. She instructed the friends to find her a house with two drawing rooms with folding doors, the back to serve as bedroom, the front for the physicians. Accordingly, 38 Manchester Street, Manchester Square – a house in a genteel neighbourhood and with enough space for her to receive friends in comfortable groups – was taken on Michaelmas day at five guineas a week.[16]

In early October, before she moved in, a circular was distributed:
> We understand the house of Mrs Southcott's accouchement is
> not finally determined upon, but in all probability it will be
> tomorrow or Tuesday. As soon as that takes place Drs Reece,

Syms [sic], and the other medical gentlemen will have immediate notice, that they may be present agreeable to their promise. The Heads of the Church will also be invited, either personly to be present, or to send their Physicians.

The accouchement is Expected to take place on the 10th or 12th of this month. Mr Wetherell, surgeon of Highgate is to be the accoucheur. Mr Phillips is in daily attendance. Her general health is lately much improved which certainly would not have been the case if the symptoms had arisen from a diseased uterus.[17]

As London supporters grouped protectively around Joanna, old and loyal friends in the country began to feel left out in the cold, especially when refused permission to attend the birth. On 1 October Foley wrote to Joanna to express his fear that he or perhaps his wife had done something to offend her, and the following day poured out his heart to Townley, who had given him the impression that Joanna was annoyed by his lack of generosity when approached for a donation towards the house.

My Very Dear Friend,

For Mrs Townley

The more I reflect upon your last short favor, the more hurt and grieved am I with myself, that I should *appear to be so ungrateful* to my beloved Spiritual Mother from whom we have experienced so many and such solid tokens of love and affection. . . . Ingratitude I abhor and detest from my very heart. . . . We are poor Creatures when left to ourselves – and my having a few guineas by me led me to make the *apparently paltry offer* towards defraying the expenses of the Furnished House and Establishment for our dear Friend, though I can assure you sincerely I did not intend to stop *at that Sum*. . . .

Another thing I did not know how my account stood with Mr Hill, the Banker, till a few days ago, and I find I am in better plight there than what I expected – and if we may be permitted, and be assured it will afford us the greatest joy and happiness to put down the £100 towards the great expenses of the House and establishment which must arise at the Confinement of our beloved Friend of the Prince of Peace, and with high pleasure shall I transmit you a draft for that sum *immediately* if we may be so greatly privileged to throw in our mite with the rest of the dear and beloved Friends in London.

I was harassed great part of last night, nor could I rest till I had written the above: my dear wife unites most cordially with me in what I have now done – and we shall be most happy in

Caricature published by Thomas Tegg, 20 September 1814 – Joanna Southcott the Prophetess Excommunicating the Bishops. Know I told thee I should begin at the Sanctuary. I will cutt them all off, having already cutt off Four Bishops for refusing to hear her Visitation. *Joanna, with her 'IC' seal around her neck, berates the episcopal bench: 'I put no more trust in Bishops as men, than I do in their Chariots and Horses, but my trust is [in] the Lord of Hosts.' Tozer is again shown as her chief accomplice.*

fulfilling the offer now made. I shall conclude with our dearest etc love to yourself, Joanna (and may she soon be safe in her bed) Mrs Underwood and to all dear beloved friends. . . .[18]

To this Joanna replied that, far from giving offence, it was most kind of Foley to send the gold (even though it 'was what I did not desire' after the very handsome presents he and Mrs Foley had made already). The fact was, much as she would have loved to have them both present at the birth, *and* Lucy Taylor, she simply could not allow one without giving offence to all the rest. Besides, it was more important for strangers rather than friends to be present so that they could be impartial witnesses. On the other hand, if he really wanted to be helpful, he could seek out some more physicians to attend her.

She also announced that, because she could not go to church to wed in public, a private marriage would take place before Shiloh was born, and in the meantime she would be moving to Manchester Street where she would live as secretly as possible, with guards on duty day and night until the time of her deliverance.[19]

Joanna's cool decision could have been taken as a snub by her old friends. Instead, faithful Foley chose to find comfort in what he called her 'heart-cheering letter' and declared himself full of joy that they had not offended her! Replying to Townley he added,

> . . . we are now quite happy in remaining quietly in our Tents till we have a happy Summons to town after dear Joanna's month is up and she well enough to see her friends and to present them to the Heavenly Babe, the Prince of Peace. . . .
>
> I am truly sorry I should have hurt your mind or have given you a moment's uneasiness in so misunderstanding your letter, but my mind was greatly agitated, as I thought we were excluded from being in London at this moment through my own want of kindness and gratitude to our Beloved Mother . . . and I could not rest until I had unburthened my mind to you upon the subject. . . .
>
> I most sincerely entreat your forgiveness and hope that everything unpleasant which has passed may be forgiven and forgotten.[20]

Foley's relief at avoiding an open quarrel with the woman he had loyally served for twelve years, the 'Woman Clothed with the Sun' who was about to give birth to the Second Messiah, is palpable. What his more pragmatic wife thought about the situation is less clear.

THE COMING OF SHILOH, Advent 1814

You see by the newspaper on Sunday that we are not to know
who the Husband is till after the Birth – Her Husband is in Heaven
that is clear, the Lord of Hosts, we are now looking for the
Proxy on Earth.

Charles Barnard to Edmund Baker, 26 October, 1814

Excitement mounted towards fever pitch after Joanna moved into 38
Manchester Street in the first week of October to be attended, not by
Townley who had keeled over under the strain and taken to her bed in
Weston Place, but by Ann Underwood and other married women.
According to the notice circulated at the beginning of the month, the
Child would be born on 10 or 12 October.[1] But the 10th arrived with no
obvious change in Joanna's condition. The 12th arrived. Still no change.
It was then rumoured that Shiloh was to be born at midnight on 19
October.[2] When the 19th arrived with still no sign of the birth, some
followers began to murmur. There must be something wrong, something
still to be done before the miracle could take place. But what?

Joanna had the answer. To reassure her friends she published an
address:

Many of the Believers in my visitation, as I have been informed,
begin to grow impatient in their expectation, as to the marriage
spoken of not having taken place and published a long time before
the child should be born; and seeing the harvest nearly ended,
'they appear ready to sink in the great deep – the seas before
them, and the Egyptian host behind them'; so that where is the
promise of either the Marriage or the Child? will soon be the cry
of the Public; and the Believers themselves will be ready to say,
'the harvest is over; the day is ended; and we are not saved'.

From this I see clearly that my enemies would soon boast and
triumph, while the Believers would be ready to sink in despair, if
the way they are stumbled in remained without being answered
and explained. In order, therefore, to do away such a state of
mind in the Believers, I take this opportunity of informing them,
that when the Marriage was first mentioned to me, it was before
I had any knowledge of what would follow; I was warned that

a private Marriage should first take place in my own house, which afterwards was to be granted to be realised in public.

This circumstance stumbled me, and also my friends who were made acquainted with it, because that time there appeared no necessity for such a private Marriage to take place in haste; but now I see cause enough from the dangers which begin to appear; so that, from my present situation, and my own feelings, I can judge the truth of the words that are already in print. For, if there be 'no Son,' there will be 'no adopted Father,' and no Marriage to be binding; because it will be but a temporary Marriage, from which death must soon release me. But who the Bridegroom is, must not publicly be made known, after the Marriage hath taken place, until the Child be born.

Thus, taking the whole into consideration, it is clear to me that the Marriage and the Birth of the Child may, and will most likely, take place within, perhaps, less than a day the one before the other; therefore the Believers may from this hint be able to form a correct judgment, and check their impatience, so as not to look for the Sixth Book immediately afer the Marriage shall have taken place; but that the Sixth and the Seventh Books, to complete the wonders, as before said, will be in order, and in right time, both after the Birth of the Child shall have taken place.

Joanna Southcott
21st October 1814.

This pronouncement reassured her followers but not the cynical reporter of the *Bristol Mirror*, who added: ' "*Qui facit per alium facit per se*," say the lawyers, and whatever the accoucheurs may think of it, Mrs Southcott, we hear, intends to lie-in by proxy.'[3]

Indeed rumours were rife. People reported pregnant women seen coming and going from Weston Place, reports no doubt connected with the recent accouchement of Underwood's daughter, Ann Barnard. And there were stories of thwarted plans made by Joanna's friends to acquire a newborn babe from a workhouse and smuggle it into her bed in a warming-pan. In Somerset it was whispered that two believers had been negotiating with a poor woman in Crewkerne to send one of her newborn twins to London to be passed off as Joanna's offspring, and the exposure of this supposed fraud gave local people substitute 'guys' for their bonfire procession.[4] Cocking a snook at their Vicar, the Reverend Hoadley Ashe who was a firm believer, the townspeople paraded effigies of Joanna through the streets before triumphantly consigning her to the flames.

Reports of such barbarities made Joanna's friends the more anxious on her behalf, especially once Mr Stokes discovered her new address and

38 Manchester Street, where Joanna died at four o'clock in the morning of 27 December 1814. Forced to move from her former abode by the mob, she asked her friends to find a house in a genteel district, with two drawing rooms with folding doors, the back to serve as bedroom, the front for the physicians. 38 Manchester Street, not far from Hertford House, home of the Prince Regent's mistress, was rented for five guineas a week.

threatened to publish it in his newspaper. Charles Barnard even suggested moving her again if her health permitted. Writing to Edmund Baker in Ilminster on 26 October, he outlined the latest instructions from Townley to the twelve doctors who were to attend Joanna at the birth; to avoid any impostures, each had been sent a special notification bearing Joanna's seal.

In the meantime, Dr Reece was calling regularly and had just pronounced himself satisfied with Joanna's condition, even though he now judged that she might go a fortnight longer before giving birth. The problem was, how to keep believers firm in the faith during this prolonged wait. Barnard wrote,

> The People in many parts begin to be very restless; but they should first assertain that the Harvest is ALL over before they complain. They will find in the North of England that it is not all in – What will they say to another fortnight?

There was also the matter of the Bridegroom to be resolved if not to be announced.

> You see by the newspaper on Sunday that we are not to know who the Husband is till after the Birth. Her Husband is in Heaven that is clear, the Lord of Hosts, we are now looking for the Proxy on Earth. . . .

Barnard concluded with news of his mother-in-law:

> I am happy to say Mrs Underwood is better than she has been, but is as usual nervous, which we must expect to continue so long as she has so much upon her mind. But our Glorious Prince will shortly arrive and bring comfort to us.[5]

When Reece next called at Manchester Street he found Joanna in bed and much weaker. Upon examination of her, he made a surprising discovery:

> The abdomen I found . . . much enlarged, but the tumour which had occupied the lower part had, to my astonishment, disappeared. There seemed great irritation of the muscles of the abdomen on the slightest pressure, accompanied with great nausea. I could not discover on the examination anything like the motion of a child, but she was however extremely tender, and could hardly bear to be touched. From this examination I could not perceive any striking change to induce me to alter the opinion I had given, although I confess I was not so much satisfied as I had been with the former one.

However, any doubts the doctor may have had were dispelled by talking to John Hows who was in the house at the time:

> I found him an intelligent person, and on interrogating me respecting her pregnancy, I informed him, much depended on her own veracity; and if confidence could be placed in her account of herself, there could be no doubt. He pledged himself on this point, for he had been acquainted with her many years, and knew her to be a woman incapable of deception.[6]

Such testimony from an apparently sensible man sent Reece away to await his summons to the birth, satisfied that his diagnosis was correct.

And so the waiting continued. 'I have no news to communicate,' wrote Barnard to Baker on 3 November, after advising him to treat all mockers with dignity and disdain. If such stoicism was hard to sustain in Ilminster where antagonism to Joanna's mission had already erupted in violence, it was no easier in London, where a scurrilous play had been performed in Tottenham Court Road the night before called 'Joanna's Hoax, or the Old Woman in the Straw', and newspapers had published and then been forced to retract false confessions in which Joanna was supposed to admit that her pregnancy was a hoax. '. . . so they go on,' Barnard complained wearily, 'but I don't think their fun will last much longer.'[7]

Jane Townley, separated from Joanna for the first time in ten years, must have felt strangely isolated and insecure, her decision to remain behind at Weston Place having the effect of excluding her from the inner circle at this critical juncture. Apart from Charles Barnard who kept her in touch with his mother-in-law, Ann Underwood, Townley's chief go-between and confidante was William Owen Pughe, who now exerted himself to bring Joanna's mundane affairs into order. His was surely the hand behind the codicil she added to her will on 4 November making alternative dispositions in case she should die childless. It read:

In the first place it is necessary to explain that Mrs Townley Mrs Underwood and myself have a joint Interest in the Books which I have published and all debts and credits appertaining thereto therefore in respect to such joint concerns I leave it wholly to the honor of these my two friends to set apart my third of such concerns after my decease leaving Issue and turn it over into the hands of my Trustees hereinafter named

In the second place with respect to presents made by my friends of Monies various Articles of Plate Apparel and other things as entered in a Book kept for that purpose and intended for the Male Child which I announced would be born of me I direct that such presents be also turned over into the hands of my Trustees I Trust if I die without Issue for them to return such presents into the hands of the Givers of them respectively

Thirdly if I should leave such a promised Child living at my decease my direction is with repect to the third part of the Interest which I have under the Will of the late James Cosins in the property consisting of certain houses recited in my above will to be bequeathed to Jane Townley Ann Underwood that my said bequest be revoked and is hereby revoked accordingly and that the said third part of my Interest in the said houses be also placed in the hands of my Trustees

And fourthly I hereby direct if I leave Issue as aforesaid that my Trustees shall for the Interest of such Child and on his behalf manage the said third part of the proceeds from the said Books after first deducting therefrom a sufficient sum to cover some tokens of love from me to my intimate friends as particularised in a certain paper Also all the said presents also the said third part of my interest in the said houses and all the property I may die possessed of and not otherwise before disposed of in my above Will

And lastly to carry into effect such Trusts as are mentioned in this Codicil I name and appoint James Spring John Hows Richard Goldsmith and William Owen Pughe to be Trustees for that purpose.

Joanna Southcott November 4th 1814

Witnesses to this Codicil –

John Tolhurst, Elizabeth Drew & Tobias Love.[8]

With this document all aspects of Shiloh's earthly affairs were set in order except one: there was still no adoptive father. The second Blessed Virgin had yet to find her Joseph. Once Joanna was married, there could be no further reason for delay. On 6 November the Spirit told her she

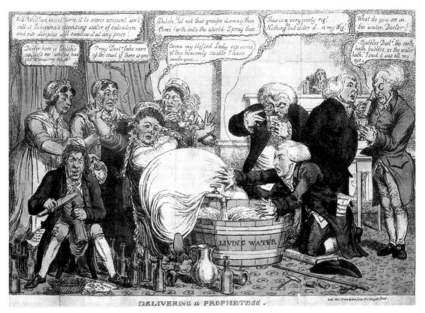

Caricature published by W.N.Jones, 1 November 1814 – Delivering a
Prophetess. *Sceptics suggested that Joanna was suffering from nothing
more than dropsy or retention of urine. Here she is shown being
supported by her three women helpers while 'living water' is drained
from her. Ever the opportunist, Tozer says, 'Well, Well! We must turn it to
some account! Wee'l call it Johanna's cleansing water of salvation and
our disciples will swallow it at any price!'*

should marry if someone was moved by the Lord to come forward and
offer. Ann Underwood wrote the words down, leaning on the bed and
sealing them up quickly so that the friends coming in to guard Joanna
could act as witnesses to this latest instruction.[9]

Meanwhile, Joanna had clearly been worrying about the possible
implications of her followers' enthusiasm for the Child. From her point
of view it was vital that no one be panicked into making medical decisions
that might endanger her life. So, on 7 November her Spirit cautioned
the believers:

> Before the end is over, everyone's faith will fail them. Her
> sufferings will be so great that she will appear as one Dead. . . .
> He that hath begun the Work will carry it through and therefore
> no violent means must be used, however great the danger may
> appear to preserve the Life of the Child by taking them; But this
> I tell thee must not be done . . . but let them consider by what
> power it is created, then let them know the same power hath
> strength to deliver and preserve the life of both, if the wisdom

and strength of men should fail, and let none be alarm'd if thou
appeared Dead for a while, for I shall Raise thee up again. . . .[10]

The words were timely, for Joanna was by now in a state of acute
distress. Confined to her bed for the past month, sick and in pain, unable
to keep anything down beyond a little malmsey wine and water, it must
have come as a tremendous relief when (as Underwood put it in a letter
to Foley) 'the sign was fulfilled in a very extraordinary way'.

In a secret letter probably intended as a legal record of the event,
Underwood described how, on Friday night, 11 November,

> a very worthy humbleminded man, a respectable friend of ours
> . . . about her own age an independant [sic] man, came to see
> me and said he was thinking very much upon our dear friend's
> situation, and most earnestly wishing for her deliverance to take
> place that she might be released from her present sufferings,
> when the thoughts came into his mind, as it was said there must
> be a temporal marriage, for some one to come forward with
> strong faith believing the visitation to be of God, that he was
> willing to be the adopted father to the child as soon as it was
> born – if this not being done . . . protracted her deliverance than
> [sic] he was willing with his hand and his heart to do any thing
> for her in any way and manner that would be of use or benefit to
> her.
>
> Unworthy of such an honour yet he humbly submitted himself
> and his intentions to the Lord who knew his motives for making
> such an offer, would pardon him if he was doing wrong – this
> pressed so forcible upon his mind and heart on Thursday night
> that he was determined to come to me on Friday morning Nov.
> 1814 and he desired me in private to mention it to our dear friend.
>
> I cannot enter wholly into the particulars of our conversation
> suffice to say I delivered his message. She was answered by the
> Spirit, she should not refuse him: neither did she feel in her mind
> to refuse him being a very respectable man and coming forward
> in the manner he did.

At long last Joanna had found her man. He may not have been the
bridegroom of her choice, but in her present state she accepted him readily
enough. Indeed she may have planned his proposal before apprising him
of the fact and then contrived the circumstances in which his offer
could be made. For the mysterious groom whose identity was to be
kept concealed was someone whom she had known for years – John
Smith, Lord Darnley's steward and owner of Rock Cottage in Blockley.

True he was no Joseph, but 'John', masculine form of her own name,
had a significance enhanced by the fact that they also had both initials in

common. Besides, John Smith was not only respectable but wealthy enough to do well by her son. And what was in it for him? The spiritual reward due to one who served a cause in which he seems wholeheartedly to have believed. Certainly, next morning he arrived in Manchester Street eager to proceed as soon as matters could be arranged and, following Joanna's directions, a contract of marriage was drawn up. Outside the day was dark and cloudy, but it was remarked that as soon as John Smith began the ceremony by reading over the service, the sun burst out. As soon as he finished, the sun withdrew behind clouds, only to burst forth again when Joanna repeated her part. The ceremony over, the skies darkened again.[11] Underwood told Foley,

> In this manner the private marriage took place last Saturday Nov 12th in the forenoon unknown to all and every one excepting myself and two friends, and this must be kept private until the Lord's appointed time come for it to be revealed, indeed till that time come no man could stand the persecution that at present prevails; all this must be a very great surprise to the friends when it comes out. Our dear friend was ordered to write to you of it, or rather that you should be (informed) but I again repeat by her desire that this letter and the contents be wholly to your bosom.[12]

Joanna woke up on Sunday a married woman. And it seemed as if her new status had done the trick when she felt unusual pains. She was just thinking of sending for Mr Wetherell when she received a surprise visit from Dr Reece, come to ask if he might examine her again. Accompanying him was Paul Assolini, Professor of Midwifery in Paris and Accoucheur to the Empress of France. He was lodging just up the road at 7 Manchester Street and had asked Reece for an introduction to Mrs Southcott.[13] Nor was this all, for on their arrival at Joanna's house, they had bumped into two foreign gentlemen about to ring the bell. Assolini immediately recognised one as General Orlov, aide-de-camp to the Emperor of Russia,[14] who introduced his companion, Prince Lieven, the Russian Ambassador.[15] Lieven explained that they were hoping to see the English prophetess. Reece had apparently gone through the motions of explaining that this would be difficult, as neither was a medical man, before agreeing to ask Mrs Southcott's favour to admit them.

So it was that Joanna, so recently dignified by marriage, was told of her eminent visitors, and agreed to see them once Reece and Assolini had completed their examination.

Meanwhile Assolini, who had seated himself next to the bed, began to quiz Joanna about her general health. He examined her belly, remarking that her stomach complaints arose from the pressure of the womb and would go off as soon as she was delivered. On leaving the room and being pressed for an opinion by Underwood, he urged the need for a proper, internal examination. When this was refused, Assolini expressed his astonishment that a person in Joanna's situation should oppose the wish of a medical man.

Reece then introduced General Orlov, who made a low bow to Joanna on his entrance and treated her with great respect. Rising magnificently to the occasion, Joanna proceeded to regale her guests with a detailed description of sufferings which, she was at pains to stress, had been visited on her for the benefit of the whole human race – at which point Prince Lieven, desiring her not to fatigue herself, declared that he and his friend had to go.

On his way out, the General offered some money to Mr Love who attended the door, but Love bowed his head and refused it. Soon afterwards Dr Reece left the house with Professor Assolini, whom he accompanied back to his own residence to inspect his surgical instruments, which he found far superior to English ones. He was amused when a woman in the house asked Assolini if he thought the newspapers were right to label Joanna an impostor.

'Pshaw!' Assolini growled. 'Don't you know that the English papers are only a black paint?' – a colloquial expression used in his own country to suggest that what papers said one day they unsaid the next.[16]

Back at Number 38 Joanna was feeling well satisfied with her morning. Reporting the visits to Foley, Underwood described how General Orlov and Prince Lieven, 'a tall, handsome looking man', had behaved in the most polite manner towards Joanna, expressing something like awe as they approached her bed and wishing her a happy deliverance when they took their leave. Underwood wrote,

> So ended our visitors, but this we are obliged to keep secret for if it was known the newspapers would have it directly – and the abominable caricatures – and very likely our house beset with inquirers more than it is at present. Mr Hows or Mr Goldsmith is constantly in the house, Mr Love & John Tolhurst. Colonel Harwood, Mr Carder & Mr Spring come of an evening. The Magistrates have been spoken to and they have given orders for protection to be sent if wanted.

Underwood's tone betrayed the tension under which the occupants of Number 38 were living. To harassment by the press had now been added the real threat of mob violence in the street outside the house. Hence her postscript:

> You had better not answer this letter at all. We have letters sent in abundance directed to our friend but we refuse them all.

Likewise boxes and baskets directed to her but they are not taken in.

Meanwhile, the person at the centre of all this commotion had apparently – at last – gone into labour. Apologising for the 'blundering manner' of her writing, Underwood explained that it was because

> our dear friend is in great pain and I am up every five minutes. I don't suppose they will leave her long together now. I pray God you may receive a letter of her safe delivery before the week is out.[17]

Underwood proved right in thinking Joanna's pains would not leave her for long, but sadly wrong in predicting an early deliverance. Saturday, 19 November, found her writing to Dr Reece:

> Sir,
>
> Mrs Southcott has had a very restless night. She desires me to say that she has something on her mind which she wishes to communicate to you. I hope therefore you will call this evening or tomorrow morning.
>
> I am, Sir, your obedient servant,
>
> Ann Underwood.

Reece called within the hour and heard that Joanna had been extremely ill. After one fit of vomiting she had passed out and found the room spinning around her when she came round. She felt so weak she feared she was dying. Uneasy at having authorised Reece to open her body, she now gave him new instructions.

If she should die her body was to be kept warm and no moves made to open it till after four days, or until putrefaction was clearly evident. It was also her wish that the same medical men who had seen her during the pregnancy should be present and the operation conducted with due decency. She told Reece,

> You will, as sure as you sit there, find *something alive* in me . . . which will prove to my friends that I am not that impostor I am represented to be.

If, on the other hand, labour came on, she wanted Mr Wetherell to attend her, and if there was any difficulty, hand her over to Dr Reece. No one else was to touch her.

Following her train of thought, Reece asked what would be her wishes if it was a case of endangering her life to save that of the child? The answer came clear and strong: Joanna forbade him to take any such action. She declared:

> If it is the work of the Lord, He will deliver me, and if it is not, it is fit it should die with me.

After turning to Underwood and shedding some tears, she charged her with seeing these instructions carried out and making sure that a proper report on the post-mortem examination was sent to her friends. Then she asked to see the five or six people waiting in the next room. Reece asked if he should withdraw. 'No, sir,' she replied, 'I particularly wish you to be present.'

Reece and Underwood helped Joanna sit up against her pillows. Her friends sat round her bed and watched while Joanna carefully adjusted the bed-clothes and placed a white handkerchief before her. When she was ready, she said:

My friends, some of you have known me nearly twenty-five years, and all of you not less than twenty. When you have heard me speak of my prophecies, you have sometimes heard me say that I doubted my inspiration. But at the same time you would never let me despair. When I have been alone, it has often appeared delusion, but when the communications were made to me, I did not in the least doubt. Feeling as I do feel, that my dissolution is drawing near, and that a day or two may terminate my life, it all appears delusion.

The exertion of making this speech left her exhausted and weeping bitterly, but after a few moments she had recovered enough to observe that it was strange the Lord should inflict such a burden on one who had spent her whole life studying the Bible.

Again she wept. Some of her friends, deeply affected, began weeping too.

'Mother, we will commit your instructions to paper,' Mr Hows suggested, 'and rest assured they shall be conscientiously followed.'

Her words were accordingly written down and Joanna, with hand on Bible, signed them with great solemnity, witnessed by Reece and four of her friends.

Mr Hows then observed, 'Mother, your feelings are *human*. We know that you are a favoured woman of God, and that you will produce the promised Child; and whatever you may say to the contrary will not diminish our faith.'

Reassured by these words, Joanna left off crying and began to laugh. Dr Reece, expecting any moment to hear her confess how she had been deluded, was much put out by this change in mood and the sudden arrival of more friends so, after writing a prescription for medicine to settle her stomach, he took his leave.

On Sunday morning he received a visit from Mr Tozer, to whom he repeated the previous day's conversation. 'Poor woman,' Tozer replied, 'how can she despair? She reasoned as a human being; but God will soon give her comfort.'

He had strong reason to believe that the Child would be cut from Joanna's side just as Woman was taken from the side of Man, he assured Reece. Moreover, to all the doctor's doubts he opposed texts from the Bible about the Child's birth. There was also the old manuscript he had just received from Hull which foretold the birth of the Child in November 1814 (Old Style), and he hinted at other overwhelming proofs which – for political reasons! – could not be divulged.

Meanwhile the world was clamouring for news from Manchester Street. Hearing that Professor Assolini had called, the editor of the *Sunday Monitor* invited him to send a report. His reply was published on 20 November:

> Sir,
>
> In reply to your letter of this morning, I have the honour to inform you that with respect to my visit to Mrs Southcott, it was only dictated by curiosity. I did not communicate with her on her situation therefore cannot form any judgment of her case. I have the honour to be, Sir,
>
> > Your obedient humble servant
> > Paulo Assolini.
>
> 7 Manchester Street.
> Thursday evening, November 18th.

A few days later Reece wrote to Underwood telling her she must persuade Joanna to submit to an internal examination. He stressed that this would be the only way to reassure her friends and help his own reputation which, he reminded her, had been put on the line by his letters to the press. He was piping to deaf adders. Joanna would not hear of the idea. Insisting that time must soon decide the matter, Underwood continued,

> She is certainly much worse, very low and weak, which must rapidly increase from her not being able to take any nourishment, neither the laudanum or kali seem to have any effect in preventing the constant retching or sickness.[18]

From early December *The Monitor* began to issue official bulletins and syndicate them to the provincial press. The first one read:

> On Thursday night Mrs Southcott rested better than she had done for some weeks past, being entirely free from pain and restlessness, and she continued so on Friday, having neither sickness nor pain. Last night, however, she became very restless and uneasy; she took one of the the opium pills, which composed her till near two o'clock in the morning, when she awaked in very great pain, and continued so for an hour; it then went off, and she slept for a short time, then waking in great pain. In this manner she has continued the whole day. The pain is not of a long duration as she very soon goes to sleep again.

Though her sickness has not returned, her appetite does not improve. She is free from fever but is faint and low.

Saturday night. 8 o'clock.[19]

This report was accompanied by a letter from Dr Reece:

Sir,

Within the last six weeks I have seen Mrs Southcott about eight times. The increasing enlargement of the Uterus, a loaded state of the mammary glands, are proofs of the progress of Pregnancy. Within the Uterus there is evidently a substance which possesses the power of moving, so that I am satisfied that if she should not produce a child, such appearances will be exhibited on dissection as will fully justify me in the opinion I have given of her being pregnant.

Messrs Wetherell and Phillip, who are in the habit of seeing Mrs Southcott three or four times a week, do not entertain the least doubt of her pregnancy.

I was not a little surprised on reading the letter that appeared in your Paper of the 20th ultimo from Professor Assolini. The Professor was introduced to Mrs Southcott by myself; and after hearing her detail of symptoms, and examining the abdomen, he accounted for the nausea at stomach and oppressure of the chest, to the pressure of a distended Uterus, and from the frequent recurrence of pains in the lumbar region, he gave his opinion that labour was approaching.

Visiting Joanna again on 6 December, Reece found her much worse. Although his last prescription had reduced her nausea, the matter being vomited was very bitter and offensive. Joanna was in resigned mood.

'Death or Life would soon end the strife,' she muttered, adding that if she was not to produce the Prince of Peace, she was at least an instrument in the hand of God to produce some good.

Concluding that the laudanum he had prescribed was affecting her head, Reece ordered opium pills instead. He was alarmed to find her pulse beginning to give way and told Colonel Harwood, waiting in the outer room, that Joanna was sinking. He also now had doubts about her pregnancy, whose truth rested largely on her word. In that case, Harwood assured him, there could be no doubt. In fact, only the previous day Mr Phillips, Mr Wetherell, Mr Forster and Mrs Lock – all experienced as medical men or accoucheurs – had examined Joanna and felt the child.

Joanna, however, sensing Reece's doubt, declared:

Well, it is of no consequence, I shall shortly produce the child, and all I ask of him is to act as a man. If he were a believer, he would not be a proper witness; and the more improbable the event, the firmer will be his conviction that it is the work of the Lord.

Her words struck home. It was all very well for Believers to hold faith – though heaven knew even theirs was being sorely strained by the passage of time. It was vital that Reece, whose testimony carried such weight, should bear witness when the event came to pass. With this in mind Colonel Harwood visited the doctor to repeat his confidence in Joanna's word. Reece again stressed the need for an internal examination, pleading that it was something she owed her friends. Colonel Harwood interrupted him: he knew no friend who would ask anything unpleasant of Joanna. Besides, no good could come of such an examination when the affair was approaching its crisis.

Next day Reece was visited by Mr Phillips, Joanna's apothecary. Phillips, though a believer, was shaken when Reece told him that he no longer thought Joanna was pregnant and admitted that Joanna had told him that she was less in size.

Behind the doors of Number 38 Ann Underwood was bearing the brunt of the responsibility involved in nursing Joanna. Her anxiety showed in a letter she sent Reece on Saturday, 10 December:

> I am sorry to inform you that Mrs Southcott still lingers on in the same distressing situation: her weakness seems rapidly to increase, from her not taking anything to support her; and the sickness having returned, and continued since Monday with very little intermission, has made a visible change in her. The extreme faintness which succeeds the retching is attended with a cold perspiration over her whole frame; she says she feels a sensation in every nerve, as if she should faint, and become insensible to her present sufferings, which she most earnestly prays may soon take place, in hope then that a few days may satisfy the minds of the public as to her real situation, and relieve her friends from their present persecution.[20]

Her sentiment did not stem from mere pananoia. Persecution was real as throughout the country effigies of Joanna and her child were being daily paraded, mutilated, then burnt; her followers – dubbed 'Joanners' – subjected to derision and violent assault. In face of these threats, Colonel Harwood came forward to steady the ranks. '[P]ermit me to advise you to consider Joanna & all her sufferings as well as the delay in the Birth only as a matter of faith,' he enjoined Edmund Baker who had sought Phillips's opinion on Joanna's situation; 'medical opinions have nothing at all to do with it; all that happens is far out of the common practice of medical men, and they know nothing about it.' In fact, it was no good trying to use one's ordinary intellect in present circumstances, for realising that

> Man by Wisdom know not God. . . . I never enter into any
> question but merely to follow on to do what duty presents itself,
> in which I believe myself to be following the Lamb whithersoever
> he goeth – and although it is impossible to be indifferent to the
> question . . . yet I keep my mind as much disingaged [sic] on
> that subject as possible. . . .

Nevertheless, even Harwood must have found it difficult to maintain
an unquestioning attitude in view of the situation he went on to describe:

> Mrs Southcott has now kept her bed two months – and seems
> reduced to the last stage of weakness it is possible to sustain
> and retain life. We do hope ere many days she must be delivered.
> At all events, according to all human judgment of the medical
> people perhaps she can not live – but according to all the faith of
> Us, who are about her, the Lord will deliver her and carry her
> through all her sufferings and . . . yourself and all true believers
> will see her as promised, with the Child in her arms and milk in
> her breast.
>
> Mrs Underwood desires to be kindly remembered to you and
> believe me your sincere friend in the Work of the Lord
>   W.Tooke Harwood. [12th December 1814][21]

The following day Underwood circulated a letter advising the friends
to keep a low profile in the present hostile climate:

> Joanna has desired me to acquaint all the Friends that it is her
> particular wish that her Believers will not wear particular marks
> in their dress, or have any *mark* by which to distinguish
> themselves. But that it will be the duty of every Believer to rejoice
> in their hearts and houses but to do nothing to cause mockery.[22]

Any cause they might have to rejoice became less certain when, two
days later, Underwood informed Dr Reece that Joanna was so ill she
could not sustain life much longer.[23] Reece called to examine her again
and was heard to exclaim:

> 'Damn me, if the child is not gone, and there is nothing left but the
> working of the muscles!'

He must have known that she was fading fast. By the following day
her mind was beginning to wander and she complained of coldness and
pain in her stomach. Devoted Underwood used hot cloths to bring some
relief, but the improvement was short-lived.

William Sharp spent two hours talking to Joanna on Monday, 19
December, and came away convinced that 'the Infant was there struggling
within her to be born.'[24] But on Dr Reece's next visit, he found Joanna
'in a rambling state, pulse extremely weak, countenance sallow and

cadaverous, with coldness of the extremities and every mark of approaching dissolution.'

When Colonel Harwood entered the room, she put out her hand and moaned, 'What does the Lord mean by this – I am *certainly dying.*'

'No, no,' Harwood smiled. 'You will not die. Or if you should, you will return again.'

His words reassured her. Turning to Reece, she said she knew her mind was wandering and, having no wish to offend, hoped he would take no notice of anything she said in her present state. And she would try to keep herself collected, she added – emphasising the point by tapping her forehead. Before he left, she had a further relapse and he formed the opinion that she would not last more than two days.[25]

The friends were now facing their greatest trial. All the time that Joanna was with them, alive in their midst, able to transmit what they regarded as the direct commands of the Lord, it was easier to adopt the unquestioning approach of Colonel Harwood. Once she had passed through the gates of death, they needed iron willpower to maintain their faith. Realising this, the friends in London quickly circulated relevant texts: 'Mrs Southcott was tranquil on Friday night last the 23th instant,' Barnard wrote to Baker, enclosing in his letter a Communication received by Joanna in 1797 that ended:

> If Death to thee should hasten on
> Thy steadfast heart shall be made known
> Faith is a Gift that comes from ME
> And thy Integrity they'll see;
> For Earth and Hell can not remove
> The Soul that walk [sic] by Faith and Love
> An untried Faith, I call it none
> Therefore thy Sorrow must come on.[26]

On Saturday, 24 December, Reece received a visit from Colonel Harwood who had been sent by Wetherell and Phillips to tell him they thought Joanna was really dying, and not, as they had previously believed, just falling into a trance. But on Christmas Day Joanna woke in great pain and cried out that the Child was coming; it was making its way through her side; its head was in the world. The nurse who was standing by immediately put her hand to the place and felt a swelling the size of a baby's head which suddenly disappeared with a kind of kick.

When Reece called on Monday, 26 December, he found to his amazement that his patient had rallied, her extremities were much warmer and her mind had recovered some steadiness and recollection. She had even taken a little nourishment and kept it down. Moreover, she had, she declared, strong labour pains which suggested that the birth would soon be accomplished.

Her friends were jubilant at the news, reminding each other how Joanna had foretold that her doctors would be puzzled and that she would enter a state that they would call death.

Eight o'clock that evening Reece visited Joanna again. This time he found her in a coma 'with laborious breathing, the expression of countenance gone, the features shrivelled and shrunk, and the pulsation of the wrist not to be felt. Still, however, the extremities were warm.'

Before leaving, Reece announced to the assembled company – Wetherell, Adams and Kent, Miss Townley, Ann Underwood, the housekeeper, and John Smith – that Joanna could not live many more hours. To his surprise they greeted the news with equanimity. It was just as she had foretold twenty years ago, they said – she would take on the appearance of death. Indeed, they declared, they would not have been satisfied if this had not happened.

In this tranquil state of mind they continued to watch as Joanna struggled through the night and at four o'clock on Tuesday morning, 27 December, breathed her last.[27]

AFTERMATH

Mr Sharp . . . gravely took him aside and told him, as a piece of good news, that 'a certain lady' had actually given birth to a son (the Shiloh, of course).

Western Flying Post, 18 October 1824

Sir,

As you desired to be present at Mrs Southcott's accouchement, had it taken place as was then expected, the friends consider it as their duty to inform you and all the medical gentlemen who had that intention, that to all appearance she died this morning exactly as the clock struck four. Care is taken to preserve warmth in the body as she directed; and it is the wish of the friends that you will see her in her present state.

Such was the dispassionate circular sent by Ann Underwood on 27 December to those doctors who had previously examined Joanna and declared their wish to be present at the birth. Its dispassionate tone masks the turmoil in her mind as the woman she loved and had gradually come to worship lay to all intents and purposes dead.

When Reece called round later that day he found Joanna lying in the same position as she had died, well wrapped up in flannels and still being kept warm by hot-water bottles. The friends pressed him for an opinion: did he think Joanna was actually dead? He examined her as well as he could within the limits imposed: he was allowed to touch her face and hands, but no other part of her body. Although in no doubt about her condition, any fears he had about conveying the news to her followers were dispelled when, on entering the drawing-room, he saw Jane Townley's smiling face and heard her declare that Joanna would return to life, as foretold twenty years ago. William Sharp, standing nearby, not only agreed but added that the believers fully expected Joanna's apparent death and would not have been satisfied had it not happened.

Taking Reece to one side, Sharp confided that no less than fifteen years previously he had purchased – specifically for that purpose – the flannel now being used to keep Joanna's body warm. After commiserating with Reece on the arduous task he had to perform, he promised that the result must greatly redound to his honour and reputation once the soul of Joanna had returned from heaven, where it had gone to legitimise the child who would be born.

Sharp's optimism was shared by all those present. They agreed that so marvellous would be the result, that a Kingdom would be born in a day, according to the words of Holy Writ, and the Millennium established. So, Sharp asked, if Joanna should be resuscitated and give birth to a boy, would Reece then believe in her mission? The doctor replied that, should such an event happen, he would certainly admit that it was the work of the Lord to answer some great purpose, but in his present frame of mind he thought it as likely that St Paul's Cathedral would ascend into the air. Sharp replied,

> 'Ah! Sir, you take only a professional view of it, but I take a spiritual one! Pray Sir, for your credit's sake, do not retract the opinion you have given, for assuredly there is a child.'

Reminded of the slur the whole affair had placed on his professional reputation, Reece now appeared rattled. Having declared it as his opinion that Mrs Southcott would not die with a child in her, he asked one of her disciples what he would do if that proved to be the case. The man replied that he had never given it a thought, for it was as likely to happen as the sky to fall down.

Dumbfounded, Reece listened as an apparently sensible woman, who had just arrived to ask about Joanna's teaching, put a similar question to Jane Townley. Townley declared that it was impossible for anything to happen other than as predicted, because all Joanna's Communications had come from the Lord.

'But, Madam,' this lady objected, 'you must allow we are all liable to be deceived.'

'Well,' replied Townley, 'if it should turn out so, I will burn my Bible, and declare the whole fabric to be nonsense!'[1]

Reece, who had now heard enough, returned home to prepare the following brief press release:

DEATH OF JOANNA SOUTHCOTT

To Mr Stokes   Tuesday afternoon
Sir –

> Agreeable to your request I send a messenger to acquaint you that Joanna Southcott died this morning precisely at 4 o'clock. The believers in her mission, supposing that the vital functions are only suspended for a few days, will not permit me to open the body until some symptom appears, which may destroy all hopes of resuscitation.

> I am, your obedient servant,

                                               Richard Reece

Piccadilly December 27, 1814[2]

Completely opposite in tone was the excited note sent by Barnard on the same day to Edmund Baker:

My Dear Friend,

The Wonders have begun. Our dear Joanna is literally dead!!! died yesterday morng. Tuesday. 4 o'clock.

The Doctors have seen her, who acknowledge that she is so – We shall know more in a few days.

We think in 3 or 4 days.

God bless you all

from your very sincerely Charles Barnard

PS It will astonish all Men.[3]

The fact that on the day of Joanna's death had come news from France of peace with America inspired her followers with fresh confidence.

'Do you not think,' said one of them, 'it is a most curious circumstance? Oh! if you did not see that God is about to do a great work you must be blind indeed!'

When, on Thursday, Reece paid his second visit to Joanna's remains he found the body beginning to be offensive, her lips and fingers turning black. However, even this change had not shaken the faith of her followers, and he was obliged to warn Mr Sharp that, as putrefaction had begun to take place, the warmth being applied would accelerate the process and make it difficult to do a proper post-mortem. Sharp told Reece to stop worrying because he could depend on it that Joanna would return to the body. If they really thought so, Reece replied wearily, then they should keep it sweet for her reception, for if her heavenly marriage ceremony lasted two days more, her earthly tenement would not be habitable on her return!

'Well then,' Sharp declared, 'the greater will be the miracle: the God that raised up Lazarus can raise her up, and that He will do so, I have not the smallest doubt.'

This time Reece had kept a parting shot: 'The evil will in this case find its own remedy, for in two or three days she will stink you all out of the house.'

Before he left, it had been decided by Sharp and Harwood that the four days which Joanna decreed must elapse between her death and post-mortem would expire the following morning at four o'clock, after which time Reece would be at liberty to open her body. For his part, Reece agreed to arrive at two o'clock next day accompanied by several medical friends – Messrs Clarke, Want, Caton and Macloud – while the Colonel undertook to inform all the other doctors who had been appointed to attend.

Reece was amazed to find that even now, in spite of all evidence to the contrary, Joanna's friends were cheerfully voicing the opinion that she was not dead but merely slept and would certainly rise again. In fact, their greatest fear was that he might do her harm in his dissection and Mr Tozer stressed that he should do it as if it were a Caesarean operation, so that all hopes of resuscitation might not be destroyed!

To this remark Reece drily replied that any power that could raise a putrid body could surely raise one that had been cut open. Then would he be sure to take care of the Child? came Tozer's next request, making it clear that he and all the disciples were confident that, even if Joanna was not raised before her body was opened, the Child would be found on dissection. Colonel Harwood even told Reece that Mr Wetherell had examined Joanna since her death and found that the impregnated womb which had been formerly on the right side was now on the left.[4]

The same kind of certainty was displayed by Mrs Drake, owner of 38 Manchester Street and a steadfast follower of Joanna, who went over to the Manchester Coffee House on Thursday night to order a gallon of rum. When Mr Lloyd, the Coffee House proprietor, expressed his sorrow for her loss, she replied with surprise, 'What loss, Mr Lloyd? . . . There's no death. She only lies in a trance, and will rise again.'[5]

By this time the friends needed to fortify themselves with something like rum, for the twelve elect had been sitting up to keep regular watch on Joanna's body since the moment she died, and even the strongest faith could not disguise their abhorrence of the awful stench. In an effort to scent the room where the body lay, the women kept vinegar boiling on the hob while each gentleman took to puffing on a pipe. Nor was it easy to step outside for fresh air, for by now the street had filled with a riotous mob, all screaming obscenities at the house and pelting any visitors with mud and filth. One poor victim turned out to be the elderly sister of Sir Charles Blicke, calling to ask whether Joanna had been resuscitated yet.[6]

Friday morning came, the day appointed for the post-mortem. A quarter of an hour before the arranged time Reece arrived to prepare the body for the operation, but was not allowed to touch it until four o'clock came. As the minutes ticked away, Joanna's friends clung to their fond and eager hope that in the last moment she would rise again. But the hour struck with no sign of renewed life.

Precisely on time, as if they had been queuing on the doorstep, other medical men arrived. In all there were fifteen professionals, including Dr Adams, Dr Sims,[7] Messrs Taunton, Clarke, Want, Caton, Mathias, and Cooke. While these waited in the anteroom, Dr Reece was taken into the apartment where the body lay, still in exactly the same state as when she died – in the bed, covered with flannel, in the same clothes and wearing her rings. Nothing had been moved. Sadly nature had shown no such forbearance, and the body had putrefied to such an extent that the limbs would not support it, and it had to be carried to the table on a sheet.

Once everything was ready, all the medical men seated themselves round the table, whilst behind them stood Joanna's disciples, some smoking tobacco to mask the smell and craning their necks to see everything. Beyond them stood others, peeping over their shoulders, desperately wanting to know what was happening. A little removed from this intense circle, waiting in the anteroom, stood Ann Underwood thinking her own thoughts.

Reece, who was in charge of opening the body, later published a full account of the 'Appearances exhibited on Dissection',

> On exposing the abdomen it appeared much distended with air, which was evidently the consequence of putrefaction after death, for previous to that the abdomen . . . was in a flaccid state.
>
> On dividing the teguments there was a considerable escape of putrid air, after which the contents of the cavity came into view. The first organ that immediately claimed attention was the womb, which contrary to all expectation was hid in the pelvis, and instead of being enlarged appeared smaller than in the natural state. It was so small, I was obliged to introduce my hand into the pelvis, and to remove the whole contents, in order to bring it out for inspection. It was of the size of a small pear. It was considered by the medical gentlemen present as uncommonly small, but I thought not more so than what it ought to be in a virgin of sixty. On examining its substance, there appeared no mark of disease. An invidious report having been spread, that Mrs S. had formerly had children, Mr Want and I next examined the ovaria, but there appeared no traces to confirm this slander.
>
> During the examination of the womb, a most interesting scene was presented. The believers were all on tiptoe to see Shiloh appear, and those who could not have a view themselves, were most anxiously making enquiries of the others. No promised child, however, appeared, which so confounded the rest that they gradually left the room abashed and dismayed.

So that was that – collapse of all their hopes, end of every dream – or so an outsider might suppose if they had not come across a faith like that of William Sharp. While Reece remained troubled by his inability to account for either Joanna Southcott's apparent pregnancy or her death, Sharp serenely observed that life was involved in mystery and although, disappointed in his hopes of seeing something divine revealed through Joanna, he was no worse off with regard to his knowledge of God for having met her.[8] Moreover, upon reflection and after recovering from initial shock, he decided that Shiloh had been born and snatched up to heaven. Indeed, meeting a friend in a fellow artist's study, he 'gravely took him aside and told him, as a piece of good news, that "a certain lady" had actually given birth to a son (the Shiloh, of course) who was then in the keeping of an angel, and who would certainly appear on earth in three years.'[9] And a notice later appeared in the press:

> Her friends know her to be dead; but the Arm of the Lord is not shortened. If He is about to do a great work on earth, as we believe He is, He can as easily raise the dead to life as awake a person from a trance.[10]

However, for the two women who had served and supported Joanna for the past decade it was hard to be so philosophical and for a time they were both inconsolable. They had so lovingly prepared the cot, the layette and arrayed all the wonderful gifts, picturing to themselves the bliss that lay ahead as they witnessed heaven being established on earth. Now, Joanna's death and the non-appearance of Shiloh left them doubly bereft. Not that any of the elect ever condemned Joanna as an impostor; one disciple immediately declared that he would always revere her memory and once a month visit the spot where she was laid with pious and reverential awe.[11] But it took a while for Townley and Underwood to become reconciled to their loss, and they did so in different ways.

Townley soon came to share Sharp's opinion that Shiloh had been born and immediately taken up to heaven, as the Book of Revelation said: 'And she brought forth a man child . . . and her child was caught up unto God, and to his throne.'[12] Looking back over recent events, she knew exactly when the birth had taken place. It had happened on Christmas Day (New Style), when Joanna had experienced pains and declared the Child was making its way through her side, that its head was in the world. Although Underwood seems not to have argued with this interpretation, her own thoughts remained far more turgid. In her mind, Joanna had been inspired by God right up until she received the false report of Pomeroy's death – and it was her failure to keep faith at that critical juncture that brought about her downfall. Such were the thoughts that Underwood poured out to Hows in a letter full of grief and despair on the day of Joanna's funeral.

> My dear Friend,
>
> I can say nothing for myself I am in that state temporally and spiritually – I know not what to do or think but I wish to inform you that the body of our dear departed friend – however she has

been deceived in this last instance – I mean respecting the marriage and the child – which I date as the first state of Satan's Power over her – hearing the sudden death of Pomeroy occasioned her to question the ways of the Lord, from that I believe Satan took the advantage. . . .

[B]ut to return to the subject the mob was very great, when the undertakers men brought the coffin, after the body was deposited, for which they used a great deal of tar, or Pitch, the Men went all out to a Public house and after some time the Mob went away, the friends sent for the Men. Six took the Body away. The Coll. [Colonel Harwood] followed them down two Streets no interruption and he came back. She is to be buried this afternoon, Goldsmith and the Coll. went yesterday to order the Grave, and the Coll, Owen, Phillips and Coles [intend?] to follow her, and see her dear remains safely deposited, which is all that can be done.

The friends I am glad to see appear to derive comfort, thinking all is right, but I cannot see anything to warrant it, yet may it please the Lord to give them comfort, as to Myself I am worse and worse I can find no comfort any where

God bless you all

I can say no more,

AU

I shall be glad to hear this day is over, that her dear remains are safely deposited which is to be done about three o'clock this afternoon.[13]

Because of the threatening attitude of the mob, the burial took place with the utmost secrecy. While the body rested at an undertaker's in Oxford Street, a grave in St John's Wood Cemetery had been booked in the name of Goddard, and not even the officiating clergyman was aware that it was the notorious Joanna Southcott he was burying until the service was due to start.[14] The hearse was followed by one coach of mourners in which sat three gentlemen – thought to be Colonel Harwood, William Sharp and William Tozer. The fearfulness of the occasion may be gauged from the fact that all wore greatcoats buttoned up to their chins, had handkerchiefs tied round the lower parts of their faces and hats pulled down over their eyes so that they should not be recognised. Not that there were many there who could have identified them, for the few idle spectators had no idea whose funeral they were watching.[15]

The usual church service was performed at the graveside, but in so perfunctory a manner that William Tozer took issue with the clergyman, complaining that he must have left something out. When the minister assured him that the customary prayer for the dead had been read, Tozer still insisted that this was not enough for so holy a woman and a prophetess. The clergyman, less than impressed, replied that he hoped he would never again have to officiate at the funeral of 'one who had lied by practising imposture and fraud, uttering blasphemies, and died unrepentant.' At this, Tozer fell silent.[16]

Amidst the gloom which descended in the ensuing days it was people like Sharp, Townley and Foley who kept the flame of Joanna's mission alight by stressing that there was no point in trying to understand what had happened, for that would be to rely on man's puny wisdom and ignore God's greater will. The friends should 'judge nothing before the time that the Lord comes who will bring to light the hidden things of Darkness,' Foley wrote in a letter which was much copied and distributed among the faithful. Swearing that he would rather die than give up his faith at that moment, Foley enjoined people to wait a while, watching to see whether Joanna's Visitation would fade away in silence like that of other false prophets, such as Ann Moore and Ann Hughes. If it did, then it was not true. If it did not, then it was true and the rest was up to God.[17]

Poor Foley! It was one thing to reassure the scattered flock, quite another to convince those within his own fold – as his diary for January shows.

> 16th: I grieve to say my wife and I are now quite opposite in our opinions respecting Joanna, and most uncomfortable in our present state.
>
> 18th: I had a violent breeze with my wife after dinner about Joanna. She asserted a most gross lie, for which and other exasperating language I was obliged to put her out of the room.[18]

While faithful Foley and those like him were content to wait and watch, others rushed in to try to fill the gap left by Joanna. Chief among these was George Turner, the merchant from Leeds who had been one of the original Seven Stars who came to Exeter in 1801. Influential from the beginning, his stature in the movement owed much to a dream he had at the time when Joanna's first prophecies were just being published to the world. He dreamt that he was sitting reading by his fire when a door opened to reveal the figure of the long-dead John Wesley who, with radiant face, gazed into the space above his head and said,

> Inform my Brethren that it is the Will of the Lord that they obey the Word of God which is made known. I am happy. Jesus is God. I know many of my Brethren will believe.

Turner interpreted this to mean that Wesley had chosen him to anoint

Joanna Southcott's memorial in St John's Wood burial ground, which was newly opened in 1814 and used until 1855. The stone stands twenty-six feet from her grave and was erected by T.P. Foley and friends in 1828 at a cost of £40. In 1965 the Panacea Society replaced the original slate stone which had become dilapidated.

Joanna as his successor – on the strength of which many Methodists went over to the Southcottian movement. Turner's own bid for leadership gained credibility from the fact that Joanna had acknowledged that some of his writings had come, like hers, from the Spirit of God. After Joanna's death, this led many to accept him as her successor and when Tozer reopened his chapel, it was to read Mr Turner's Communications to the congregation. Reporting this development to Charles Taylor on 26 April 1815, Foley writes almost apprehensively as if afraid that this friend too might have joined the Turner faction. Foley complained,

> Our dear Joanna's writings are quite neglected, and the lyes they invent about Underwood, me, and those that don't rely on them would much surprise you. . . . Tozer says he has Visitations, so it is fine Confusion. Miss Townley desires her opinion of Mr Turner's Communications to be made as public as possible. . . .[19]

Foley had no doubt where his allegiance lay; it was, as ever, with the 'Woman clothed with the Sun'. For him, as for so many of the friends, no one could ever take her place. Joanna remained their spiritual guide, and since she had commanded in the previous year: 'No more preaching or meetings of the friends after Sunday next, August 28, are to be holden until after the birth of Shiloh,' they would continue patiently to wait.

One year to the day after this injunction – and ten weeks after the battle of Waterloo marked the overthrow of the man whom Joanna had identified as Antichrist – a circle of friends met together in a place far removed from the turmoil still prevailing among the groups in London. Broadway Tower, a sham castle built by the Earl of Coventry in the Cotswolds, stands more than a thousand feet above sea-level,

*Rock Cottage, the home of John Smith, at Blockley, Gloucestershire.
There is no documentary evidence that Joanna lived in Blockley, but her
spirit has pervaded the place since her death. Local Southcottians (their
names include Smith, Troup, Herbert and Bull) lie buried in Blockley
churchyard and for over a century Rock Cottage remained in the
possession of families connected with Joanna's mission. After Alice
Seymour bought Rock Cottage in 1917, it became the headquarters of the
Southcott Society. Coincidentally Rock Cottage was gutted by fire in
1971, the year in which 'Joanna's Cottage' in Gittisham also burnt down.*

commanding a view over thirteen counties from its rooftop gallery. It is
just a few miles from Blockley, the home of John Smith, the man who
married Joanna, and a place which more than any other to this day
retains powerful links with her mission. For generations there have been
stories linking Joanna with Blockley, persistent rumours that she came

here – perhaps during the course of her visits to the Foleys at Oldswinford or Stanhope Bruce at Inglesham – both within easy reach. Perhaps together with Townley and Underwood she used it as a quiet country refuge when alarmed by the crime-rate in London. Although there is no documentary evidence to prove that Joanna actually lived in Rock Cottage, there is plenty to suggest that her spirit has pervaded the place ever since her death.[20]

On 28 August, 1815, a party consisting of John Smith, and his niece and nephew, John Hows and his son, Mrs Carder, Mr Malkin, 'Mr George from London' (possibly George Troup), and the Reverend Thomas Foley drove up to Coventry Tower on Broadway Hill to drink tea and admire the magnificent views. According to Foley, it was a happy, friendly gathering after which, as they were on their way back to Rock Cottage 'the beautiful villa of Mr Smith at Blockley,' they found themselves threatened by a tremendous thunderstorm. Seeing the dark clouds piling all around, they had to ride and drive for all they were worth, and as the thunder, lightning and rain burst upon them, they blessed the Lord for protecting them until they found shelter under Mr Smith's 'most hospitable and friendly roof'.[21]

The strange thing is, that over the years there have been friends of Joanna gathering together in every generation and every quarter of the globe – looking towards the Final Millennium in a mood of wistful expectancy.

NOTES

CHAPTER 1

1. Southcott, *The Trial of Joanna Southcott, During Seven Days* [Book 25], London,1804, p.45, where the young Joanna was described by her brother Joseph as 'of a mild placid disposition.' A sample of Joanna's hair was worked into her patchwork quilt made in 1808, now in Royal Albert Memorial Museum, Exeter [see photograph].
2. Southcott, *Fourth Book of Wonders* [Book 62], London, 1814, p.58.
3. Quoted in *Southcott Express*, June 1927, p.142.
4. Ottery St Mary Parish Records, DRO:
   Lucy, dau. of Wm & Hannah Southcott, buried 14/5/1748.
   Susanna, dau. of Wm & Hannah Southcott, baptised 14/8/1748.
   Joanna, dau of Wm & Hannah Southcott, baptised 6/6/1750.
   John, son of Wm & Hannah Southcott, baptised 22/10/1752.
   Gittisham Parish Records, DRO:
   Joseph, son of William & Hannah Southcott, baptised 14/5/1755.
5. In April 1928 a party of Southcottians took a motor-trip to Joanna's home in Gittisham – see *Southcott Express*, June 1928, p.37. The son of the then owner recalled this event in conversation with the author. The cottage [see photograph] was destroyed by fire in the 1970s.
6. Southcott, *Second Book of Wonders* [Book 58], London, 1813. See p.95-100 onwards for a detailed account of William Southcott's farming difficulties.
7. Diary of Revd J. Swete published in *Devon's Age of Elegance*, ed. Peter Hunt, p.40.
8. Southcott, *Copies & Parts of Copies of Letters & Communications* [Book 22], London, 1804, p.13.
9. Southcott, *Second Book of Wonders* [Book 58], London, 1813. See pp.88-96 for saga of the lost Southcott fortune.
10. Southcott, *Copies & Parts of Copies of Letters & Communications* [Book 22], London, 1804, p.11.
11. Elias Carpenter, *Nocturnal Alarm, being an Essay on Prophecy and Vision*, London, 1803, p.67.
12. After studying Joanna's handwriting, Alice Seymour concluded 'that her schoolmaster was of German origin, from those settled in England by foreign influx at the time of the Hanoverian succession of George I' – *Southcott Express*, June 1928, p.28.
13. Southcott, *The Answer of the Lord to the Powers of Darkness* [Book 12], London, 1802, p.79.
14. Southcott, *Second Book of Wonders* [Book 58], London, 1813, p.101.
15. Southcott, *The Controversy of the Spirit with the Worldly Wise* [Book 54], London, 1811, p.3. 'brought up to industry from my early age. . .'.
16. Southcott, *A True Picture of the World & A Looking-Glass for All Men* [Book

52], London, undated ?1809, p.8. 'When I lived with my parents it is known to my brothers and sister that I studied as much their peace and happiness as I did my own. . . .'.

17. Southcott, *The Answer of the Lord to the Powers of Darkness* [Book 12], London, 1802, pp.79-80.

18. Southcott, *Copies & Parts of Copies of Letters & Communications* [Book 22], London, 1804, pp.63-5.

19. Southcott, *The Answer of the Lord to the Powers of Darkness* [Book 12], London, 1802. See p.126 for explanation of the Devonshire words 'Stroil' [weeds, especially roots of couch grass, raked together for burning], 'Moule' [choking roots], and 'Sull' [ox-drawn plough].

20. Southcott, *A Dispute between the Woman & the Powers of Darkness* [Book 11], London, 1802, pp.83-4.

21. Southcott, *Strange Effects of Faith, with Remarkable Prophecies* [Book 5], Exeter, 1801, pp.203-4.

22. Southcott, *Controversy of the Spirit with the Worldly Wise* [Book 54], London, 1811, p.3.

23. Seymour, *The Express*, London, 1909, p.116.

24. Southcott, *Second Book of Wonders* [Book 58], London, 1813, p.100.

CHAPTER 2

Note: All dialogue and quotations have been taken from contemporary documents, although in this chapter the colloquial nature of Joanna's speech and internal musings may suggest otherwise. The main source for her courtship by Noah Bishop is *Letters & Communications* [Book 24]. Other quotes have been taken from *Strange Effects of Faith* [Book 5]; *Copies and Parts of Copies of Letters and Communications* [Book 22]; and *Mr Joseph Southcott Will Now Come Forward* [Book 23].

1. Seymour, *The Express*, p.143.

2. Southcott, *The Second Book of the Sealed Prophecies* [Book 36], p.60.

3. Southcott, *The Second Book of the Sealed Prophecies* [Book 36], p.72. *Express Leaflet*, No.13, p.4. 'Tail corn' was inferior grain, separated by the winnowing machine as not fit for market.

4. Southcott, *Letters & Communications* [Book 24], pp.63-6.

5. *Mr Joseph Southcott Will Now Come Forward* [Book 23], pp.43-4.

6. Southcott, *Letters & Communications* [Book 24], pp. 27-35 for Joanna's courtship by Noah Bishop.

7. Fanny Wickers was probably the Frances Wickers whose marriage to Robert Stone was recorded at Sidmouth, 30/12/1771. (IGI, Devon).

8. Southcott, *Letters & Communications* [Book 24], p.65.

9. Southcott, *Second Book of Sealed Prophecies* [Book 36], p.61. Cf. Southcott, *Second Book of Wonders* [Book 58], p.16. In May 1779 Noah Bishop married his sister-in-law, Ann West, at Sidmouth and the following year their son was baptized John at Harpford where Noah became a churchwarden. '[H]is name is handed down to posterity on the boards containing the Ten Commandments, dated 1827' – *Express & Echo*, 9/1/1914. Noah Bishop died, apparently Harpford's oldest inhabitant, in 1836, his wife Ann died a few months later – *Devon & Exeter Gazette*, 20/9/1926.

10. Extract taken from Blockley Coll. 787 (33). Exell in *Joanna Southcott at Blockley*

and the Rock Cottage Relics quotes further from this document: 'Joanna says they are verses that she used to go out in the fields, looking to heaven, saying to herself, when she felt her heart attached to any earthly object to draw her heart from the Lord . . . they were verses composed by her grandfather's sister, Sally Southcott.' For Sarah Southcott's life, see Southcott, *Second Book of Wonders* [Book 58], pp.89-90.

11. Southcott, *A True Picture of the World etc.* [Book 52], p.8. 'Mr and Mrs Brown both said I acted as much for their interest as though I had been their own child, and as such they always treated me.' Robert Portbury, friend and follower of Joanna, refers to Mr Brown in a manuscript note: 'This Gentleman kept trade at Honiton, Devon. My Father bound his books for him.' (WCSL, S920 SOU A/ 1, p.53).

12. See advertisements in *Exeter Flying Post*, 13/1/1775; 5/1/1776.

13. Southcott, *Copies & Parts of Copies* [Book 22], pp.48-9.

14. Southcott, *Copies & Parts of Copies* [Book 22]. p.15.

15. For description of Hannah Southcott's death, see Southcott, *Strange Effects of Faith* [Book 5], pp.204-5.

16. *Sixth Book of Wonders*, p.59. [Not published by Joanna Southcott but compiled by Daniel Jones after her death and regarded as spurious by some of her followers.]

17. LMA Acc. 1040/78. There is an inscription to Joanna's parents, dated 1835, which includes a faded manuscript note 'about the year [blank] she was buried at the Independent Chaple [sic] Ottery St Mary.' Records of the Meeting House Yard, Ottery St Mary, show burials for John Godfrey, 18/7/1748, and Mrs Godfrey (widow), 25/6/1762.

18. Southcott, *Copies & Parts of Copies* [Book 22], pp.15-16.

CHAPTER 3

Note: The main sources for this chapter, including direct speech and quotes, are *Copies & Parts of Copies* [Book 22]; *Second Book of Wonders* [Book 58]; and *Strange Effects of Faith* [Book 5].

1. On 7 May 1771 Hannah Southcott and Nicholas Paige, husbandman of Sidbury, were married by the Rev. William Putt at Gittisham church. Their daughter, Susanna, was christened at Black Torrington, 15/9/1771. Hannah had given birth to a son, James, and another daughter, Charlotte, by December 1774 (Parish Records, DRO). The Paige family have been recorded in Black Torrington church registers since 1578. Land Tax Assessments show Nicholas Paige as owning Broompark and farming Fishley estate as a tenant for the next twenty years (DRO).

2. Southcott, *Copies & Parts of Copies* [Book 22], pp.16, 20-1 for details of Joanna's dalliance with Mr Rigsby.

3. Nathaniel Bishop married Margaret West at Sidmouth, 22/4/1770 (Parish Records, DRO).

4. Southcott, *Copies & Parts of Copies* [Book 22], pp.17-18 for details of Joanna's dalliance with Peter West.

5. Southcott, *Second Book of Wonders* [Book 58] p.98 for Susanna's unwanted admirer.

6. Southcott, *Second Book of Wonders* [Book 58], p.99.

7. In October 1771 John, baseborn son of Jemima, was christened at Gittisham. His reputed father was John Southcott (Parish Records, DRO).

8. Southcott, *Second Book of Wonders* [Book 58], p.99.
9. WCSL – Southcott Family Cuttings File – includes an undated, unattributed newspaper extract: 'Most of Joanna Southcott's prophetic work was executed at Exeter, and she gained a wide local reputation as a harvest prophet. It is said that for miles around the farmers based all their operations on her forecasts. At Newton Market the farmers would greet each other with, "Well, what has Joanna for us this time?"'
10. Southcott, *Strange Effects of Faith* [Book 5], pp.205-6.
11. Southcott, *Copies & Parts of Copies* [Book 22], pp.12-14 for a detailed account of the incident of the cider house which includes, 'I thought to myself he might well say "my dear love".'
12. For Joanna her mother's memory was sacrosanct. She never refers directly to a relationship between her father and another woman but her writings contain hints that William Southcott took a mistress. See Hopkins, *A Woman to Deliver Her People*, p.230, note 26. Also, 'if I prolong the reign of the King he will soon find his subjects like thy Father's Mistress weary of him' in BL Add. MS 32634 f.59. In BL Add. MS 47799, f.24v a footnote identifies Mary Hood as the 'simple woman he did chuse'.
13. Southcott, *Letters & Communications* [Book 24], pp.65-6.
14. Southcott, *Controversy Between Joanna Southcott & Elias Carpenter* [Book 38], p.4.
15. Southcott, *An Answer to a Sermon Published & Preached by Mr Smith* [Book 50], p.64.
16. Southcott, *Strange Effects of Faith* [Book 5], pp.206-7.
17. Southcott, *Strange Effects of Faith* [Book 5], pp.207-8.

CHAPTER 4

Note: The main sources for this chapter, including direct speech and quotes, are *Strange Effects of Faith* [Book 5]; *Copies & Parts of Copies* [Book 22]; and *Joseph Southcott Will Now Come Forward* [Book 23].

1. Southcott, *Strange Effects of Faith* [Book 5], p.208.
2. George, son of Nicholas & Hannah Paige, was christened, 18/6/1777, at Black Torrington (Parish Records, DRO).
3. John Rigsby married Jane Littlejohns, 4/5/1777, at Black Torrington (Parish Records, DRO).
4. William Carter married Susanna Southcott, 11/11/1777, at Sidmouth (Parish Records, DRO).
5. Southcott, *Strange Effects of Faith* [Book 5], p.208.
6. See Advertisement in *Exeter Flying Post*, 2/8/1787, for detailed list of William Wills's stock.
7. *Mr Joseph Southcott Will Now Come Forward* [Book 23], pp. 69-101 for 'the History of Joanna while she continued with Mr Wills.'.
8. Moreton Hampstead Parish Records (DRO) show:
    20/8/1758   marriage of William Wills to Sarah Connett.
    11/3/1759   baptism of Sarah, daughter of William & Sarah Wills.
    5/7/1761   baptism of William, son   ditto.
    30/1/1763   baptism of Ann, daughter   ditto.
    25/12/1784   baptism of Mary, daughter   ditto.
    William Wills, whose business apparently flourished in Exeter, died in 1813

possessed of several properties. See Probate of his Will, 1/2/1814 (DRO – 53/ 6 Box 99).

9. Southcott, *Copies & Parts of Copies*, [Book 22], p.18.

10. *Mr Joseph Southcott Will Now Come Forward* [Book 23], p.72.

11. 'This Parson Sanderson was a man I well knew about five feet two inches high, rather thin in body and countenance, had a swaggering walk and I have seen him go to Wills's House when the City talk'd Commonly of them, and I believe not without reason.' Note penned by Robert Portbury in Book 23 (WCSL, S920 SOU A/3). See Hopkins, *A Woman To Deliver Her People*, pp.37-44 for an assessment of Sanderson's character and career in Exeter.

12. *Mr Joseph Southcott Will Now Come Forward* [Book 23], pp.80-1.

13. *Mr Joseph Southcott Will Now Come Forward* [Book 23], pp. 79-82.

14. John Wesley, *Journal*, VI, p.365.

15. *Mr Joseph Southcott Will Now Come Forward* [Book 23] p.79.

16. Southcott, *Full Assurance That the Kingdom of Christ is at Hand* [Book 44], pp.18-19.

17. *Mr Joseph Southcott Will Now Come Forward* [Book 23], p.79.

18. William Southcott of Gittisham married Mary Webber at Ottery St Mary, 9/7/ 1783 (Parish Records, DRO).

19. ECA Book 73a, Quarter Sessions Minute Book, p.133 (DRO).

20. Southcott, *Copies & Parts of Copies* [Book 22], p.20.

21. ECA Book 73a, Quarter Sessions Minute Book, p.136 (DRO).

22. *Mr Joseph Southcott Will Now Come Forward* [Book 23], p.82. Cf.Seymour *The Express*, p.240. 'Joanna's brothers and sisters at first were strongly averse to her writings, and did all they could to prevent her.'

CHAPTER 5

Note: Where not otherwise attributed, quotes in this chapter referring to Joanna's conflict with John Eastlake and his Methodist class in Exeter are taken from *Strange Effects of Faith, being a Continuation of Joanna Southcott's Prophecies* [Book 8], pp.85-92.

1. Southcott, *Trial of Joanna Southcott* [Book 25], pp.45-6.

2. Southcott, *Second Book of Wonders* [Book 58], p.84.

3. Southcott, *Strange Effects of Faith, being a Continuation of Joanna Southcott's Prophecies* [Book 8], p.85.

4. Southcott, *True Picture of the World* [Book 52], pp.12-13. See also, Seymour *The Express*, p.248.

5. *Exeter Flying Post*, 17/10/1777, for marriage of Anthony Tremlett's daughter to Mr Rexford, merchant of Manchester. Anthony Tremlett had married Mary White at St Sidwell, Exeter, 16/9/1750 (IGI, Devon). For further references to him, see *Exeter Flying Post* Indexes in WCSL.

6. 5/12/1784   burial of Richard, son of William Southcott.
14/7/1785   burial of Susannah, wife of William Southcott.
17/7/1785   baptism of Hannah, daughter of William Southcott. (Aylesbeare Parish Records, DRO).

7. See *The Express*, pp.248-9. *Exeter Flying Post*, 1/2/1787, reported that Anthony Tremlett's wife had died 'last Thursday.'

8. 8/5/1781 marriage of Sarah Channon to Charles Minifie at Talaton (Parish Records, DRO). For details of Charles Minifie's business affairs see *Exeter Flying Post*, 6/11/1778; 10/3/1780; 19/8/1784; 24/11/1785.

9. *Exeter Flying Post*, 24/7/1783 and 10/10/1793.

10. 6/2/1785 marriage of Mary Channon to John Wolland at Heavitree (Parish Records, DRO).

11. *Exeter Flying Post*, 20/12/1787.

12. Southcott, *The Trial of Joanna Southcott* [Book 25], p.57.

13. Southcott, *True Picture of the World* [Book 52], p.12.

14. *Southcott Express*, June, 1928, p.43.

15. Quoted in Elijah Chick, *A History of Methodism in Exeter*, p.39.

16. Southcott, *Strange Effects of Faith, being a Continuation of Joanna Southcott's Prophecies* [Book 8], p.85.

17. J. W. Thomas, *Reminiscences of Methodism in Exeter*, p.28. *The Exeter Journal, 1796*, includes in its list of tradespeople: 'J. Eastlake, tailor, Musgrave's Alley.'

18. Elijah Chick, *A History of Methodism in Exeter*, p.88.

19. Southcott, *Strange Effects of Faith, being a Continuation of Joanna Southcott's Prophecies* [Book 8], pp.85-7.

20. *Mr Joseph Southcott Will Now Come Forward* [Book 23], pp.102-3.

21. Southcott, *Strange Effects of Faith, being a Continuation of Joanna Southcott's Prophecies* [Book 8], pp.87-92.

CHAPTER 6

Note: Main sources for this chapter are *Full Assurance That the Kingdom of Christ is at Hand* [Book 44], pp.2-12; *Strange Effects of Faith* [Book 1], pp.5-17.

1. Letter to Doctor Waters, 24 May 1809, referring to Mr Cowlard, a new curate in Exeter, who had refused the Sacrament to the Taylors because of their association with Joanna Southcott. Published in Jones, *Southcott's Prophecies*. [DRO 3703Z/Z16.]

2. Southcott, *A Warning to the World* [Book 20], pp.3-4.

3. Southcott, *Full Assurance That the Kingdom of Christ Is at Hand* [Book 44], pp.2-3.

4. 12 December 1772, burial of Elizabeth Channon at Ottery St Mary; 16 March 1780, burial of Edward Channon at Ottery St Mary. (Parish Records, DRO).

5. Edward Channon's Will is cited in the Will of Sarah Minifie who died 5 August 1814. (DRO).

6. Southcott, *Full Assurance That the Kingdom of Christ Is at Hand* [Book 44], p.4.

7. Southcott, *The Fourth Book of Wonders* [Book 62], pp.56-7.

8. Southcott, *Strange Effects of Faith* [Book 1], pp.5-6.

9. Advertisements in *Exeter Flying Post*, 20 September 1792, p.3; 23 March 1799, p.3.

10. For Henry Tanner, see J. K. Hopkins, *A Woman to Deliver Her People*, pp.49-57. When Henry Tanner died, aged 88, he was described as one 'who has for more than fifty years officiated as minister to a congregation of Methodists in Exeter. He was a very pious, respectable man.' (*Exeter Flying Post*, 28 March 1805.)

11. Southcott, *An Answer to a Sermon Published* [Book 50], pp.7-8.

12. Southcott, *A Warning to the World* [Book 20], p.24. John Leech [sic] appears in the 1793-4 list of Itinerant Preachers sanctioned in the Tiverton and Cullompton circuit of which Exeter formed part before 1808.

13. Southcott, *Strange Effects of Faith* [Book 1], p.6.

14. *Exeter Flying Post*, 19 August 1784, p.3.

15. *Exeter Flying Post*, 1 December 1785, p.3.

16. *Exeter Flying Post*, 24 November 1785, p.3.

17. Southcott, *Full Assurance That the Kingdom of Christ Is at Hand* [Book 44], pp.4-7.

18. Southcott, *Full Assurance That the Kingdom of Christ Is at Hand* [Book 44], p.8.

19. *Exeter Flying Post*, 3, 10, & 24 October 1793.

20. Southcott, *A Warning to the World* [Book 20], p.26. Cf. Southcott, *Full Assurance That the Kingdom of Christ Is at Hand* [Book 44], pp.8-9 and Southcott, *Copies & Parts of Copies* [Book 22], p.34.

21. Balleine describes Joseph Pomeroy as 'a handsome, middle-aged man, a very popular preacher, who often came to stay with his parents in Exeter,' *Past Finding Out*, p.20.

22. Southcott, *Strange Effects of Faith* [Book 1], p.7.

23. Southcott, *Full Assurance That the Kingdom of Christ Is at Hand* [Book 44], p.12.

24. Southcott, *Strange Effects of Faith* [Book 1], pp.7-8.

25. Tobin, P.J., *The Southcottians in England*, p.81.

26. Letter to Doctor Waters, 24 May 1809, in Jones, *Southcott's Prophecies*. [DRO 3703Z/Z16.]

27. Southcott, *Wisdom Excelleth the Weapons of War* [Book 60], p.26.

28. Southcott, *A Warning to the World* [Book 20], p.25.

29. *Southcott Despatch*, No.15, p.5.

30. Southcott, *Strange Effects of Faith* [Book 2], p.55.

31. Southcott, *Strange Effects of Faith* [Book 1], p.17.

32. Explanation of Mr Shannon [sic] being driven mad by the Devil, 3 January 1795, BL Add. MS 32635, f.174.

33. BL Add. MS 47800, f.40.

34. Blockley MS 515, reverse pagination, p.35.

35. Wednesday, 25 February, 1795, was appointed by the King for a General Fast, a day of prayer and supplication for divine aid in times of national danger. Joanna mistakenly gives the date as 28 February 1795.

36. Southcott *Prophecies. A Warning to the Whole World* [Book 14], pp.24-6.

37. WCSL – Southcott Cuttings File – unattributed newspaper dated June 1928. '"Joyless June", Tennyson said. . . . The summer of 1795 was worst of all. It was in effect partly composed of real winter.'

38. BL Add. MS 32634 f.136v.

39. Southcott, *Strange Effects of Faith* [Book 1], pp.8-11.

40. Southcott *Prophecies. A Warning to the Whole World* [Book 14], pp.43-4.

41. Southcott, *Letters & Communications* [Book 24], pp.26-7.

42. Southcott, *Divine & Spiritual Letters of Prophecies* [Book 9] p.21.

43. Blockley Mss. 515, p.48.

44. Southcott, *Second Book of Sealed Prophecies* [Book 36], p.11.

45. Southcott, *Strange Effects of Faith* [Book 1], pp.12-13.

46. Southcott, *On the Prayers for the Fast Day* [Book 21], p.17.

47. *Express Leaflet*, No.36.

48. Southcott, *Controversy between Joanna Southcott & Elias Carpenter* [Books 38-42], p.95.

49. Southcott *Prophecies. A Warning to the Whole World* [Book 14], p.122.

50. BL Add. MS 47799, f.19v.

51. Southcott, *Second Book of Sealed Prophecies* [Book 36], pp.102-3.

52. Southcott, *Strange Effects of Faith* [Book 1], pp.18-19.
53. *Southcott Express*, 1927, pp.184-5.
54. Southcott *Prophecies. A Warning to the Whole World* [Book 14], pp.14-15.
55. BL Add. MS 47799, f.24v.
56. BL Add. MS 32635, f.178.
57. Southcott, *Prophecies. A Warning to the Whole World* [Book 14], pp.40-1.
58. Southcott, *Second Book of the Sealed Prophecies* [Book 36], p.33.
59. Southcott, *Second Book of the Sealed Prophecies* [Book 36], pp.118-9.
60. Southcott, *Strange Effects of Faith* [Book 1], p.19.
61. Southcott, *Second Book of the Sealed Prophecies* [Book 36], pp.127-8. 'Hat' is West Somerset dialect for covering several sheaves of corn with a kind of thatch to prevent them from sprouting while at the same time allowing the wind to pass through to dry the straw [see Elworthy, F.T., *The West Somerset Word Book,* p.326].
62. Southcott, *Second Book of the Sealed Prophecies* [Book 36], pp.79-80.

CHAPTER 7

1. BL Add. MS 47799, f.32v.
2. *Watch*, No.2, 1935, p.12.
3. Southcott, *Second Book of Sealed Prophecies* [Book 36], p.87.
4. BL Add. MS 47799, f.34v.
5. Southcott, *Second Book of Sealed Prophecies* [Book 36], p.86.
6. Southcott, *Second Book of Sealed Prophecies* [Book 36], p.39.
7. Southcott, *Prophecies. A Warning to the Whole World* [Book 14], p.57
8. Southcott, *Second Book of Sealed Prophecies* [Book 36], p.111.
9. Southcott, *A Warning to the World* [Book 20], p.30. See Parish Records, DRO, for: 12 July 1795 marriage of John Southcott & Margaret Pleace at St Mary's, Exeter; 24 July 1797 burial of John Southcott at St David's, Exeter.
10. Southcott, *Second Book of Sealed Prophecies* [Book 36], p.115.
11. *Express Leaflets*, No.38, p.9.
12. BL Add. MS 47799, f.30v.
13. BL Add. MS 32634, f.36.
14. Southcott, *Second Book of Sealed Prophecies* [Book 36], pp.66-71.
15. BL Add. MS 47799, f.29.
16. BL Add. MS 32634, f.155.
17. Doctor Reece, who attended Joanna in August 1814, wrote that 'her regular monthly appearance had left her for at least fifteen years.' See Seymour *The Express*, No.2. p.357.
18. Southcott, *Second Book of Sealed Prophecies* [Book 36], pp.60-6.
19. Southcott, *Communication sent in a Letter to Rev. Mr P. in 1797* [Book 64], pp.1-11.
20. Southcott, *A Warning to the World* [Book 20], p.31.
21. BL Add. MS 32635, f.177.
22. BL Add. MS 32635, f.185.
23. Marriage of Joseph Southcott & Sarah Hall at St Paul's, Bristol, 21/12/1797. (Parish Records, Bristol Record Office).
24. Southcott, *Copies of Letters sent to the Clergy of Exeter* [Book 59], p.35.
25. Southcott, *A Warning to the World* [Book 20], pp.31-2.
26. Southcott, *Second Book of Letters* [Book 10], p.53.
27. *Southcott Despatch* (1920), No.22, p.5.

28. BL Add. MS 32635, f.184.

29. *Mr Joseph Southcott Will Now Come Forward* [Book 23], pp.17-18.

30. Southcott, *Second Book of Letters* [Book 10], pp.54-6.

31. *Express Leaflets*, March 1912, No.13, pp.10-11.

32. BL Add. MS 32635, f.188.

33. *Southcott Despatch* (1919), No.4.

34. Southcott, *Divine & Spiritual Letters of Prophecies* [Book 9], p.29.

35. BL Add. MS 32634, f.48v.

36. Southcott, *Divine & Spiritual Letters of Prophecies* [Book 9], pp.29-30.

37. Southcott, *Controversy of the Spirit with the Worldly Wise* [Book 54], p.6.

38. *Exeter Flying Post*, 5 September 1799, p.3. announced the death of 'Mrs Pomery wife of the Reverend Joseph Pomery, vicar of St Kew, who though labouring for many years under the constant pressure of a variety of bodily pains and sufferings, persevered in a patient discharge of all her relative and social duties; and after having expressed with true Christian fortitude a strong presentiment of her approaching dissolution cheerfully resigned her spirit into the hands of Him who gave it. . . .' She had given birth to six children, of whom three survived to adulthood.

39. Southcott, *A Warning to the World* [Book 20], p.33.

40. Southcott, *Second Book of Letters* [Book 10], p.86.

41. Southcott, *Second Book of Sealed Prophecies* [Book 36], p.134.

42. Southcott, *Copies of Letters sent to the Clergy of Exeter* [Book 59], p.24.

43. Exell, *Joanna Southcott at Blockley*, p.17.

44. Balleine held the opinion that Joanna was in love with Pomeroy and hoped that he would marry her, see *Past Finding Out*, p.25.

45. Southcott, *Copies of Letters sent to the Clergy of Exeter* [Book 59], p.25.

46. Derrett, *Prophecy in the Cotswolds*, p.53.

47. Communication to Joanna, 9 January 1800, published in Jones, *Southcott's Prophecies*. [DRO 3703Z/Z16.]

48. Southcott, *Copies of Letters sent to the Clergy of Exeter* [Book 59], pp.27-32.

49. *Mr Joseph Southcott Will Now Come Forward* [Book 23], p.104.

50. BL Add. MS 32634, f.156.

51. Southcott, *Controversy of the Spirit with the Worldly Wise* [Book 54], pp.6-7.

52. BL Add. MS 47799, f.13v.

53. Communication to Joanna, 10 August 1800, in Jones, *Southcott's Prophecies*. [DRO 3703Z/Z16.]

54. 15 December 1800 – burial of Nicholas Paige at Black Torrington (Parish Records, DRO). In 1804 Joanna described a dream that she was going to marry 'Brother Paige that is dead. . . . He first made love to me and then married my sister.' Southcott, *Letters & Communications* [Book 24], p.72.

55. Southcott, *A Warning to the World* [Book 20], p.20.

56. *Mr Joseph Southcott Will Now Come Forward* [Book 23], pp.7-8.

57. Southcott, *A Warning to the World* [Book 20], pp.19-20.

CHAPTER 8

1. Foley, *An Epistle to the Reverends*, the Vice-Chancellors of Cambridge and Oxford, printed as a pamphlet for circulation among the Heads of the Church and State, by the Revd. Thos.P.Foley, Rector of Oldswinford, Worcs, on 27 December 1803, p.5. Also quoted in *Watch* (1937) No.4, p.11ff. .

2. For details of T.P.Foley, see Gunning *Reminiscences of Cambridge*, Vol.1. and

Oldswinford Parish Records (WCRO); also, *Alumni Cantab.*

3. Southcott, *Continuation of the Controversy with the Worldly Wise* [Book 55], p.45.
4. Communication on the Likeness of Men to the Fallen Angels, 1 May 1801, published in Jones, *Southcott's Prophecies.* [DRO 3703Z/Z16.]
5. Southcott, *Divine & Spiritual Letters of Prophecies* [Book 9], pp.1-3.
6. *Watch* (1937) No.4, p.11.
7. Southcott, *Divine & Spiritual Letters of Prophecies* [Book 9], see pp.3-15 for this and following letters till 1 August 1801.
8. Southcott, *Continuation of Prophecies by Joanna Southcott* [Book 7], p.5.
9. Southcott, *Divine & Spiritual Letters of Prophecies* [Book 9], see pp.17-20 for the text of this and previous letter to Stanhope Bruce.
10. Southcott, *Continuation of Prophecies by Joanna Southcott* [Book 7], pp.6-8.
11. Southcott, *Divine & Spiritual Letters of Prophecies* [Book 9], pp.20-24.
12. For details of William Sharp see DNB and W.S.Baker's *Life of Sharp.*
13. Southcott, *Divine & Spiritual Letters of Prophecies* [Book 9], p.25.
14. Southcott, *Divine & Spiritual Letters of Prophecies* [Book 9], pp.24-5.
15. Southcott, *Divine & Spiritual Letters of Prophecies* [Book 9], pp.33-4.
16. Southcott, *Divine & Spiritual Letters of Prophecies* [Book 9], p.28.
17. Southcott, *Divine & Spiritual Letters of Prophecies* [Book 9], p.32.
18. Southcott, *Divine & Spiritual Letters of Prophecies* [Book 9], p.37.
19. Southcott, *Divine & Spiritual Letters of Prophecies* [Book 9], pp.37-8.
20. Southcott, *Divine & Spiritual Letters of Prophecies* [Book 9], p.39.
21. Southcott, *Divine & Spiritual Letters of Prophecies* [Book 9], p.42.
22. Southcott, *Continuation of Prophecies by Joanna Southcott* [Book 7], p.28.
23. Southcott, *Divine & Spiritual Letters of Prophecies* [Book 9], p.42.
24. Southcott, *Divine & Spiritual Letters of Prophecies* [Book 9], pp.46-8.
25. Southcott, *Divine & Spiritual Letters of Prophecies* [Book 9], pp.48.
26. Southcott, *Continuation of Prophecies by Joanna Southcott* [Book 7], pp.21-30.
27. Southcott, *Second Book of Letters* [Book 10], pp.49-53.
28. BL Add. MS 32634 f.53.
29. Southcott, *Second Book of Letters* [Book 10], pp.56-67.

CHAPTER 9

1. *Watch* (1937) No.4, p.12.
2. Foley, *An Epistle to the Reverends*, etc. op. cit., p.6ff.
3. *Watch* (1937) No.4, pp.12-13.
4. Southcott, *Trial of Joanna Southcott during Seven Days* [Book 25], p.76.
5. Southcott, *An Answer to the World* [Book 43], pp.4-5.
6. Southcott, *Second Book of Letters* [Book 10], pp.74-80.
7. Southcott, *Second Book of Letters* [Book 10], p.75.
8. Quoted in Southcott, *Second Book of Letters* [Book 10], p.76.
9. BL Add. MS 47799, f.9.
10. Southcott, *Second Book of Letters* [Book 10], pp.77-9.
11. Southcott, *Second Book of Letters* [Book 10], p.68.
12. Joanna Southcott to Mrs Bruce, February 1802, in Jones, *Book of Letters*, p.99. [DRO 3703Z/Z14].
13. Southcott, *Copies & Parts of Copies* [Book 22], p.24.
14. Southcott, *Second Book of Letters* [Book 10], pp.68-9.
15. Joanna Southcott to T.P. Foley, 19 February 1802, in Jones, *Book of Letters*,

p.65. [DRO 3703Z/Z14].

16. Southcott, *Second Book of Letters* [Book 10], pp.80-1.
17. *Southcott Despatch* (1919) No.8. pp.7-8.
18. Mr Sharp's Journal for part of 1802 in BL Add. MS 57860, f.11. Cf. BL Add. MS 47795, f.3, where Joanna compares her 'entry into the Metropolis of the Kingdom with our Blessed Saviour's triumphant entry into Jerusalem sitting on an ass.'
19. Foley, *An Epistle to the Reverends, etc.* op. cit., p.10.
20. Southcott, *Strange Effects of Faith* [Book 8], p.103.
21. Southcott, *Strange Effects of Faith* [Book 7], p.23. Basil Bruce to Joanna Southcott, 20 October 1801, writes 'my wife's sentiments are in perfect unity with my own . . . six amiable and well-disposed children are the fruit of our happy union.'
22. Southcott, *The Continuation of the Prophecies (A Word in Season)* [Book 15], p.3.
23. For details of Nathaniel Brassey Halhed, see DNB.
24. Mr Sharp's Journal in BL Add. MS 57860, f.11.
25. Communication to Joanna Southcott, 24 May 1802, published in *Express Leaflet*, No.30, pp.3-4.
26. Foley, *Epistle to the Reverends, etc.* op.cit., p.10.
27. *Southcott Despatch* (1921) No.33, p.8.
28. Mr Sharp's Journal in BL Add. MS 57860, f.12.
29. BL Add. MS 47801B, f.18.
30. Mr Sharp's Journal in BL Add. MS 57860, f.15.
31. BL Add. MS 47795, f.59.
32. John Mossop (?1760-1834) was curate of Deeping St James 1778-1830, Vicar of Baston 1781 and of Langtoft 1801 (all in Lincolnshire).
33. BL Add. MS 47801B, ff.2-11.
34. BL Add. MS 47799, f.71.
35. Southcott, *Second Book of Letters* [Book 10], pp.88-92.
36. *Southcott Despatch* (1921) No.25, p.11.
37. BL Add. MS 47801B, ff.13-13v.
38. BL Add. MS 47801B, ff.19v-22.
39. Foley, *Epistle to the Reverends, etc.* op.cit. p.11.
40. *Southcott Despatch*, No.7, pp.7-9.
41. Communication to Joanna, 25 July 1802, in Jones, *Southcott's Prophecies*. [DRO 3703Z/Z16.]
42. BL Add. MS 32636, f.57v.
43. BL Add. MS 47795, f.59.
44. Foley, *Epistle to the Reverends, etc.* op.cit. pp.12-13.
45. BL Add. MS 47795, f.59.
46. Southcott, *Dispute Between the Woman & the Powers of Darkness* [Book 11], pp.83-93.

CHAPTER 10

1. BL Add. MS 32636, ff.13v-19.
2. Southcott, *Answer of the Lord to the Powers of Darkness* [Book 12], p.56.
3. See Foley's Diary, 11 October 1802, for list of people included in Joanna's note for sealing. Foley sent details to his sister who replied that, 'It was above her Comprehension and she declined signing it.' (Blockley 515, p.4.)
4. Southcott, *Answer of the Lord to the Powers of Darkness* [Book 12], p.58. For

the rest of this episode, see pp.56-60.

5. BL Add. MS 32636, ff.21-3.
6. Southcott, *Answer of the Lord to the Powers of Darkness* [Book 12], p.4.
7. Southcott, *Answer of the Lord to the Powers of Darkness* [Book 12], p.118.
8. BL Add. MS 47794, ff.5-6.
9. Southcott, *Trial of Joanna Southcott during Seven Days* [Book 25], pp.xxiii-xxiv.
10. Hopkins, *A Woman to Deliver Her People*, p.189.
11. *Southcott Despatch* (1920) No.17, p.6.
12. BL Add. MS 32633, f.116.
13. Foley's Diary, Blockley 515, p.16.
14. Bramall, *A Review of the Prophecies of Mrs Joanna Southcott*, p.6., in Jones, *Book of Letters*. [DRO 3703Z/Z14.]
15. Foley's Diary, Blockley 515, p.20.
16. BL Add. MS 47794, f.7.
17. Foley's Diary, Blockley 515, pp.20-22.
18. BL Add. MS 47799. f.72v-73v.
19. BL Add. MS 47795, f.59.
20. BL Add. MS 47794, f.7v.
21. Foley's Diary, Blockley 515, p.23ff.
22. Foley's Diary, quoted in Exell, p.23.
23. BL Add. MS 47799, ff.72-3 – where names and addresses of the judges and jurymen are listed, as well as those who were invited but did not come.
24. Foley's Diary, Blockley 515, pp.48-70. For Foley's use of 'cast', see Psalm 18:42, v.42: 'Then did I beat them small as the dust before the wind: I did cast them out as the dirt in the street.' See also Revelation 20:10: 'And the devil that deceived them was cast into the lake of fire and brimstone, where the beast and the false prophet are. . . .'

CHAPTER 11

1. Southcott, *Prophecies: A Warning to the Whole World* [Book 14], pp.71-2.
2. BL Add. MS 47795, f.5.
3. For details of Elias Carpenter and Joseph Prescott, see Hopkins, *A Woman To Deliver Her People*, pp.127-133.
4. Carpenter, *Apology for Faith*, etc. p.35.
5. Southcott, *A Warning to the World* [Book 20], p.66.
6. Southcott, *Strange Effects of Faith* [Book 1], p.25.
7. BL Add. MS 47795, f.6.
8. Southcott, *The Continuation of the Prophecies (A Word in Season)* [Book 15], pp.19-36.
9. *Southcott Express* (March 1927) No.5, p.108.
10. *Southcott Despatch* (1921) No.33, p.3.
11. BL Add. MS 47799, f.77.
12. *Southcott Express* (March 1927) No.5, pp.108-111.
13. BL Add. MS 47799, f.79.
14. *Southcott Despatch* (1921) No.33, pp.4-5.
15. BL Add. MS 47795, f.59v.
16. Hopkins, *A Woman to Deliver Her People*, p.63.
17. BL Add. MS 32635, f.191v.
18. BL Add. MS 47799, f.81v.
19. Southcott, *Trial of Joanna Southcott during Seven Days* [Book 25], p.48.

20. BL Add. MS 47795, f.59v.
21. Foley, *Epistle to the Reverends, etc.* op.cit., p.16.
22. Law, *Copy of an Epistle . . . sent to Henry Addington, Prime Minister of the United Kingdom.*
23. *The Two Witnesses* (November 1916) No.21, p.9.
24. The Temporal & Spiritual Sword, a letter from Joanna to William Sharp, dated 25 July 1803, in Jones, *Southcott's Prophecies.* [DRO 3703Z/Z16.] cf. Answer to Mrs Foley, dated 26 July 1803 in BL Add. MS 32633, f.182v.
25. *The Two Witnesses* (November 1916) No.21, pp.3-5.
26. *The Two Witnesses* (June 1915) No.4, p.11.
27. Dream dated 1 September 1803 published in Jones, *Southcott's Prophecies.* [DRO 3703Z/Z16.]
28. BL Add. MS 47799, f.87v.
29. Letter dated 4 August 1803 in BL Add. MS 57860, f.25.
30. Mary Joanna, daughter of Thomas and Elizabeth Foley, christened at Oldswinford, 26 August 1803. (Parish Records, WRO.)
31. These words feature on the first page of the first edition of Southcott, *A Word to the Wise* [Book 17], but were omitted in some later editions.
32. Southcott, *Divine & Spiritual Communications* [Book 18], pp.11-20.
33. BL Add. MS 32636, f.33v.
34. BL Add. MS 47799, f.104.
35. BL Add. MS 47794, f.9.
36. BL Add. MS 47795, f.59v.
37. BL Add. MS 32634, f.93.
38. BL Add. MS 47795, f.59v.
39. BL Add. MS 47795, f.7.
40. BL Add. MS 32636, f.33v.
41. BL Add. MS 47795, f.7.
42. *Express Leaflet* (June 1913) No.28, p.3.
43. BL Add. MS 32636, f.34.
44. Southcott, *A Warning to the World* [Book 20], p.57.
45. Southcott, *Sound An Alarm* [Book 19], p.24: 'and now there are eight thousand one hundred and forty-four, whose names stand for Satan's destruction.'
46. *Express Leaflets* (April, 1914) No.38, p.7.
47. BL Add. MS 47794, f.14.
48. *Express Leaflets* (April 1914) No.38, pp.5-8.
49. BL Add. MS47794, ff.17-18.
50. BL Add. MS 47795, f.8, f.10.
51. Southcott, *Sound An Alarm* [Book 19], p.12.
52. BL Add. MS 47799, ff.116-117.
53. BL Add. MS 47795, f.10.
54. Southcott, *Sound An Alarm* [Book 19], p.12.
55. BL Add. MS 32633, f.205v.
56. BL Add. MS 47795, ff.10-10v.
57. Southcott, *Answer to Thomas Paine's Age of Reason* [Book 56], p.51.
58. Letter to Carpenter, 10 April 1804, in BL Add. MS 32633, f.239v.
59. *Southcott Express* (December 1927) No.8, p.194. Also Townley, *Letter to the Editor of the Council of Ten*, p.4.
60. Communication, 27 March 1804, in *Express Leaflets* (1911) No.3.
61. BL Add. MS 47795, f.59v. Cf. BL Add. MS 32636, f.48v.

CHAPTER 12

1. BL Add. MS 32636, ff.50-57.
2. Blockley 577 (43).
3. BL Add. MS 32636, ff.60v-63.
4. *Southcott Express* (December 1927) No.8, p.194.
5. BL Add. MS 32633, f.240v.
6. Townley, *Letter to the Editor of the Council of Ten*, p.6. Also, *Southcott Express* (December 1927) No.8, p.195.
7. BL Add. MS 32636, f.63v.
8. BL Add. MS 47794, f.19v.
9. *Southcott Express* (December 1927) No.8, p.195.
10. BL Add. MS 32636, f.63v.
11. Southcott, *The Full Assurance that the Kingdom of Christ Is at Hand* [Bk 44], pp.21-3.
12. Southcott, *On the Prayers for the Fast Day* [Book 21], pp.29-30.
13. *Southcott Express* (December 1927) No.8, p.195.
14. BL Add. MS 32636, ff.67-71 for Jane Townley's letter to the Bishop of London and Joanna's accompanying letter.
15. Townley, *Letter to the Editor of the Council of Ten*, p.6.
16. Southcott, *On the Prayers for the Fast Day* [Book 21], pp.15-16.
17. Townley, *Letter to the Editor of the Council of Ten*, p.8.
18. Southcott, *On the Prayers for the Fast Day* [Book 21], p.15.
19. Bristol *Trade Directories* show:
    1803 Joseph Southcote –Umbrella-maker – Address: Pipe Street.
    1805   ditto   ditto   9 Trinity St.
    1806   ditto   ditto   69 Broad Quay.
    1808   ditto   ditto   ditto.
    1809   ditto   ditto   Philadelphia St.
    1810 Sarah Southcote   Stationer   34 Old Market St.
20. Southcott, *Copies & Parts of Copies, etc.* [Book 22], pp.30-33.
21. Southcott, *On the Prayers for the Fast Day* [Book 21], pp.43-8.
22. *Southcott Despatch* (1919) No.3, p.4. Booth's identity remains obscure.
23. Southcott, *On the Prayers for the Fast Day* [Book 21], pp.33-5.
24. Southcott, *Letters & Communications* [Book 24], pp.11-19 shows Joanna's fraught state.
25. Communication On the Oath, 14 June 1804, in Jones, *Southcott's Prophecies.* [DRO 3703Z/Z16.]
26. Southcott, *Letters & Communications* [Book 24], p.29.
27. BL Add. MS 47800, f.228v.
28. Southcott, *Letters & Communications* [Book 24], pp.29-30.
29. Southcott, *Letters & Communications* [Book 24], p.70. An ink note on page 70 of Book 24 held in Exeter's WCSL declares: 'Writ to Mr Pomeroy by me Robt. Portbury and returned again without answering a word therein.'
30. Southcott, *Copies & Parts of Copies* [Book 22], pp.46-7.
31. Southcott, *Letters & Communications* [Book 24], p.72.
32. Southcott, *Copies & Parts of Copies* [Book 22], pp.52-80.
33. Southcott, *Letters & Communications* [Book 24], p.97.
34. BL Add. MS 47794, ff.21-2.
35. BL Add. MS 32633, f.32.

36. Southcott, *Letters & Communications* [Book 24], pp.109-115.
37. *Mr Joseph Southcott Will Now Come Forward* [Book 23], pp.28-9.

CHAPTER 13

1. BL Add. MS 32633, where Joanna's letter to Foley, 6 July 1804, contains a description of her dream which includes this dialogue.
2. BL Add. MS 47794, ff.25-6.
3. *Mr Joseph Southcott Will Now Come Forward* [Book 23], pp.29-30.
4. Southcott, *Trial of Joanna Southcott During Seven Days* [Book 25], p.52.
5. *Mr Joseph Southcott Will Now Come Forward* [Book 23], pp.30-32.
6. *Bristol Gazette & Public Advertiser*, 19 July 1804, p.3.
7. *Mr Joseph Southcott Will Now Come Forward* [Book 23], pp.63-85.
8. Blockley Collection 596.
9. BL Add. MS 47797, ff.76-7.
10. *Mr Joseph Southcott Will Now Come Forward* [Book 23], p.97.
11. Southcott, *True Explanation of the Bible* [Books 28-33], pp.184-190.
12. Communication dated 22 August 1804 in BL Add. MS 32636, f.72v.
13. BL Add. MS 47795, f.59v.
14. BL Add. MS 47797, ff.78-9.
15. BL Add. MS 32634, f.204v.
16. Joanna's dream, 2-3 September 1804, in BL Add. MS 32633.
17. BL Add. MS 32634, f.200.
18. *Southcott Despatch* (1921) No.24, pp.4-5.
19. BL Add. MS 47794, f.35.
20. BL Add. MS 32636, f.78v.
21. BL Add. MS 47794, f.35.
22. Blockley Collection 567, p.20.
23. WCSL, S920 SOU A/4, where a manuscript note signed Robert Portbury on page 10 of *Joanna Southcott's Answer to the Five Charges in the Leeds Mercury* states: 'The samples of corn, barley and beans here spoken of as sent to Archdeacon Moore was gather'd and sent by me to him, with a letter to convince him of the truth contained in Joanna's Prophecy's, the Copy of it is among my writings.'
24. BL Add. MS 32636, ff.81-97v.
25. Southcott, *True Explanation of the Bible* [Books 28-33], pp.41-2.
26. WCSL, S920 SOU A/7, where a manuscript note signed Robert Portbury on p.42 of Southcott, *Second Book of Wonders* reads: 'Having journies through Cornwall, I waited on Mr Pomeroy at his house in Bodmin two separate times but could get no other satisfaction from him then what is written in the above letter (Pomeroy to Stanhope Bruce, 1 October, 1804) as touching Mrs Southcott's Prophetic writings that was placed in his hands at his own request, by Mr Jones, at my reasoning with him he turned pale and went away to the staircase.'
27. Southcott, *Second Book of Wonders* [Book 58], pp.41-2.
28. Southcott, *True Explanation of the Bible* [Books 28-33], pp.75-80.
29. Southcott, *True Explanation of the Bible* [Books 28-33], p.365.
30. The Communication on the Parable of the Highwayman was finished at nine o'clock 'after candlelight' on 6 November 1804 – see its publication in Jones, *Southcott's Prophecies*, pp.1-2. [DRO 3703Z/Z16.]
31. BL Add. MS 32636, ff.103-104v.
32. BL Add. MS 47794, ff.47-48v.

CHAPTER 14

1. A Christian Henry Fischer is listed in the records of the Moravian Church in Great Britain, but there is no further information or record of any Moravian minister of that name.
2. Tobin, *The Southcottians in England*, pp.108-9.
3. Southcott, *Trial of Joanna Southcott, during Seven Days* [Book 25], pp.41-137, for details of events at Neckinger House.
4. Southcott, *Controversy between Joanna Southcott & Elias Carpenter* [Books 38-42], p.184.
5. Quoted in Hopkins, *A Woman to Deliver Her People*, p.188.
6. BL Add. MS 32636, f.126.
7. Derrett, *Prophecy in the Cotswolds*, p.97, note 49.
8. BL Eg. MS 2399, f.84. Also, BL Add. MS 32636, f.134.
9. BL Add. MS 32636, f.146v.
10. BL Add. MS 47800, f.218.
11. BL Add. MS 47794, f.53.
12. *Southcott Express* (December 1927) No.8, p.196.
13. BL Add. MS 47794, f.53.
14. Southcott, *Second Book of the Sealed Prophecies* [Book 36], p.22.
15. Sketch of Rev. W. Tozer published anonymously in *Memoirs of the Life & Mission of Joanna Southcott* (1814).
16. Quoted in Hopkins, *A Woman to Deliver Her People*, p.131.
17. BL Eg. MS 2399, ff.154v-155.
18. Southcott, *Controversy between Joanna Southcott & Elias Carpenter* [Books 38-42], p.11.
19. Southcott, *Controversy between Joanna Southcott & Elias Carpenter* [Books 38-42], pp.30-34.
20. Communication 2 June 1805 published in *Southcott Despatch* (1922) No.38, pp.2-5.
21. *Express Leaflets* (1914) No.42, pp.8-9.
22. BL Add. MS 32636, ff.156-69.
23. BL Add. MS 47794, f.55v.
24. BL Add. MS 32636, f.177v.
25. BL Add. MS 47795, f.20.
26. *Answer of Rev. T. P. Foley to the World* [Book 37], p.22.
27. Blockley Coll. 577/59.
28. Letter to Mrs Taylor 6 August 1805 in Blockley 596, p.14.
29. Southcott, *Controversy between Joanna Southcott & Elias Carpenter* [Books 38-42], p.34.
30. BL Add. MS 32637, ff.55-9. Also, BL Eg. MS 2399, ff.45-6.
31. Southcott, *Controversy between Joanna Southcott & Elias Carpenter* [Books 38-42], pp.50-51.
32. BL Add. MS 32636, ff.179v-180v.
33. Southcott, *Controversy between Joanna Southcott & Elias Carpenter* [Books 38-42], pp.234.
34. Letter to Tozer, 25 October 1805, quoted in Hopkins, *A Woman to Deliver Her People*, p.98.
35. Southcott, *Controversy between Joanna Southcott & Elias Carpenter* [Books 38-42], p.152.
36. BL Add. MS 32636, f.181.

37. BL Add. MS 32637, f.64.
38. BL Add. MS 47795, ff.22-22v.
39. BL Add. MS 32637, f.83.
40. BL Add. MS 47795, f.22.
41. BL Add. MS 47794, f.72.

CHAPTER 15

1. Dr Benjamin Moseley (1742-1819) in DNB.
2. Townley, *Letter to the Editor of the Council of Ten*, p.4.
3. *Southcott Express* (December 1927) No.8, pp.193-4.
4. BL Add. MS 47794, f.31v.
5. In Answer to a Circumstance Which Caused Some Dispute, in Jones, *Southcott's Prophecies*.[DRO 3703Z/Z16.]
6. Hopkins, *A Woman to Deliver Her People*, p.254, n.29.
7. BL Add. MS 32636, ff.189-190.
8. Southcott, *The Long-Wished-For Revolution* [Book 46], pp.15-49.
9. BL Add. MS 32637, ff.87v-90.
10. *Southcott Despatch* (1921) No.25, pp.4-7.
11. England May Be a Happy Land, copy of a letter dated 1 April 1806, in Jones, *Southcott's Prophecies*. [DRO 3703Z/Z16.]
12. BL Add. MS 47794, ff.78-108.
13. BL Add. MS 32637, f.99.
14. John Finlayson (1770-1854) in DNB.
15. BL Add. MS 57860, f.101.
16. Joanna Southcott in DNB.
17. William Owen Pughe (1759-1835) in DNB.
18. Blockley Coll. 577.
19. *Express Leaflets* (1914) No.41, p.10.
20. BL Add. MS 47800, ff.68v-70.
21. BL Add. MS 47795, f.28.
22. BL Add. MS 32634, f.281.
23. Lane, *Bibliography of Joanna Southcott*, p.776.
24. Southcott, *A Few Remarks & Inquiries on a Sermon* [Book 45], pp.6-11.
25. BL Add. MS 32637, f.110v.
26. Southcott, *Answer to Mr Brothers' Book* [Book 47], pp.32-43.
27. BL Add. MS 32637, f.179v.
28. BL Add. MS 47797, f.123.
29. BL Add. MS 32635, f.176v.
30. BL Add. MS 47800, f.37.
31. BL Add. MS 32636, f.194.
32. BL Add. MS 47797, ff.129-130.
33. BL Add. MS 47795, ff.32-9.
34. Foley to Pidcock, 28 January 1807, in BL Add. MS 57860, ff.117-8.
35. BL Add. MS 47795, ff.43-4.
36. Southcott, *A Caution & Instruction to the Sealed* [Book 48], p.6.
37. Letter dated 6 December 1806 in Jones, *Southcott's Prophecies*. [DRO 3703Z/Z16.]
38. BL Add. MS 47797, f.139.
39. BL Add. MS 47800, ff.89v-90.

CHAPTER 16

1. Southcott, *An Account of the Trials on Bills of Exchange* [Book 49], pp.1-58.
2. BL Add. MS 47797, f.143.
3. BL Add. MS 47795, f.45.
4. BL Add. MS 47797, f.144.
5. BL Add. MS 32637, f.191.
6. BL Add. MS 47795, f.45.
7. BL Add. MS 47794, f.102.
8. BL Add. MS 47795, f.46v.
9. BL Add. MS 26038, f.35v.
10. BL Add. MS 32637, ff.199-203v.
11. BL Add. MS 32635, f.21v.
12. BL Add. MS 32637, f.206.
13. BL Add. MS 47797, f.160v.
14. BL Add. MS 32635, ff.15v-17.
15. BL Add. MS 47794, ff.104-5.
16. BL Add. MS 47795, ff.47-9.
17. BL Add. MS 32636, f.195v.
18. BL Add. MS 47800, f.41.
19. *Pulman's Weekly News*, nd, Southcott Cuttings, WCSL.
20. *Southcott Express* (1927) No.6, pp.142-3.
21. Letter dated 22 October 1807, in Jones, *Southcott's Prophecies*. [DRO 3703Z/Z16.]
22. Letter dated 1 October 1807, in Jones, *Southcott's Prophecies*. [DRO 3703Z/Z16.]
23. BL Add. MS 32635, f.50.
24. Letter dated 11 June 1808, in Jones, *Southcott's Prophecies*. [DRO 3703Z/Z16.]
25. BL Add. MS 32635, ff.18v-19v.
26. Marriage of William Carter of Staple, Somerset, widower, to Eleanor Mylard, widow, dated 19 June 1806. (South Molton Parish Register, DRO).
27. Solomon, son of Eleanor Mylard, christened at South Molton on 25 October 1807. (Parish Register, DRO.)
28. BL Add. MS 47802, f.110.
29. BL Add. MS 32635, f.21v; and BL Add. MS 47800, f.117v.
30. BL Add. MS 47802, ff.111-6.
31. BL Add. MS 47797, f.164v.
32. BL Add. MS 57860, ff.126-7.
33. BL Add. MS 47797, f.165v.
34. Southcott, *Answer to a Sermon Preached by Mr Smith* [Book 50], pp.4, 25, 70-71.
35. BL Add. MS 47794, f.108.
36. BL Add. MS 47798, f.13.
37. BL Add. MS 47797, f.143.
38. BL Add. MS 47794, f.114.
39. BL Add. MS 47802, f.35v.
40. BL Add. MS 47800, ff.126-31.
41. BL Add. MS 47795, ff.53-4.

CHAPTER 17

1. BL Add. MS 47800, f.136-7; BL Add. MS 32635, f.73, and *Southcott Express* (1928) No.9, pp.11-16.
2. Balleine, *Past Finding Out*, p.55.
3. Southcott, *An Answer to Thomas Paine* [Book 56], p.51.
4. Hopkins, *A Woman to Deliver Her People*, p.105.
5. Southcott, *Copies and Parts of Copies* [Book 22], p.44.
6. BL Add. MS 47794, ff.116-8.
7. Orders About Believers Going to Church, dated 24 May 1809, in Jones, *Southcott's Prophecies*. [DRO 3703Z/Z16.]
8. BL Add. MS 47794, f.119.
9. BL Add. MS 47794, f.83.
10. Dream, 10 June 1809, in Blockley Coll. 585.
11. BL Add. MS 32634, ff.260v-264v.
12. Southcott, *Fifth Book of Wonders* [Book 63], p.4.
13. Latimer, *Annals of Bristol in the Nineteenth Century*, p.25.
14. *Southcott Despatch* (1922) No.36, pp.4-7.
15. Answer to Hann's False Assertions published in Southcott, *True Explanations of the Bible, 7th Part* [Book 53], pp.608-9. Also BL Add. MS 57860, ff.129-30.
16. BL Add. MS 47802, ff.32-4.
17. Pair of glass Communion Beakers in Royal Albert Memorial Museum, Exeter. [See illustration].
18. Southcott, *True Explanations of the Bible, 7th Part* [Book 53], p.624.
19. BL Add. MS 47802, f.83.
20. Patchwork preserved in the Rougemont Museum, Exeter. [See illustration].
21. Announcement of the marriage of J.W.Luscombe to Frances Taylor, daughter of Mr Taylor of Exeter, cabinet-maker, 'last Thursday', *Exeter Flying Post*, 26 July 1810.
22. BL Add. MS 26038, ff.40-50 for details of Joanna's quarrel with Field.
23. BL Add. MS 47794, f.122.
24. Announcement of the death of John Wolland, maltster of Heavitree, *Exeter Flying Post*, 27 September 1810.
25. Will of Sarah Minifie of Ottery St Mary, died 5 August 1814. (DRO.)
26. BL Add. MS 32635, f.78.
27. BL Add. MS 47798, ff.35-6.
28. Letter, dated 21 March 1811, in Blockley Coll. 596/16.
29. Letters from Richard Law to Jane Townley, dated 13 May and 14 June 1816, in BL Add. MS 47796, f.5.
30. BL Add. MS 47794, f.124.
31. BL Add. MS 47798, f.39.
32. Southcott, *Continuation of Controversy with the Worldly Wise* [Book 55], p.51.
33. Southcott, *An Answer to Thomas Paine* [Book 56], pp.51-2.
34. *Express Leaflets* (1913) No.28, Preface.
35. BL Add. MS 47800, f.149.
36. BL Add. MS 32635, f.88.
37. BL Add. MS 47794, f.124.
38. BL Add. MS 47800,f.146v.

CHAPTER 18

1. BL Add. MS 47798, f.39v.
2. Quoted in Hopkins, *A Woman to Deliver Her People*, p.98.
3. BL Add. MS 57860, ff.161-9.
4. Blockley Coll. 596/15-16.
5. For background to Harwood's lawsuit against Horne Tooke see Patterson, *Sir Francis Burdett and His Times*, vol.1, p.125.
6. BL Add. MS 57860, ff.173-7.
7. Southcott, *An Answer to Thomas Paine* [Book 56], pp.24-25, 2, 53.
8. Southcott, *Third Book of Wonders* [Book 61], pp.61-2.
9. Will of James Cosins, proved 5 January 1813 – PROB11/1540.
10. Jones, *Sixth Book of Wonders*, pp.31ff.
11. BL Add. MS 57860, ff.183-193.
12. BL Add. MS 47795, f.63.
13. BL Add. MS 57860, ff.175v-195.
14. BL Add. MS 47795, ff.63-4.
15. BL Add. MS 57860, ff.195-6.
16. Letter dated 16 July 1816, BL Add. MS 47796, ff.14v-15r.
17. Letter dated 5 April 1813, BL Add. MS 26038, f.59.
18. Letter dated 2 June 1813, Blockley Coll. 596/18.
19. Will of Joanna Southcott, proved 28 April 1815 – PROB11/1567.
20. Southcott, *Wisdom Excelleth the Weapons of War* [Book 60], pp.38-40.
21. Southcott, *Book of Wonders, Marvellous and True* [Book 57], p.39.

CHAPTER 19

1. Southcott, *Second Book of Wonders* [Book 58], pp.3-4.
2. Jones, *Sixth Book of Wonders*, pp.6-30.
3. Southcott, *Second Book of Wonders* [Book 58], p.4.
4. Jones, *Sixth Book of Wonders*, pp.15-73.
5. Southcott, *Second Book of Wonders* [Book 58], pp.4-5.
6. Jones, *Sixth Book of Wonders*, pp.43-73.
7. Letter to the Bishops, 27 September 1813, in Jones, *Southcott's Prophecies*, pp.1-2. [DRO 3703Z/Z16.]
8. BL Add. MS 20638, ff.61-2. The erasures in the original letter show its author's efforts to ensure that her tone was not too humble or importunate.
9. Jones, *Sixth Book of Wonders*, p.82.
10. Southcott, *Second Book of Wonders* [Book 58], pp.16, 83, 109.
11. Southcott, *Third Book of Wonders* [Book 61], p.6.
12. Explanation of the Conception, 28 February 1814, in Jones, *Southcott's Prophecies*, pp.1-2. [DRO 3703Z/Z16.]
13. Southcott, *Third Book of Wonders* [Book 61], p.58.
14. Answer to Foley's Letter, 16 October 1813, in BL Add. MS 32635, ff.180-181.
15. Southcott, *Copies of Letters sent to the Clergy of Exeter* [Book 59], pp.3-38.
16. WCSL, S920SOU A/8, where a manuscript note signed 'Robert Portbury' on p.41 of Southcott, *Copies of Letters sent to the Clergy of Exeter* states, 'I am witness to these words from the mouth of Bishop Pelham at his palace when I waited on him to ask a question – if it was right for the clergy to ridicule individuals from the pulpit.'

17. Southcott, *Copies of Letters sent to the Clergy of Exeter* [Book 59], pp.42-5.
18. Southcott, *Wisdom Excelleth the Weapons of War* [Book 60], pp.1-13.
19. BL Add. MS 57860, f.201.
20. Southcott, *Wisdom Excelleth the Weapons of War* [Book 60], pp.1-9.
21. Southcott, *Fifth Book of Wonders* [Book 63], pp.65-7.

CHAPTER 20

1. Fourth Letter of Prophecy, 19 November 1813, published in Southcott, *Copies of Letters sent to the Clergy of Exeter* [Book 59], p.40.
2. Southcott, *Third Book of Wonders* [Book 61], p.4.
3. BL Add. MS 32635, f.131v.
4. Cf. A.E.Waite, *The Holy Kabbalah*, p.348. 'The complete integration . . . of all branches of the Sephirotic Tree will not take place till He comes Who shall be called Man, that is, Adam or SHILOH.'
5. Southcott, *Third Book of Wonders* [Book 61], p.6.
6. Southcott, *Third Book of Wonders* [Book 61], p.63.
7. An Explanation of Joanna's Illness, 26 August 1814, in Jones, *Southcott's Prophecies*, pp.1-2. [DRO 3703Z/Z16.]
8. Southcott, *Fifth Book of Wonders* [Book 63], pp.61-6. Joanna had been mistaken about Pomeroy's death, now she was misled about his marriage. The 'Mrs P.' who returned all letters and was so protective, was not Pomeroy's wife but his daughter. He had not remarried.
9. Southcott, *Fourth Book of Wonders* [Book 62], p.53.
10. LMA Acc. 1040/81.
11. Southcott, *Fifth Book of Wonders* [Book 63], p.16.
12. Communication on the Cot, 10 May 1814, in Jones, *Southcott's Prophecies*, pp.1-2. [DRO 3703Z/Z16.]
13. Southcott, *Fifth Book of Wonders* [Book 63], p.59.
14. LMA Acc. 1040/24.
15. Southcott, *Fifth Book of Wonders* [Book 63], pp.3-7, 39-50, 68-71.
16. Letter to Pomeroy, 18 June 1814, in BL Add. MS 26038, f.65.
17. BL Add. MS 26039, ff.37-44.
18. Southcott, *A Communication Sent in a Letter*, etc., [Book 64], pp.6-7.
19. WCSL, Southcott Cuttings. [See Illustration]
20. Blockley Coll. 577/42, p.39.
21. Sarah Minifie, aged 75, died at Ottery St Mary on 5 August 1814. [Parish Records, DRO.]

CHAPTER 21

1. Joseph Adams, M.D. (1756-1818) in DNB.
2. Richard Reece, physician (1775-1831) in DNB.
3. Dr Reece's Statement of the Circumstances that attended the Last Illness and Death of Mrs Southcott, published by Seymour in *The Express*, Vol.2, pp.354-99.
4. WCSL, S920SOU A/9 – manuscript note on p.2.
5. Letter, 24 August 1814, in Jones, *Southcott's Prophecies*. [DRO 3703Z/Z16].
6. Foley's Diary, 16 July to 26 August 1814, published by Seymour in *The Express*, Vol.2, pp.345-53.

7. BL Add. MS 47800, f.172v.
8. Southcott Cuttings, WCSL, includes a critical reference to Joanna's love of eating well and alleged that she endulged a fad for asparagus during her 'pregnancy' by eating 160 heads at one meal.
9. Communication on the Vision of the Candle, Also An Explanation of Joanna's Illness, 26 August 1814, in Jones, *Southcott's Prophecies*. [DRO 3703Z/Z16].
10. Letter, 25 August 1814, published by Seymour in *The Express*, Vol.2, p.363.
11. Seymour, *The Express*, Vol.2, p.364.
12. Southcott, *Prophecies Announcing the Birth of the Prince of Peace* [Book 65], pp.38-40.
13. Charles William, son of Charles Vincent and Ann Barnard, christened 7 September 1814 in St Pancras, Old Church. (IGI, London.)
14. Southcott, *Prophecies Announcing the Birth of the Prince of Peace* [Book 65], pp.34-5.
15. BL Add. MS 32636, f.208.
16. BL Add. MS 32635, f.190.
17. BL Add. MS 32636, f.204.
18. BL Add. MS 57860, ff.213-4.
19. BL Add. MS 32635, ff.190-191.
20. BL Add. MS 57860, ff.215-6.

CHAPTER 22

1. BL Add. MS 32636, f.204.
2. *Pulman's Weekly News*, nd, Southcott Cuttings, WCSL.
3. *Bristol Mirror*, 29 October 1814.
4. *Pulman's Weekly News*, nd, Southcott Cuttings, WCSL.
5. LMA Acc. 1040/25.
6. Dr Reece's Statement of the Circumstances that attended the Last Illness and Death of Mrs Southcott, published by Seymour in *The Express*, Vol.2, p.376.
7. LMA Acc. 1040/26.
8. Joanna Southcott's Will, PROB11/1567, p.340.
9. Underwood to Foley, 14 November 1814, Blockley Coll. 779.
10. BL Add. MS 32633, f.149.
11. On Joanna's Marriage, LMA Acc. 1040/78.
12. Blockley Coll. 779.
13. Paolo Assolini (1759-1840), an eminent Neapolitan doctor who had delivered Napoleon's son, the Duke of Reichstadt. See *Enciclopedia Italiana*, Vol.4; *Annual Register* (1814).
14. Count Alexis Orlov (1787-1862), natural son of Count Theodore Orlov (1741-1796), fought against Napoleon and was afterwards Russian Ambassador at Constantinople. His interest in medical matters is seen in *Letters of King George IV, 1812-1830*, ed. A.Aspinall, where Letter No.485 from Dr Jenner to Colonel McMahon (13 September 1814) had been 'written at the request of Count Orlof' who wanted a concise outline of the origin of vaccination to present to the Tsar.
15. Christopher Andreievitch (1774-1839), Count de Lieven, inherited the title of Prince in 1826 and was Ambassador in London, 1812-34. His wife exerted influence over the Prince Regent. 'In November 1814 we were at Brighton where the Prince Regent had invited us to pass some weeks ... We came every

day to take lunch, to walk and to dine with the Regent.' (*Unpublished Diary & Political Sketches of Princess Lieven,* p.33.) The Lievens' close connection with the English court at this time could be significant in the light of the letter sent by Jane Townley to Mrs Tozer on 26 September 1814 to be forwarded to George Troup, a devout follower of Joanna and page to the Prince Regent for over forty years.

> Sir,
>
> I have a favour to request of you, as you have access to His Royal Highness the Prince Regent I shall be obliged if you will take an opportunity of informing him that the Prediction in the Third Book of Wonders which Mrs Southcott was ordered to send to the Prince Regent last March is now likely to be realised and it was for the Heads of the Nation to bear testimony of the Truth that she was ordered to send a letter and her Portrait to them, in order that they may send their Physicians at the time of her delivery to be witnesses of the Birth of the Child . . . therefore she wishes to know whether His Royal Highness the Prince Regent will appoint one of his Physicians to attend to be present at the Birth. [LMA Acc. 1040/206].

It is not known whether Townley's letter had the desired effect, but there have been persistent rumours that the Prince Regent was interested in Joanna and 'made some generous gifts to help the Cause.' (Seymour, *Voice in the Wilderness,* p.viii).

16. Dr Reece's Statement, in Seymour *The Express*, Vol.2, pp.376-8.
17. Blockley Coll. 779.
18. Dr. Reece's Statement, in Seymour *The Express*, Vol.2, pp.378-82.
19. *Sunday Monitor*, 4 December 1814.
20. Seymour *The Express*, Vol.2, pp.383-402.
21. LMA Acc. 1040/29.
22. Letter, 13 December 1814, in Jones, *Southcott's Prophecies*. [DRO 3703Z/ Z16].
23. Dr. Reece's Statement, in Seymour *The Express*, Vol.2, p.386.
24. Letter, 25/12/1815, in BL Add. MS 47800.
25. Dr. Reece's Statement, in Seymour *The Express*, Vol.2, pp.386-7.
26. LMA Acc. 1040/17.
27. Dr. Reece's Statement, in Seymour *The Express*, Vol.2, pp.387-9.

CHAPTER 23

1. Seymour, *The Express*, pp.388-90.
2. Southcott Cuttings, WCSL.
3. LMA Acc. 1040/27.
4. Seymour, *The Express*, pp. 390-91.
5. *Bristol Mirror*, 7 January 1815, p.4.
6. Southcott Cuttings, WCSL.
7. John Sims, M.D. in DNB. In November 1817 Dr Sims was summoned to Claremont to assist in the accouchement of Princess Charlotte, see *Letters of King George IV*, Vol.2, p.211.
8. Seymour, *The Express*, pp.391-4.
9. *Western Flying Post*, 18 October 1824, in Southcott Cuttings, WCSL.
10. Balleine, *Past Finding Out*, p.68.

11. Seymour, *The Express*, p.394.

12. Townley, *Letter to the Editor of the Council of Ten*, pp.8 ff. where she admits to feeling shocked when Joanna died. 'Had I not been mercifully blinded, I would not have supported myself during those anxious days, between her death and the time of dissection; and through the night that followed that operation, the confusion and distress of my mind were greater than I can express.' But by the following morning, 'it was clear to my mind that it was a spiritual birth we were to look for.'

13. BL Add. MS 26039, ff.55-6.

14. Southcott Cuttings, WCSL.

15. *Bristol Mirror*, 14 January 1815, p.4.

16. Southcott Cuttings, WCSL.

17. BL Add. MS 47798, ff.70-71.

18. Foley's Diary in WRO. Extracts published in *Notes & Queries*, 5 July 1952, pp.295-6.

19. BL Add. MS 47795, ff.51-66.

20. Exell, *Joanna Southcott at Blockley*, pp.5-9.

21. BL Add. MS 47801A, f.1v.

Appendix 1
SOUTHCOTT FAMILY TREE

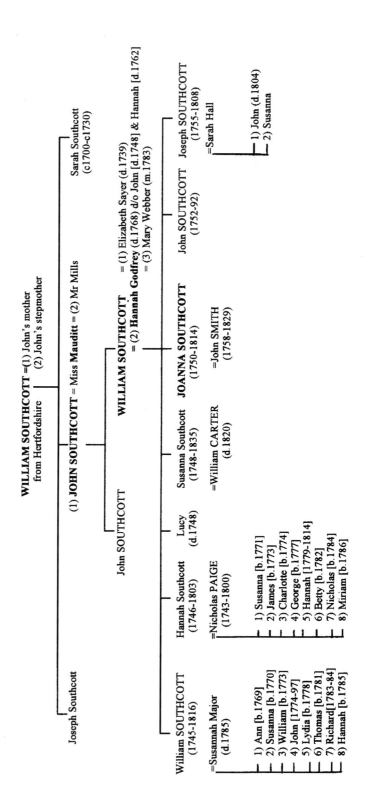

WILLIAM SOUTHCOTT =(1) John's mother
from Hertfordshire   (2) John's stepmother

Joseph Southcott

Sarah Southcott
(c1700-c1730)

(1) JOHN SOUTHCOTT = Miss Mauditt = (2) Mr Mills

John SOUTHCOTT

WILLIAM SOUTHCOTT   = (1) Elizabeth Sayer (d.1739)
= (2) Hannah Godfrey (d.1768) d/o John [d.1748] & Hannah [d.1762]
= (3) Mary Webber (m.1783)

JOANNA SOUTHCOTT
(1750-1814)
=John SMITH
(1758-1829)

John SOUTHCOTT
(1752-92)

Joseph SOUTHCOTT
(1755-1808)
=Sarah Hall

1) John (d.1804)
2) Susanna

Susanna Southcott
(1748-1835)
=William CARTER
(d.1820)

Lucy
(d.1748)

Hannah Southcott
(1746-1803)
=Nicholas PAIGE
(1743-1800)

1) Susanna [b.1771]
2) James [b.1773]
3) Charlotte [b.1774]
4) George [b.1777]
5) Hannah [1779-1814]
6) Betty [b.1782]
7) Nicholas [b.1784]
8) Miriam [b.1786]

William SOUTHCOTT
(1745-1816)
=Susannah Major
(d.1785)

1) Ann [b.1769]
2) Susanna [b.1770]
3) William [b.1773]
4) John [1774-97]
5) Lydia [b.1778]
6) Thomas [b.1781]
7) Richard[1783-84]
8) Hannah [b.1785]

Appendix 2
BIOGRAPHICAL NOTES ON PRINCIPAL CHARACTERS

Revd Hoadley Ashe (1751-1826)
Anglican clergyman and supporter of Joanna. A learned and pious man, son of Revd Robert Ashe, a prebendary of Winchester. In 1775 he was appointed perpetual curate of Crewkerne and Misterton in a part of Somerset that became a hotbed of Southcottian activity. He assumed the name Hoadley in 1798 on the death of his aunt, daughter-in-law of Bishop Hoadley of Winchester. First met Joanna in 1807 and was immediately converted to her cause, but this led to bitter conflict with his parishioners. Died 3 May 1826, aged 75, and buried in Crewkerne churchyard.

Richard Brothers (1757-1824)
Prophet. Born in Newfoundland, son of a gunner. After being educated at Woolwich, entered the navy at fourteen and became a lieutenant in 1783. Discharged on half-pay, he married Elizabeth Hassall in 1786, but soon left her. In September 1787 he came to London where he lived quietly until, refusing to draw his pension because it meant swearing loyalty to the crown, he fell into debt and was sent to a workhouse. Announcing himself as 'Nephew of the Almighty', he published *A Revealed Knowledge of the Prophecies and Times* (1794) and proceeded to swamp the world with such inflammatory pamphlets that he was arrested for treason and confined as a criminal lunatic. Supported by N.B.Halhed and William Sharp until they fell under the sway of Joanna Southcott, his most steadfast disciple was John Finlayson, whose exertions secured his release from the asylum in 1806. From 1815 he lived with Finlayson in his house at Marylebone, where he died in January 1824 and was buried in St John's Wood at the far side of the cemetery from Joanna.

Revd Stanhope Bruce (1730-1823)
Anglican clergyman and supporter of Joanna. Vicar of Inglesham in Wiltshire for sixty years. One of the Seven Stars who visited her at Exeter to judge whether she was genuine. His son Basil embraced the cause at the same time but died in 1801. Stanhope Bruce married as his second wife Esther Elizabeth Dix in 1803. After Joanna's death he remained true to the cause espoused by Townley and Sharp.

Elias Carpenter (fl.1805)
Wealthy owner of Neckinger house and adjoining paper mill at Bermondsey. Became a Southcottian in 1802 and gave ample financial support to the movement before quarrelling with Joanna over his power to interpret the visions of Joseph Prescott – a prerogative Joanna claimed for herself. As a

result Carpenter left the society in 1805. Afterwards established a Church on similar lines, calling himself 'Elias Paul Gabriel' and continued 'sealing' the people on his own account.

Revd Samuel Eyre (1776-1853)

Anglican clergyman and supporter of Joanna. Born in Wylye, Wiltshire, youngest son of Revd John and Susanna Eyre. He heard of Joanna Southcott when he arrived in Bristol in 1804, immediately embraced her cause and remained faithful till his death. He died at his residence, Stoke's Croft, in Bristol and was buried in Arnos Vale cemetery.

John Finlayson (1770-1854)

Writer and ardent disciple of Richard Brothers (q.v.). Born in Scotland, he moved to London after coming under Brothers' influence in 1797. He married Elizabeth Anne, daughter of Colonel Basil Bruce. After dying in poverty he was buried in the same grave as Brothers at St John's Wood.

Revd Thomas Philip Foley (1758-1839)

Anglican clergyman and guardian of Joanna's Box. Son of Revd Philip Foley, Rector of Shelsley, Worcestershire, and kinsman of Thomas, Baron Foley. Educated at Repton School and Jesus College, Cambridge, he became Rector of Oldswinford, Worcestershire, in 1797, and married Elizabeth Bache. An adherent of Richard Brothers, in 1798 he backed Brothers' prophecy that there would be no more monarchy in France. After meeting Joanna in 1801, he embraced her cause and maintained his belief in her mission to the end of his life.

His son Richard Foley (1801-1861) was Rector at North Cadbury, Somerset, for nearly twenty years and succeeded his father as guardian of Joanna's Box.

Nathaniel Brassey Halhed (1751-1830)

Orientalist and pioneer of modern philology. Born at Westminster, son of William Halhed, a director of the Bank of England. Educated at Harrow and Christ Church, Oxford. In India, working for the East India Company, he translated Sanskrit law codes, the mystical *Upanishads*, and compiled a Bengali grammar. Served as M.P. for Lymington, Hampshire, 1791-1796. In January, 1795, he became a disciple of Richard Brothers, seeing in his teaching similarities with oriental mysticism. Having embraced Joanna's cause, after her death he acknowledged George Turner as her successor. Halhed's collection of oriental manuscripts was purchased by the British Museum.

Colonel William Tooke Harwood (born 1757)

Staunch supporter of Joanna during her life time. Born in Norwich, son of Thomas and Elizabeth Harwood. Married Ann Holcroft in June 1797. Joined the Society for Constitutional Information and was the intimate friend of reformers such as Horne Tooke, William Godwin, and Thomas Holcroft. Kept vigil at Joanna's deathbed and followed her coffin to the grave despite the fact that his faith had been shattered.

Thomas Holcroft (1745-1809)
Dramatist, novelist and ardent millenarian. Born in Leicester Fields, London, son of a shoemaker turned pedlar. At thirteen became a stable-boy at Newmarket. Later joined a company of strolling players and drew on his experiences in his first novel, published 1780. *The Road to Ruin*, his most successful play, was performed at Covent Garden in 1792 – the year in which he joined the Society for Constitutional Information. Indicted for high treason, he served time in Newgate before being discharged without trial. His daughter Ann married William Tooke Harwood in 1797.

Revd Joseph Pomeroy (1749-1837)
Anglican clergyman. Born at Lanton in Cornwall 6 November, 1749, son of John and Grace Pomeroy. Joseph married Melloney Scobell in 1778 at Madron. She died on 30 August, 1799, and his father died three days later. Persecuted by Southcottians for his alleged betrayal of Joanna. For over sixty years he was Vicar of St Kew in Cornwall, where he lies buried in a granite coffin specially prepared and laid in the ground during his lifetime.

William Owen Pughe (1759-1835)
Welsh antiquary and lexicographer. Known in early life as William Owen. Born at Tynybryn in Merioneth, son of a skilled singer to the harp. Arrived in London in 1776 and after 1783 began to collect materials for his Welsh-English dictionary, published in 1803. Three years later he succeeded to a small estate at Nantglyn, near Denbigh, and assumed the surname of Pughe. He had married Sarah Elizabeth Harper in 1790 and they had a son, Aneurin Owen, and two daughters. Friend of William Blake, an adherent of Joanna Southcott, and for many years secretary/adviser to Jane Townley. 'In erudition no student of theWelsh language and literature has ever surpassed him' – DNB.

Richard Reece (1775-1831)
Physician and writer. Son of William Reece, Vicar of Bosbury in Herefordshire. Member of Royal College of Surgeons (1796). Recipient of Royal Humane Society silver medal in1799. Married Kitty, daughter of Judge Blackborow, and had established a prestigious practice in London by the time Joanna consulted him about her 'supernatural' pregnancy in 1814. Author of numerous works, including a popular *Medical Guide* that went into seventeen editions.

William Sharp (1749-1824)
Celebrated engraver, friend of Thomas Paine, at one time a believer in Swedenborg, afterwards in Richard Brothers. His place of business was 50 Titchfield Street and he later lived at Chiswick. Born in London, son of a

gunmaker, and apprenticed to an engraver of firearms, from 1787 he published his own work. He achieved international fame and was elected an honorary member of the Imperial Academy at Vienna and the Royal Academy at Munich. Became a staunch supporter of Joanna Southcott, whom he brought from Exeter and maintained at his own expense for a considerable time. The last of her followers to admit the reality of her death, Sharp never lost faith in her divine mission nor expectation of her reappearance. He died of dropsy and was buried in Chiswick Churchyard.

John Smith (1758-1829)

'Husband' of Joanna. Son of Richard and Ann Smith of Blockley, Worcestershire, he became Steward to the Earl of Darnley and owned a perfumery in Princes Street, Cavendish Square. He became an adherent of Joanna Southcott with whom on 12 November, 1814, he went through a private marriage service at 38 Manchester Street. After Joanna's death he remained true to the group led by Townley and Sharp. He died at Rock Cottage, Blockley, in December 1829, and was buried in the churchyard in what became the family grave of his brother Samuel Smith (1752-1837).

Jane Townley (1761-1825)

Companion of Joanna. Born at Belfield Hall, near Rochdale, daughter of Colonel Richard Townley, High Sheriff of Lancashire, and his first wife Ann (née Western), who died in 1761. Christened at St Chad's on 19 August, 1761, Jane was regarded as an invalid when she met Joanna in 1803 and became her life-long supporter. She provided Joanna with a home for more than ten years, acting as her amanuensis and close friend. After Joanna died Jane became convinced that she herself was now the recipient of divine communications which revealed Shiloh's true identity – he was, in fact, the Prince Regent! Jane Townley died at Weston Place, St Pancras, on 25 March, 1825, and was buried privately at St Martin's Burying Ground, Camden Town, her coffin followed only by Dr Pughe and Mr Bancroft.

William Tozer (d.1828)

Southcottian minister. An eloquent, if rough-tongued, lay-preacher. Born in Devon, William Tozer arrived in London in 1804 and allied himself with Carpenter before joining the Southcottian movement. After taking Joanna's side in her dispute with Carpenter, Tozer replaced the latter as minister at the Southcottian chapel in Duke Street, St George's Fields, where his former trade of lath-render came in useful for the new building programme. He was buried in the same grave as Joanna Southcott at St John's Wood.

George Troup (1763-1838)

Supporter of Joanna. Son of Alexander and Helen Troup, George was born in Aberdeen in 1763 and married Ann Kent at Brighton in November, 1797. Ann died in 1820 after giving birth to at least four children, including Helen Shove who married John Smith (nephew of the man who 'married' Joanna Southcott).

George Troup was 'Pagesman' to the Prince of Wales in 1788, promoted to Wardrobe Keeper in 1800, and in 1812 was page-in-ordinary of H.M.Backstairs [CRO LC3/68 (139)]. When he retired with a pension of £200 a year in September 1824 his address was given as: Stable yard, St James Palace, but by 1828 he had moved to 8 Upper Berkeley Street, and was living at 29 Edgware Road in 1834 when he made his will. He was buried at Blockley. He had a brother William (possibly his twin), with whom he was often confused. A loyal Southcottian, he kept faith with Townley and Sharp after Joanna's death.

George Turner (d.1821)

Leeds merchant and disciple of Brothers. Turner was one of the Seven Stars who went to Exeter to judge Joanna's writings in 1801. He acted as a judge at her trials and was her host when she visited Yorkshire. Acknowledged as Joanna's successor by Southcottian groups in Yorkshire, Lancashire and the West Country, he was rebuffed by Sharp, Foley and Harwood. After his predictions grew increasingly, wild he was committed to a Quaker asylum where he published fourteen books and gradually resumed the direction of the Movement. Turner regained his liberty in 1820 and promptly promised the appearance of Shiloh in London on 14 October. He died September, 1821, bitterly disappointed.

Ann Underwood (1766-1825)

Devoted servant of Jane Townley and Joanna Southcott's chief amanuensis. Widowed young, she had a daughter, Ann, who married Charles Vincent Barnard, another fervent Southcottian. She appeared genuinely fond of Joanna, whom she nursed to the bitter end. Then, after wearing herself out nursing Townley through her last illness, she herself died six weeks later and was buried at St Martin's Burying Ground, Camden Town, in the grave that already held her daughter.

Revd Thomas Webster

Anglican clergyman and supporter of Joanna. Lived in Falcon Court, High Street, Borough. One of the seven men who visited Exeter in 1801 to examine Joanna's writings, he wrote *The Anagogue* (1813) in which he discussed the probability of earth being inhabited by angels before the creation of man. His grandson, Revd Walter Begley (1846-1905) would inspire and support Alice Seymour, who did so much to revive Joanna's cause in the twentieth century.

Appendix 3
CUSTODIANS OF JOANNA SOUTHCOTT'S BOX

First Custodian	1801–1816	William Sharp, Titchfield Street, London
Second Custodian	1816–1825	Jane Townley, Weston Place, St Pancras
Third Custodian	1825–1839	Thomas Foley, Oldswinford, Worcestershire
Fourth Custodian	1839–1861	Richard Foley, North Cadbury, Somerset
Fifth Custodian	1861–1876	Samuel Jowett, Leeds, Yorkshire
Sixth Custodian	1876–1898	John Marshall Jowett, Bradford, Yorkshire
Seventh Custodian	1898	Sealey Stuckey, Burnham, Somerset (died 1898)
Eighth Custodian	1898–1925	Robert Stuckey, Bridgwater, Somerset
Ninth Custodian	1925–1926	Edwin Armstrong Jowett, Morecambe, Lancs
Tenth Custodian	1926–1957	Cecil K. Jowett, Cheadle, Cheshire
Eleventh Custodian	1957	Maud Jowett (Cecil's widow)
Twelfth Custodian	1957 to present day	The Panacea Society, Bedford

A NOTE ON SOURCES

The main sources for Joanna Southcott's life are the sixty-five works of her canon (originally indexed by Philip Pullen in 1815) and unpublished materials held in collections by the following:

(1) British Library, London [BL]
(2) London Metropolitan Archive [LMA]
(3) Humanities Research Centre, University of Texas, Austin
(4) West Country Studies Library, Exeter [WCSL]
(5) Blockley Antiquarian Society, Blockley, Gloucestershire
(6) Harry Price Library, University of London
(7) John Rylands University Library, Manchester
(8) Guildhall Library, London
(9) Devon Record Office [DRO]
(10) Gloucestershire Record Office [GRO]
(11) Worcestershire Record Office [WRO]
(12) Local Studies Library, Taunton
(13) Princeton University Library

Other collections of manuscripts exist in private hands. Many of these are copies by her followers of Joanna's 'communications'.

WORKS BY JOANNA SOUTHCOTT OR RECOGNISED AS PART OF HER CANON:

The Strange Effects of Faith, With Remarkable Prophecies (Made in 1792, etc) of Things Which Are to Come: Also, Some Account of My Life. Exeter. Published in six parts: parts 1-5, 1801; part 6, 1802. [Books 1-6]

A Continuation of Prophecies by Joanna Southcott from the year 1792 to the present time. Exeter, 1802. [Book 7]

The Strange Effects of Faith; being a Continuation of Joanna Southcott's Prophecies of Things Which Are to Come. London, 1802. [Book 8]

Divine & Spiritual Letters of Prophecies, Sent to Reverend Divines, etc. London, nd. [Book 9]

Second Book of Letters. London, nd. [Book 10]

A Dispute between the Woman & the Powers of Darkness. London, 1802. [Book 11]

The Answer of the Lord to the Powers of Darkness. London, 1802. [Book 12]

A Communication Given to Joanna, in Answer to Mr Brothers' Last Book, Published the End of This Year. London, 1802. [Book 13]

Prophecies. A Warning to the Whole World, from the Sealed Prophecies of Joanna Southcott, and Other Communications, etc. [also known as: The First Book of the Sealed Prophecies]. London, 1803. [Book 14]

The Continuation of the Prophecies of Joanna Southcott. A Word in Season to a Sinking Kingdom. London, 1803. [Book 15]

The Second Book of Visions. London, 1803. [Book 16]

A Word to the Wise or a Call to the Nation, That They May Know the Days of Their Visitation, etc. Stourbridge, 1803. [Book 17]

Divine & Spiritual Communications, Written by Joanna Southcott On the Prayers of the Church of England, etc. London, 1803. [Book 18]

Sound an Alarm in My Holy Mountain. Leeds, 1804. [Book 19]

A Warning to the World. Joanna Southcott's Prophecies. London, 1804. [Book 20]

On the Prayers for the Fast Day, May 1804. Letters on Various Subjects from Mrs Joanna Southcott to Miss Townley. London, 1804. [Book 21]

Copies & Parts of Copies of Letters & Communications, Written from Joanna Southcott and Transmitted by Miss Townley to Mr W. Sharp in London. London, 1804. [Book 22]

Mr Joseph Southcott, the Brother of Joanna Southcott, Will Now Come Forward as Dinah's Brethren Did, etc. London, 1804. [Book 23]

Letters & Communications of Joanna Southcott, the Prophetess of Exeter, Lately Written to Jane Townley. Stourbridge, 1804. [Book 24]

The Trial of Joanna Southcott, during Seven Days, Which Commenced on the Fifth, and Ended on the Eleventh of December, 1804. At Neckinger House, Bermondsey, Near London. London, 1804. [Book 25]

Joanna Southcott's Answer to Garrett's Book, Entitled, 'Demonocracy Detected', etc. London, 1805. [Book 26]

Joanna Southcott's Answer to Five Charges in the Leeds Mercury, etc. London, 1805. [Book 27]

The True Explanation of the Bible, Revealed by Divine Communications to Joanna Southcott, etc. Published in six parts. London, 1804-5. [Books 28-33]

An Explanation of the Parables Published in 1804 by Joanna Southcott; Also an Answer to a Book by L. Mayer, etc. London, 1806. [Book 34]

The Kingdom of Christ is at Hand etc. London, 1805. [Book 35]

The Second Book of the Sealed Prophecies. London, 1805. [Book 36]

The Answer of the Rev. Thomas P. Foley, to the World, Who Hath Blamed His Faith, etc. Stourbridge, 1805 [by Thomas Foley]. [Book 37]

The Controversy between Joanna Southcott and Elias Carpenter, One of Her Judges, Made Public. Published in five parts. London, 1805. [Books 38-42]

An Answer to the World for Putting in Print a Book in 1804 Called Copies & Parts of Copies, etc. London, 1806 [by William Sharp]. [Book 43]

The Full Assurance That the Kingdom of Christ Is at Hand, from the Signs of the Times. London, 1806. [Book 44]

A Few Remarks & Inquiries on a Sermon Preached by the Rev. Joseph Cockin, Independent Minister at Halifax, Being the Contents of a Letter, etc. Leeds, 1806. [Book 45]

The Long-Wished-For Revolution, Announced to Be at Hand in a Book Lately Published by L. Mayer . . . Explained by Joanna Southcott, etc. London, 1806. [Book 46]

Answer to Mr Brothers' Book, Published in September, 1806. . . . Also a Letter Sent to Mr Huntingdon, etc. London, 1806. [Book 47]

A Caution & Instruction to the Sealed, That They May Know for What They Are Sealed. London, 1807. [Book 48]

An Account of the Trials on Bills of Exchange, Wherein the Deceit of Mr John King and His Confederates . . . Is Exposed, etc. London, 1807. [Book 49]

An Answer to a Sermon Published & Preached by Mr Smith . . . at Beersheba Chapel, etc. London, 1808. [Book 50]

No Title [known as: *Answer to False Doctrine & the Crying Sins of the Nation*] London, 1808. [Book 51]

A True Picture of the World & A Looking-Glass for All Men. London, nd, ?1809. [Book 52]

True Explanations of the Bible. Part 7. London, 1810. [Book 53]

The Controversy of the Spirit with the Worldly Wise, As Given through Joanna Southcott. London, 1811. [Book 54]

A Continuation of the Controversy with the Worldly Wise. London, 1811. [Book 55]

An Answer to Thomas Paine's Third Part of the Age of Reason . . . Likewise to S. Lane . . . & to Hewson Clarke, etc. London, 1812. [Book 56]

The Book of Wonders, Marvellous & True. London, 1813. [Book 57]

The Second Book of Wonders, More Marvellous Than the First. London, 1813. [Book 58]

Copies of Letters Sent to the Clergy of Exeter from 1796 to 1800, with Communications & Prophecies Put in the Newspapers in 1813. London, 1813. [Book 59]

Wisdom Excelleth the Weapons of War . . . Judgments Are the Strange Works of the Lord, But Mercy His Darling Attribute. London, 1814. [Book 60]

The Third Book of Wonders, Announcing the Coming of Shiloh; With a Call to the Hebrews, etc. London, 1814. [Book 61]

The Fourth Book of Wonders, Being the Answer of the Lord to the Hebrews. London, 1814. [Book 62]

The Fifth Book of Wonders, Announcing the Event Having Taken Place Which Was Promised in the Fourth Book Should Be in May. . . . Also an Answer to the Address of the Rev. James Hearn, etc. London, 1814. [Book 63]

A Communication Sent in a Letter to the Reverend Mr P. in 1797, with an Explanation Thereon Now Given. London, 1814. [Book 64]

Prophecies Announcing the Birth of the Prince of Peace, Extracted from the Works of Joanna Southcott, etc. London, 1814. [Book 65]

PRIMARY WORKS

Anon., 1814 *Memoirs of the Life & Mission of Joanna Southcott etc. to which is added a Sketch of the Rev. W. Tozer.* London, 1814.

Aspinall, A. [ed.] *Letters of King George IV, 1812-1830.* Cambridge, 1938.

Bramall, James. *A Review of the Prophecies of Mrs Joanna Southcott taken by James Bramall late Secretary to St Ann's Sunday School.* Manchester [in *Book of Letters* DRO 3703 Z/14].

Brothers, Richard. *A Revealed Knowledge of the Prophecies and Times.* 2 parts. London, 1794.

Carpenter, Elias. *Nocturnal Alarm, being an Essay on Prophecy and Vision, etc.* London, 1803.

Carpenter, Elias. *An Apology for Faith, and Detection of Existing Errors Subversive of the Truth, etc.* 2 parts. London, 1814.

Copas, Thomas. *An Address to the Believers in Joanna Southcott's Mission, partly in Answer to Mr Samuel Jowett of Leeds.* London, 1843.

Fairburn, J.F. *The Life of Joanna Southcott, the Prophetess.* London, 1814.

Foley, T.P. *An Epistle to the Reverends*, printed as a pamphlet, 1803.

Grant, Johnson. *Grant's History of the English Church.* Vols.2 & 3. London, 1814.

Gunning, Henry. *Reminiscences of the University, Town & County of Cambridge from the Year 1780.* Vol.1. London, 1854.

Hughson, D. *The Life of Joanna Southcott.* London, 1814.

Jones, D. [comp.] *The Sixth Book of Wonders, being a verbatim copy of the Six Sealed Letters dated September 1813 announcing "This Day the Rev. Joseph Pomeroy married to Joanna Southcott, the Great Prophetess, and the Wonder of the World".* Bath, 1852.

Jones, D. [comp.] *Southcott's Prophecies,* Bradford-on-Avon, 1853-1860. [DRO 3703 Z/16]

Jones, D. [comp.] *Book of Letters, Joanna Southcott and others,* 1803-1853. [DRO 3703 Z/14]

Kirby, R. S. *Kirby's Wonderful and Eccentric Museum; Or Magazine of Remarkable Characters, Including All the Curiosities of Nature and Art, from the Remotest Period to the Present Time.* London, 1820.

Law, Richard. *Copy of an Epistle of the Most Extraordinary Nature; Sent to the Right Hon. Henry Addington, etc. July 19th, 1803.* London, nd.

Order of Service for January 12th. The Uplifting of Hands. According to the Command Given to Joanna Southcott. Plymouth, 1913.

Polwhele, Richard. *The History of Devonshire,* Vol.1. London, 1797.

Priestley, Joseph. *The Present State of Europe Compared with Ancient Prophecies,* London, 1794.

Pullen, P. *Index to the Divine & Spiritual Writings of Joanna Southcott.* London, 1815.

Quennell, P. [ed.] *Private Letters of Princess Lieven to Metternich (1820-1826).* London, 1937.

Reece, Richard. *A Correct Statement of . . . the Last Illness and Death of Mrs. Southcott.* London, 1815.

Roberts, D. *Observations relative to the Divine Mission of Joanna Southcott.* Gloucester, 1807.

Seymour, Alice. [comp.] *The Express.* 2 vols. London, 1909.

Seymour, Alice. [comp.] *The Voice in the Wilderness.* Ashford, 1933.

Sibley, Samuel. *A Copy of the Articles of Faith, as Acknowledged and Believed by the Children of the Faithful, Belonging to the House of faith, Or Philadelphian Church; Well Known by the Name of the Followers of the Divine Mission of Joanna Southcott,* London, 1819.

Southey, Robert. *Letters from England, By Don Manuel Alvarez Espriella.* 3 vols. London, 1807.

Strachey, L & R. Fulford. *The Greville Memoirs.* London, 1938.

Temperley, H. [ed.] *Unpublished Diary of Princess Lieven.* London, 1925.

Townley, Jane. *A Letter from Mrs Jane Townley to the Editor of the Council of Ten in Answer to His Remarks and Misrepresentations Respecting the Mission of Joanna Southcott.* London, 1823.

Townley, Richard. *A Journal Kept in the Isle of Man.* 1791.

Wesley, John. *The Journal of the Rev. John Wesley.* Vol.VI. London, 1914.

Wilson, H., and J. Caulfield. *The Book of Wonderful Characters: Memoirs and Anecdotes of Remarkable and Eccentric Persons in All Ages and Countries.* London, 1870.

PERIODICALS, BOOKLETS & NEWSPAPERS

Antiquarian Book Monthly, February 1996 – G. Lindsay: 'Mary Roberts, A Neglected Naturalist'.

Bell's Weekly Messenger [29/5/1814; 1/1/1815]

Bristol Gazette & Public Advertiser [19/7/1804]

Bristol Mirror [29/10/1814; 7/1/1815; 14/1/1815]
Country Life, 9/6/1955; 16/6/1955 – C.Hussey: 'Combe, Devon'.
Devon & Exeter Gazette, 20/9/1926
Devon Life, April 1976 – P.Thompson: 'Your Own Messiahs in the West'.
Edinburgh Review, Vol. XXIV, February 1815.
Exeter Flying Post (*Trewman's*) – see individual references in Notes.
*Exeter Pocket Journal,*1796 [WCSL]
Express & Echo, 9/1/1914
Gentleman's Magazine, Vol. LXXXV, January 1815.
Morning Advertiser [26/8/1814]
Morning Chronicle [3/9/1814]
Morning Herald [15/11/1813]
Notes & Queries, 5/7/1952 – H.J. Haden:'Thomas Philip Foley'.
The Observer, [3/4/1814]
Proceedings of the Devon Archaeological Society I, 1929-1932 – F.C. Tyler: 'The
    Rolling Stone on Gittisham Hill'.
Pulman's Weekly News, November 1814.
Southcott Society publications:
        A. Seymour [Ed.] *Express Leaflets* [1911-1914]
        The Two Witnesses [1915-1918]
        The Southcott Despatch [1919-1922[
        The Southcott Express [1926-1929?]
        Watch [1935-1938?]
Sunday Monitor [20/11/1814; 4/12/1814]
The Times [25/8/1814; 30/8/1814]
West Briton, or Truro Advertiser [August 1813]
Western Flying Post [18/10/1824]
Worcester Herald [5/5/1809]

SECONDARY WORKS

Alumni Cantabrigienses, compiled by John Venn & J.A. Venn. Cambridge, 1922.
Alumni Oxonienses, compiled by Joseph Foster. London, 1888.
Armytage, W. H. G. *Heavens Below: Utopian Experiments in England, 1560-1960*.
    Toronto, 1961.
Ashton, John. *The Dawn of the XIXth Century in England*. London, 1906.
Baker, W. S. *William Sharp*. Philadelphia, 1875.
Balleine, G. R. *Past Finding Out: The Tragic Story of Joanna Southcott & Her
    Successors*. London, 1956.
Baring-Gould, S. *Devonshire Characters & Strange Events*. London, 1908.
Bindman, David. *Blake as an Artist*. Oxford, 1977.
Brockett, A. *Nonconformity in Exeter, 1650-1875*. Manchester, 1962.
Carpenter, S. C. *Eighteenth-Century Church & People*. London, 1959.
Carr, Glenda. *William Owen-Pughe*. Cardiff, 1983.
Chick, Elijah. *A History of Methodism in Exeter & the Neighbourhood From the Year
    1739 until 1907*. Exeter, 1907.
Cohn, Norman. *The Pursuit of the Millennium*. London, 1970.
Cole, G.D.H. & Raymond Postgate. *The Common People*. London, 1956.
Coleridge, Lord John. *The Story of a Devonshire House*. London, 1905.
Cooper, J.H. The Moravian Church – History, Beliefs & Practices. London, 2000.

Derrett, J.D.M. *Prophecy in the Cotswolds, 1803-1947*. Shipston-on-Stour, 1994.

Elworthy, F.T. *The West Somerset Word Book, A Glossary of Dialectal and Archaic Phrases used in West Somerset and East Devon*. London, 1888.

Exell, A.W. *Joanna Southcott at Blockley & The Rock Cottage Relics*. Shipston-on-Stour, 1977.

Forth, Brent. *And the Lord Spake unto Joanna Southcott*. London, 1937.

Fox, Rachel. *Joanna Southcott's Place in History: A Forecast*. Plymouth, 1925.

Fox, Rachel. *How We Built Jerusalem in England's Green & Pleasant Land*. 2 vols. Bedford, 1931.

Fulford, R. *George the Fourth*. London, 1949.

George, Dorothy. *England in Transition*. London, 1953.

George, Dorothy. *London Life in the Eighteenth Century*. London, 1966.

Guest, R. & A.V. John. *Lady Charlotte*. London, 1989.

Harrison, J.F.C. *The Second Coming*. London, 1979.

Hopkins, J.K. *A Woman to Deliver Her People*. Austin, 1982.

Hoskins, W.G. *Industry, Trade & People in Exeter, 1688-1800*. Exeter, 1968.

Jackman, F.W. *Deviating Voices:Women and Orthodox Religious Tradition*. Cambridge, 2002.

James, William. *The Varieties of Religious Experience*. London, 1985.

Jones, L.E.C. [ed.] *The Time for Worshipping in the Spirit, Illucidated from the Visitation of Prophecy to Joanna Southcott during the years 1792-1814*. Bradford-on-Avon, 1853.

Lamont, William. *Godly Rule: Politics & Religion, 1603-1660*. London, 1969.

Lane, C. *Life of Joanna Southcott & Bibliography of Joanna Southcott*. Reprint. Exeter, 1912.

Latimer, John. *Annals of Bristol in the Nineteenth Century*. Bristol. 1887.

Le Messurier, B. *History of the Mint Methodist Church*. Exeter, 1962.

Lewis, Val. *Satan's Mistress: The Extraordinary Story of the Eighteenth-Century Fanatic Joanna Southcott and her Lifelong Battle with the Devil*. London, 1997.

Margary, Harry. *A to Z of Regency London*. London, 1985.

Matthews, Ronald. *English Messiahs*. London, 1936.

Maxted, I. *Devon Book Trades, A Biographical Dictionary*. Exeter, 1991.

Palmer, A. *Life & Times of George IV*. London, 1972.

Patterson, M.W. *Sir Francis Burdett & His Times*. London, 1931.

Robertson, Mary S. *The True Story of Joanna Southcott*. Ashford, 1923.

Robertson, Mary S. *Authentic History of the Great Box of Sealed Writings left by Joanna Southcott*. Plymouth, 1925.

Robertson, Mary S. *The Way to God*. Ashford, 1935.

Rudé, George. *Hanoverian London*. London, 1971.

Street, James. *The Mynster of the Ile*. Taunton, 1904.

Thomas, J.W. *Reminiscences of Methodism in Exeter*. Np, 1870?

Thomas, Keith. *Religion & the Decline of Magic*. London, 1971.

Tobin, P.J. *The Southcottians in England* – unpublished M.A. thesis, University of Manchester, 1978.

Waite, A.E. *The Holy Kabbalah*. New York, 1965.

Warne, Arthur. *Church & Society in Eighteenth-Century Devon*. Newton Abbot, 1969.

Whitlock, Ralph. *The Folklore of Devon*. London, 1977.

Willey, Basil. *The Eighteenth-Century Background*. London, 1965.

Wilson, Mona. *The Life of William Blake*. Oxford, 1971.

Wright, E.P. *A Catalogue of the Joanna Southcott Collection at the University of Texas*. Austin, 1968.

Index

Numbers in italics refer to monochrome plates; Roman numbers refer to colour plates